NEW TESTAMENT
SURVEY

NEW TESTAMENT SURVEY

Robert G. Gromacki

BAKER BOOK HOUSE
Grand Rapids, Michigan

First printing, September 1974
Second printing, May 1975
Third printing, April 1976
Fourth printing, January 1977
Fifth printing, January 1978
Sixth printing, July 1979
Seventh printing, February 1981
Eighth printing, March 1983
Ninth printing, January 1984
Tenth printing, March 1985
Eleventh printing, February 1986
Twelfth printing, May 1987
Thirteenth printing, August 1988
Fourteenth printing, April 1989
Fifteenth printing, September 1989

Copyright © 1974

Baker Book House Company

ISBN: 0-8010-3677-1

Library of Congress Card Catalog Number: 74-83793

Title Page—

View of the Old City of Jerusalem, looking northwest from the Jewish cemetery on the Mount of Olives.

To
All My
New Testament Students
Past, Present, and Future

Contents

List of Illustrations

List of Maps

List of Charts

Illustration Credits

Preface

The purpose of a survey is to give a Christian a working understanding of the message of the New Testament books. For that reason, it must include the results of New Testament Introduction without getting involved in the technical discussions. It must incorporate historical and cultural background, gleaned from Bible dictionaries and encyclopedias, without becoming a book of manners and customs. It must come to grips with the actual text of Scripture without becoming a verse by verse commentary. As an introductory discipline, it seeks to lay an adequate foundation for detailed book studies and passage exegesis later on in the experience of the students. This, then, becomes the challenge of both the teacher and the student. The latter should be aware of the goals and extent of this study and the former should neither skim the surface nor get bogged down in insignificant details.

As a survey teacher of college freshmen for over thirteen years, the author has observed that many graduates of the Sunday school know *what* happened in the New Testament era, but not *why* those things occurred. Interpretative significance must always be attached to historical fact. Some students may know the meaning of an individual verse or passage, but they are unable to relate it to the theme of the book. Synthesis must precede analysis.

In this text the author has attempted to present a readable, understandable survey. His goal has been to make the complex simple and to say much in few words. It has been designed to meet the needs of survey students at the freshman and sophomore levels of Christian liberal arts colleges, Bible colleges, and Bible institutes. In addition, it could serve as an adequate text and study guide for adult Sunday school and Training Union classes, local church evening Bible institutes, and home Bible classes.

The text has been written from a firm evangelical persuasion that the Bible is the inerrant, inspired Word of God, the basis of the faith and practice of each believer. The hermeneutic approach is that of moderate dispensationalism.

The first chapter provides necessary background data: both inter-testamental and first-century history, social and economic conditions, Gentile religions and philosophies, and Judaistic practices. The next two chapters view the entire New Testament at a glance and the Gospels in particular.

Each book is discussed in its own chapter following the known order of the New Testament. Who wrote the book? What do we know about his life? To whom did he write? What is known about the life of the recipient? If the book was written to a church, how did the church get started? What is known about the city in which the church was located? Where was the author when he wrote? What caused him to write? Who took the letter from him to the destination? What is distinctive about each book? What contribution does it make to the canon that no other book makes? Answers to these questions will be given in organized paragraphs and supported by Biblical references. Following these introductory data are a detailed outline and a summary commentary of each book. In the survey section, passage divisions are noted in the margin next to the beginning of each paragraph. It is highly recommended that the student read the relevant portion of Scripture, read the survey comments, and then reread the Scripture to get the maximum benefit of the study. In this way, both the Scripture and the text will take on additional meaning.

Each chapter concludes with an "Increase Your Learning" section. First, projects to be done by the student are listed. These will cause him to mark his Bible purposefully. Topics for group discussion are then suggested. These can be used either by the teacher to stimulate interest or by buzz groups. Finally, a list of recommended commentaries for further reading is given. A selective bibliography of over three hundred volumes is found at the conclusion of the book. These books represent mainly evangelical scholarship; critical liberal books have been deliberately omitted. For the most part, the books listed are still in print. An individual on his own could profit greatly from a serious study of the Biblical books and this text and a pursuit of the suggested projects.

All Scripture references and quotations are to the Authorized Version of the Bible (King James Version) since this is still regarded as *the* text of fundamentalism.

Special thanks must be given to the author's wife, Gloria, who faithfully labored for many hours over the typewriter to prepare this manuscript. It is his hope and prayer that God will use this book to bring believers into a greater understanding of the New Testament and into a dedicated love for the Lord Jesus Christ.

Robert Glenn Gromacki

NEW TESTAMENT
SURVEY

This pottery juglet filled with thirty-five silver tetradrachmas formed the private "bank" of a Shechem resident of the second century B.C., when Palestine was under control of the Ptolemaic dynasty in Egypt. The coins cover a minimum of ninety years, from at least the last year of Ptolemy I (285 B.C.) to the tenth year of Ptolemy V (193 B.C.).

1

BACKGROUNDS

Intertestamental History

To have a full, adequate understanding of the New Testament, one must have a working knowledge of Israel's closing kingdom years, the seventy years of the Babylonian exile, the postcaptivity era, and the period between the testaments. This latter period has sometimes been called the "four hundred silent years" because there was no oral or written revelation communicated directly by God. Between the prediction of Elijah's coming (Mal. 4:5) and the angelic announcement of the birth of John the Baptist (Luke 1:11-20), however, God was preparing the world for the advent of His Son. In the last two hundred years of Israel's canonical history and the subsequent four-hundred-year interval, many significant political and religious developments occurred. For example, the Sadducees and the Pharisees were very prominent during Christ's earthly ministry, but where did they come from? They are not mentioned anywhere in the Old Testament. The last historical book, Nehemiah, relates that Persia controlled Palestine, but the Gospels reveal the presence of Rome in Jerusalem. How did this Western empire come to have political influence in the East? Answers to these questions and others similar to them can only be found in the six centuries before Christ.

Babylon (626-539 B.C.)

After the conquest of the northern kingdom of Israel by Assyria (722 B.C.), Judah continued to function as a single political entity until Babylonian influence began to be felt in Palestine. Immediately after Babylon conquered Egypt at the second battle of Carchemish, Judah came under the political dominion of Nebuchadnezzar, king of Babylon (605 B.C). At this time the first deportation of exiles, including Daniel, occurred (Dan. 1:1-6). Much of the temple wealth was also confiscated and removed to Babylon. Shortly after, Jehoiakim, king of Judah, rebelled, but he was bound and carried off to Babylon. His son and successor, Jehoiachin, reigned only three months because he likewise rebelled (597 B.C.). At this time the second major deportation took place. Not only was Jehoiachin carried away to Babylon, but also his mother, wives, military consultants, soldiers, and craftsmen (II Kings 24:6-16; II Chron. 36:8-10). The remaining wealth of the temple and palace was removed, A young priest, Ezekiel, was also taken at this time (Ezek. 1:2). Only the poor remained in the land. Nebuchadnezzar then placed Jehoiachin's uncle, Mattaniah, on the throne and changed the latter's name to Zedekiah (II Kings 24:17-20). Against the advice of Jeremiah, Zedekiah aligned himself with Egypt in an attempt to overthrow the Babylonian yoke. When Egypt failed to support Judah, the city of Jerusalem fell to the Babylonians after a lengthy, tragic siege. After Zedekiah saw his sons slain, his eyes were blinded, and he was dragged in chains to Babylon. Solomon's temple was then burned down, the walls of the city were destroyed, and the remaining inhabitants were led away in the third major deportation (586 B.C.; II Kings 25:1-21). The temple vessels were broken and carried away. The few people who remained were placed under the governorship of Gedaliah who was later assassinated by members of the royal family (II Kings 25:22-26). The Jewish kingdom which began with Saul about five hundred years before was now over. Henceforth there would not be a royal aspirant to the throne of David until Jesus' offer of Himself to Israel as her king.

The seventy years of exile (605-535 B.C.) gave birth to orthodox Judaism. Since the temple and the sacrificial system had been destroyed, the exiles congregated themselves into assemblies or synagogues for the worship of God, the study of the Old Testament, and fellowship. In the centuries that followed, synagogues sprouted throughout the Mediterranean world wherever the Jews emigrated. They were never designed to become a substitute for the temple. Sacrifices were never offered in them because Jerusalem was the only God-appointed place of sacrifice. When the missionary outreach of the apostles began, these synagogues became strategic preaching centers. Out of them came the first Christian converts, believers who were Jews and Gentile proselytes to Judaism.

The captivity also saw the rise of the scribe. Since the priests could not practice their ministry, they undertook a serious study and copying of the Old Testament Scriptures. The more they copied, the more they learned. Soon they became the "theologians" of orthodox Judaism.

The Exile also produced the Diaspora. Later, when the exiles and their families were permitted to return to the land, many of the Jews chose to remain in Babylon. Whereas Jews were formerly located only in

Palestine, the Exile saw the beginning of Jewish residence outside of the land. This takes on significance when one realizes that these converted, Diaspora Jews formed the nucleus of New Testament churches scattered throughout the Roman empire.

Idolatry, the chief cause of divine judgment, came to an abrupt end in the captivity. This sin which had plagued the nation ever since its inception (Exod. 32:15-28) no longer was a part of the national life. Chastisement produced this worthy fruit of repentance.

Persia (539-331 B.C.)

The Jews came under the dominion of the Medo-Persian empire when Cyrus conquered Babylon and Belshazzar in 539-538 B.C. (Dan. 5). Cyrus, once king of Anshan, a tributary to Media, rose to power with his conquest of Media. He then made claim to Assyria, Mesopotamia, Armenia, and Cappadocia. Later he defeated Lydia, took Greek Asia Minor, and moved eastward, absorbing into his empire Hyrcania, Parthia, Drangiana, Arachosia, Margiana, and Bactria. The Jews found in Cyrus a kind benefactor, however. He issued a decree permitting the exiles to return to Palestine with the express purpose of rebuilding the temple (Ezra 1-4). Under the leadership of Zerubbabel, 42,360 Jews and 7337

The Ishtar Gate of Babylon reconstructed. The structure is housed at the State Museum at Berlin.

servants returned (Ezra 2:64-65) and laid the foundation of a new temple. When external opposition interrupted the work, labor ceased for the next fifteen years.

In this interval, Cyrus died and was replaced by Cambyses who secretly murdered his brother, Smerdis. Cambyses defeated Egypt and advanced into Ethiopia. When a report came that a usurper, known as Pseudo-Smerdis, had taken the throne, he made haste to return to Persia. On the way back, however, he died. When the army of Cambyses came home, it put to death the usurper and placed Darius I on the throne.

During the reign of Darius, God raised up the prophets Haggai and Zechariah to convict the returned exiles of their sin of procrastination. Under the combined leadership of the prophets and Zerubbabel, the people returned to the reconstruction of the temple (Ezra 5-6). When the provincial governors questioned their actions, the Jews appealed to Darius to honor the decree of Cyrus. When Darius discovered the decree in the court records, he not only granted permission to the Jews but he authorized that the work should be subsidized with government funds (Ezra 6:7-12). With this encouragement, the Jews completed the task of rebuilding the temple in 516-515 B.C. This temple, later enlarged and renovated by Herod the Great (John 2:20), stood for the next five centuries; it was the prominent temple of New Testament activities.

On this high mountain ledge, near Bihistun (Bisitun), the Persian ruler Darius the Great had his autobiography carved in rock. The trilingual inscription unlocked the Assyrio-Babylonian system of cuneiform writing.

Darius, politically ambitious, moved against Thrace, Macedonia, and the Scythians. Defeated by the Greeks at the battle of Marathon, he retreated to the mainland. This battle was significant, however, because it produced the first major encounter between East and West, the Persian empire and the Greek city states. His successor, Xerxes, after putting down rebellions within the empire in Babylon and in Egypt, also moved against Greece and succeeded in taking Athens. However, his fleet was defeated at the battle of Salamis. Xerxes then retreated, leaving the Greeks in control of their own land. In Biblical history, Xerxes is known as Ahasuerus, Esther's husband. Although hostile to the Greeks, through the diplomacy of Esther and Mordecai he proved to be the deliverer of the Jews from the plot of Haman to exterminate all Jews.

His successor, Artaxerxes I, permitted Ezra the scribe to return to Palestine to teach the law to the returned exiles (Ezra 7-10). Shortly after Ezra's return (458-457 B.C.), Nehemiah asked the king for permission to return to Jerusalem to rebuild the walls which were still in a state of disrepair (Neh. 1-2). When it was granted, Nehemiah led an expedition back to Palestine, organized the laborers, and reconstructed the walls of Jerusalem (445-444 B.C.). Then, under the combined leadership of Ezra and Nehemiah, a revival broke out. Certain features of the Feast of Tabernacles were reinstituted; confession of sin and separation from the Gentiles occurred; and a covenant was signed, pledging the obedience of the people of God in the instruction of their children, the observance of the Sabbath and the Sabbatical year, and the financial support of the temple (Neh. 8-10). With his work completed, Nehemiah returned to Persia. Upon his second visit to Palestine, he discovered that the people had broken their pledge. Under his supervision the offenders were disciplined (Neh. 13). At this point, the recorded history of the Old Testament ends. The Jews were back in the land with a rebuilt temple and reconstructed walls around Jerusalem. The prophetic era, begun with Moses, was also over. For the next four hundred years, no divinely authenticated prophet proclaimed new, authoritative truth.

History, however, continued. Persian dominion lasted another hundred years until the rise of Philip of Macedon and his son, Alexander.

Greece (331-323 B.C.)

Philip of Macedon laid the foundation for the Greek empire. He succeeded where others had failed before him in uniting the Greek city states under a single ruler. Upon his death his ambitious son, Alexander, took over. Alexander looked eastward to the vast areas controlled by the Greeks' ancient enemy, the Persians. Leading his army, he crossed the Hellespont and defeated the Persians at the strategic Granicus River. This victory opened up the entire region of Asia Minor to him. He then

5

A CHART OF
INTERTESTAMENTAL HISTORY

Babylon

Nabopolassar	626-605 B.C.
Nebuchadnezzar	605-562 B.C.
Evil-Merodach	562-560 B.C.
Neriglissar	560-556 B.C.
Labishi-Marduk	556 B.C.
Nabonidus	556-539 B.C.
Belshazzar	553-539 B.C.

Persia

Cyrus	550-530 B.C.
Cambyses	530-522 B.C.
Smerdis (Bardiya)	522-521 B.C.
Darius I	521-486 B.C.
Xerxes I	486-464 B.C.
Artaxerxes I	464-423 B.C.
Darius II	423-404 B.C.
Artaxerxes II	404-359 B.C.
Artaxerxes III	359-338 B.C.
Arses	338-336 B.C.
Darius III	336-331 B.C.

Greece

Philip	359-336 B.C.
Alexander	336-323 B.C.

Ptolemies

Ptolemy I Soter	323-285 B.C.
Ptolemy II Philadelphus	285-246 B.C.
Ptolemy III Euergetes	246-222 B.C.
Ptolemy IV Philopator	222-203 B.C.
Ptolemy V Epiphanes	203-181 B.C.

Seleucidae

Antiochus III	223-187 B.C.
Seleucus IV Philopator	187-175 B.C.
Antiochus IV Epiphanes	175-164 B.C.

Maccabees-Hasmoneans

Mattathias	166 B.C.
Judas	166-160 B.C.
Jonathan	160-142 B.C.
Simon	142-135 B.C.
John Hyrcanus	135-104 B.C.
Judah Aristobulus	104-102 B.C.
Alexander Jannaeus	102- 76 B.C.
Alexandra and Hyrcanus II*	76- 67 B.C.
Aristobulus II	67- 63 B.C.

Roman Influence

Hyrcanus II*	63- 40 B.C.
Antigonus	40- 37 B.C.
Herod the Great	37- 4 B.C.

Same Person

6

encountered and defeated the Persian armies at Issus. Faced with a choice to go either east or south, Alexander advanced southward and gained Phoenicia, Palestine, and Egypt. Tradition states that he spared the city of Jerusalem because Jaddua, the high priest, showed him out of the prophecy of Daniel (ch. 8) that he would conquer Persia. Whether this tradition is historically correct is difficult to determine, but it is a fact that Jerusalem was not destroyed even though other conquered cities were. Alexander then retraced his steps northward, moved east, and conquered the Persians for the third time in the decisive battle of Arbela. This victory opened up the Persian heartland; his army then quickly moved through Babylon and Persia and extended itself as far as India. On the return trip to Greece, Alexander succumbed either through malaria or drunkenness or both. Although Alexander is mainly known as a great military strategist, his main contribution was in spreading the Greek culture and language to the Near East. The Hellenization was so complete that the next six hundred years (300 B.C.—A.D. 300) saw Greek become the *lingua franca* of the Mediterranean world. A highly sophisticated language with its many declensions, conjugations, and grammatical technicalities, it was the perfect medium in which the New Testament could be written. Thus, when that time came, the apostles could speak and write in a language that everyone in the Roman world

The site of the grand temple of Apollo, at Delphi, Greece.

Two silver drachmas bearing the image of Alexander the Great.

could understand. This period of the formation of the Greek language is known as the *Koine* period (the Greek word *koine* means "common").

When Alexander died, he left no heir old enough to take over the empire. After seven years of internal struggle, the conquered territory was divided into four sections under the control of four generals (cf. Dan. 8:8, 22): Antigonus took northern Syria and Babylon; Cassander ruled Macedonia; Ptolemy controlled southern Syria and Egypt; and Lysimachus reigned over Thrace and western Asia Minor. In 315 B.C. Ptolemy, Cassander, and Lysimachus formed an alliance to check Antigonus who aspired to be a second Alexander. Ptolemy demanded that Antigonus yield Babylon to Seleucus, the former's general. When Antigonus resisted, he was defeated and Seleucus obtained Babylon by force. This action began the Seleucidae dynasty, a family of rulers that eventually ruled the Jews. Later, in 301 B.C., a new alliance of Seleucus, Lysimachus, and Cassander defeated and killed Antigonus. It had been agreed beforehand that Palestine would be assigned to Ptolemy in the event of victory over Antigonus. However, since Ptolemy had not taken part in the fighting, the other three allies decided that the territory should be assigned to Seleucus. Before Seleucus could occupy the land, however, Ptolemy annexed the territory to his Egyptian domain. Thus Seleucus and Ptolemy, who were once friends, became bitter enemies. Their descendants, the Seleucidae and the Ptolemies, continued that hostility and engaged in many wars, with Palestine being the battlefield and the prize of victory.

Ptolemies (323-198 B.C.)

Jews prospered during the Ptolemaic occupation. The absorption of the Grecian culture by a great number of Jews necessitated the translation of the Hebrew Old Testament into the Greek language. During the reign of Ptolemy II Philadelphus (285-246 B.C.), the Septuagint (also known as the LXX) was published. It became the Bible for the Diaspora Jews since they were being gradually weaned away from the Hebrew text. In the New Testament period, it was widely circulated throughout the Mediterranean world, used in the synagogues by both Jews and Gentile proselytes. Therefore, when the early churches, composed mostly of Gentile Christians, were established, they had the authoritative text of the Old Testament in a language they could read immediately. Before the writing of the Gospels and the Epistles, it was the Bible of the young church.

Seleucidae (198-166 B.C.)

Constant battles took place between the Seleucidae and the Ptolemies (275, 245, 240, 219, 217 B.C.). A lengthy war (202-198 B.C.) was climaxed at the battle of Panion. With this victory the Seleucidae finally gained control of Palestine, much to the disfavor of the Jews. During the years of subsequent occupation, the Jews were severely persecuted because they refused to submit to pagan, Hellenizing pressures.

Roman political influence first began to be felt in the East during this time. When Hannibal of Carthage was defeated by the Romans (202 B.C.), he fled eastward and took refuge in the court of Antiochus III. Full of vengeance, Hannibal encouraged Antiochus to invade Greece to

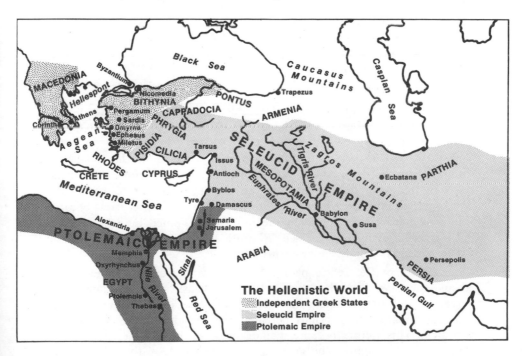

The Hellenistic World
Independent Greek States
Seleucid Empire
Ptolemaic Empire

gain more territory. Rome interfered, defeated Antiochus, forced him to withdraw and took his son as a political hostage to Rome.

Twelve years later the son, Antiochus IV Epiphanes, was released, returned to Syria, and shortly after was crowned king. Full of ambition, he invaded Egypt, the realm of the Ptolemies. However, Rome again intervened. Pressured to leave Egypt, he took out his rage upon the Jews in Jerusalem. He killed many, prevented others from observing religious rites, and polluted the temple by erecting a pagan altar in its midst and by offering a pig as a blood sacrifice.

Unknown to the Seleucidae, they had stimulated a spirit of nationalism among the Jews. Tired of oppression and years of Gentile dominion, they prayed and conspired to be free. This determination not only produced the Maccabean revolt but permeated Jewish thought into the New Testament era up to the time of Bar-Cochba (A.D. 135). Among the orthodox developed a longing for a military, political messiah who would smash the Gentile war machines. This is why so many were disenchanted with Jesus' teachings and actions.

Another significant development of this era was the growth of Antioch in Syria in population and influence. As the capital of the Seleucidae empire, it prospered. By the time of Jesus, it had become the third largest city in the Roman empire. The first major outreach of the gospel occurred in Antioch (Acts 11:19-26); it was there that believers were first called "Christians." It became the site of Paul's home church and the base of his missionary operations.

Maccabees (166-135 B.C.)

After Antiochus Epiphanes' intolerable pollutions of the temple in 168 B.C., further abuses were heaped upon the Jews. The deplorable conditions reached a pinnacle when a Syrian official tried to force Mattathias, an old priest, to offer a pagan sacrifice in the village of Modin. The priest refused and when an apostate Jew volunteered to do so, Mattathias killed him and the government envoy, destroyed the altar, and fled into the wilderness with his three sons. The priest became a national hero overnight. Soon the family was joined by other zealots and a guerilla army was formed. Mattathias died shortly after, but he had lit the spark for a major insurrection.

Leadership of the rebels passed to Judas who was nicknamed Maccabeus, meaning "the hammer." In early clashes the Syrians were victorious, but the zealots continued to increase in experience and in numbers. Finally the guerillas defeated the Syrian army and liberated Jerusalem. This victory became memorialized in the Feast of Hanukkah, or the Feast of Lights. The city was later besieged by the Syrians, but an offer of peace was extended to the Jews because the Syrians were concerned about another enemy that was marching toward their capital, Antioch. However, traitors developed within the Jewish ranks, and civil war broke out once again. This time Judas died in battle and was replaced by Jonathan, his brother.

Both the Jews and the Syrians were marked by political intrigue. There was much inner rivalry as well as visible battles. Finally, through diplomacy Jonathan became the ruling high priest in Judea and a member of the Syrian nobility. Conflict persevered, however, until Simon, Jonathan's brother, secured a treaty with Rome (139 B.C.) and arranged for the granting of political freedom to the Jews by Demetrius II, an aspirant to the Seleucidae throne. Simon then gained for himself and his family official recognition as the high priestly order. This act legitimized a new dynasty, a hereditary high priesthood that came to be known as the Hasmoneans.[1] Political power thus came to be invested in the priests. This dual role (civil-religious) continued and caused the priests to become wealthy, powerful men. With their rise, the royal family of David sank to a new low so that by the time of the New Testament, its members were obscure and insignificant (e.g., Joseph the carpenter).

Hasmoneans (135-63 B.C.)[2]

The death of Simon, the last son of Mattathias, ended the Maccabean era of struggle; the ascent of John Hyrcanus, the son of Simon, marked the beginning of the dynasty of Hasmonean ruling priests. The next hundred years of political freedom were marred by jealousy, greed, and suspicion. The failure of the family to rule itself was manifested in the civil disorder and the military weakness which eventually led to a Roman takeover.

During the reign of John Hyrcanus, two religious-political parties emerged. The Hasidim represented the conservative wing who wished to retain Jewish religious and national liberty and to resist the influence of Greek culture. This separatist group was the forerunner of the Pharisees. On the other hand, the Hellenizers were willing to surrender some of their Jewish distinctives to gain some desired qualities of the Greek way of life. This group matured into the sect of the Sadducees. Before his death, John Hyrcanus repudiated his Pharisaical affiliation and declared himself to be a Sadducee.

Later, at the outset of the reign of Alexander Jannaeus, the Pharisees asked the Syrians for help in overthrowing Alexander and were victorious. When the Pharisees realized that the Syrians might be political opportunists and that they might continue to occupy Jerusalem, they

---

1. Named after Hasmon, the great, great grandfather of Mattathias.
2. The division between the Maccabees and the Hasmoneans is arbitrary. They can be combined into a single period or kept separate.

repented of their initial action. Thinking that Alexander and the Sadducees had been punished enough, they joined forces with Alexander to drive out the Syrians. However, Alexander, bitter over the initial Pharisaical conspiracy, retaliated. He captured the leaders of the rebellion and crucified eight hundred before the Sadducees at a victory banquet. Tradition states that he instructed his wife to dismiss his Sadducean advisors after his death and to reign with the aid of the Pharisees.

Both Alexandra and her son, Hyrcanus II, favored the Pharisees when they assumed control. The Pharisees, crying for vengeance for what Alexander had done, succeeded in getting the civil officials to put to death many of the Sadducees. The rule of Hyrcanus II was brief because his brother Aristobulus II conspired with the Sadducees for his removal. When his mother died, Hyrcanus II fled for his life and found refuge in the house of Aretas, the king of the Nabatean Arabs.

Roman Influence (63-4 B.C.)

In exile Hyrcanus II became acquainted with Antipater, an Idumean, whose son became Herod the Great. Antipater persuaded Hyrcanus II that he had been unjustly deposed and deprived of his hereditary rights by his younger brother. He informed Hyrcanus II that the latter could be restored to the ruling high priesthood by a movement of the army of the Nabatean Arabs against Jerusalem. Hyrcanus II agreed and started back to the Jewish capital. At this time Rome, which had observed the political strife from a distance, intervened, decided in favor of Hyrcanus II, defeated Aristobulus II, and restored Hyrcanus II to the priestly office. Thus, Antipater was introduced to Jewish political life through Rome and Hyrcanus II. The influence of his family in the politics of Palestine continued for the next four generations. Antipater actually became the chief counselor and the real power behind the throne.

Antigonus, the son of the deposed Aristobulus II, later conspired with the Parthians to capture Jerusalem. When he was made king and priest, young Herod, the son of Antipater, fled to the city of Rome. There he won the favor of Mark Antony who conferred upon him the title of "the King of the Jews." With Roman support Herod returned to Jerusalem, drove out the Parthians, and established himself as the political ruler of Palestine. The Hasmonean priesthood that had exercised civil power for one hundred years lost it when Herod came to the throne and never regained it. Although the priests had much power among the Jewish populace, the iron hand of Rome was there to stay.

The constant jealousy of the Hasmonean priests, the struggle between the Pharisees and the Sadducees, and intervention of Gentiles (Syrians, Parthians, Idumeans, and Romans) created a genuine spirit of unrest among the people. They longed for a person to lead them to peace and freedom. Into this world Jesus came (Gal. 4:4). It is no wonder that Herod and all of Jerusalem were troubled when they heard the prophetic question of the Magi (Matt. 2:2).

First Century History

The Mediterranean world in the time of Christ and the apostles was a Roman world. The empire extended from Babylon in the east to Spain in the west and from northern Europe to north Africa. Ever since 265 B.C. when Rome gained control of Italy, it had sought to extend its political influence. When it destroyed Hannibal and the Carthaginian empire, it absorbed Spain and northern Africa. Moving toward the east, through more wars and voluntary surrenders, it annexed Macedonia, Achaia, Asia Minor, Syria, and Judea. The northern border was extended with the conquest of Gaul.

Rome did not superimpose a uniform governmental procedure upon its conquered territories. All areas were naturally subject to the emperor and to the Roman armies, but many localities were permitted to govern their own affairs as long as they did not violate Roman sovereignty or directives. For example, there was fear in Ephesus over the legality of the town meeting called by the angry silversmiths (Acts 19:35-41).

An ancient Roman-built road, a short distance west of Jerusalem.

13

If such meetings were suspected by the Romans as the beginnings of insurrection, they would be put down by force.

Conquered areas were generally organized into provinces. These are mentioned in the New Testament: Cilicia (Acts 6:9), Cyprus (Acts 13:4), Pamphylia (Acts 13:13), Bithynia (Acts 16:7), Macedonia (Acts 16:9), Asia (Acts 20:4), Lycia (Acts 27:5), Illyricum (Rom. 15:19) or Dalmatia (II Tim. 4:10),[3] Spain (Rom. 15:24), Achaia (Rom. 15:26), Galatia (Gal. 1:2), Syria (Gal 1:21), Judea (Gal. 1:22), Pontus (I Peter 1:1), and Cappadocia (I Peter 1:1). These provinces were ruled in two different ways. Proconsuls (Acts 13:7; 18:12), who were responsible to the Roman senate, ruled over those areas where the inhabitants were passive and basically submissive to Roman law. Those provinces that were regarded to be troublesome and possible breeding places for rebellion (e.g. Judea) were ruled by governors called procurators, propraetors, or prefects. Proconsuls gained and kept their positions by annual appointment and renewal; procurators were assigned directly by the emperor and kept their offices as long as the emperor wanted them there.

When New Testament history began, Caesar Augustus was the Roman emperor (Luke 2:1). He had survived a struggle of rivals to gain that position. His reign was marked by political, military, social, and religious reforms. His importance to students of the Gospels lies in the fact that he issued the decree that forced Joseph to take the pregnant Mary to

A CHART OF FIRST CENTURY ROMAN EMPERORS		
Dates	Names	Scriptures
30 B.C.—A.D. 14	Augustus	Luke 2:1
A.D. 14-37	Tiberius	Luke 3:1
A.D. 37-41	Caligula	
A.D. 41-54	Claudius	Acts 11:28; 18:2
A.D. 54-68	Nero	Acts 25:10; 28:19
A.D. 68	Galba	
A.D. 69	Otho	
A.D. 69	Vitellius	
A.D. 69-79	Vespasian	
A.D. 79-81	Titus	
A.D. 81-96	Domitian	
A.D. 96-98	Nerva	
A.D. 98-117	Trajan	

---

3. Two designations for the same province.

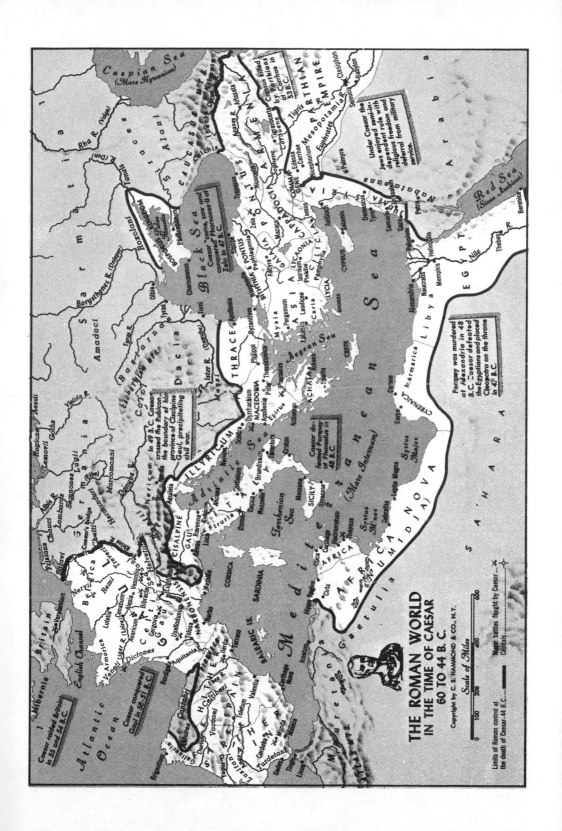

THE ROMAN WORLD
IN THE TIME OF CAESAR
60 TO 44 B.C.

Copyright by C.S. HAMMOND & CO., N.Y.

Scale of Miles
0   100   200   300   400   500

Limits of Roman control at
the death of Caesar-44 B.C.
Major battles fought by Caesar ......✕
Capitals......■

Caspian Sea
(Mare Hyrcanium)

ARMENIA

Crassus killed Parthians at
Tigranocerta. Parthians by Carrhae in
53 B.C.

PARTHIAN EMPIRE

Mesopotamia

Ctesiphon   Babylon
Seleucia

Arabia

Under Caesar the
Jews enjoyed semi-
dependent rule with
religious freedom and
deferral from military
service.

Red Sea
(Sinus Arabicus)

Nabataeans

SYRIA   Palmyra
Damascus   Tyre   Petra
Samaria   Gaza   Pelusium   Berenice

EGYPT
Naucratis   Heliopolis
Alexandria   Memphis
Nile R.
Thebes

Pompey was murdered
at Alexandria in 48
B.C. Caesar defeated
the Egyptians and placed
Cleopatra on the throne
in 47 B.C.

Black Sea

PONTUS   Pharnaces II of
Zela came, saw and
conquered Pharnaces II of
Zela in 47 B.C.

CAPPADOCIA   COMMA-
GENE   Edessa   Carrhae
Nicephorium   Nicosia

CILICIA   Tarsus   Antioch

CYPRUS   Salamis

Libya

Mediterranean Sea
(Mare Internum)

CYRENAICA   Cyrene   Barca
Marmarica

SAHARA

THRACE   Byzantium

MACEDONIA   Philippi
Thessalonica   Pella
Dyrrachium   Apollonia

Aegean Sea

ASIA   Pergamum   Smyrna
Mysia   Ephesus   Laodicea
Lydia   Caria   LYCIA
Rhodes   CRETE

ACHAIA   Athens   Sparta
Corinth

Caesar de-
feated Pompey
at Pharsalus in
48 B.C.

Syrtis Major

AFRICA NOVA   Caerulia

Adriatic Sea

ILLYRICUM

Noricum. In 49 B.C. Caesar
crossed the Rubicon,
the boundary of his
province of Cisalpine
Gaul, precipitating
civil war.

Aquileia   Ravenna
CISALPINE GAUL
Rubicon R.
Genua   Etruria
Rome   Ostia
Corsica   SARDINIA

Tyrrhenian Sea
SICILY   Messana   Syracuse

AFRICA   Utica   Carthage
Hippo Regius   Cirta

NUMIDIA

Mauretania

Atlantic Ocean

Britain

Caesar raided Britain
in 55 and 54 B.C.

Hibernia
English Channel

Germania
Rhine R.

BELGICA
CELTIC GAUL
Lutetia   Alesia   Gergovia
Avaricum   Uxellodunum
Bibracte

NARBONENSIS
Narbo   Massilia

SPAIN
Tarraco   Valentia   Ilerda
Corduba   Gades   Malaca

Caesar conquered
Gaul in 58-51 B.C.

BALEARIC IS.

A CHART OF
THE HERODIAN DYNASTY*

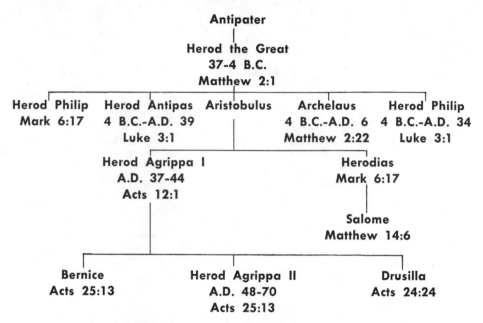

Antipater
|
Herod the Great
37-4 B.C.
Matthew 2:1

Herod Philip	Herod Antipas	Aristobulus	Archelaus	Herod Philip
Mark 6:17	4 B.C.-A.D. 39		4 B.C.-A.D. 6	4 B.C.-A.D. 34
	Luke 3:1		Matthew 2:22	Luke 3:1

Herod Agrippa I
A.D. 37-44
Acts 12:1

Herodias
Mark 6:17

Salome
Matthew 14:6

Bernice	Herod Agrippa II	Drusilla
Acts 25:13	A.D. 48-70	Acts 24:24
	Acts 25:13	

Only those names mentioned in the Bible are listed here.

Bethlehem where Jesus was born. This demonstrates how God can use the decisions of unsaved men to accomplish the fulfillment of His word (cf. Mic. 5:2). The decree ordered that all enter their names on a census roll which would later be used for taxation. To placate the Jews, permission was granted to them to return to their tribal seats of government rather than to Roman seats of authority.

At this time Herod the Great ruled as the King of the Jews in Judea (37-4 B.C.). Given that title and office by Mark Antony, he became a shrewd politician, switching his allegiance to Augustus when the downfall of Antony and Cleopatra became evident. A ruthless person, Herod murdered anyone who dared to question or to remove his authority. Included among his victims were: Aristobulus, a brother-in-law; Joseph, his wife's uncle; Mariamne, his wife; Alexandra, his mother-in-law; and three of his sons. In order to appease the Jews, he enlarged and beautified the temple of Zerubbabel, a project that involved forty-six years (John 2:20). However, he never became a genuine Jewish proselyte; his actions were totally political. When the Magi came west to worship the infant Messiah, they inquired at Herod's court about His location (Matt. 2:1-23). Full of jealous suspicion, Herod also wanted to find Him in order to destroy Him. He may have thought that the baby was born to the deposed Hasmonean clan or possibly to the insignificant royal family of David. When the wise men failed to return, in his rage he declared the decree that all male infants under two years of age in the environs of Bethlehem should be killed. Joseph, warned about Herod's animosity, then took Mary and the infant Jesus to escape the jurisdiction of Herod.

At the death of Herod, a struggle for power among his heirs erupted, insurrections by the Jews occurred, and Jewish pressure against Rome for political autonomy developed. Augustus decided that Archelaus, son by Malthace, should be made the ethnarch of Judea, Samaria, and Idumea. His full brother, Herod Antipas, was appointed tetrarch of Galilee and Perea. Herod Philip, son by Cleopatra, was recognized as the tetrarch of Batanea, Trachonitis, and Auranitis, regions northeast of the Jordan River and the Sea of Galilee.

When Joseph heard that Herod the Great was dead, he returned to Nazareth in Galilee although he feared the wrath of Archelaus as much as that of his father (Matt. 2:22). The Jews so reacted to the reign of Archelaus (4 B.C—A.D. 6) that they succeeded in forcing Augustus to remove him from that position and to replace him with a procurator, Coponius. The next twenty-five-year segment of history was not recorded in the New Testament.

> Now in the fifteenth year of the reign of Tiberius Caesar, Pontius Pilate being governor of Judaea, and Herod being tetrarch of Galilee, and his brother Philip tetrarch of Ituraea, and of the region of Trachonitis, and Lysanias the tetrarch of Abilene, Annas and Caiaphas being the high priests, the word of God came unto John the son of Zacharias in the wilderness (Luke 3:1-2).

These verses identify the main rulers during the ministries of John the Baptist and Jesus. Although Tiberius was not directly involved in the life of Jesus, his presence and power were felt (Matt. 22:17, 21; Mark 12:14, 16, 17; Luke 3:1; 20:22, 24, 25; 23:2; John 19:12, 15). When the Pharisees and the Herodians tried to trick Jesus with the question about the payment of tribute, He replied: "Render therefore unto Caesar [Tiberius] the things which are Caesar's . . ." (Matt. 22:21). One of the accusations made against Jesus before Pilate by the Jews was that He refused to pay taxes to Tiberius (Luke 23:2). The Jews strongly asserted that if Pilate released Jesus he would be the enemy of Caesar and subject to punishment (John 19:12, 15).

On the other hand, Herod Antipas was inseparably connected with the Gospel period activities (Matt. 14:1, 3, 6; Mark 6:14, 16, 17, 18, 20, 21, 22; 8:15; Luke 3:1, 19; 8:3; 9:7, 9; 13:31; 23:7, 8, 11, 12, 15). He ruled those areas, Galilee and Perea, where Jesus grew from childhood to maturity and where He performed most of His miracles. Jesus nicknamed Herod "that fox" (Luke 13:32). It was Herod who beheaded John the Baptist at the request of his adulterous wife Herodias. Later, when he heard about Jesus' ministry, in his fear and superstition he concluded that Jesus had to be John the Baptist resurrected from the dead. Jesus and Herod Antipas never met until Pilate sent Christ to Herod because Christ was from Galilee, Herod's jurisdiction. Antipas hoped that Jesus would perform a miracle to satisfy his curiosity, but when Jesus did nothing and remained silent, Herod sent Him back to Pilate.

Pilate gained immortal notoriety through the trials of Jesus held before him. Born in Seville, Spain, he lived in Caesarea where he was appointed procurator of Judea (A.D. 26-36). During the Jewish feasts, he went to Jerusalem to supervise personally the peace. The Jews disliked him because he had robbed the temple treasury and had used the funds to build an aqueduct to bring water into the city. Various revolts broke out against him; each time he retaliated by killing off some Jews (cf. Luke 13:1). At the time of Jesus' trial, he was under investigation by Roman authorities. Subsequently, he was banished to Gaul by Caligula; there he committed suicide. In addition to references to him in the records of the four Gospel writers, he is mentioned elsewhere in the New Testament (Acts 3:13; 4:27; 13:28; I Tim. 6:13). Along with

The replica of the theater inscription that includes the name of Pontius Pilate. The original, discovered at Caesarea, was taken to Jerusalem for protective purposes.

A CHART OF FIRST CENTURY PROCURATORS OF JUDEA		
Dates	Names	Scripture
A.D. 6-10	Coponius	
A.D. 10-13	M. Ambivius	
A.D. 13-15	Annius Rufus	
A.D. 15-26	Valerius Gratus	
A.D. 26-36	Pontius Pilate	Luke 3:1; 23:1
A.D. 36-38	Marcellus	
A.D. 38-41	Maryllus*	
A.D. 44-46	Cuspius Fadus	
A.D. 46-48	Tiberius Alexander	
A.D. 48-52	Ventidius Cumanus	
A.D. 52-59	M. Antonius Felix	Acts 23, 24
A.D. 59-61	Porcius Festus	Acts 24:27
A.D. 61-65	Albinus	
A.D. 65—Destruction of Jerusalem (A.D. 70)	Gessius Florus	
Destruction of Jerusalem— A.D. 72	Vettulenus Cerialis	
A.D. 72-75	Lucilius Bassus	
A.D. 75-86	M. Salvienus Flavius Silva	
A.D. 86	Pompeius Longinus	
*Herod Agrippa I ruled over Judea in A.D. 41-44.		

Herod Antipas, the Romans, and the Jews, he was held morally and legally responsible for the death of the innocent Jesus (cf. Acts 4:27).

Early apostolic ministry (Acts 1-12) occurred during the reigns of Tiberius, Caligula, and Claudius, the Judean governorships of Pilate, Marcellus, and Maryllus, and the dominion of both Herod Antipas and Herod Agrippa I. When Antipas was banished to Gaul by Caligula, the former's kingdom was given to Agrippa. Earlier, Caligula had given the tetrarchy of Philip to the favored Agrippa. When Caligula was murdered, Agrippa supported Claudius and for this favor was granted the territories of Judea and Samaria (A.D. 41-44). Thus he ruled over the same territory that once belonged to Herod the Great. Agrippa seemed to be a sincere Jewish proselyte. He opposed all attempts to impose pagan idolatry upon the Jews and became the first political ruler to oppress Christianity (Acts 12:1-25). He killed the apostle James, the brother of John, imprisoned Peter, and planned to murder him after the Passover feast. After an angel released Peter, Agrippa in his anger killed the guards.

Because of his persecution and blasphemous pride, God smote him with an incurable disease.

The missionary activities of Paul (Acts 13-21) happened during the reigns of Claudius (A.D. 41-54) and Nero (A.D. 54-68). During the rule of Claudius, a great famine occurred in the Roman empire (Acts 11:28). This event caused the church at Antioch to send financial relief to the church at Jerusalem by Paul and Barnabas. Later, in his zeal to reinstitute the ancient religion to Roman society, Claudius issued a decree forcing all Jews to leave the city of Rome. This caused Aquila and Priscilla to leave Rome and to move to Corinth where they came in contact with Paul (Acts 18:1-3). Although the emperor Nero was not mentioned by his proper name, he was referred to as "Caesar" (Acts 17:7; 25:8, 10, 11, 12, 21; 26:32; 27:24; 28:19; Phil. 4:22) and "king" (I Peter 2:13, 17). In these years (A.D. 41-64), the Christian was able to evangelize and to mature without any official, imperial suppression or persecution.

When Paul was wrongfully arrested in Jerusalem for an alleged violation of temple worship (Acts 21:17-40), he was able to give defenses or apologies of his Christian beliefs to Herod Agrippa II, the Roman procurators Felix and Festus, and Nero himself (Acts 23:23—28:31). With the death of Agrippa I, Judea reverted to rule by assigned procurators: Fadus (A.D. 44-46), Alexander (A.D. 46-48), Cumanus (A.D. 48-52), Felix (A.D. 52-59), and Festus (A.D. 59-61). After Paul was arrested, he was sent to Caesarea, the main Roman headquarters of Palestine, where he was imprisoned and where he appeared before Felix. The Jews charged Paul with insurrection tendencies (Acts 24:2-9), but the apostle formally denied them (Acts 24:10-23). Later Paul gave a strong witness to Felix and his wife Drusilla, one of the daughters of Herod Agrippa I. Felix had frequent contacts with Paul, hoping that the apostle would give him bribery money in order to effect a release (Acts 24:24-26). After two years of imprisonment at Caesarea, Paul was able to give another defense of his convictions to Festus, Felix's successor, when formal charges by the Jews against him were renewed (Acts 25:1-7). In order to avoid a fixed trial at Jerusalem, Paul exercised his rights as a Roman citizen and asked to be tried by Nero (Acts 25:9-12). Later Paul reiterated his defense and appeal before Herod Agrippa II and his sister Bernice who came to visit Festus (Acts 25:13—26:32). Both Festus and Agrippa agreed that Paul could have been released if he had not made a formal appeal to Caesar. Agrippa's dominion at this time included parts of Galilee and Perea and the former tetrarchies of Philip and Lysanias.

Paul had two direct encounters with Nero. Paul's appeal took him to Rome where he spent two years under house arrest (Acts 28:16-31).

This panel on the Arch of Titus, in Rome, shows Roman soldiers carrying off furnishings from the temple at Jerusalem. The scene records the destruction of Jerusalem by the Romans under the emperor Titus in A.D. 70. (See also page 323.)

Since Paul had not violated any Roman civil decree, he was acquitted and released. Later, when a fire destroyed a large section of Rome (A.D. 64), Nero blamed it on the Christians who believed in a future destruction of the world by fire. He arrested and murdered many Christians at this time, including Paul and Peter. This was the first official imperial persecution.

In the closing years of Nero's reign, the Jewish war against the Romans broke out (A.D. 66-73). Vespasian, a Roman general, in order to suppress the rebellion, besieged the city of Jerusalem. While this was taking place, a revolt broke out in Rome. Nero was overthrown and killed. Civil war followed, with a rapid succession of emperors being assassinated: Galba (A.D. 68), Otho (A.D. 69), and Vitellius (A.D. 69). Finally, the army of Vespasian killed Vitellius and made the general their emperor. When Vespasian left Jerusalem, his son Titus continued the siege and finally destroyed the city and the temple in A.D. 70. The Jewish War ended in A.D. 73 with the final conquest of Masada.

New Testament history is basically silent about the latter third of the first century. The last living apostle, John, was finally banished to Patmos by the emperor Domitian in the second major imperial persecution (Rev. 1:9). This is the last historical allusion. The New Testament, although written against a historical background, was not designed to become a textbook of history. The authors referred to civil authorities

21

and events only when they made a positive contribution to an understanding of the activities of both Christ and the apostles.

Socio-Economic World

Class Structure

In the Roman world there was a great gulf between the rich and the poor. The wealthy consisted of the political and ruling families and the landowners who controlled public lands, bought private acreage at a low price from the financially destitute, and exploited conquered territories. The middle class was almost nonexistent. Some craftsmen thrived (Acts 18:3; 19:24), but most middle-bracket people soon became poor, dependent upon public welfare. The poor were everywhere. Without the basic necessities of food, clothing, and shelter, they were driven to lives of crime (cf. Luke 10:30; Eph. 4:28).

It has been estimated that the majority of the Roman world consisted of slaves. They became such by conquest, birth to slave parents, or inability to pay debts. Slaves came from all strata of society: rich and poor, male and female, and learned and ignorant. Because of the great supply, most slaves were inhumanely treated; they were looked upon as things, objects of possession to be sold, bought, and killed at will, instead of as human beings. However, there were some warm, considerate slave-master relationships. Some slaves were given wages so that they could later purchase their freedom; others were released directly by the will of the master out of love and compassion. Many of the early Christian converts came out of the slave class. Throughout the Epistles can be found instructions as to how Christian slaves and Christian masters should conduct themselves (I Cor. 7:21-22; 12:13; Gal. 3:28; Eph. 6:5-8; Col. 3:11; 3:22—4:1; I Tim. 6:1-2; Titus 2:9; Philem.; I Peter 2:18-25). The apostles never attacked nor defended the institution of public slavery; rather, they addressed themselves only to Christians who were directly involved. The concepts of redemption from bondage to sin and of equality in Christ, however, provided embryonic patterns for the eventual release of slaves by Christian masters.

Although slavery was widely practiced in the Old Testament era, it had practically disappeared from Jewish life by the first century. Most Jews in Palestine were free and poor. They made their living by farming, fishing, herding, and various crafts (e.g., pottery making, carpentry). The rich aristocracy was composed of the families of the priests and rabbis. Their major income came from the control of the lucrative temple commerce (John 2:13-17; Matt. 21:12-16). They exchanged Gentile coin for Jewish shekels for a fee and at a rate in their favor; they sold animals and birds for sacrificial use; they inspected the animals for a fee before sacrifice; and they received kickbacks from those who operated these concessions in the temple area. Wealth was looked upon as a sign of divine favor and inner spirituality, but Christ shocked both the rich and the poor with His repudiation of that assumption (Matt. 6:19-24; Luke 16:13-31; 18:18-30).

Languages

Because of Alexander's conquests, the Roman occupation of the Mediterranean world, and the constant migration of people, most individuals were bilingual or multilingual. In the midst of many languages and dialects (Acts 2:4-11), four major tongues emerged. Latin was spoken only by native Romans and key political subjects. It was used by lawyers, authors, and poets, mainly in the western section of the Roman empire. Its usage never filtered down to the ordinary man. The language most spoken and read throughout the Mediterranean area was Greek. Archaeologists have uncovered innumerable papyrus documents and fragments showing its usage in letters, business affairs, and mundane matters. In Palestine and throughout the Near East, Aramaic was very popular. Jesus doubtless spoke it (cf. Matt. 27:46). Hebrew was no longer spoken and read by the average Jew; the orthodox, including the rabbis of the Pharisaical order, still embraced its usage. The apostles were probably bilingual (Greek and Aramaic) with the exception of Paul who because of his training must have been able to read Hebrew (Acts 21:37; 22:2). Since there was such a language mix, public documents had to be written in several languages in order to reach all of the people. This is why the crime of Jesus, written as a superscription over His head, was inscribed in three languages (John 19:20).

Education

Education was private, not public. The families that could afford it either hired a teacher or bought an educated slave to serve as a tutor for the children in the family. Instruction was given in homes or in private schools (Acts 19:9). Paul used the concept of the tutor or "schoolmaster" (paidagogos, Greek) as an educational metaphor to prove that regenerated believers were no longer under the supervision of the law (Gal. 3:24—4:5). When a child reached an appointed age (usually twenty-one), he became an adult with full acceptance of the responsibilities and privileges pertaining thereto. Until that day the child, even though destined for rulership, was under the discipline of the tutor. Later, some education was taken by youths of rich families at famous Greek universities (e.g. Athens, Tarsus, Alexandria). In the early years of formal education, the basics of reading, writing, and mathematics were gained; later, attention was given to speech, law, philosophy, and literature.

Jewish education differed somewhat. The main textbook was the Old

Testament; Jewish youths read, recited, and copied it. Less orthodox families exposed their children to some pagan literature. Wealthy families sent their male children to study with famous rabbis. Paul left his home in Tarsus and studied in Jerusalem under Gamaliel (Acts 22:3). Emphasis upon earning a living by using one's hands accompanied the intellectual pursuits. For instance, Paul, although extremely learned, could make tents to support himself (Acts 18:3). He no doubt learned this as a lad in his hometown either from his father or a close friend.

Religions

Gentile

Idols and temples to the pantheon of Greek-Roman gods still were in vogue in New Testament times. In Athens Paul became burdened when he saw a "city wholly given to idolatry" (Acts 17:16). In order not to offend any god that might have been overlooked, the Greeks had even constructed an altar with this inscription: "To the Unknown God" (Acts 17:23). These devotees believed that the gods could dwell among men. When Paul healed the cripple at Lystra, the pagans thought that

The Parthenon at Athens.

he was Mercury and that Barnabas was Jupiter (Acts 14:8-18) and almost offered animal sacrifices to them. Later at Malta when Paul was not affected by the bite of a poisonous snake, the inhabitants believed him to be a god (Acts 28:1-6). The city of Ephesus identified patriotism with worship of its distinctive goddess, Diana, in the temple dedicated to her (Acts 19:23-41). Some of the early converts turned from such pagan idolatry to the living God (I Thess. 1:9).

Emperor worship was part of the state religion of Shintoism in Japan before the Second World War. Patriotism was manifested in total obedience to him. The refusal to worship Hirohito was looked upon not as a matter of religious conscience, but as an issue of treason. The same situation had its beginnings in the Roman empire during the first century. Several emperors (Caligula, Nero, and Domitian) tried to ascribe deity to themselves with limited success. Some rulers were deified at death. Such worship of the Caesars, either living or dead, was more political than religious. It fostered loyal allegiance on the part of the subjects. Most polytheistic pagans had no problem in adding another deity, but Christians could not participate. They could not call any man "God," "Savior," or "Lord." These titles belonged only to the triune God of the Scriptures. For this reason, some imperial persecution came to them during the days of Nero, but the real pressure did not arrive until the second century when they were exposed to severe martyrdoms by the Roman populace. There is no reference in Scripture to the worship of the emperor and/or state.

The influence of the occult was strong then. All men, both civilized and barbaric, were basically superstitious. These fears and beliefs gave rise to the use of means to contact the supernatural world of demons and bodiless human spirits, to ascertain the future, and to control their destinies. Astrology, magic, exorcism (casting out demons by a secret formula), augury (predicting the future by an examination of the inner organs of sacrificed animals or by observation of bird migration), and necromancy (consulting the spirits of dead men) all fascinated and gripped the minds of unregenerate men. Both Israel and the church were warned against involvement with such satanic practices (Deut. 18:9-14; I Cor. 10:20-21; Eph. 5:11-12). Simon of Samaria, a professed convert, had been involved in sorceries and witchcraft (Acts 8:9-24). Paul inflicted blindness upon Elymas, a sorcerer, and identified him as a "child of the devil" when the latter opposed the apostle's ministry (Acts 13:6-11). Paul cast a spirit of divination out of a woman who was being used by her masters to gain money through fortune telling (Acts 16:16-18). Jewish exorcists tried to imitate Paul by casting out demons in the name of Christ and failed (Acts 19:13-17). Many Ephesian converts once involved in the occult brought their magical books and arts and burned them publicly, even though they were expensive, as a testimony to others (Acts 19:19).

Many pagan intellectuals had become thoroughly disenchanted with their religious heritage and had moved into philosophical speculation. Paul encountered such at Mars Hill in Athens. Luke reports: "For all the Athenians and strangers which were there spent their time in nothing else, but either to tell, or to hear some new thing" (Acts 17:21). Although these erudite scholars had the time, money, and intelligence to engage in such pursuits, the average pagan in the home, farm, or marketplace was too concerned about eking out a living to get involved. These philosophies seldom filtered down to the world of blood, sweat, and tears. Nevertheless, these philosophies did influence some Christian thinking and some converts brought into their new faith faulty mental concepts framed by these pagan ideas. Many false teachers had wedded some misinterpreted Scriptural concepts with Greek philosophy and had penetrated the churches with their intellectual message. Several Epistles were written to warn believers about the errors of this syncretism (e.g. Colossians, I John, and Jude). Paul admonished: "Beware lest any man spoil you through philosophy and vain deceit, after the tradition of men, after the rudiments of the world, and not after Christ" (Col. 2:8). He claimed that although the Greeks desired to hear human wisdom he would continue to exalt the cross (I Cor. 1:22-23).

The philosophies had many forms and emphases. Gnosticism (Greek *gnosis* means "knowledge") deprecated the value of the material world and exalted the soul or mind. At death the soul was released from the prison of the body. Since the body was temporary, it could be dissipated through lustful use or its appetites could be starved in order to fulfill the wishes of the mind. The beginnings of pseudo-Christian, Gnostic heresies can be seen in the background of Colossians and I John. Such a philosophy would naturally deny the creation of the material universe by God directly, the incarnation of Christ, His bodily resurrection, the residence of God within the believer's body, and the bodily resurrection of all men. In this system, salvation was gained through knowledge by an elite few with no attention given to sin, guilt, and faith.

The Stoics and the Epicureans were two opposing groups of philosophers (Acts 17:18). Stoicism, begun by Zeno (340-265 B.C.), taught that the world was governed by rational purpose, not by chance, although it denied the existence of a personal God who created and superintended the world. The goal of man was to adjust himself to that purpose. This belief in fate developed self-control and a high level of morality among its adherents. On the other hand, Epicureanism, begun by Epicurus (342-271 B.C.), believed that the world came into being by chance through the cosmic collision of atoms. Since there was no purpose, there was no absolute good. The pursuit of pleasure, not truth, became the quest of man. Whatever brought happiness and satisfaction and removed pain was to be embraced.

The influence of Platonism, cynicism, and skepticism was evident in some pockets of society. Cynics were the beatniks of the first century. They reacted to the economic pursuits of society, believing that the highest goal was to have no human wants or desires. Skeptics denied the reality of absolutes and claimed that everything was relative. The latter dealt with beliefs; the former more with behavior patterns. Platonism denied the reality of the material universe, seeing it only as a mental copy of the real world of ideas.

All of these attempts for truth began and ended with man. In none of these systems was there any place for oral or written revelation from a God who controlled history and the destinies of men.

Jewish

The Jewish concept was just the opposite. The Jews believed in a personal God who had revealed Himself through miraculous interventions into history, in oral pronouncements of divinely authenticated prophets, and in inscripturated truth. To them, the Old Testament was not a collection of ancient religious literature; rather, it was the Word of God, the basis of their morality, religious observances, and civil government. Their Bible consisted of the Law, Prophets, and Writings. This threefold division did not represent three degrees of inspiration or three periods of canonization. Actually, the cause of this division is unknown. Many

Detail of a stone carving of the six-pointed "Star of David," found at Capernaum.

CHART OF THE HEBREW CANON			
Law	Genesis Exodus Leviticus	Numbers Deuteronomy	
Prophets (eight books)	Former Prophets (four) Joshua Judges Samuel Kings	Latter Prophets (four) Major (three) Isaiah Jeremiah Ezekiel Minor (one)* Hosea Nahum Joel Habakkuk Amos Zephaniah Obadiah Haggai Jonah Zechariah Micah Malachi	
Writings (eleven books)	Poetical (three) Psalms Proverbs Job	Five Rolls (five) Song of Solomon Ruth Lamentations Ecclesiastes Esther	Historical (three) Daniel Ezra-Nehemiah Chronicles

The twelve minor prophets were regarded as one book, called "The Twelve."

evangelicals believe that the divisions developed out of liturgical use in the synagogues; whereas others think that the Law was written by Moses, the pattern for all future prophets, that the Prophets were composed by men who had both the prophetic office and gift, and that the third section of Writings was penned by men who had the prophetic gift but not the office.[4] The Hebrew canon consisted of twenty-two or twenty-four books,[5] corresponding to the present thirty-nine.

Since Christianity was an extension of God's program through Israel, the early church also accepted the Old Testament as its authoritative

---

4. For example, David's office was that of king, but God enabled him to prophesy.
5. Some joined Lamentations to Jeremiah and Ruth to Judges.

basis of faith and practice. In time, the New Testament books were added one by one to the growing canon. Christ's teaching was saturated with direct quotations and allusions to the Old Testament. He declared it to be final, authoritative, infallible, and irrevocable (Matt. 5:18; John 10:35). The New Testament books are full of references to it. The apostles equated "The Scripture says" with "God says" (Gal. 3:8), identified the word of the prophets with the word of God (Acts 4:24-25; cf. Ps. 2:1; Acts 28:25), and regarded their own writings as equal in authority with the old canon (I Tim. 5:18; II Peter 3:16).

Neither Israel nor the Church accepted the apocrypha as canonical. These books contain romantic tales, philosophical proverbs, devotional expressions, and historical data. Not once did a New Testament writer quote from them. They are full of historical, chronological, geographical and doctrinal errors. Jesus (Luke 24:44), Philo (A.D. 40), Josephus (A.D. 90) and the Prologue to Ecclesiasticus (130 B.C) all referred to a threefold division of the Old Testament canon, not a fourfold one. Although included in the Septuagint, they were not elevated to the status of Scripture until the Roman Catholic Church did so at the Council of Trent (A.D. 1545-1546). These fifteen books were apparently written about 300 B.C.—A.D. 100:

1. Wisdom of Solomon
2. Ecclesiasticus
3. Tobit
4. Judith
5. I Esdras
6. II Esdras
7. I Maccabees
8. II Maccabees
9. Baruch
10. Letter of Jeremiah
11. Additions to Esther
12. Prayer of Azariah or Song of Three Young Men
13. Susanna
14. Bel and the Dragon
15. Prayer of Manasseh

Of these, three were not given canonical status (I Esdras, II Esdras, and Prayer of Manasseh). The remaining eleven were so combined that the net addition to the Catholic Douay Version was seven: Baruch and the Letter of Jeremiah were made one; the additions to Esther were added to the canonical Esther; the Prayer of Azariah was inserted between the canonical Daniel 3:23 and 3:24, making it 3:24-90; and both Susanna and Bel and the Dragon were added to Daniel as chapters thirteen and fourteen respectively.

In circulation during the New Testament era were also pseudepigraphal books, including some apocalyptic literature. They were so named because they bore the names of authoritative Old Testament figures long deceased and because they were designed to encourage the Jewish populace to endure persecution until God's messianic kingdom was established.

They were more removed from canonical status than even the apocrypha. Here is their listing:

1.	Assumption of Moses	10. Martyrdom of Isaiah
2.	II Baruch	11. III Maccabees
3.	III Baruch	12. IV Maccabees
4.	I Enoch	13. Paralipomena of Jeremiah
5.	II Enoch	14. Psalms of Solomon
6.	Jubilees	15. Sibylline Oracles
7.	Letter of Aristeas	16. Testament of Job
8.	Life of Adam and Eve	17. Testimony of the Twelve
9.	Lives of the Prophets	Patriarchs

Two of these (Assumption of Moses and Enoch) were quoted in the book of Jude (vv. 9, 14-15). Mere quotation, however, does not establish the authenticity of all of their content.[6]

The obedience of the Jew to the Book was centered in two places of worship: the synagogue and the temple. Although not mentioned in the Old Testament, the synagogue was at the center of Jewish life in New Testament times (Mark 1:21; 6:2; Luke 4:16, 31; 6:6; 13:10; Acts 13:14, 27, 42, 44; 15:21; 16:13; 17:2; 18:4). Synagogues were not only in Palestine; they also existed throughout the Roman world. James observed: "Moses of old time hath in every city them that preach him, being read in the synagogues every sabbath day" (Acts 15:21). It is difficult to determine whether the first synagogue was organized during the Babylonian captivity, in the postexilic testamental period, or during the intertestamental era, although the first option seems most logical because the need for congregated fellowship, instruction, and worship existed among the exiles. Synagogues could only be started when there were at least ten adult Jewish males in the community. The buildings were preferably located outside the cities and near rivers or lakes in order to facilitate proselyte baptism. In structure they were simple. Generally rectangular, they contained an elevated platform where the reading desk was located, a chest or closet which housed copies of the law and other canonical literature, lamps for lighting, and benches for the congregation. The elders of the community voted for one to become "the ruler of the synagogue" (e.g., Jairus; Mark 5:22). His responsibilities were to preside over the meetings, to introduce visitors (Acts 13:15), to arbitrate disputes (Luke 13:14), to appoint those who would read the Scripture and pray, and to select those who would preach. Either he or an assistant, the synagogue attendant *(hazzan),* was in charge of the physical care of the building. In addition, the attendant blew the

---

6. See discussion under Jude.

trumpet to announce the beginning and end of the Sabbath day, lit the lamps, removed and returned the scrolls to the chest, and sometimes served as principal of the synagogue school. The order of service rarely varied and usually included the recitation of the *Shema* or doctrinal creed (Deut. 6:4-9; 11:13-21; Num. 15:37-41) with benediction both before and after, a prayer, the reading of the Law, the reading of the Prophets, a sermon or discourse, and the final blessing or benediction. Often guests were invited to bring the message (Luke 4:16; Acts 13:14-15). This provided the apostles choice opportunities to show the fulfillment of the prophetic hopes in Christ. Quite often they were invited back for several Sabbaths to continue their exposition (Acts 13:42).

The synagogue was the center of instruction, but the temple was the place of sacrifice. There were many synagogues, but there was only one temple. The first temple, built by Solomon (949 B.C.), was destroyed by the Babylonians (586 B.C.). Under the combined leadership of Zerubbabel, Haggai, and Zechariah, a second temple was constructed after many labor setbacks (516-515 B.C.). The Talmud states that five key items from the first temple were absent from the second: the ark of the covenant, the Shekinah cloud of glory, the divine fire, the Holy Spirit, and the Urim and Thummim. This second edifice was plundered by Antiochus Epiphanes and defiled when a pagan altar was erected in its midst (168 B.C.). Shortly after, it was recovered, cleansed, and fortified by Judas Maccabeus. It was seized by Pompey and the Romans (63 B.C.) and subsequently by Herod the Great (37 B.C.). Herod began a renovation program of enlargement and beautification in the eighteenth year of his reign (20-19 B.C.). Work on the temple proper was completed by the priests in a year and a half; the courts were finished in eight years. Auxiliary buildings were constantly being added up to the reigns of Herod Agrippa II and Albinus (A.D. 64). The work had been in operation for forty-six years (John 2:20) when Jesus first cleansed it.

Its architectural specifications can be gleaned from the writings of Josephus and the Talmud. The temple area covered about twenty-six acres. The main building and its courts were arranged in terraces, with the temple found on the highest one. Thus the temple was clearly visible to all within the city of Jerusalem and to those outside with an unobstructed view of the city. The outer court, known as the court of the Gentiles, was frequented by Gentiles, unclean persons, and merchants. It was surrounded by a high wall with several gates on the western side and porticoes all around it. This was probably the area in which the money exchangers and the sellers of sacrificial animals were located. On the inner side was a rampart surrounded with a stone parapet which also formed the outer boundary of the inner temple area. A short distance away from the rampart was a wall which surrounded

Herodian Jerusalem (a model) including the temple area in the background.

the temple and the inner courts. Through the eastern gate of this wall one could enter into the court of the women. This gate, higher and wider than the eight others, was made of Corinthian brass and probably was known as the "Beautiful Gate" (Acts 3:2). A wall separated the court of the women from the court of the Israelites. Within the court of the Israelites was the court of the priests with the temple sanctuary. Within the court of the priests was the altar of sacrifice and the laver. The temple was on a terrace, twelve steps higher than the inner court. It was built upon massive blocks of white marble, gilded with gold decorations both inside and out. The temple was divided into two sections: the Holy Place and the Holy of Holies. The Holy Place was sixty feet long, thirty feet wide, and ninety feet high. It contained one golden candlestick, a table of showbread, and an altar of incense. The Holy of Holies was thirty feet long, thirty feet wide, and ninety feet high. It did not contain any furniture because the ark of the covenant disappeared during the time of the Babylonian invasion. A wooden partition and a thick double veil separated the two holy places.

Only during the religious feasts did large numbers of people come to the temple area. It was designed for sacrificial ceremonies, not for congregational worship. However, individuals could go there for prayer (Luke 2:37; 18:10). Some teaching occurred there when a leading rabbi was present (cf. Luke 20:1). The priests were permitted by the Romans to maintain a police force to guard the inner sanctuary, to keep unauthorized persons out of certain designated areas (e.g., Gentiles out of the inner court), and to maintain order in the courts (Matt. 26:47; Acts 4:1; 5:24-26). This force, led by Judas, may have arrested Christ in Gethsemane and removed Him to the house of Annas.

Jewish religious observances were based upon the directives of the Old Testament. The Sabbath, or the seventh day of the week, was to be kept holy through rest and instruction in the Law (Exod. 20:6-11). In defining work, the scribes had imposed upon the Sabbath such strict regulations that works of compassion and necessity were ruled out. This led to their criticism of Jesus' actions and to their claim that He had broken the Sabbath (Matt. 12:1-14; 23:2-4). The religious calendar was marked by these feasts:

Date	Title	Scripture
April 14	Passover	Exod. 12:1-20; Lev. 23:5
April 15	Unleavened Bread	Lev. 23:6-8
June 6	Pentecost	Lev. 23:15-21
October 1	Trumpets	Lev. 23:23-25
October 10	Atonement	Lev. 23:26-32
October 15	Tabernacles	Lev. 23:33-44
December 25	Dedication	John 10:22
March 14	Purim	Esther 9:26-28

The religious year began with Passover, whereas the civil year began with the Feast of Trumpets. The first six feasts were ordered by God through Moses; Purim began after the Babylonian captivity in the postexile era; and the Feast of Dedication started in the intertestamental period. The feasts were holy, patriotic seasons in which the people were reminded of their national heritage and the works of God in their behalf.

The Feast of Passover was the oldest and most important. It was their "Independence Day" (cf. our July 4). It commemorated their deliverance from Egyptian bondage under the leadership of Moses (Exod. 12:1-28), an event that marked the beginning of their national life through the redemptive purpose of God. It became identified with the Feast of Unleavened Bread to form an eight-day festival, known sometimes as the days of unleavened bread or merely as Passover (Matt. 26:2, 17). As a youth, Christ attended this feast in Jerusalem (Luke 2:41-52).

In His ministry He cleansed the temple during Passover (John 2:13-17), and He was crucified during that season (cf. I Cor. 5:7). Passover, Pentecost, and Tabernacles formed the three great annual festivals.

Pentecost (Exod. 23:16; Lev. 23:15-22; Num. 28:26-31; Deut. 16: 9-12) was also known as the Feast of Harvest, the Feast of Weeks, and the Day of First Fruits. It occurred fifty days after Passover. It marked the anniversary of the giving of the law to Moses on Mt. Sinai and a thanksgiving for the conclusion of the harvest. During the observance, loaves of bread were made from the recently harvested grain and offered to God on the altar. Not mentioned in the Gospels, it holds significance because on the Day of Pentecost that followed Christ's death, resurrection, and ascension, the Holy Spirit descended in fulfillment of Christ's pledge (Acts 2:1).

The Feast of Trumpets, or *Rosh Hashanah,* marked the beginning of the Jewish New Year (cf. our Jan. 1) or crop year. It came after the harvest of the previous year and before the sowing of the crops for the new year. It was celebrated with the blowing of trumpets and horns in the temple from morning to evening. Since it was not a required feast, most Jews stayed at home and observed it in the synagogues rather than at the Jerusalem temple. This feast is not mentioned in the New Testament.

The Day of Atonement, perhaps the most sacred holy day for the pious Jew, was the day appointed for a yearly, general, and perfect expiation for all those unatoned, uncleansed sins of the past year. It was a day during which the nation of Israel was reconciled to God. It became a day of fasting for the people, a period devoted entirely to confession, repentance, and prayer (Acts 27:9). On this day only did the high priest enter the Holy of Holies, taking the blood of the sin offering with him. This day provided the historical and theological background against which the Book of Hebrews contrasts the priestly work of Christ.

The third of the great annual feasts, the Feast of Tabernacles, was an eight-day festival that began just five days after the Day of Atonement (Lev. 23:36; Deut. 16:13; Ezek. 45:25; Neh. 8:18). It was also known as the Festival of Tents, the Feast of Ingathering, and the Festival of Jehovah. It commemorated the forty years of wilderness wanderings during which their ancestors lived in tents. It also was an expression of thanksgiving for the ingathering of the harvest and fruits. During the week, the people lived in handmade booths in imitation of their forefathers' experience. On the last day of the feast (John 7:37), two outstanding ceremonies occurred. The first was the lighting of a great candelabra in the court of the women; this symbolized the pillar of fire which led Israel by night (Exod. 13:21). The second involved a procession that brought a pitcher of water from the pool of Siloam. This water was then poured out at the foot of the altar in the court of the priests; this action symbolized the two times when God gave Israel water out of the rock (Exod. 17:5-6; Num. 20:11). This feast formed the background for Jesus' debate with His critics and for two of His major sermons (John 7:2—8:59).

The Feast of Dedication, also known as the Feast of Lights or *Hanukkah,* had its origin in the Maccabean period. It commemorates that time when Judas Maccabeus delivered Jerusalem from the Syrians and reopened, cleansed, and rededicated the temple (164 B.C.). Tradition states that the oil supply for the temple lampstand, enough for only one day, lasted for eight days; thus, an eight-day festival was established. Corresponding to the Christian Christmas, it was celebrated by the brilliant lighting of Jewish houses and the temple area. Today, exchange of gifts is also involved. Jesus apparently attended one of these feasts (John 10:22-39).

The Feast of Purim[7] remembered the exploits of Esther and Mordecai in delivering the Jews from the plot of the Persian Haman to exterminate them (Esther 9:20-32). During the two-day feast, the entire Book of Esther was read publicly in the synagogue. Some scholars detect one possible reference to this feast in the New Testament (cf. John 5:1).

Although New Testament Judaism had one Book, one temple, and one sacred calendar, there were many religious and political sects with differing beliefs and practices. The strict, conservative element was the Pharisees. The title means "separated ones." Some have traced their origin to the postexilic period when Israel separated itself from the heathen of the land under the influence of Ezra and Nehemiah (Ezra 6:21; 9:1; 10:11; Neh. 9:2; 10:28). Most, however, identify them with the Hasidim of the Hasmonean period, a group that resisted the Hellenization of Jewish life. They placed great emphasis on a strict observance of the law, equated the tradition of the elders or the scribal interpretations of the law with the Mosaic law itself, and regarded themselves as very righteous and others as sinners (Luke 18:11-12). They religiously prayed, fasted, tithed, and observed the weekly Sabbath (Matt. 12:1-2; 23:23; Luke 11:42). They believed in the existence of angels, in life after death, and in the resurrection of the body (Acts 23:6, 8; 24:15). They were involved in the conspiracy to put Christ to death.

The liberal religious sect was the Sadducees, the archenemy of the Pharisaical party. The origin of their name is debatable. Some have

---

7. A Hebrew word meaning "lots." This title was attached to the feast because Haman cast lots to determine when he should carry out the decree to massacre the Jews within Persia (Esther 9:24).

traced it to Zadok, the priest who was faithful to David and Solomon when Abiathar, another priest, defected to Adonijah (I Kings 1:32-43); others link it to the sons of Zadok who were the priestly powers during the exile (II Chron. 31:10; Ezek. 40:46). Others feel that the linguistic parent is a Hebrew word meaning "righteous" or "desolation." In any case, the doctrines of the Sadducees were more important than the derivation of the name. They accepted the Law as final authority, placing it above even the Prophets and the Writings. They took the Law literally, rejecting the allegorical interpretations of the Pharisees and the scribal traditions. However, they denied the existence of angels, the immortality of the spirit, and the resurrection of the body (Matt. 22:23; Acts 23:8). In their antisupernaturalistic rationalism, they absorbed many Greek philosophical concepts into their belief. Most of the priests belonged to the Sadducees; therefore, the latter enjoyed much political power in New Testament times. With the destruction of Jerusalem (A.D. 70), their power and existence died.

Scribes probably first appeared during the Babylonian captivity (Ezra 7:6). Initially, they were professional copyists of the law. The more they copied the more they came to know about the Scriptures. Soon they developed into the teachers and interpreters of the law. Whenever a case developed with no direct Scripture bearing upon its solution, they passed an oral judgment upon the situation. They later communicated this oral, traditional law to their pupils. In their teaching they always referred to the judgments of past, learned rabbis (Matt. 7:28-29). Other names for this group included lawyers, jurists, teachers of the law, and rabbis (Matt. 22:35; Luke 5:17; 7:30; 10:25; 11:45, 52; 14:3; Acts 5:34). The most learned of them became the "doctors of the law." Most scribes belonged to or were sympathetic to the Pharisees.

The Herodians (Matt. 22:16; Mark 3:6; 12:13) were an influential political group, composed mainly of the aristocratic, Sadducean priests that supported the Herodian dynasty and Roman rule in Palestine. Greatly opposed to the Pharisees, they nevertheless joined with them in a common effort to crucify Christ.

The Sanhedrin originated during the Greek period of occupation, although many rabbis traced its beginning to the council of seventy elders named by Moses. In New Testament times it was the Jewish supreme court. Biblical writers named it by these terms: "rulers," "chief priests and rulers," "chief priests and elders and scribes," and "council." The high priest presided over a membership of seventy, consisting of high priests, members of families from which the high priests came, tribal and family heads, scribes, Pharisees, and Sadducees (Matt. 26:3, 57, 59; Mark 14:53; 15:1; Luke 22:66; Acts 4:5; 22:30). Council sessions were not held at night, on the Sabbath, or during the various religious feasts. They normally met in the temple area daily, although some claim that they congregated only on Monday and Thursday. In religious cases they had the power to impose and to execute the death sentence upon Gentiles who trespassed into unauthorized temple courts and upon Jews who invited Gentiles into the Jewish temple areas. In civil cases their verdicts of capital punishment had to be referred to the Roman procurator for execution. Christ appeared before the Sanhedrin on a charge of blasphemy (Matt. 26:65). The council also heard the charges against Peter and John (Acts 4:5, 6; 5:27), against Stephen (Acts 6:13), and against Paul (Acts 23:1). It controlled a police force that could make arrests (Matt. 26:47; Mark 14:43; Acts 4:3; 5:17-18). It even had the power to issue warrants to the synagogues of Damascus for the seizure of Christians in their midst (Acts 9:2; 22:5; 26:12).

Although not mentioned in the Gospels, the Essenes were a well-known sect in the time of Jesus. They formed a monastic community on the western shore of the Dead Sea near Engedi. Organization was strict with unconditional obedience demanded of its members. Three years of probation were required before full membership was granted. Since they abstained from marriage, converts came through adoption of others' children or proselytization. Pure communal living was practiced: common food, meals, clothes, and treasury. Since trading was forbidden, they

Ruins of the domestic sections of the Qumran community. A mill for grinding grain is in the foreground.

The sheer east slope of Masada rock, the site of Herod's famed fortress by the Dead Sea.

engaged in agriculture and crafts to support themselves. Furthermore, they repudiated slavery, swearing, and anointing with oil; bathed in cold water before each meal; practiced modesty at all times, and wore white clothing. They had not only withdrawn from a Roman-controlled society, but they also refused to offer sacrifices at the temple because they believed that the priests were corrupt. Instead, they sent gifts of incense to the temple. They were far more legalistic than the Pharisees. Some have conjectured that either Jesus or John the Baptist (or both) had been influenced by the Essenes, but there is no objective, Scriptural proof that this happened. The discovery of the Dead Sea Scrolls in 1947 led to the disclosure of the Qumran community on the western shore of the Dead Sea. Scholars have debated whether the Qumran community belonged to the Essene sect. There are both similarities and differences between their respective beliefs and practices. If they were not identical, then they probably were two branches of the same ascetic sect.

The Zealots were political revolutionaries. Committed to the overthrow of Roman rule, they refused to pay taxes and started frequent revolts (cf. Acts 21:38). Barabbas was probably one (Mark 15:7). One of Jesus' disciples, Simon, was a converted political revolutionary (Luke 6:15; Acts 1:13). Their strength was located in Galilee and in other remote areas. Their power came to an abrupt end in the Jewish War (A.D. 66-73) at the infamous siege of Masada.

As a result of the Assyrian (722 B.C.) and the Babylonian (586 B.C.) conquests of Palestine, Jews were scattered throughout the Mediterranean world. They were divided into two groups: the Hebraists and the Hellenists. The Hebraists were Jews who were committed to orthodox Judaism, and who spoke Hebrew or Aramaic and closely followed Hebrew rituals (e.g., Paul; Acts 22:3; Phil. 3:5). On the other hand, the Hellenists were those Jews who continued to embrace the faith of Judaism but who adopted the customs of their Gentile neighbors.

Increase Your Learning

By Discussing

1. Should history be called "His Story"?
   How can God carry out His plan for the ages without the violation of human freedom?
2. Contrast the social and economic conditions of the first century with those of the present.
3. Do any contemporary religious and philosophical movements have counterparts in the first century? Do men think and worship any differently today?
4. What can evangelicals learn from the various religious sects that existed within first-century Judaism?

By Reading

Pfeiffer, Charles F. *Between the Testaments.* Grand Rapids: Baker Book House, 1959 .

Tenney, Merrill C. *New Testament Times.* Grand Rapids: Wm. B. Eerdmans Publishing Co., 1965.

Byblos, the ancient Phoenician seaport.

2

INTRODUCTION

Title

Christians are men and women of *the Book*. The Muslim people have the Koran, the Hindus have the Rig-Veda, but Christians base their faith and practice upon the Bible. But why is this group of sixty-six books called the Bible? Why not some other name? The title is based upon the word *biblos,* the name of the papyrus or byblos reed used in ancient times for making scrolls or writing paper. In fact, the ancient Phoenician city of Byblos was so named because it was the commercial center for the manufacture and shipping of this precious writing material. The magnificent ruins of Byblos can still be visited in modern Lebanon today. Daniel regarded the prophecy of Jeremiah as one of the books *(ta biblia* in the Septuagint, the Greek translation of the Hebrew Old Testament; Dan. 9:2) by which he understood the length of the Babylonian captivity. From his Roman prison Paul charged Timothy to bring "the books, especially the parchments" (II Tim. 4:13). Both of these references show the use of *ta biblia* for some of the Old and New Testament books. Very early in church history Christians called the Scriptures "The Books." The dominance of the Roman church fostered the use of the Latin word *biblia* which is the same in the French language. By the thirteenth century, The Books (plural) came to be known as The Book (singular). Our English word "Bible" is, then, based upon the Latin and French with an Anglicized ending. This title shows the basic authority and unity of all of the books within the two testaments. Christians do not regard the New Testament as a second Bible; they follow one book, with two major divisions of equal value and authority.

Jesus Christ referred to the Old Testament books as the "scriptures" (Matt. 21:42) or the "scripture" (John 10:35), using both the singular and plural designations. The word "scripture" is the translation of the Greek word *graphe,* which basically means "a writing." Christ regarded the written, prophetic word to be authoritative and divinely inspired. New Testament writers did likewise (Acts 18:24; Rom. 15:4). Paul even called them "the holy scriptures" (II Tim. 3:15; Rom. 1:2), and "the oracles of God" (Rom. 3:2). Now, the question is, Were the New Testament books also so entitled? When Paul claimed that all scripture was divinely inspired or God-breathed (II Tim. 3:16), over fifteen of the New Testament books had already been written. Would not these books also be profitable for Timothy's spiritual growth? It would certainly appear so. Earlier, in proving that elders should be supported financially, Paul quoted from two books (Deut. 25:4; Luke 10:7) and referred to them under the singular title, "the scripture" (I Tim. 5:18). Paul thus regarded Luke's Gospel as the authoritative equal of Moses' fifth book; he also saw the two testaments as a single unit. Peter cautioned against twisting the Epistles of Paul ". . . as they do also the other scriptures, unto their own destruction" (II Peter 3:15-16). Note that Peter knew of Paul's letters and of their collection into a single group. His use of "other" is very critical here; he must have valued Paul's Epistles as scripture also. For example, a person may say, "I read *Life, Time,* and other magazines." This is a proper use of "other" because *Life* and *Time* are magazines. Therefore, another fitting title for the New Testament is that of "Scripture."

The second half of our English Bible is more commonly called the New Testament. Tertullian, an early Church Father (c. 200), first employed the Latin *Novum Testamentum* to indicate this section. It was a translation of the Greek *He Kaine Diatheke.* The word "testament" can include the ideas of will, covenant, or contract. The Old Testament was called the book of the covenant (Exod. 24:8; II Kings 23:2). Paul named it "the old testament" (II Cor. 3:14). Jeremiah predicted that the old covenant would be supplanted by a new one (Jer. 31:31). Jesus claimed that the new covenant would be established in the blood of His sacrificial death (Matt. 26:28). Later writers continued the contrast between the old covenant made with Israel and ratified by animal blood, and the new covenant made with the church through Christ's blood (I Cor. 11:23-25; Heb. 8:6-8). It was only natural that the two sections of the Bible would come to be known as the Old and the New Testaments.

Evangelicals, however, consistently argue for the continuity of the two sections within God's progressive written revelation. The two are vitally connected as attested by this familiar poem:

The New is in the Old contained,

INTRODUCTION

The Old is in the New explained;
The New is in the Old concealed,
The Old is in the New Revealed.

Classifications

Any classification of these twenty-seven books of the New Testament must admittedly be arbitrary because they were not so catalogued when originally written. However, it has been convenient to group the books by their content and literary style. The present order of the books within our English New Testament has produced this very common listing:

Biography	History	Pauline Epistles	General Epistles	Prophecy
Matthew	Acts	Romans	Hebrews	Revelation
Mark		I Corinthians	James	
Luke		II Corinthians	I Peter	
John		Galatians	II Peter	
		Ephesians	I John	
		Philippians	II John	
		Colossians	III John	
		I Thessalonians	Jude	
		II Thessalonians		
		I Timothy		
		II Timothy		
		Titus		
		Philemon		

This is a natural division. The New Testament, as should be expected, begins with the four Gospels which depict the advent of the eternal Son of God into the world, His life and ministry here on the earth, His vicarious death and resurrection, and His bodily ascension into heaven. The Book of Acts then records the early history of the church as the gospel is carried by the apostles from Jerusalem to Rome. Once the historical foundation and background of Christianity have been established, its doctrinal significance is then set forth in the Epistles. Since Paul was the most prominent apostle in extending the gospel message throughout the Roman empire, his thirteen Epistles are listed first. There is a question about the human authorship of Hebrews (most believe that Paul wrote it), so it is found right after Paul's letters and before the acknowledged General Epistles. The term "general" applies both to the content of the books and to their readers. Paul's letters were sent to specific churches and individuals, whereas the General Epistles, for the most part, had a general circulation. All of the Epistles present solutions to the doctrinal and moral problems of the early church. The New Testament appropriately concludes with the prophetic Book of Revelation.

43

This final book anticipates the ultimate triumph of God's plan for the ages, the establishment of the kingdom of God on earth, and the eventual creation of the righteous eternal state.

The literary style of the books has also been used as a basis for classification. The first five books are obviously *historical* in character: Matthew, Mark, Luke, John, and Acts. However, these books contain more than just history; they are full of doctrinal and prophetic truths. Because many of the books were written to local churches or groups of believers, they have a distinct *ecclesiastical* character. These are Romans, I and II Corinthians, Galatians, Ephesians, Philippians, Colossians, I and II Thessalonians, Hebrews, James, I and II Peter, I John, and Jude. These books, however, do contain some historical data, a few personal allusions, and much doctrinal and prophetic material. In fact, the Book of Revelation could be included in this category because it was originally sent to the seven churches of Asia. Some books were sent to individuals and thus have a *personal* character: I and II Timothy, Titus, Philemon, II and III John. However, even these books deal with local church problems, contain historical information, and present great doctrinal and prophetic passages. Since both Luke and Acts were sent to Theophilus, they could possibly be classified here. Although Revelation is definitely *prophetic* or *apocalyptic* in character, the prophetic strain can also be found in the sermons of Christ and the apostles, in the historical narratives, and in the doctrinal exhortations of the Epistles. It must be seen then that these classifications apply only to the general style or character of the books.

Late in his life, the apostle John was instructed by an angel: "Worship God: for the testimony of Jesus is the spirit of prophecy" (Rev. 19:10). Jesus Himself, on the night of His resurrection, told His wondering disciples: "These are the words which I spake unto you, while I was yet with you, that all things must be fulfilled, which were written in the law of Moses, and in the prophets, and in the psalms, concerning me" (Luke 24:44). Look at those final two words again: *concerning me*. The major theme of the Scriptures is Christ. Through the Bible one comes to know Christ and through Christ he comes to worship and to know God in all His fullness. The following outline expresses this spiritual theme:

> Preparation for Christ—Old Testament
> Manifestation of Christ—Gospels
> Propagation of Christ—Acts
> Explanation of Christ—Epistles
> Consummation in Christ—Revelation

Some unknown author has aptly written: "If the Old Testament bears witness preeminently to the one who *is* to come, the New Testament bears witness to the One who *has* come."

Writers

The twenty-seven New Testament books were written by nine different men. Evangelicals are disagreed over the authorship of Hebrews. If Paul wrote it, then only eight men were directed by the Holy Spirit to give us these books. This chart lists the writers with their respective books.

Writer	Book		
Matthew	Matthew		
Mark	Mark		
Luke	Luke Acts		
John	John I John	II John III John	Revelation
Peter	I Peter II Peter		
James	James		
Jude	Jude		
Paul	Romans I Corinthians II Corinthians Galatians Ephesians	Philippians Colossians I Thessalonians II Thessalonians I Timothy	II Timothy Titus Philemon
?	Hebrews		

It is quite obvious that all of the writers were men. They were all Jews, with the possible exception of Luke; however, some feel that he was a Jew with a Greek name (cf. Timothy who had a Jewish mother and a Greek father; Acts 16:1).

Matthew, John, and Peter were members of the original band of twelve apostles (Matt. 10:1-4). Paul became an apostle by the direct revelation and commission of the resurrected Christ (Gal. 1:1, 11-12). Paul called James an apostle and mentioned that James had also seen the risen Lord (I Cor. 15:7; Gal. 1:19). Luke, although not an apostle, was closely connected with Paul in the latter's apostolic, missionary ministry. The young church at Jerusalem, including the apostles, met in the home of John Mark (Acts 12:12) who later was identified with the ministries of Paul and Peter (Acts 13:5; Philem. v. 24; I Peter 5:13). Jude was the brother of James (Jude v. 1). Therefore, the New Testament was written by apostles, men directly appointed by Christ, and by others closely associated with these same apostles.

Both James and Jude were half-brothers of Christ, probably born to Mary and Joseph after the birth of Jesus (Mark 6:3; Gal. 1:19). Of the eight known authors, only two (Paul and Luke) did not know Jesus during His earthly ministry. Vocationally, John and Peter were commercial fishermen before their apostolic call. Matthew was a publican or tax-collector. Luke was a physician; Paul was a religious Pharisee. Nothing is known about the prior occupations of Mark, James, and Jude. Perhaps the latter two were carpenters like Joseph, their father.

A second look at the chart will reveal that Paul wrote about one-half of the New Testament books, a remarkable achievement considering the fact that he began his ministry much later than the others. In fact, he wrote more books than all of the original apostles put together. Both Paul and Peter used amanuenses or secretaries at times to compose some of their books (Rom. 16:22; I Peter 5:12).

Order of Writing

The New Testament books were not written in the order in which they appear in our English Bibles (consult the chart). The Gospels were not written before the Epistles, nor were all of Paul's letters necessarily penned before the General Epistles. In fact, the Pauline Epistles were not composed in their listed order either. It is generally acknowledged by evangelicals that James was the first and that Revelation was the last to be published.

It is difficult to date all of the books accurately. Because some do not contain any pertinent historical date (II Peter, Jude), it is hard to fit them into the proper first-century background. The Gospels, of course, deal with the life and ministry of Christ without any references to contemporary historical events at the time of writing (cf. the publication of a Lincoln biography today). For this reason, men have debated for decades whether Matthew or Mark was written first.

Using the chart as a guide, notice that no inspired books were produced during the earthly life of Jesus Christ. Neither He nor His apostles wrote then. There is a good possibility that some noninspired accounts of isolated events in our Lord's life were recorded then and that these were later used as source materials in the composition of at least one Gospel (Luke 1:1-2). There is almost total agreement that no book was written during the first fifteen years of apostolic ministry, a time

Approximate Dates of New Testament Books

DATES	30	47	49	52	56	58	61
EVENTS	Life of Christ	Paul's First Journey	Paul's Second Journey	Paul's Third Journey	Paul's Caesarean Imprisonment		Paul's First Roman Imprisonment
ACTS	1-12	13-14	15-18	18-21	22-26		28
BOOKS	James	Galatians, I Thessalonians, II Thessalonians	Matthew?	I Corinthians, II Corinthians, Romans		Luke	Ephesians, Philippians, Colossians, Philemon, Acts

DATES	61	64	67	70	85	95
EVENTS	Paul's Release	Paul's Second Roman Imprisonment				
ACTS						
BOOKS	I Timothy, Titus, I Peter, II Peter		II Timothy	Hebrews, Mark?, Jude		John, I John, II John, III John, Revelation

when the gospel message was practically restricted to Palestine proper (A.D. 30-45; found in Acts 1-12). The Epistles of Paul must be seen against the historical background of his three missionary journeys and two Roman imprisonments (c. 47-67; Acts 13-28). He wrote none during his first trip (A.D. 47-48; Acts 13-14). His first book, Galatians, was probably written in the interval between his first and second journeys. He wrote two books during his second trip (A.D. 49-52; Acts 15:36—18:22), three during his third journey (A.D. 52-56; Acts 18:23—21:17), and none in his Caesarean imprisonment (A.D. 56-58; Acts 22-26). After a troubled, plagued voyage, Paul spent two years in Rome under house arrest, during which time he wrote four books (c. 59-61). After his acquittal, Paul traveled freely in the Mediterranean world and had time to write two more books. When Christianity became a capital offense against the Roman government, Paul was arrested and taken to Rome a second time. During this final imprisonment, he wrote his last book. Outside of James, most of the non-Pauline letters were written late, probably after Paul's three journeys were over.

It would appear then that twenty-two of the New Testament books were composed during a concentrated period of twenty-five years (A.D. 45-70). This is especially striking when one realizes that the thirty-nine Old Testament books were written over a period of one thousand years (c. 1500-400 B.C.). In the next fifteen years (A.D. 70-85), no books were published. There are probably several reasons for this: The early Christians began to experience the Roman imperial persecutions; the apostolic leaders were being martyred; and survival was foremost in the mind of the church. After the Zerubbabel-Herod temple in Jerusalem was destroyed by the Romans in fulfillment of Christ's prophecy (Matt. 24:1-2), the Christians lived in expectation of Christ's imminent return. There was an early tradition that Peter would die and that John would not before the second coming of Jesus Christ (John 21:18-24). The martyrdom of Peter and the prolonged life of John would naturally quicken the faith and hope of the early church. Such a background of persecution and expectation would obviate the composition of more books at this time. Late in the first century (85-95), however, the last living apostle, John, wrote the last five books. John had to dispel the notion that he would not die before Christ's coming (John 21:23). Through him God's progressive written revelation, begun in Genesis, would end with the writing of Revelation (Rev. 22:18-19). With John's writings and death in the past, the foundation of this church age had been firmly established (Eph. 2:20). There would be no need for further revelation; the need, from the second century on, would be to promote the written message of God through translation and evangelization.

Inspiration and Authority

Why do Christians value the New Testament so highly? Why are they often erroneously charged with the sin of bibliolatry (worship of the book)? It is because they believe that both of the testaments are the inspired word of God.

What is inspiration? This theological term is based upon the Greek word *theopneustos,* found only once in the Bible and translated as "given by inspiration of God" (II Tim. 3:16). It literally means "God-breathed." Evangelicals believe that the written Bible is just as authoritative and just as much the word of God as the oral pronouncements of God Himself. This authority extends equally to all of the sixty-six books and to every word contained within those books. This means that the Christian must regard the entire Bible as the basis of his faith and practice. To him it is inerrant truth, no matter in what area it speaks (theology, ethics, history, science, etc.). The evangelical argues that inspiration refers to what was originally written by the prophets and apostles, not to the men themselves nor to the effect produced within the life of the reader. Although the original texts have been destroyed through various means, the essential text of Scripture has been preserved in the thousands of copies discovered by archaeologists and protected in modern museums and libraries. The science of textual criticism has demonstrated the validity of our present Hebrew and Greek texts upon which our English translations are based. The contemporary Christian can look upon his English Bible with confidence, knowing that he holds in his hands the genuine Word of God without essential loss.

The doctrine of inspiration has not been superimposed upon the Biblical books. This is what they claim for themselves. Critics may reject the claim, but they cannot deny that the claim has been made. Both Paul and Peter made such clear assertions. Paul stated: "All scripture is given by inspiration of God" (II Tim. 3:16). Peter added: "For the prophecy came not in old time by the will of man: but holy men of God spake as they were moved by the Holy Ghost" (II Peter 1:21). The Bible was not conceived by man's imagination and desire; Spirit-moved men produced the God-breathed writings. The human authors recognized that they were divinely blessed and controlled men. Moses knew that he spoke and wrote the words of the Lord (Exod. 24:3-4). David asserted: "The spirit of the Lord spake by me, and his word was in my tongue" (II Sam. 23:2). More than one prophet knew that the word of the Lord came unto him (Jer. 32:26; Zeph. 1:1; Hag. 1:1). These men were supernaturally authenticated both by miracles and by the fulfillment of their predictions. Israel acknowledged them as genuine divine spokesmen.

Jesus Christ Himself put His stamp of approval upon the Old Testament. His sermons and conversations were saturated with its contents.

He used it as a defensive weapon against the satanic temptations (Matt. 4:4, 7, 10). In His debates with His critics, He treated it as the final, authoritative word on the subject at hand (cf. Matt. 12:2-5). He boldly argued that the Scripture could not be broken (John 10:35). He further claimed that not one jot (smallest letter of the Hebrew alphabet) or tittle (a stroke of the pen that distinguished one letter from another) would ever pass from the law (Matt. 5:17-18). The liberal critics have theorized that Jesus accommodated Himself to the naive, ignorant beliefs of His day, but there is no concrete evidence that He ever did. In fact, that would be contrary to His entire life and purpose. He was the truth, He lived the truth, and He spoke the truth.

Christ's authentication of the Old Testament forms the basis of His preauthentication of the New Testament. Late in His ministry Jesus affirmed: "Heaven and earth shall pass away, but my words shall not pass away" (Matt. 24:35). How would we know what His words were if they had not been written down? Do not these words contain a hint of future Scripture writing? The real preauthentication of the New Testament can be seen in Christ's promise of the ministry of the Holy Spirit in the lives of His apostles. In the upper room on the eve of His crucifixion, He assured His own with these words: "But the Comforter, which is the Holy Ghost, whom the Father will send in my name, he shall teach you all things, and bring all things to your remembrance, whatsoever I have said unto you" (John 14:26). Later, He added: "I have yet many things to say unto you, but ye cannot bear them now. Howbeit when he, the Spirit of truth, is come, he will guide you into all truth: for he shall not speak of himself; but whatsoever he shall hear, that shall he speak: and he will shew you things to come. He shall glorify me: for he shall receive of mine, and shall shew it unto you" (John 16:12-14). These verses clearly anticipate the content of the Gospels (all things to your remembrance whatsoever I have said unto you), the Epistles (teach you all things; all truth), and the prophetic section, including Revelation (show you things to come).

The apostles recognized that the content of their teaching and writing was divinely revealed (I Cor. 2:9-10). Paul clearly stated: "Now we have received, not the spirit of the world, but the spirit which is of God; that we might know the things that are freely given to us of God. Which things also we speak, not in the words which man's wisdom teacheth, but which the Holy Ghost teacheth; comparing spiritual things with spiritual" (I Cor. 2:12-13). These verses show that Paul saw the fulfillment of Christ's promise within his own ministry. He knew that God had invested him with divine authority (I Cor. 14:37; II Cor. 10:8). Each apostle, himself divinely authenticated, recognized the divine authority of the other: Peter of Paul (II Peter 3:15-16); Paul of Luke

(I Tim. 5:18); and Jude of Peter (Jude vv. 17-18; cf. II Peter 3:3). They regarded the books of the two testaments to be of equal authority (in I Tim. 5:18 Deuteronomy and Luke are so equated).

As an obedient Christian, a child of God must share Christ's attitude toward the Old Testament and His preauthentication of the New. To him the Bible is no mere human composition; it is the living word of the living God. He needs it to sustain his spiritual life. He needs it in order to know what to believe and how to live. This is why he studies it with a deep respect.

Increase Your Learning

By Discussing

1. Do you believe that any new inspired books could be produced today? Defend your answer.
2. What would be your reaction if archaeologists claimed to have found a lost book of the Bible? How could the authenticity of that book be treated?
3. Many sects (e.g. Mormons, Seventh Day Adventists) have elevated their own books to the status of Scripture. How would you disprove their positions?

By Reading

Geisler, Norman L. and William E. Nix. *A General Introduction to the Bible*. Chicago: Moody Press, 1968.

Lightner, Robert P. *The Saviour and the Scriptures*. Nutley, N.J.: Presbyterian and Reformed Publishing Co., n.d.

Pinnock, Clark H. *Biblical Revelation*. Chicago: Moody Press, 1971.

Tenney, Merrill C. *New Testament Survey*. Grand Rapids: Wm. B. Eerdmans Publishing Co., 1961. pp. 123-131, 401-427.

Warfield, Benjamin Breckinridge. *The Inspiration and Authority of the Bible*. Nutley, N.J.: Presbyterian and Reformed Publishing Co., 1948.

Bethlehem across terraced Judean countryside.

3

THE GOSPELS

Although Jesus Christ is the central person of history, very little information about Him can be learned from sources outside of the four Gospels and the rest of the New Testament. Since the first thirty years of His life were lived in obscurity and the latter three or four years of His ministry were localized in Palestine, it would be very unlikely for secular historians and men of literature, residing in Rome, to have written about Him. However, as Christianity spread throughout the Mediterranean world during the first and second centuries, these pagan writers could not ignore the presence of Christians in their midst. Men like Tacitus, Pliny, and Lucian described the new religious sect and traced it back to its founder, Jesus Christ. These early writers, though, made only brief, general allusions to Christ's teachings, trial, death, and influence upon His followers. A first-century Jewish historian, Josephus, wrote this striking paragraph about Christ, but many textual critics believe it to be spurious, an interpolation inserted by later Christians into his text:

> Now there was about this time Jesus, a wise man, if it be lawful to call him a man, for he was a doer of wonderful works, a teacher of such men as receive the truth with pleasure. He drew over to him both many of the Jews, and many of the Gentiles. He was the Christ. And when Pilate, at the suggestion of the principal men among us, had condemned him to the cross, those that loved him at the first did not forsake him; for he appeared to them alive again the third day; as the divine prophets had foretold these and ten thousand other wonderful things concerning him. And the tribe of Christians so named from him are not extinct at this day.[1]

It is true that apocryphal gospels were circulated among the early

1. Josephus, *Antiquities* (Whiston edition), XVIII, iii, 3.

churches, but they were rejected because they did not meet the tests of canonicity. They were not inspired and infallible, free from moral, doctrinal, and historical error. They were not written by authenticated apostles or by their associates. Rather, they contained fanciful legends and mere repetition of canonical truth. They were probably written to enhance and to advance certain heretical viewpoints.

To learn about the life and ministry of the Savior, the believer must look to the Bible, especially to the four Gospels. But why do Christians have any gospel records of the life of Christ? How and why were they composed? These questions and others like them have given rise to the synoptic problem.

The Synoptic Problem[2]

The word "synoptic" comes from two Greek words: *sun,* meaning "with" or "together," and *optanomai,* meaning "to see." The word is applied to the first three Gospels (Matthew, Mark, and Luke) because they present a common approach to the life of Christ. The Gospel of John is omitted because it contains much distinctive content.

Definition of the Problem

The Synoptic Gospels record a lot of material that is common to all three of them or is found in at least two of them. From his study Westcott[3] determined these percentages of differences and similarities:

	Differences	Agreements
Matthew	42%	58%
Mark	7%	93%
Luke	59%	41%
John	92%	8%

Practically the entire Book of Mark can be found within the others. The content of Matthew and Luke is about equally divided between agreements and peculiarities, with Luke having more unique material. The great bulk of John's narrative is found only within his book. It has been calculated that of the 661 verses in Mark, 610 are parallel to Matthew and Luke. Of the eighty-eight separate paragraphs in Mark, only three are absent from Matthew and Luke.

This bulk of common material has given rise to the synoptic problem

---

2. The synoptic problem is a very technical study, usually treated in texts and courses on New Testament Introduction rather than New Testament Survey. However, survey students should have a general familiarity with the problem and its various solutions. For an in-depth treatment, consult Everett F. Harrison, *Introduction to the New Testament* (Grand Rapids: Wm. B. Eerdmans Publishing Co., 1964), pp. 131-156.

3. B. F. Westcott, *An Introduction to the Study of the Gospels,* 7th ed. (London: Macmillan & Co., 1888), p. 191.

with its various questions. How were these pieces of literature constructed? Did the three originate and develop independently of each other? If they did, how can one account for the many similarities among them? Did the writers read each other's books? Did they incorporate sections of the others into their own volume? Did the writers talk to each other about their respective purposes in writing a life of Christ? Did they have access to a common written source or sources? Did they interview eyewitnesses? Could the Holy Spirit direct two or three men to write the same things, yet independently of each other? Finally, why is there material distinctive to each writer, some content common to all three, and other sections found in only two of them?

Various Proposed Solutions

Most critical work on the synoptic problem has been done from the liberal viewpoint, although some conservatives have also been involved in the study. The solutions offered by liberal scholarship usually reflect a humanistic, naturalistic explanation for the literary composition of the Gospels. Little stress if any is placed upon the guiding work of the Holy Spirit in the lives of the writers. The liberals' solutions are based upon two major presuppositions. The first is that the writers incorporated unwritten, oral tradition that had been transmitted from the apostles to the churches. The second is that the writers utilized written, documentary sources to structure their content. Naturally, there could be a combination of the two methods. A third alternative is that the writers copied or borrowed from each other's writings.

The *interdependence* theory concludes that the first Biblical author used oral tradition as the basis of his Gospel, that the second writer consulted the first Gospel for his content, and that the third author researched both written Gospels to structure his narratives. Although this view has a ring of plausibility, there is no positive evidence that one writer read and used the written Gospel of another. By itself, this concept cannot explain the omissions and differences of content within the Synoptic Gospels.

The *oral transmission of tradition* theory claims that the direct source of each Gospel was oral tradition received from the preaching ministry of the apostles. As each generation of converts was taught concerning the life of Christ, the tradition became fixed through constant repetition. It is true that the apostles repeated their oral message many times before the first Gospel was penned. Tradition in fact identified Mark and Luke with the preaching ministries of Peter and Paul respectively. However, this view cannot account for the unique material of each writer either. If the oral tradition was so fixed and authoritative, then why did the authors use such liberty in adding and subtracting material? With such a common base, one would expect to find more total agreement on the details involved in the major events of Christ's life (e.g., trials, death, and resurrection appearances).

Most explanations involve the use of some written sources by the Biblical authors. The *fragment* theory states that each writer used a large number of short written narratives as the basis of his volume. Although Luke claimed that many gospelettes were in existence before he wrote (Luke 1:1-4), he did not say that he incorporated all or parts of them into his book. Even if he did consult these sources, this does not mean that the other two synoptic writers did likewise. Since the Gospels do manifest a general agreement of event sequence, it would be difficult to see how this could be achieved through an arbitrary employment of random fragments. The *urevangelium* theory says that there was an original, written gospel or gospelette from which all three synoptic writers drew their materials. This position, however, cannot explain the differences and/or omissions in the common accounts within the three books. The main objection is that there is no objective, manuscript evidence for the existence of this unknown, original gospel. No Biblical or patristic writer ever refers to it. A very popular approach is the *two-document* hypothesis which states that Matthew and Luke used two main written sources: the Gospel of Mark and another document entitled "Q" by literary critics.[4] The Q document became the basis of that material common to Matthew and Luke, but not found in Mark. A *four-document* theory later developed out of this approach. In this concept, added to Mark and "Q" were an "M" document that was the source of material found only in Matthew and an "L" document containing that content found only in Luke. First of all, it is difficult to prove the priority of Mark. Tradition favors a late date for Mark (A.D. 65). This would mean that Matthew and Luke wrote after A.D. 70 with no reference to the destruction of Jerusalem. If Luke used Mark and wrote his Gospel in the late sixties or seventies, then this creates real problems with the dating of Acts, a book that followed Luke. Luke apparently wrote Acts when Paul was in Rome (c. A.D. 61); the Gospel had to be written in the fifties. Actually, most tradition favors the priority of Matthew. Second, there is no positive, objective manuscript evidence for the existence of such documents designated Q, M, or L. Their existence was never mentioned by the Biblical authors or the Church Fathers. Archaeologists have not unearthed them. Third, it would be difficult to account for the agreements of Matthew and Luke against Mark. If the former two used Mark, why do they agree in some places contrary to Mark? The Gospel of Mark should have served as a

---

4. The letter "Q" is assigned to this document because it is the first letter of the German word *quelle,* meaning "source."

check on them. In the final analysis, this approach is based upon a human, evolutionary development of Scripture.

A contemporary critical view is that of the *Formgeschichte* school.[5] It attempts to determine the beginnings of the material upon which the various documentary sources are based. It goes beyond the written documents to the oral tradition, the apostolic repetition of the teachings of Jesus. The latter, according to its proponents, can be detected in sermonic stories or epigrams and various historical recitals, such as a recounting of Christ's death at the observance of the Lord's Supper. This various biographical data was gathered, collated, structured into a literary framework, and written into a document which became a source for the Gospels.

An Evangelical Answer

Do conservatives have an adequate explanation for the synoptic problem? Are they able to account for the striking similarities of the first three Gospels and the unique distinctiveness of John's Gospel? A concept of strict, verbal dictation by God to human stenographers is incapable of explaining the synoptic phenomena.[6] However, the methods of human expertise that were superintended by the divine Spirit in the production of Holy Writ can be perceived and outlined.

Since two and possibly three of the writers were eyewitnesses of Christ's activities, they had direct knowledge of those conversations, sermons, and events they recorded. Both Matthew and John were numbered among the twelve apostles. Like Peter, they preached and wrote what they personally observed (John 19:35; cf. Acts 10:37-43; I Peter 5:1; II Peter 1:14-18). Since Mark was a resident of Jerusalem, he may have heard the teaching of Jesus when He was in the temple and/or the environs of that city. Luke, of course, would not have had any firsthand acquaintance with Christ.

Since the Gospels were written between twenty-five and sixty years after the events had actually occurred, some have argued that even eyewitnesses would not have been able to remember the events accurately. Men, especially aging men, are prone to memory failure. If the Bible were nothing more than a mere human composition, then this argument would carry some weight. However, such critics disregard the promise of Christ to His apostles, including Matthew and John: "But the Comforter, which is the Holy Ghost, whom the Father will send in my name,

---

5. A German word meaning "form history."
6. The evangelical doctrine of the verbal, plenary inspiration of the Scriptures does not necessitate a dictation approach. Most informed evangelicals do not embrace this concept, although liberal critics of fundamentalism often charge the latter with that belief.

57

he shall teach you all things, and bring all things to your remembrance, whatsoever I have said unto you" (John 14:26). The ministry of the Holy Spirit enabled the apostles to remember, to preach, and to write accurately the oral ministry of Christ. The science of cybernetics claims that the human brain is like a computer, storing up all data impressed upon it. The Spirit so programmed their memory banks that they were able to remember graphically His words at the critical moment of writing.

Other material could have been gleaned through personal contacts and conversations with those who were eyewitnesses. Matthew doubtless heard from other apostles what the latter witnessed in Matthew's absence. For example, only Peter, James, and John observed the transfiguration of Christ (Matt. 17:1-2); however, they reported it to the others after the resurrection of Christ (Matt. 17:9). Mark could have easily talked to the apostles since they established their headquarters in Jerusalem for the propagation of the gospel. Luke journeyed with Paul to Jerusalem (Acts 21:17); therefore, he would have had opportunity to talk with a few of the apostles. During the two years of Paul's Caesarean imprisonment, he would have had ample time to interview many residents of Palestine who had witnessed Christ's ministry.[7] There is a strong possibility that he could have even consulted with Mary, the mother of Jesus.[8] Eyewitnesses were available (Luke 1:2), so all four writers could have talked with such people.

Naturally, some material could have been gained through the hearing of apostolic sermons. Mark doubtless heard many if not all of the apostles' preaching. Luke heard Paul many times. Although Paul was not a firsthand observer, he had infrequent contacts with the original apostles. However, in his case, the message was given to him directly by Jesus Christ through postresurrection appearances (I Cor. 15:1-8; Gal. 1:11-12). Mark and Luke were together with Paul in Rome (Philem. v. 24); therefore, Mark could have told Luke about the life of Christ as given in the content of apostolic sermons which he heard.

As previously mentioned, Luke admitted that there were gospelettes or short narratives of Christ's life in circulation at the time he decided to write (Luke 1:1-4). It is difficult to say how many were known to him and what their contents were. Archaeologists have not discovered any of them. They probably were accounts of isolated events (e.g., a diary account of the cleansing of a leper; Luke 5:12-14) written by men not directed by the Spirit.

---

7. Luke's language contains subtle hints that this was so. He identified Mnason as an old disciple (Acts 21:16).
8. Note the statement: "But Mary kept all these things, and pondered them in her heart" (Luke 2:19; cf. 2:51). Would not Mary reveal to a physician that which she would not tell to others?

It is not even inconceivable that the Holy Spirit could have revealed truth to these writers totally unknown to them. If such a revelation were given to Paul, then the procedure could also be partially true of them. However, in the final analysis, it must be admitted that in all cases the writer consulted sources, both oral and written, scrutinized them, selected material, and wrote under the direct influence of the Holy Spirit. These were not mere human compositions; they were the Word of God inscripturated through human penmen.

The Content of the Gospels

The Gospels do not contain needless repetition. Their content cannot be summed up in the following popular statement: "If you have read one, you've read them all." Each Gospel is a distinctive unit by itself. Each was written at a different time for a different readership for a different purpose. A reading of one Gospel will not reveal the total life of Christ. No Gospel writer determined to write an exhaustive, chronological biography. Rather, each selected from a vast reservoir of material those events that would best relate to his purpose (cf. John 20:30-31). These events were then arranged for effect rather than for chronological sequence. The authors were actually writing interpretative commentaries upon Christ's life rather than a daily chronicle. This is why Mark and John omitted references to Christ's birth and developmental years; these events did not suit their purpose. This is why John included only eight of Christ's miracles; the others, although known to him, were not relevant to his literary needs.

To follow Christ's earthly ministry from His incarnation to His ascension, one must harmonize the Gospels into a coherent whole. At times, this is difficult to do. Insufficient data are available to make a firm judgment about the exact time that an event occurred. However, the general movement of Christ's life can be expressed. The following outline is one attempt to correlate the many paragraphs of the four Gospels into a logical, chronological sequence.

	MATTHEW	MARK	LUKE	JOHN
GOSPEL PROLOGUE:			1:1-4	1:1-18
I. THE EARLY YEARS				
A. Genealogies of Jesus	1:1-17		3:23-38	
B. Birth announcement of John			1:5-25	
C. Birth announcement of Jesus			1:26-38	
D. Visit of Mary to Elizabeth			1:39-56	
E. Birth of John			1:57-80	
F. Explanation to Joseph	1:18-25			
G. Birth of Jesus			2:1-7	
H. Worship of the shepherds			2:8-20	
I. Circumcision of Jesus			2:21-38	
J. Visit of the Magi	2:1-12			

	MATTHEW	MARK	LUKE	JOHN
K. Flight to Egypt	2:13-18			
L. Return to Nazareth	2:19-23		2:39-40	
M. Passover visit			2:41-51	
N. Development			2:52	
II. PUBLIC PRESENTATION				
A. Ministry of John	3:1-12	1:1-8	3:1-18	
B. Baptism of Jesus	3:13-17	1:9-11	3:21-23	
C. Temptation of Jesus	4:1-11	1:12-13	4:1-13	
D. Confession of John				1:19-28
E. John's evaluation of Jesus				1:29-34
F. First disciples of Jesus				1:35-51
III. EARLY GALILEAN MINISTRY				
A. Turning water into wine				2:1-11
B. Visit to Capernaum				2:12
IV. EARLY JUDEAN MINISTRY				
A. Cleansing of the temple				2:13-22
B. Talk with Nicodemus				2:23— 3:21
C. Testimony of John				3:22-36
D. Departure from Judea	4:12		3:19-20	4:1-3
E. Ministry in Samaria				4:4-42
V. MINISTRY IN GALILEE				
A. Arrival	4:17	1:14-15	4:14-15	4:43-45
B. Healing the nobleman's son				4:46-54
C. Synagogue at Nazareth			4:16-30	
D. Visit to Capernaum	4:13-16		4:31	
E. Calling disciples	4:18-22	1:16-20		
F. Casting out demons		1:21-28	4:31-37	
G. Healing Peter's mother-in-law	8:14-15	1:29-31	4:38-39	
H. Healing multitudes	8:16-17	1:32-34	4:40-41	
I. Preaching tour		1:35-39	4:42-44	
J. Calling disciples			5:1-11	
K. Healing a leper	8:2-4	1:40-45	5:12-16	
L. Tour summary	4:23-25			
VI. REASONS FOR OPPOSITION				
A. Forgiving sins	9:2-8	2:1-12	5:17-26	
B. Eating with publicans	9:9-13	2:13-17	5:27-32	
C. No observance of fasts	9:14-17	2:18-22	5:33-39	
D. Healing the paralytic				5:1-16
E. Claiming equality with God				5:17-47
F. Plucking grain	12:1-8	2:23-28	6:1-5	
G. Healing withered hand	12:9-14	3:1-6	6:6-11	
H. Withdrawal	12:15-21	3:7-12		
VII. SERMON ON THE MOUNT				
A. Choosing the twelve		3:13-19	6:12-16	
B. Introduction	5:1-2		6:17-20	
C. Beatitudes	5:3-12		6:20-26	
D. Salt and light	5:13-16			

	MATTHEW	MARK	LUKE	JOHN
E. Relationship to the law	5:17-20			
F. Hatred and murder	5:21-26			
G. Adultery and divorce	5:27-32			
H. Oaths	5:33-37			
I. Vengeance	5:38-42		6:29-30	
J. Love	5:43-47		6:27-28, 32-36	
K. Perfection	5:48			
L. Giving	6:1-4			
M. Prayer	6:5-15			
N. Fasting	6:16-18			
O. Treasures	6:19-24			
P. Anxiety	6:25-34			
Q. Judgment	7:1-5		6:37-42	
R. Asking and receiving	7:7-11			
S. Golden rule	7:12		6:31	
T. Warnings	7:13-23		6:43-45	
U. Two foundations	7:24-27		6:46-49	
V. Conclusion	7:28— 8:1			

VIII. SECOND TOUR OF GALILEE

	MATTHEW	MARK	LUKE	JOHN
A. Healing the centurion's servant	8:5-13		7:1-10	
B. Raising the widow's son			7:11-17	
C. Doubt of John	11:2-6		7:18-23	
D. Praise of John by Jesus	11:7-15		7:24-30	
E. Woes upon the cities	11:16-24		7:31-35	
F. Invitation to believe	11:25-30			
G. Anointing by the sinful woman			7:36-50	
H. Completion of tour			8:1-3	

IX. INCREASING OPPOSITION

	MATTHEW	MARK	LUKE	JOHN
A. Concern of his friends		3:19-21		
B. Blasphemy of the Pharisees	12:22-37	3:22-30		
C. Sign of Jonah	12:38-45			
D. Natural relationships denied	12:46-50	3:31-35	8:19-21	
E. Parable of the sower	13:1-9	4:1-9	8:4-8	
F. Reasons for parables	13:10-17	4:10-12	8:9-10	
G. Interpretation of sower parable	13:18-23	4:13-20	8:11-15	
H. Parable of the tares	13:24-30			
I. Parable of the lamp		4:21-25	8:16-18	
J. Parable of rapid growth		4:26-29		
K. Parable of the mustard seed	13:31-32	4:30-32		
L. Parable of the leaven	13:33			
M. Purposes of parables	13:34-35	4:33-34		
N. Interpretation of the tares	13:36-43			
O. Parable of the treasure	13:44			
P. Parable of the pearl	13:45-46			
Q. Parable of the fish	13:47-52			

	MATTHEW	MARK	LUKE	JOHN
R. Calming the storm	13:53; 8:18-27	4:35-41	8:22-25	
S. Healing the demoniac	8:28-34	5:1-20	8:26-39	
T. Request of Jairus	9:1, 18-19	5:21-24	8:40-42	
U. Healing of woman with issue of blood	9:20-22	5:25-34	8:43-48	
V. Raising Jairus' daughter	9:23-26	5:35-43	8:49-56	
W. Healing two blind men	9:27-31			
X. Healing a dumb man	9:32-34			
Y. Unbelief of Nazareth	13:54-58	6:1-6		
X. Third Tour of Galilee				
A. Commission of the apostles	9:35—11:1	6:7-13	9:1-6	
B. Fear of Herod	14:1-12	6:14-29	9:7-9	
C. Return of the apostles		6:30	9:10	
D. Feeding the five thousand	14:13-21	6:31-44	9:10-17	6:1-13
E. Withdrawal of Jesus	14:22-23	6:45-46		6:14-17
F. Walking on the water	14:24-33	6:47-52		6:17-21
G. Sermon on the bread of life				6:22—7:1
H. Healing of the multitudes	14:34-36	6:53-56		
I. Criticism of the Pharisees	15:1-20	7:1-23		
J. Deliverance of the Syrophoenician woman's daughter	15:21-28	7:24-30		
K. Healing a deaf and dumb man	15:29-31	7:31-37		
L. Feeding the four thousand	15:32-39	8:1-9		
M. Sign of Jonah repeated	15:39—16:4	8:10-12		
N. Leaven of the Pharisees	16:4-12	8:13-21		
O. Healing a blind man		8:22-26		
P. Prediction of the church	16:13-20	8:27-30	9:18-21	
Q. Announcement of His death and resurrection	16:21-23	8:31-33	9:22	
R. Essence of discipleship	16:24-28	8:34—9:1	9:23-27	
S. Transfiguration of Christ	17:1-8	9:2-8	9:28-36	
T. Explanation of Elijah	17:9-13	9:9-13		
U. Healing a demonic boy	17:14-21	9:14-29	9:37-43	
V. Second death announcement	17:22-23	9:30-32	9:43-45	
W. Payment of temple tax	17:24-27			
X. Humility and greatness	18:1-5	9:33-37	9:46-48	
Y. Occasions of stumbling	18:6-14	9:38-50	9:49-50	
Z. Principles of forgiveness	18:15-35			
XI. Later Judean Ministry				
A. Unbelief of His brethren				7:2-9
B. Rejection by the Samaritans	19:1-2	10:1	9:51-56	
C. Lessons on discipleship			9:57-62	

	MATTHEW	MARK	LUKE	JOHN
D. Parable of the widow			18:1-8	
E. Parable of the Pharisee and the publican			18:9-14	
F. The faith of children	19:13-15	10:13-16	18:15-17	
G. The rich young ruler	19:16-26	10:17-27	18-18-27	
H. Request of Peter	19:27-30	10:28-31	18:28-30	
I. Parable of the laborers	20:1-16			
J. Third death announcement	20:17-19	10:32-34	18:31-34	
K. Request of James and John	20:20-28	10:35-45		
L. Healing of blind Bartimaeus	20:29-34	10:46-52	18:35-43	
M. Salvation of Zacchaeus			19:1-10	
N. Parable of the pounds			19:11-28	

XV. THE LAST WEEK

Friday

A. Arrival at Bethany				11:55— 12:1

Saturday

	MATTHEW	MARK	LUKE	JOHN
A. Supper at Bethany	26:6-13	14:3-9		12:2-8
B. Plot of the Jews				12:9-11

Sunday

	MATTHEW	MARK	LUKE	JOHN
A. Triumphal entry	21:1-11	11:1-11	19:29-44	12:12-19
B. Request of the Greeks				12:20-36
C. Return to Bethany		11:11		12:36

Monday

	MATTHEW	MARK	LUKE	JOHN
A. Cursing the fig tree	21:18-19	11:12-14		
B. Cleansing of the temple	21:12-13	11:15-18	19:45-48	
C. Healing the multitudes	21:14-16			
D. Return to Bethany	21:17	11:19		

Tuesday

	MATTHEW	MARK	LUKE	JOHN
A. Withering of the fig tree	21:19-22	11:20-26		
B. Question over authority	21:23	11:27-28	20:1-2	
C. Evaluation of John's authority	21:24-27	11:29-33	20:3-8	
D. Parable of the two sons	21:28-32			
E. Parable of the husbandmen	21:33-46	12:1-12	20:9-19	
F. Parable of the marriage feast	22:1-14			
G. The tribute question	22:15-22	12:13-17	20:20-26	
H. The resurrection question	22:23-33	12:18-27	20:27-40	
I. The commandment question	22:34-40	12:28-34		
J. The Messiah question	22:41-46	12:35-37	20:41-44	
K. Woes upon the Pharisees	23:1-39	12:38-40	20:45-47	
L. Unbelief of Israel				12:37-50
M. The widow's mite		12:41-44	21:1-4	
N. Prediction of the temple's destruction	24:1-2	13:1-2	21:5-6	

	MATTHEW	MARK	LUKE	JOHN
O. Signs of Christ's return	24:3-42	13:3-33	21:7-36	
P. Parable of the watchful servant		13:34-37		
Q. Parable of the thief	24:43-44			
R. Parable of the steward	24:45-51			
S. Parable of the virgins	25:1-13			
T. Parable of the talents	25:14-30			
U. The sheep-goat judgment	25:31-46			
V. Summary of activities			21:37-38	
W. Plot of the Jews	26:1-5	14:1-2	22:1-2	
X. Betrayal of Judas	26:14-16	14:10-11	22:3-6	

Wednesday
  no record

Thursday

A. Passover preparation	26:17-19	14:12-16	22:7-13	
B. Eating the Passover meal	26:20	14:17	22:14-18	13:1
C. Washing the disciples' feet			22:24-27	13:2-17
D. Exit of Judas	26:21-25	14:18-21	22:21-23	13:18-32
E. Institution of the Lord's Supper	26:26-29	14:22-25	22:19-20	
F. Prediction of denial	26:31-35	14:27-31	22:28-38	13:33-38
G. Teaching on comfort				14:1-31
H. Vine and the branches				15:1-16
I. Future relationships				15:17—16:33
J. Prayer of intercession				17:1-26
K. Prayer in Gethsemane	26:36-46	14:32-42	22:40-46	18:1

Friday

A. His arrest	26:47-56	14:43-52	22:47-53	18:2-12
B. Trial before Annas				18:13-14, 19-23
C. Trial before Caiaphas	26:57-68	14:53-65	22:54, 63-65	18:24
D. Denials of Peter	26:58, 69-75	14:54, 66-72	22:54-62	18:15-18, 25-27
E. Trial before the council	27:1	15:1	22:66-71	
F. Suicide of Judas	27:3-10			
G. Trial before Pilate	27:2, 11-14	15:1-5	23:1-5	18:28-38
H. Trial before Herod			23:6-12	
I. Trial before Pilate	27:15-26	16:6-15	23:13-25	18:39—19:16
J. Mockery of the soldiers	27:27-30	15:16-19		
K. En route to Golgotha	27:31-32	15:20-21	23:26-32	19:17
L. Arrival at Golgotha	27:33-34	15:22-23	23:33	19:17
M. First three hours on the cross	27:35-44	15:24-32	23:33-43	19:18-27
N. Last three hours	27:45-50	15:33-37	23:44-46	19:28-30

	MATTHEW	MARK	LUKE	JOHN
O. Confession of the centurion	27:51-56	15:38-41	23:47-49	
P. Piercing of Jesus				19:31-37
Q. Burial of Jesus	27:57-61	15:42-47	23:50-56	19:38-42
Saturday				
A. Permit of a guard	27:62-66			
XVI. The Resurrection Events				
A. Coming of the women	28:1	16:1		
B. The earthquake	28:2-4			
C. Despair of Mary Magdalene				20:1-2
D. Angelic vision to the women	28:5-8	16:2-8	24:1-11	
E. Visit of Peter and John to the tomb			24:12	20:3-10
F. Appearance to Mary		16:9-11		20:11-18
G. Appearance to the women	28:9-10			
H. Alarm of the Jews	28:11-15			
I. Appearance to the two		16:12	24:13-32	
J. Report of the two		16:13	24:33-35	
K. Appearance to the ten			24:36-43	20:19-23
L. Appearance to the eleven		16:14		20:24-31
M. Appearance to the seven				21:1-25
N. Great Commission	28:16-20	16:15-18	24:44-49	
O. His ascension		16:19-20	24:50-53	

A quick scan of the above chart will show the selective purposes of the respective writers. Only a few major events were recorded by all four: the feeding of the five thousand, the triumphal entry, and the passion week. Although only John recorded the teaching emphases of the Upper Room Discourse, he completely omitted two major addresses: the Sermon on the Mount and the Olivet Discourse. Luke paid special attention to Christ's ministry in Perea. Since all four spent much time on Christ's last week, with the real focus on His death and resurrection, this is what they deemed to be the major purpose of His incarnation. He came to conquer sin and death through His crucifixion and resurrection.

4

MATTHEW

Writer

Who ever heard of an internal revenue agent writing a best seller? That is exactly what happened in the composition of this first Gospel. From human standards, Matthew would have been considered an unlikely candidate for the apostolic band, much less a biographer of Christ's life. But God's ways are not man's ways.

Matthew was a publican or customs-house officer (Matt. 9:9; Mark 2:14; Luke 5:27). His responsibility was to collect tolls levied on merchandise carried by caravans through his district with its center at Capernaum, a town on the northern tip of the Sea of Galilee. His position alienated him from the great majority of Jewish people who regarded publicans as apostate traitors and who treated them as sinful outcasts. Yet Jesus drafted Matthew to become a disciple, and the latter immediately obeyed. No doubt as a testimony to his new faith, Matthew hosted a supper for Jesus, His disciples, and a great company of friends, including both publicans and sinners (Luke 5:29-30). Shortly thereafter, from among the multitude of His disciples, Jesus chose twelve to form His inner circle of apostles (Matt. 10:1-4; Mark 3:13-19; Luke 6:12-16). Matthew was one of those twelve, listed as the seventh or eighth. From this point on, although not mentioned directly in the Gospels, Matthew walked with the Lord, sharing in the same privileges and responsibilities as the other apostles. After Christ's death, resurrection, and ascension, he was still numbered with the apostles, waiting for the descent of the Holy Spirit (Acts 1:13). His name again disappears from the Scriptural record. Since the apostolic band continues to be mentioned in Acts, it must be implied that Matthew had an active ministry in the early church.

Tradition states that he preached in Judea for about fifteen years, and then went as a missionary to foreign countries, including Ethiopia, Persia, and Parthia. Nothing certain is known about his death.

Like the other Gospel writers, Matthew does not mention himself as the writer of this book; these men hid behind their message. Several of the early Church Fathers (Justin Martyr, Papias, Irenaeus, Origen) regarded him as the author. Since Matthew was a rather obscure apostle, it would be strange for tradition to ascribe the book to him if he, in fact, had not written it. Certainly a forger would have used a more prominent name.

There are some indications within the book that point to Matthew as the real author. Both Mark and Luke refer to his surname, Levi, as well as to his apostolic name, Matthew (Mark 2:14; Luke 5:27). Matthew did not include this double identification, probably because his readers doubtless knew it. According to Mark, the testimonial dinner was held in "his house" (Mark 2:15); Luke said that Levi prepared the feast in "his own house" (Luke 5:29). Matthew, however, simply says that "Jesus sat at meat in the house" (9:10). The omission of the possessive pronoun "his" would argue that the readers knew that it was Matthew's house because he had told them about that personal experience. His inclusion and use of monetary terms (three words for money not found elsewhere in Scripture) definitely reflect his secular background as a tax collector. Interestingly, this is the only Gospel to contain the account of Jesus' payment of the temple tax (17:24-27). All of these little details add up to a strong internal confirmation of the traditional view that Matthew, the publican turned apostle, composed this book.

Original Language

A related problem that also sheds some light on the authorship question deals with the original language of the Gospel. It revolves around this statement allegedly made by Papias, an early Church Father: "Matthew composed [some read "collected"] the oracles in the Hebrew language, and each one interpreted them as he was able."[1] No matter how this statement is explained, it does suggest that Matthew wrote something. This cannot be disputed, but what did Matthew write? The problem centers in the meaning of "oracles" (logia in the Greek text). Some scholars believe that the logia or the sayings of Christ were written in Aramaic (probable meaning of "Hebrew") by Matthew and that a later writer (or writers) used this document plus other sources to compose the Greek Gospel of Matthew. This view naturally denies the Matthaean authorship of the entire book. Some believe that Matthew

---

1. Quoted by Eusebius, *Ecclesiastical History,* III, xxxix, 16.

Latin inscription on one of the columns of the synagogue at Capernaum. This synagogue, built in the second century A.D., likely stands on the same site of the earlier synagogue building where Jesus worshiped and spoke.

wrote the entire Gospel in Greek with the exceptions of Christ's discourses; these were in Aramaic. Still others think that Papias meant that Matthew wrote the book in Greek but according to Hebrew literary style. Another explanation has Matthew writing two Gospels, one in Aramaic and the other in Greek, with only the Greek text being preserved in the manuscripts. Salmon thinks that Papias was right in saying that Matthew wrote it, but wrong in the language used. Everett F. Harrison even suggests that Papias, like Jerome, confused the *Gospel According to the Hebrews,* a noncanonical book, with Matthew's Gospel.[2] A popular view, expounded by Zahn, states that Matthew was originally written in Aramaic, that someone later translated the entire Gospel into Greek, and that only the Greek translation has survived down through the centuries. Although this view seems plausible, there are some apparent difficulties with it. First of all, there are no Aramaisms in the book. Second, the author clarifies customs which would not need explanation if the book had been originally written in Aramaic and if it had been sent to Palestinian, Aramaic readers (27:7-8, 15). Furthermore, why should the author give the Aramaic word and its corresponding Greek translation in some cases if the entire Gospel was actually a

2. Everett F. Harrison, *Introduction to the New Testament* (Grand Rapids: Wm. B. Eerdmans Publishing Co., 1964), p. 159.

69

translation (cf. 1:23)? As someone has pointed out, the Greek text of Matthew reads more like an original edition than like a translation. Harrison correctly observes: "Despite this tradition of a Semitic original, the Fathers have no information on the translation of it into Greek. What they knew and used for themselves was a Greek Gospel."[3] The statement by Papias is intriguing, but until more objective evidence is forthcoming, the position that Matthew wrote the entire book in Greek must stand.

Time and Place

No one can be dogmatic here. There is no clear Scriptural solution to the geographical and chronological background of the book. Speculation over the place of origin generally centers in either Syrian Antioch or Judea. In all fairness, the place of writing must be listed as unknown.

The time of writing is even more controversial. Liberal critics, who deny the concept of predictive prophecy, naturally date the book late in the first century. Since Jesus predicted the destruction of Jerusalem (accomplished in A.D. 70 by the Romans), they date the book after that event, generally in the eighties or nineties. They see in the parable of the marriage feast a subtle inference of a post-A.D. 70 date: "But when the king heard thereof, he was wroth: and he sent forth his armies, and destroyed those murderers, and burned up their city" (22:7). Jesus told this story, however, to illustrate the future judgment that would fall upon Jerusalem and Israel's leaders for their willful rejection of Him. The predictive element within the parable must be seen as divine revelation, later verified by history.

Most evangelicals set the date of writing in the middle of the first century (between 50 and 70), setting as the limits the first dispersion of Jewish Christians (Acts 8:4) and the destruction of Jerusalem (predicted, but not described in ch. 24). They feel that the book was basically designed for Jewish readers living in Palestine and that this purpose could only be fulfilled if the book had been written before A.D. 70.

The question as to the earliest written Gospel also bears on Matthew's date. If the Gospel of Mark were written first and possibly used by Matthew, then the latter's book must necessarily have been written later (closer to 70). However, if Matthew's Gospel was the first, then the date must be pushed forward, possibly into the fifties. Some Church Fathers even dated the book in the late thirties and forties. Irenaeus placed its writing in the reign of Nero when Paul and Peter, in his opinion, were in Rome.

Harrison, arguing for a 70-80 date, believes that the book itself sug-

---

3. Ibid., p. 158.

gests that a considerable interval had elapsed between the events surrounding Christ's death and resurrection and the time of writing.[4] He refers to the purchase and use of the potter's field for the burial of strangers (27:7-8) and to the widespread report that the disciples had stolen Christ's body (28:13, 15). However, how much time is needed to accomplish these two facts? Certainly, within a space of twenty to thirty years (leaving a date of 50-60), the reputation of the burial ground would have been established and the rumor would have had ample time to become fixed within the Jewish community. The 50-70 date must still be considered as the most plausible of the several options.

Purposes

The content and organization of each canonical book reflect some definite purposes behind its writing. These books were not aimless; the authors developed certain themes and goals. So it is with Matthew.

The opening verse of the book clearly points out his first purpose: "The book of the generation of Jesus Christ, the son of David, the son of Abraham" (1:1). He wants to demonstrate that Christ is the rightful heir to the promises of the Abrahamic and Davidic covenants. God promised Abraham a great nation, material prosperity, personal greatness, divine protection, and the land of Palestine (Gen. 12:1-3; 13:14-18; 15:18-21; 17:1-8). He also added that in Abraham "shall all families of the earth be blessed." Paul argued that these promises were given not only to Abraham, but also to his seed, namely Jesus Christ (Gal. 3:16). The Davidic covenant included the blessings of an eternal house, kingdom, and throne (II Sam. 7:11-16). Gabriel told Mary that her child, Jesus, would be the recipient of these special promises (Luke 1:32-33). Matthew demonstrates how all of this can be possible. Throughout the book he establishes the fact that only Christ could fulfill the requirements of this messianic office.

Another purpose, akin to the first, was to present Jesus Christ as the King of Israel in exact fulfillment of Old Testament prophecies. Although Matthew does portray Christ as a teacher of men and the savior of sinners, he puts great emphasis upon Jesus' royalty and upon His relationship to the kingdom. The message: "Repent ye: for the kingdom of heaven is at hand," rings throughout the book. The "kingdom of heaven" is mentioned thirty-three times; the "kingdom of God" is mentioned five times. The royal, messianic title "Son of David" is found nine times. Matthew must have written for the Jewish reader because of his frequent quotations of and allusions to the Old Testament (cf. 1:22; 2:5, 15, 17, 23). He definitely paints the life of Christ against a historic, prophetic background. Fulfilled prophecy was one of the proofs he used to establish

---

4. Ibid., p. 165.

his purpose. Christ, as the messianic king, had to be born of a virgin (1:23) in Bethlehem (2:6), to go into Egypt (2:15), to reside in Nazareth (2:23), to be announced by John the Baptist, His forerunner (3:3), to minister basically in Galilee (4:15-16), to perform miracles of healing (8:17), to be humble (12:18-21), to speak in parables (13:35), to offer Himself to Israel as the lowly king (21:5), to be arrested (26:56), and to be crucified (27:35). Such frequent mention of the Old Testament is not coincidental nor incidental; it was specifically planned.

The earthly teaching ministry of Christ had a double thrust. Matthew indicates this twofold emphasis with two key verses that both begin with these words: "From that time. . . ." Shortly after Jesus' baptism and temptation, He withdrew into Galilee because John the Baptist had been imprisoned by Herod Antipas. Matthew then recorded: "From that time Jesus began to preach, and to say, Repent: for the kingdom of heaven is at hand" (4:17). Our Lord then began an active, public ministry to Israel. He supported His offer of Himself to Israel as the rightful Jewish king with His sinless life, His miraculous works, and His authoritative words. When He sent His apostles out on their first preaching mission, He limited their audiences to Jews, excluding both the Samaritans and the Gentiles (10:5-7). In spite of all the proofs for His claims, the official Jewish leadership rejected Him, claiming that He was satanically controlled (12:24). This verdict caused Jesus to announce that the next public sign-miracle for that Jewish generation would be the sign of the prophet Jonah, a disguised allusion to His coming death and resurrection (12:38-39). Hereafter Jesus began an intense private ministry to His disciples. For the first time, He announced a new program: "I will build my church" (16:18). Then Matthew observed: "From that time forth began Jesus to shew unto his disciples, how that he must go unto Jerusalem, and suffer many things of the elders and chief priests and scribes, and be killed, and be raised again the third day" (16:21). From this point Jesus was carefully preparing His disciples for the events surrounding His death and for the new responsibilities that would befall them in the new church age. His preparation culminated in the Great Commission to preach the gospel throughout the world to all peoples.

Distinctive Features

Just as each member of the human body has some appointed function to perform, so each canonical book makes a distinctive contribution to God's written revelation. The Biblical books were not needlessly duplicated; each one contains spiritual truth and perspective not found elsewhere. In studying, one should always ask this question: What is found in this book that is not expounded elsewhere?

There are some events found only in Matthew: the explanation of

Mary's pregnancy to Joseph by an angel in a dream (1:18-25), the journey of the Magi to Palestine (2:1-12), the flight into Egypt by Joseph, Mary, and the baby Jesus to avoid Herod's decree to slay all Jewish male infants (2:13-15), the killing of those infants (2:16-18), the suicidal death of Judas by hanging (27:3-10), the dream of Pilate's wife concerning the innocence of Jesus (27:19), the resurrection of the bodies at the time of Christ's death and resurrection (27:51-53), and the bribery of the Roman guard to spread the rumor that Christ's body was stolen by the disciples (28:12-15).

The classic chapter on the parables of the kingdom is located in this book (ch. 13). Certain parables are recorded only here: the wheat and the tares (13:24-30, 36-43), the treasure hidden in the earth (13:44), the merchant and the pearl (13:45-46), the net and the fish (13:47-50), the unmerciful servant (18:23-35), the vineyard workers (20:1-16), the two sons (21:28-32), the marriage feast of the king's son (22:1-14), the wise and the foolish virgins (25:1-13), the talents (25:14-30), and the sheep and the goats (25:31-46).[5]

There are three miracles performed by Jesus that are mentioned only in this book: the healing of two blind men (9:27-31), the deliverance of the dumb demoniac (9:32-33), and the coin found by Peter in the fish's mouth (17:24-27).

Although the New Testament is basically a Christian-church document, the word "church" nowhere occurs in the Gospels except for two references in Matthew (16:18; 18:17). The first refers to the Church as that universal body of believers who have a common faith in the deity and redemptive work of Jesus Christ; the second refers to the discipline of a professing believer by the local assembly.

Christ preached many sermons during His earthly ministry. Most of these, although in condensed form, are found throughout the four Gospels. However, seven found in Matthew are treated in detailed depth and scope. On their respective subjects they are the key Scriptural passages. These are the famous Sermon on the Mount (5:1—7:29), the commission to the twelve apostles preceding their first preaching journey (10:1-42), the parables on the kingdom of heaven (13:1-52), the spiritual necessity of humility and forgiveness (18:1-35), the condemnation of religious hypocrisy (23:1-36), the Olivet Discourse describing the signs of the second advent of Christ (24:3—25:46), and the Great Commission given by the resurrected Christ (28:16-20). All Christians should know the content and the location of these discourses.

Matthew selected these sermons and arranged them at strategic inter-

---

5. Some evangelicals do not regard the account of the sheep and the goats as a parable.

vals for the benefit of his readers. For five, he carefully notes their conclusion with words similar to these: ". . . when Jesus had ended these sayings . . ." (7:28; 11:1; 13:53; 19:1; 26:1). The content of the book must therefore be related to the literary placement of these discourses.

Outline

I. THE BIRTH OF THE KING (ch. 1)
  A. His genealogy (1:1-17)
  B. His birth (1:18-25)

II. THE RECEPTION OF THE KING (ch. 2)
  A. By the wise men (2:1-12)
  B. By Herod the Great (2:13-23)

III. THE DEDICATION OF THE KING (ch. 3)
  A. His forerunner (3:1-12)
  B. His baptism (3:13-17)

IV. THE TEMPTATION OF THE KING (ch. 4)
  A. His test (4:1-11)
  B. His ministry (4:12-25)

V. THE MESSAGE OF THE KING (chs. 5-7)
  A. His beatitudes (5:1-16)
  B. His relationship to the law (5:17-20)
  C. His interpretation of the law (5:21-48)
  D. His rebuke of hypocrisy (6:1—7:6)
  E. His invitation (7:7-29)

VI. THE POWER OF THE KING (chs. 8-10)
  A. Authority over disease (8:1-17)
  B. Authority over nature (8:18-27)
  C. Authority over demons (8:28-34)
  D. Authority to forgive sin (9:1-8)
  E. Authority over the will of man (9:9-13)
  F. Authority over death (9:14-26)
  G. Authority over blindness and dumbness (9:27-34)
  H. Authority to delegate authority (9:35—10:42)

VII. THE OPPOSITION OF THE KING (chs. 11-12)
  A. Doubt of John the Baptist (11:1-15)
  B. Opposition of the cities (11:16-30)
  C. Opposition of the Pharisees (12:1-24)
  D. Rejection of the nation by Christ (12:25-50)

VIII. THE PARABLES OF THE KING (ch. 13)

IX. THE INSTRUCTION OF HIS DISCIPLES (chs. 14-20)
  A. Reassurance of the disciples (14:1—16:12)
  B. Prediction of the church (16:13-20)
  C. First announcement of His death (16:21-27)
  D. His transfiguration (16:28—17:21)
  E. Second announcement of His death (17:22-23)
  F. Teachings on offenses, humility, and forgiveness (17:24—20:16)
  G. Third announcement of His death (20:17-34)

X. THE FORMAL PRESENTATION OF THE KING (21:1-22)
  A. The triumphal entry (21:1-11)
  B. The cleansing of the temple (21:12-17)

C. The cursing of the fig tree (21:18-22)
XI. THE REJECTION OF THE KING (21:23—23:39)
    A. The rejection of Christ by the nation (21:23—22:46)
    B. The rejection of the nation by Christ (23:1-39)
XII. THE PROPHECY OF THE KING (chs. 24-25)
    A. Signs of His coming (24:1-44)
    B. Parable of the wise servant (24:45-51)
    C. Parable of the virgins (25:1-13)
    D. Parable of the talents (25:14-30)
    E. Judgment of the sheep and goats (25:31-46)
XIII. THE PASSION OF THE KING (chs. 26-27)
    A. His anointing (26:1-13)
    B. His passover (26:14-30)
    C. His agony in Gethsemane (26:31-46)
    D. His arrest (26:47-56)
    E. His trials (26:57—27:26)
    F. His crucifixion (27:27-56)
    G. His burial (27:57-66)
XIV. THE RESURRECTION OF THE KING (ch. 28)
    A. His resurrection (28:1-15)
    B. His commission (28:16-20)

Survey

1:1-17

For an understanding of Matthew's genealogy, a comparison with that recorded by Luke is necessary (3:23-38). Luke traces the line of Christ back to Adam, whereas Matthew begins with Abraham and comes forward to Christ. Luke goes from son to father; Matthew from father to son. Women are mentioned only in Matthew. Matthew gives the royal family of David through Solomon and the kings of Judah; Luke traces the Davidic family through a nonruling son, Nathan. Some see contradictions in these two lists, but close scrutiny will reveal beautiful harmony. Actually, Matthew is giving the physical ancestry of Joseph, whereas Luke records Mary's descent. These two lists were absolutely necessary to demonstrate that only Christ could be the rightful Jewish king and messiah. God had placed a curse upon the descendants of Jehoiachin, prohibiting any of them from ever ruling over Israel (1:11; cf. Jer. 22:24-30). The dilemma of Israel was this: How could she have a Jewish king, even if permitted by the Roman empire, if a divine curse rested upon the royal line? The only way that this difficulty could be solved was through the virgin conception. Jesus gained His physical rights to the throne of David through Mary. As the legal, but not actual, firstborn son of Joseph, He received the legal, royal rights without being involved in the curse.

1:18-25

When Joseph discovered Mary's pregnancy, he faced a moral paradox.

He did not want to disgrace Mary because of his great love toward her; however, he could not marry her because of her supposed infidelity. Mary could not logically explain her condition; therefore, the angel explained to Joseph the cause and the purpose of this virgin birth. The explanation clearly shows that the Messiah had to be more than the son of Adam, the son of Abraham, and the son of David; he also had to be divine, the Son of God. By naming the child, Joseph was claiming before his peers, legal paternity. Since Joseph was called "the son of David" (a messianic title), the royal right inherent in that title was included in the birthright passed on to Jesus.

2:1-23

Only the wise men recognized the significance of the unusual star. They knew that it signaled the advent of God's Son (cf. Num. 24:17; Dan. 9:24-27). They knew that the Messiah had to be both human and divine; this is why they came to worship one who had been born. We do not know their names, number, or native land. Contrary to tradition, they did not follow a star for weeks from their country to Palestine. They saw the star; it disappeared; they traveled by faith to Jerusalem, making an obvious inquiry at Herod's palace; the star then reappeared and led them to the house (not the manger) where Jesus and Mary

Bethlehem from the area today referred to as Shepherds' Fields.

were. The star probably first appeared at the moment of the conception or birth; their visit may have occurred almost two years later.

The worship of the Magi is offset by the hatred of Herod. This double reception was to be seen throughout Christ's ministry; some would believe, but others would reject. Herod, established as the Jewish king by the Roman leaders Antony and Octavian, would naturally feel threatened by the announcement of the birth of the Jewish Messiah-King. A highly suspicious man, he had earlier killed many relatives because of imagined conspiracy against him. His decree to murder all male children under two years of age was designed to destroy the Christ child; however, Joseph took Jesus and Mary to Egypt to escape the decree. After the death of Herod, the family settled in Nazareth.

3:1-12

There is a time interval of almost thirty years between chapters 2 and 3. Almost no attention is given to Christ's human development years. The silence is broken by the ministry of John the Baptist. As the forerunner (Isa. 40:1-5; Mal. 4:5-6), John had the responsibility of calling out from Israel a believing remnant who would be spiritually prepared for the coming of the Messiah-King. The earthly kingdom to be established by the Messiah could only be entered by those who were first members of the spiritual kingdom through repentance and faith. This inner experience had to be manifested publicly through baptism. Although many responded to his invitation, the Jewish officials refused.

3:13-17

The baptism of Jesus marks His official identification as the divine-human Messiah by the Father and His initial introduction to the believing remnant (John 1:31-34). It ended His period of obscurity and thrust Him into His public ministry. At this time He was anointed by the Holy Spirit for His messianic tasks (Isa. 61:1-2; Acts 10:38). His baptism was much different than others because He had no sins to confess.

4:1-11

Theologians have argued for years over the nature of Christ's temptation. Was He not able to sin or was He able not to sin? The former rests upon His divine essence; the latter is based upon His yielded human will. In either case, the temptation demonstrated that Christ neither possessed a sinful nature nor that He did or thought any evil thing. It further shows His moral right to be the Jewish king. Satan tempted Christ as to the lust of the flesh, the pride of life, and the lust of the eyes (I John 2:16), but in each instance, Jesus was completely submissive to the Holy Spirit and totally obedient to the will of God revealed in the Scriptures.

4:12-25

Jesus' active ministry began after the imprisonment of John the Baptist by Herod Antipas. His message was the same as that of John. He appealed for men to repent before the kingdom was established. His ministry had a triple impact: teaching, preaching, and healing. Not only did the converts of John begin to follow Him, but also new crowds were attracted to Him.

5-7

The Sermon on the Mount has been approached in several ways. Some see it as the gospel message to the unbelieving world. Others view it as the rule of life for the Christian today. Many dispensationalists identify it as the law of the future, messianic, earthly kingdom. Jesus Himself explained its significance: "For I say unto you, That except your righteousness shall exceed the righteousness of the scribes and Pharisees, ye shall in no case enter into the kingdom of heaven" (5:20). He was laying down the spiritual requirements for entrance into His kingdom, both in its spiritual and physical aspects. The sermon is just as applicable and relevant today as in Christ's day. To enter the spiritual kingdom today and the eternal kingdom in the future, one must not have a Pharisaical type of righteousness; rather, one must be clothed with the imputed righteousness of God.

This sermon demonstrates Christ's legislative, judicial, and administrative rights to the Jewish throne. As the King, He had the rights to make up the laws of His kingdom, to interpret those laws, and to execute them. He embodied within Himself the threefold aspects of the democratic process.

5:1-16

The Beatitudes reveal the moral and spiritual qualities of those who would enter His kingdom. Such virtues were never exhibited by the religious hypocrites. As salt and light, His subjects were to have spiritual influence upon others. Their presence in the world should retard moral corruption and point darkened minds to the light of the world, even Christ.

5:17-20

Christ came to fulfill the Old Testament, not to destroy it, as was commonly charged of Him. Christ indicated His acceptance of the total inspiration, authority, and inerrancy of the Scriptures with His reference to the jot and tittle. The jot referred to the smallest letter of the alphabet and the tittle to the stroke of the pen that distinguished one letter from another.

The southern end of the Sea of Galilee, from an elevated site looking east-ward to the mountains of Syria.

5:21-48

The Pharisees stressed outward conformity to the demands of God, but Jesus said that true obedience to the law involves the attitudes of the inner self. The attitude produces the action. In a series of six contrasts introduced by the recurring phrases, "Ye have heard that it was said . . . but I say unto you" (5:21-22, 27-28, 31-32, 33-34, 38-39, 43-44), Jesus contrasted His interpretation with that of the Pharisees concerning murder and hatred, adultery and lust, divorce and re-marriage, oaths, personal retaliation, and love and hatred toward enemies. Sin involves the thought as well as the deed.

6:1—7:6

The Pharisees paraded their religiosity. They gave, prayed, and fasted before men, to be seen of men, and to have the glory of men. According to Jesus, such hypocrisy will never be rewarded by God. Genuine righteousness counts not its gifts, regards prayer as a secret devotion, and does not try to impress men with its sacrifices. The Pharisees regarded personal riches as a mark of divine favor, but Jesus said that spiritual wealth is what God desires of men. A genuine believer will not worry about material possessions, but rather will seek to be spiritual. In so doing he has the assurance that his heavenly Father will meet all his needs. The Pharisees were guilty of judging others for petty matters, but were ignorant of their own major spiritual faults.

7:7-29

In the conclusion to His sermon, Jesus set forth the two options open to His listeners. His interpretation of the righteousness that God demands is likened to the strait gate, the narrow way, and the rock foundation; only a few will find eternal life through it. The interpretation of the Pharisees, called false prophets, is seen in the wide gate, the broad way, and the sand foundation; many will experience eternal destruction because of it. Jesus warned against mere profession; a genuine, personal relationship with Christ is absolutely necessary for entrance into His kingdom. The people were amazed because Jesus spoke authoritatively; the scribes often quoted recognized rabbinical authorities, but Jesus said, "*I* say unto you."

8:1—10:42

To prove that Jesus was the rightful king of Israel, Matthew now presents a group of miracles. Jesus' miracles were His credentials, proving that He was what He claimed to be (cf. John 10:38; Acts 2:22). In other words, His works support His words. They demonstrate that He has authority in every realm of life. He healed men of all physical problems: leprosy, palsy, fever, death, blood disease, and blindness. He healed both the source and the after-effects; no therapy or recuperation was necessary. He healed both in public and in private. He healed with His touch and with His Word; His physical presence was not always required. He could control nature or the demonic world. As God, He had the authority to forgive sins and to call men from their chosen vocations to His discipleship. A mark of genuine authority is one's ability to delegate that power to another. When Jesus sent the Twelve out to preach, He gave to them the authority to do exactly what He did (10:7-8). He restricted their itinerary to the Jews because at this time the kingdom offer was not open to the non-Jewish world; He was still offering Himself to Israel as her king (10:5-6). In His ordination address, He anticipated for them the same responses to their ministry as to His; there would be both reception and rejection. In this way they could more fully identify with their master.

In spite of the mounting evidence of His sinless life, His gracious words, and His miracles, Christ encountered opposition from the Jewish people. They wanted a political king who would overthrow the Romans, not a spiritual king who spoke only of repentance and righteousness.

11:1-15

Even John the Baptist began to doubt. "Art thou he that should come, or do we look for another?" (11:3) he asked. Earlier at Christ's baptism, John had been convinced of His divine messiahship; but why was he wavering now? His problem was simple: How could the kingdom of heaven be established when the forerunner was in prison and when the supposed Messiah was being rejected? John expected the earthly kingdom to be instituted in his own lifetime. To assure John, Christ performed miracles in the presence of John's messengers and pointed out that these fulfilled messianic prophecy (cf. Isa. 61:1-2). Christ then called upon John to trust Him and the purpose of God even though he could not understand all that was happening. Christ then recognized the positional greatness of John; the Old Testament prophets wrote about the coming Messiah, but John personally introduced Him to Israel. If Israel had received Christ as her king, then John would have fulfilled those prophecies concerning the coming of Elijah (Mal. 4:5-6).

11:16-30

The parable of the children in the marketplace shows that the generation in Jesus' day resisted both the invitation of John and Jesus. No matter what approach was taken, that generation found excuses to reject the kingdom offer. Because those cities repented not in the face of the presence and power of Christ, their accountability was greater and their judgment would be more severe than those ancient cities who rejected the messages of godly men. In spite of national opposition, however, Jesus continued to give an invitation to individuals to find spiritual rest in Him.

12:1-24

The opposition of the Pharisees centered in alleged violations of the Sabbath both by Christ and His disciples. Actually, they did not break the fourth commandment; they broke the traditional, Pharisaical interpretation of the Sabbath. When the disciples plucked heads of grain, rubbed them in their hands, blew the chaff away, and ate the kernels, the Pharisees accused them of working on the Sabbath (harvesting, threshing, and winnowing). Jesus defended the disciples by appealing to the actions of David and the priests. As the Lord of the Sabbath, He could determine the purpose of that day; it was designed for man's benefit, not to be a yoke around his neck. Doing good was always permissible on the Sabbath; therefore, healing on the seventh day was not morally wrong. The Pharisees, full of prejudice, plotted to destroy Christ because of His antitradition policies. After Jesus cast a demon out of a blind and dumb man, the people began to wonder: "Is not this the son of David?" (12:23). The Pharisees had seen and heard enough. They now pronounced their official verdict as to their evaluation of the person and work of Christ. To them, He was an insane demoniac. They agreed that Jesus had supernatural power, but that His power was of Satan, not of God's Spirit.

12:25-50

Christ charged them with committing the unpardonable sin. To say that Jesus performed miracles by Satan and not by the Holy Spirit is both unforgivable and blasphemous. When the leaders requested a further miracle-sign, Jesus announced that no more miracles would be done as public signs for Israel. The next national sign would be that of Christ's death and resurrection, alluded to in the metaphor of Jonah and the fish. The parable of the unclean spirit (12:43-45) reveals that Israel was now in a far worse spiritual condition than before the ministries of John and Jesus. Henceforth, natural relationships would hold no significance for Christ; only spiritual ones would be important.

13:1-58

Now that a climax had been reached in the relationship between Christ and the religious leaders, through a series of parables He began to show His disciples the form which the kingdom would take on earth during the rejection of the King Himself by Israel. The parables were designed to reveal truth to believers and to hide truth from prejudiced unbelievers. Although parables are difficult to understand at times, there seems to be a general scheme behind these parables on the mystery form of the kingdom of heaven. During the king's absence and rejection, there will be a preaching of the word with multiple responses from the hearts of men (sower and seed). It will be very difficult to differentiate between the saved and the unsaved; both will be found within professing Christendom (wheat and tares). Christianity will have a great outward development from small beginnings (mustard seed), but will experience inward corruption (leaven). During this time, spiritual treasures will be gained (earthen treasure and pearl). The period will end with the separation of the saved from the lost and with salvation for the former and judgment for the latter (dragnet of fish).

14:1—16:12

In the midst of national opposition, the disciples needed reassurance, especially after John the Baptist was beheaded by Herod Antipas. The feeding of the five thousand reflected Christ's compassion upon the

82

PALESTINE IN THE TIME
OF CHRIST

Copyright by C. S. HAMMOND & CO., N. Y.

Scale of Miles

Perennial Rivers
Seasonal Rivers & Streams
Cities of the Decapolis

Capitals
Roads & Trade Routes

* The Decapolis and Ascalon retained
  their independence under the Roman
  governor of the province of Syria.

The Great Sea

(Mediterranean Sea)

Archelaus, upon Herod's death
became ruler of Judaea, Samaria and
Idumaea. His reign lasted until 6 A.D.
when he was removed and exiled.
His territory then was placed under
a Roman procurator.

Salome, Herod's sister, was given
Jamnia, Azotus and Phasaelis. They,
in turn, passed to Livia, wife of Augustus and then to Emperor Tiberius.

Horns of Hattin
(Kurûn Hattin) is a
possible site of the
Sermon on the Mount.

The Dead Sea Scrolls
were found in a cave
here; also the ruins of
an Essene monastery.

Here John the Baptist
was imprisoned and
beheaded by order
of Herod Antipas.

Residence of
Roman procurators.

ABILENE
Abila
Damascus
Sidon
Sarepta
(Zarephath)
MOUNT LEBANON
Leontes R.
River Jordan
MT. HERMON
PANIAS
Dan Caesarea Philippi
TRACHONITIS
Tyre
Cadasa
(Kedesh)
ULATHA
Lake
Semechonitis
Gischala
Seleucia
GAULANITIS
BATANAEA
BASHAN
Raphana
Ptolemais
(Accho)
Ladder
of Tyre
Chorazin
Bethsaida
(Julias)
Jotapata
Cana
Magdala
(Dalmanutha)
Capernaum
Tabigha
Gergesa
Gamala
Dion
MT. CARMEL
GALILEE
Sepphoris
Nazareth
Tiberias
Sea of
Galilee
Hippos
AURANITIS
Philoteria
Yarmuk R.
Abila
Edrei
Kishon R.
Plain of
Esdraelon
Mt.
Tabor
Nain
Gadara
Capitolias
Dora
Bethabara
GILEAD
Caesarea
En-gannim
(Ginaea)
Scythopolis
(Beth-shan)
Pella
DECAPOLIS
SAMARIA
Samaria
(Sebaste)
Mt. Ebal
Shechem
Mt. Gerizim
Sychar
Jacob's Well
River Jordan
Amathus
Jabbok R.
Gerasa
Plain of Sharon
Apollonia
Antipatris
Joppa
Phasaelis
PERAEA
Arimathaea
(Ramathaim)
Lydda
(Diospolis)
Gophna
Archelais
Ephraim
Philadelphia
(Rabbath-ammon)
Beth-nimrah
Jamnia
Gezer
(Gazara)
Bethel
Ramah
Jericho
Julias
(Livias, Beth-haram)
Hesbon
AMMON
Ekron
Nicopolis
(Emmaus)
Emmaus
Jerusalem
Mt.
of Olives
Bethany
Khirbet
Qumran
Azotus (Ashdod)
Bethlehem
Herodium
Ascalon
JUDAEA
Mareshah
(Marisa)
Hebron
Ziph
Callirhoe
Machaerus
Dibon
Gaza
Juttah
Carmel
En-gedi
Wilderness of Judah
Salt or Dead Sea
(L. Asphaltitis)
Rabbath Moab
(Areopolis, Rabba)
Gerar
Masada
Kir-moab
(Kir-hareseth)
Raphia
Beersheba
IDUMAEA
Arnon R.
Zered
NABATAEANS
MOAB

hungry, but it also demonstrated His creative ability to His own. He was God even though the nation did not recognize Him. This truth needed to be reinforced in the hearts of the apostles. The walking on the water and the calming of the storm added to their conviction. Jesus' defense of the disciples' eating manners must have encouraged them. More miracles were performed by Christ, not as public signs, but as responses to personal faith and as teaching tools for the disciples.

16:13-20

Popular opinion, rejecting the Pharisaical, blasphemous charge, regarded Jesus as a holy spokesman for God, but that evaluation was not even adequate. In reply to Christ's inquiry, Peter answered: "Thou art the Christ, the Son of the living God" (16:16). The only reason why Peter could recognize the divine-human Person was that God had revealed that spiritual truth to him. Jesus then announced: "Thou art Peter, and upon this rock I will build my church; and the gates of hell shall not prevail against it" (16:18). The church was not built upon the person of Peter[6] or upon his confession, but rather upon the person and redemptive work of Jesus Christ. The Church is composed of all believers, both Jew and Gentile, saved since Calvary and Pentecost, united to each other and to Christ by the baptism in the Holy Spirit (cf. I Cor. 12:13; Eph. 1:22-23; 2:19-22). The power of hell could not prevent the foundation or the construction of the Church from coming to pass. When Peter preached the gospel at Pentecost and in Cornelius' house (Acts 2, 10), he opened the door of access into the present expression of the kingdom of heaven (the Church) to the Jew and to the Gentile. Since Israel was to receive no more signs and since her rejection of Christ was now inevitable, the disciples were to remain silent about Christ's real identity.

16:21-27

Matthew now indicates the second major purpose of Christ's earthly ministry with these introductory words: "From that time forth began Jesus to shew" (16:21; cf. 4:17). For the first time, Christ clearly declared His intention to die and to be raised. The disciples did not perceive that the cross had to precede the crown, that Christ had to suffer before He could reign. Genuine discipleship also includes such self-denial.

---

6. Since there is only one word in the Aramaic for *rock*, many have argued that Jesus must have regarded Peter as the foundation. If that is so, then why did Matthew, directed by the Holy Spirit, use two Greek words instead of one? Christ evidently made a play on words. Peter was a small rock (Greek masculine gender) hewn out of the large rock mountain (Greek feminine gender). Peter recognized this difference (I Peter 2:4-8).

16:28—17:23

Jesus' transfiguration fulfills His prediction: "There be some standing here, which shall not taste of death, till they see the Son of man coming in his kingdom" (16:28). Peter, James, and John got a preview of Christ's coming to the earth to establish His kingdom in glory (II Peter 1:15-18). This event demonstrated that Christ's divine glory was veiled in human flesh during His earthly sojourn and that He was, in fact, God's beloved Son. The thrill of this experience was soon removed by the disciples' inability to cast out a demon and Jesus' second announcement of His death and resurrection. Note their sorrow.

17:24—18:35

Since Christ's death, resurrection, and ascension into heaven were now before Him, He had to instruct His own concerning proper spiritual qualities. Although Christ did not have to pay the tribute money because He was the king, He nevertheless did so in order not to offend; thus believers should be prepared to do for the sake of public testimony that which is not required. Humility and concern for the lost should always mark the Christian. Restoration of sinning brethren should be encouraged. Christians should be quick to forgive one another; after all, if Christ forgave them such a great debt of sin, should they not forgive others for small wrongs?

19:1-15

Christ did not mediate between the Shammai school of Phariseeism which taught that unfaithfulness was the only grounds for divorce and the liberal Hillel school which regarded incompatibility as sufficient grounds. Instead, He went back to the original purpose of marriage. Man and woman were to live together until death separated them. Divorce was simply permitted to prevent greater evils, wife beating or murder, from happening. If Jesus allowed divorce, He may have been referring to fornication committed during the betrothal period (cf. 1:18-19). Problems are inherent in marriage, but marriage is never wrong in the will of God; however, marriage is not necessary for every person.

19:16—20:16

To show that heaven cannot be gained by human effort, Jesus charged the rich young ruler to sell his possessions, give the sale money to the poor, and follow Christ. The ruler loved himself far more than his neighbor or his God; he had not kept the commandments. His refusal showed that he trusted what his riches could do for him, not what Christ could provide for him. Jesus then announced that the disciples would rule over the twelve tribes of Israel during the kingdom because of

JERUSALEM
IN NEW TESTAMENT TIMES

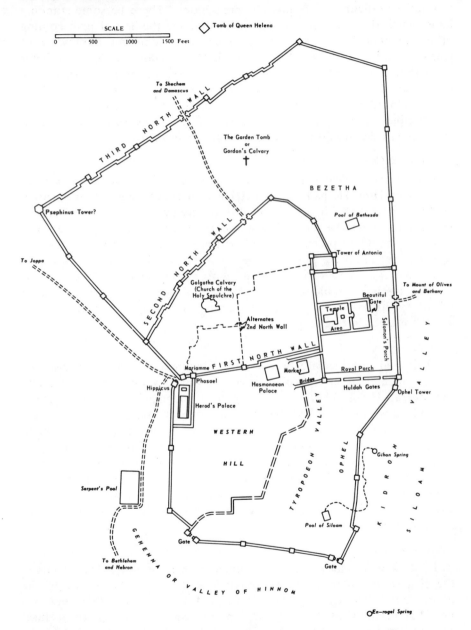

SCALE

Tomb of Queen Helena

0   500   1000   1500 Feet

To Shechem
and Damascus

THIRD NORTH WALL

The Garden Tomb
or
Gordon's Calvary
✝

BEZETHA

Psephinus Tower?

Pool of Bethesda

To Joppa

SECOND NORTH WALL

Tower of Antonia

Golgotha Calvary
(Church of the
Holy Sepulchre)

Beautiful
Gate

To Mount of Olives
and Bethany

Temple
Area

Alternates
2nd North Wall

Solomon's Porch

Mariamme   FIRST NORTH WALL

Market

Royal Porch

Phasael

Bridge

Hasmonaean
Palace

Huldah Gates

Ophel Tower

Hippicus

Herod's Palace

WESTERN

HILL

TYROPOEON VALLEY

OPHEL

Gihon Spring

KIDRON VALLEY

SILOAM

Serpent's Pool

Pool of Siloam

To Bethlehem
and Hebron

GEHENNA OR VALLEY OF HINNOM

Gate

Gate

En-rogel Spring

This map is used by permission graciously granted by Dr. G. Frederick Owen and Beacon Hill Press, Kansas City, Missouri. Reproduced from Dr. Owen's book, Jerusalem, *p. 29.*

86

their faithful service. The parable of the laborers demonstrates that Christ has a perfect right to reward men as He sees fit, that equal rewards will be given for equal faithful service, and that many called to Christian life and service late in this era will be rewarded before those called earlier.

20:17-34

On the way to Jerusalem Jesus again reiterated His intention to die and to be raised. He definitely knew what lay before Him. The request of the mother of James and John to have her sons sit on the choice thrones no doubt was provoked by Christ's earlier announcement (19:28). In His answer Jesus taught that spiritual greatness is not achieved by pride and self-assertion, but by humility and service to others. Even He "came not to be ministered unto, but to minister, and to give his life a ransom for many" (20:28). It is amazing that the blind men *saw* the messiahship of Christ when Jerusalem was blinded to that truth. Jesus healed them out of His compassion for their need and in response to their faith.

21:1-22

The Triumphal Entry into Jerusalem marked Christ's formal and final presentation of Himself to Israel as the king of the Jews (cf. Zech. 9:9). Although many praised Him for being the son of David, the majority opinion of the city was: "This is Jesus the prophet of Nazareth of Galilee" (21:11). They saw Him only as a mere man. His first action within the city was to drive out the money changers and those who sold birds and animals within the temple courts. They had turned His house into a religious racket; therefore, He had the right to purify His temple (cf. Mal. 3:1-3). Jesus cursed the fig tree because it had the outward signs of life but no fruit to offer to its creator. The fig tree symbolized Israel, a nation with outward religiosity, but no spiritual fruit.

21:23—22:14

Christ's cleansing of the temple brought Him into open conflict with the priests who questioned His authority to do so. Jesus answered their question with a question: Where did John the Baptist get his authority? He had trapped them and unmasked their bias. They had rejected John without reason, and now they were doing the same to Jesus. Jesus then set forth three parables to show the relationships that existed between Israel's leaders and God. They could be seen in the son who professed obedience with the lip, but who disobeyed with the life. They were like the husbandmen who refused to obey the servants of the householder and who killed the son (Christ) to gain what did not belong to them.

Just as the husbandmen were destroyed by the householder, so Israel would be destroyed by God (accomplished A.D. 70). They were like those bidden to the marriage feast of the son who made excuses why they could not come.

22:15-22

In an attempt to pressure Jesus into saying something that could be used against Him, the Pharisees and the Herodians threw three difficult questions at Him. They asked whether taxes should be paid to Rome. They thought that if Jesus answered negatively, they could charge Him with treason and that if He answered positively, the restless Jews would become disenchanted with Him. However, Jesus distinguished between the church (God) and the state. A man is obligated to honor both as long as they operate in their God-given realms; there is no conflict between being a good citizen and a good member of the family of God.

22:23-33

The Sadducees asked a theological question about life after death. Jesus stated that resurrection does not restore natural, earthly relationships. There will be no need for family life in heaven; service and fellowship with God will occupy our attention there. Jesus challenged their denial of the resurrection by appealing to the power of God to do so and to the Scriptural teaching of that fact (Job 19:25-27; Isa. 26:19; Dan. 12:2).

22:34-40

A lawyer asked Jesus to identify God's greatest commandment. Instead, Jesus condensed all of the commandments into two: Love God and love man with all that you are. These two form the essence of all of God's precepts.

22:41—23:36

Now that Jesus had adequately answered all of their hardest questions, it was His turn to quiz them: "What think ye of Christ? whose son is he?" (22:42). When this leading question brought the reply, "The son of David," Jesus then asked why David called his son "Lord" under the inspiration of the Holy Spirit. The only logical answer would be that David knew that the Messiah would be both human and divine, that he would be both the son of David and the Son of God. The leaders rejected Christ's claims to deity, and yet the Old Testament described the two natures of the Messiah. Their sinful prejudice caused Jesus to pronounce a series of woes upon their religious hypocrisy. Because of their unbelief, Israel could only expect the judgment of God. The clash for the moment was over; they had repudiated Him and He had rejected them.

23:37—24:31

Because Israel willfully rejected Him, Christ predicted a time of absence from the nation, a visible return, and a later spiritual acceptance by them. He also announced that the temple would be completely devastated. These disclosures stimulated the disciples to ask these questions: "Tell us, when shall these things be? and what shall be the sign of thy coming, and of the end of the world?" (24:3). These are basically two questions. The first deals with the temple, whereas the second deals with a sign that will precede His second advent and end the age (better translation than "world") of His absence and rejection. This famous teaching, called the Olivet Discourse, was thus given to reveal the conditions that would prevail on the earth prior to Christ's return to establish His kingdom. Dispensationalists believe that these signs will have their ultimate fulfillment in the seven-year tribulation period, although the embryonic beginnings of these events can be seen in the latter days of this church age.

Jesus predicted the presence of war, famine, pestilence, and earthquakes (cf. seal judgments, Rev. 6). Persecution of the saved, treason, and religious deception will mark this period. Some of the positive features are that many righteous will be delivered through the persecutions and that the kingdom message will be heard universally. The event that will signal the great tribulation will be the manifestation of the antichrist (24:15; cf. Dan. 9:24-27). This tragic period will end when Jesus Christ returns to the earth (24:27-30).

24:32—25:46

In a series of parables, Jesus revealed what attitudes a believer should have toward this great event. Although he cannot know the exact day and hour, the Christian should be sensitive to world conditions around him and to the possibility of prophetic fulfillment in his lifetime. Some have suggested that the putting forth of leaves by the fig tree represents the establishment of the State of Israel (1948) and that the generation born then will live to see the fulfillment of Jesus' words. Others see it as a guarantee that the race or generation of Jews will survive until that day. Just as the flood surprised Noah's generation, so Christ's return will catch unsaved men unprepared. The believer, on the contrary, should be watching (24:37-44), faithfully doing the master's will (24:45-51), prepared (25:1-13), and discharging his spiritual responsibilities (25:14-30). When Christ returns to the earth, He will separate all living Gentiles into two groups: the saved (sheep) and the lost (goats). The saved will share in the blessings of His earthly kingdom, whereas the lost will be cast into hell. During the tribulation, men will express their faith in the messiah of Israel by their actions toward the Jews.

26:1-16

The closing events of Christ's earthly ministry were now upon Him. The plot to crucify Him had intensified and solidified. Of all His followers, it would appear that only Mary understood the full significance of Christ's frequent references to His death. As an act of love and worship, she anointed Him, anticipating His death and burial. Judas, probably frustrated because the Romans were not overthrown, bargained with the priests to deliver Christ into their hands for thirty pieces of silver.

26:17-56

On the night before His crucifixion, Jesus ate the Passover feast with His disciples secretly in the upper room. On this occasion Jesus revealed His knowledge of Judas' betrayal. After the feast, Christ instituted the ordinance of the Lord's Supper, symbolizing His body and blood with the bread and wine. From the house they went to the Mount of Olives where Jesus announced that all of His disciples would forsake Him that night. The denial of Peter was especially stressed. Later, in the Garden of Gethsemane, Christ agonized over the nature of His coming sacrificial death. Three times He prayed: "O my Father, if it be possible, let this cup pass from me: nevertheless not as I will, but as thou wilt" (26:39).

A view southeast over the Old City of Jerusalem, from the Lutheran Tower.

At the conclusion of His prayer, Judas came with the temple guard to seize Jesus. Instead of resisting, Christ willingly yielded to the demands of the soldiers. The disciples fled as Jesus predicted.

26:57—27:26

A comparison of the four Gospels will reveal that Christ underwent six "trials" during that night and early the next day. The first three occurred before religious authorities: Annas, Caiaphas, and the Sanhedrin. The second three took place before the civil rulers: Pilate, Herod Antipas, and Pilate again. The trials were a mockery of justice. They took place at the wrong time (night), in the wrong place (private homes), without benefit of counsel, before false witnesses, and accompanied by beatings, and He was sentenced to death contrary to the evidence.

The religious leaders convicted Him because of His prediction of the destruction of the temple and His claim to be the Son of God. They saw Christ as a blasphemer and beat Him without mercy. During these trials, Peter denied Christ three times as predicted. Judas tried to reverse the terrible sequence of events by returning the money, but it was too late. Full of remorse, he hanged himself.

Pilate recognized the political innocence of Christ. He did not see Christ's claim to be the king of the Jews as a threat to the Roman empire. However, under tremendous pressure by the religious leaders, he delivered Christ to be crucified and released Barabbas at their request.

27:27-50

After being mocked by the Roman soldiers, Jesus was taken to Golgotha to be crucified. He was on the cross for about six hours (9 A.M.—3 P.M.). He refused a narcotic drink that would deaden some of the pain; rather He chose to suffer for sins consciously. The soldiers divided His garments and gambled for His coat. The crowd, led by the priests, continued to mock Him. During this experience, Jesus uttered His famous sayings:

1. Father, forgive them; for they know not what they do (Luke 23:34).
2. Verily I say unto thee, To day shalt thou be with me in paradise (Luke 23:43).
3. Woman, behold thy son; Behold thy mother! (John 19:26-27).
4. My God, my God, why hast thou forsaken me? (Matt. 27:46).
5. I thirst (John 19:28).
6. It is finished (John 19:30).
7. Father, into thy hands I commend my spirit (Luke 23:46).

27:51-56

Some strange phenomena accompanied His death. Darkness covered

Palestine during the last three hours on the cross (27:45). The inner veil of the temple was ripped from the top to the bottom showing that God was through with the system of animal sacrifices. An earthquake broke rocks and opened graves. The bodies of some believers appeared in Jerusalem, possibly after His resurrection.

27:57-66

The body of Jesus was removed from the cross by Joseph of Arimathaea and Nicodemus (John 19:38-42), anointed and wrapped for burial, and placed into the former's private tomb. The tomb was sealed and guarded at the request of the Jewish leaders to keep the disciples from stealing the body.

28:1-15

Again, all four Gospels must be studied together for a complete account of Christ's resurrection appearances. It is impossible to be dogmatic about the exact chronological order of the appearances, but here is a plausible sequence:
1. To Mary Magdalene (John 20:14-18).
2. To the women (Matt. 28:8-10).
3. To Peter (Luke 24:34; I Cor. 15:5).
4. To the two disciples on the Emmaus road (Luke 24:13-31).
5. To the ten apostles (Luke 24:36-43; John 20:19-24).
6. To the eleven apostles (John 20:24-29).
7. To seven apostles by the Sea of Galilee (John 21:1-23).
8. To five hundred brethren (I Cor. 15:6).
9. To James (I Cor. 15:7).
10. To the eleven, on the day of ascension (Matt. 28:16-20).

These appearances occurred during the forty days between His resurrection and ascension. He was now in a real, physical, immortal, incorruptible body that could be seen, heard, and touched.

28:16-20

On the day of His ascension, Christ commissioned the apostles to make disciples of all nations through evangelization ("Go"), baptism, and teaching. Ten days after Christ went into heaven the Holy Spirit came, and the disciples were enabled to carry out this command (Acts 2).

Increase Your Learning

By Doing

1. Since Matthew emphasizes the kingdom theme, underline these terms wherever they are found in his Gospel: king, kingdom of heaven, and Son of David.
2. Since Matthew stresses the fulfillment of prophecy in Christ's ministry, underline those Old Testament quotations throughout his book.

By Discussing

1. Could genuine Christianity exist apart from the factuality of the virgin birth of Christ? How essential is that doctrine?
2. Is it possible to fulfill the beatitudes today in the midst of modern pressures?
3. How can we relate the commands to love and to pray for our enemies with American involvement in wars? Can a Christian conscientiously be a combat soldier or must he be a pacifist?
4. Compare the nature of Christ's miracles with the claims of modern faith healers. Are they the same? Different? In what ways?
5. Compare the popularity of Jesus today among the youth with that expressed by the multitudes in His day. Cite similarities and differences.

By Reading

Gaebelein, A. C. *The Gospel of Matthew.* New York: Our Hope Press, 1916.

McNeile, Alan Hugh. *The Gospel According to St. Matthew.* London: Macmillan Co., 1955.

Morgan, G. Campbell. *The Gospel According to Matthew.* Westwood, N.J.: Fleming H. Revell Co., 1929.

Plummer, Alfred. *An Exegetical Commentary on the Gospel According to St. Matthew.* Grand Rapids. Wm. B. Eerdmans Publishing Co., 1956.

Tasker, R. V. G. *The Gospel According to St. Matthew.* Grand Rapids: Wm. B. Eerdmans Publishing Co., 1961.

5

MARK

Writer

Of the New Testament authors Mark was probably the youngest at the time he wrote his Gospel. His given name was John and his Latin surname was Mark, with the latter name being more prominent in Scripture. Nothing is known about his father, but his mother was Mary, a resident of Jerusalem and a sister to Barnabas (Acts 12:12; Col. 4:10). His family must have had some wealth, for Mary owned a house large enough to accommodate many Christians gathered together for prayer (Acts 12:12), and Barnabas, a Levite of Cyprus, owned sizeable acreage (Acts 4:37).

Although Mark is not mentioned by name in the Gospels, there is plausible speculation that he knew the apostles and Jesus during the latter's earthly ministry. Some have suggested that it was his house that had the upper room where Jesus met with His disciples the night before His crucifixion (14:12-16) and where the disciples waited for the descent of the Holy Spirit (Acts 1:12—2:2). Because only Mark's Gospel contains the account of a young man who followed Jesus after His arrest in Gethsemane and who later fled naked when apprehended by the arresting crowd (14:51-52), many identify that young man as an anonymous reference to Mark himself.

He is first mentioned in the Bible at the time of James' martyrdom and Peter's imprisonment (Acts 12:12-17). The house of his mother probably was a popular meeting place for the early Christians since Peter went there directly after his release by the angel. Through this contact Mark must have been fairly familiar with the personal teaching of the apostles themselves. He may have been a direct convert of Peter because the apostle later identified him as his son (I Peter 5:13), a son in the faith (cf. Paul and Timothy) and not a natural son.

His active ministry began when he accompanied Paul and Barnabas from Jerusalem to Antioch and later from Antioch to Cyprus during Paul's first missionary journey (Acts 12:25; 13:3-13). However, when the team moved into Pamphylia (central Turkey today), he "departing from them returned to Jerusalem" (Acts 13:13). Several reasons have been given for Mark's defection. Since the Holy Spirit only separated Paul and Barnabas for this evangelistic task (Acts 13:2), some believe that Mark did not feel "called." His lack of personal conviction may have caused emotional distress. Others detect a growing dislike for Paul especially since the leadership influence of his uncle Barnabas was declining. The most plausible view is that the Gentile emphasis in the Pauline outreach bothered Mark's Jewish feelings and prejudice. When Paul and Barnabas planned their second missionary journey (Acts 15:36-41), Barnabas wanted to take Mark again, but Paul disagreed. Luke records that "the contention was so sharp between them, that they departed asunder one from the other: and so Barnabas took Mark, and sailed unto Cyprus; and Paul chose Silas..." (15.39-40a). For about the next ten years, the Bible is silent on the activities of Mark. During this time, Mark must have matured in the faith and the differences between him and Paul must have been resolved because he is later associated with Paul during the latter's first Roman imprisonment (Col. 4:10; Philem. v. 24). In fact, Paul identified him as a fellow-laborer. Either before or shortly after this experience in Rome with Paul, Mark was working with Peter in Babylon (I Peter 5:13). When Paul was imprisoned in Rome a second time awaiting his martyrdom, he asked Timothy: "Take Mark, and bring him with thee: for he is profitable to me for the ministry" (II Tim. 4:11). Mark had overcome his early failures to become an effective servant of God. Whether Timothy and Mark ever arrived in Rome before Paul's death is difficult to say. Tradition states that Mark went to Egypt and established the churches in Alexandria. It sets his death as a Christian martyr during the reign of Nero.

Although not an apostle, Mark, the companion of two leading apostles, has been recognized by early church tradition as the author of the second Gospel. Irenaeus said that "after the death of Peter and Paul, Mark delivered to us in writing things preached by Peter."[1] Others, including Papias, Justin Martyr, Clement of Alexandria, Tertullian, Origen, and Eusebius, agree that Mark wrote the book and that Peter was somewhat

1. Irenaeus, *Against Heresies,* III. i. 1.

involved in its composition. Many have retitled this book "Peter's Gospel" because of this early tradition. Since the Jerusalem church met at Mark's house and since Mark did work with Peter in Babylon, Peter no doubt was one of the sources of Mark's material. This could explain the rather obvious personal reference to Peter in the angel's words to the women: "But go your way, tell his disciples and Peter . . ." (16:7). Some have also seen in Peter's sermon before Cornelius (Acts 10:34-43) the skeleton outline for the entire Book of Mark. The Markan authorship seems rather sure. There would be no good reason why early church writers would ascribe the book to Mark, a non-apostle, if he did not write it. In fact, the title *Kata Markon* ("According to Mark") is found in some of the earliest Greek manuscripts.

Internal evidence, though slight, confirms this conclusion. The account of the flight of the young man (14:51-52), found only in Mark, takes on special significance if that youth was really Mark. The detailed description of the upper room (14:12-16) is noteworthy if that room was in the house owned by Mark's mother. Unless there is stronger opposition, it is safe to conclude that John Mark was the author of this book.

Time and Place

There is much disagreement among scholars over the date of its writing. Since the date of composition is involved in the synoptic problem, those who argue for the priority of Mark would date it as early as A.D. 45. Others, who see Matthew as the first Gospel, would date it near the martyrdom of Peter and before the destruction of Jerusalem, approximately A.D. 67-68. We admit that we do not possess enough data for a precise dating. Early church traditions ascribed it to periods both before and after Peter's death. There is no good reason to project the book into the latter third of the first century.

There is a hint within the book suggesting a composition date in the middle third of the first century. On the way to Gologtha, the soldiers compelled "Simon a Cyrenian, who passed by, coming out of the country, the father of Alexander and Rufus, to bear his cross" (15:21). If this is the same Rufus as the one saluted by Paul during his third journey (Rom. 16:13), then the intended readers of Mark's Gospel must have known the two sons of Simon. Otherwise, why would Mark have included the mention of the two sons when they have no historical significance in the life of Christ?

This verse also argues for a Roman destination or origin. Either Mark was writing to believers in Rome where Rufus lived or else he was writing from Rome to readers who knew the family of Alexander and Rufus.

Purposes

The opening verse presents the first obvious purpose: "The beginning of the gospel of Jesus Christ, the Son of God" (1:1). In his biographical study of the life and ministry of Christ, Mark outlines a double thrust: "For even the Son of man came not to be ministered unto, but to minister, and to give his life a ransom for many" (10:45). His ministry of teaching and healing occupies the first part of the book (chs. 1-10), whereas the events surrounding His crucifixion are found in the lengthy second half (chs. 11-16). The comparison of content in the two sections will reveal that Mark clearly emphasized the redemptive nature of Christ's death and resurrection.

He also intended to convince the Roman mind and reader of the deity and mission of Jesus Christ. The reader must have been unfamiliar with Palestinian geography and customs. Mark points out that the Jordan was a river (1:5), that the Pharisees used to fast (2:18), and that the Mount of Olives overlooked the temple area (13:3). He translated several Aramaic expressions for the benefit of his readers (3:17; 5:41; 7:34; 14:36; 15:34). Latinisms are inserted throughout the book: *modius* for "bushel" (4:21); *census* for "tribute" (12:14); *centurio* for "centurion" (15:39, 44-45); and others. Since there were good Greek equivalents for these words, the readers must have had a Roman orientation. He even occasionally used a Latin term to explain a Greek word (12:42; 15:16).

The purposes were both evangelism and edification. The book was designed to convince the new reader of Christ's deity and sacrificial death and to educate the converts about the significance of Christ's person and ministry.

Distinctive Features

This is a book of action. Since the Roman mind was interested in power, Mark deliberately omitted the birth and childhood accounts and moved quickly into the miraculous ministry of Christ. The Roman mind would be far more impressed with what Jesus did than with His genealogical record or teaching. Mark could then argue from Christ's miracles to His deity and then to the greatest miracle and display of power that the world has ever seen—His death and resurrection.

The Greek adverb *euthus* (translated in several ways: "straightway," "immediately," "forthwith," and "anon") is used forty-two times in the book, more than all of the rest of the New Testament put together. Christ is seen as a man of activity, as a man who gets things done.

Since over 90 percent of the content of Mark is found elsewhere in Matthew and Luke, there are very few unique passages in this book. However, these accounts are not found in the other Gospels: the parable of the seed growing secretly (4:26-29), the healing of the blind man at Bethsaida (8:22-26), and the flight of the young man (14:43-52).

Ending of Mark

There is a textual controversy over the ending of the book. Although this problem is best fitted to the science of textual criticism, survey students should have a working knowledge of the issue. These are the questions: Did the original text or manuscript end at 16:8? If so, did Mark end his writing here or has the original ending been lost? If not, what is the true ending of Mark? Is the well-known ending (16:9-20) genuine or an interpolation? If it is an interpolation, is the content of that section true, false, or a mixture? The extant Greek manuscripts contain at least three different endings: the abrupt ending (concluding at 16:8), a short ending, adding one verse, and the long ending (16:9-20).

Generally, debate centers around the abrupt and the long endings. The long ending has the support of long years of acceptance by the Church[2] and of much manuscript evidence, although critics date these manuscripts late. Textual critics point out that the acknowledged best manuscripts (recently found) do not contain the long ending. They argue that if the long ending were original, it would be difficult to explain its omission in the oldest manuscripts. They also argue that if the abrupt ending were original, it would be easy to explain the addition of material to polish the ending. In observing the content of the long ending, it must be pointed out that the Greek word for "week" in verse 9 is not the same as in verse 2. The description of Mary Magdalene (16:9) does not seem natural here after her earlier introduction into the narrative (16:1). If the long ending were genuine, one would expect to find something more about Peter, especially since he was singled out (16:7). Many evangelicals note that some of the details of the Great Commission are not found elsewhere and seem to be inconsistent with Scriptural teaching (16:15-18).

There does not appear to be a solution in sight. Most would admit that if the long ending is genuine, it is more like an epilogue than a conclusion to a continuing narrative. Since the science of textual criticism favors the abrupt ending, it would seem best not to base doctrine or practice upon these verses (16:9-20). The passage may be genuine, but until it can be conclusively proven, doctrinal support should be found elsewhere.

---

2. The Greek manuscripts used in the translation of the 1611 Authorized Version (King James Version) had the longer ending. For a recent defense of this version, see David Otis Fuller, *Which Bible?* (Grand Rapids: Grand Rapids International Publications, 1970).

MARK

Outline

(The outline is built around the concept of Christ as the Servant of Jehovah: Isa. 52:13; Zech. 3:8.)

I. THE INTRODUCTION OF THE SERVANT (1:1-13)
   A. His forerunner (1:1-8)
   B. His baptism (1:9-11)
   C. His temptation (1:12-13)
II. THE MINISTRY OF THE SERVANT (1:14—5:43)
   A. Calling disciples (1:14-20)
   B. Casting out demons (1:21-28)
   C. Removing a fever (1:29-31)
   D. Healing the masses (1:32-34)
   E. Showing concern for others (1:35-39)
   F. Cleansing a leper (1:40-45)
   G. Healing the palsy (2:1-12)
   H. Calling Levi (2:13-22)
   I. Defending His disciples (2:23-28)
   J. Restoring the withered hand (3:1-5)
   K. Healing the masses (3:6-12)
   L. Ordaining twelve apostles (3:13-21)
   M. Warning against blasphemy (3:22-35)
   N. Relating parables (4:1-34)
   O. Calming the storm (4:35-41)
   P. Delivering the maniac (5:1-20)
   Q. Raising the daughter of Jairus (5:21-43)
III. THE OPPOSITION TO THE SERVANT (6:1—8:26)
   A. Unbelief of Nazareth (6:1-6)
   B. Warnings to the Twelve (6:7-13)
   C. Murder of John by Herod (6:14-29)
   D. Feeding of the five thousand (6:30-44)
   E. Walking on the water (6:45-52)
   F. Healing of the masses (6:53-56)
   G. Traditions of the Pharisees (7:1-23)
   H. Healing of the Syrophenician girl (7:24-30)
   I. Healing of a deaf and dumb man (7:31-37)
   J. Feeding of the four thousand (8:1-9)
   K. Leaven of the Pharisees (8:10-21)
   L. Giving of sight to the blind man (8:22-26)
IV. THE INSTRUCTION OF THE SERVANT (8:27—10:52)
   A. Confession of Peter (8:27-33)
   B. Essence of true discipleship (8:34-38)
   C. His transfiguration (9:1-13)
   D. Necessity of faith (9:14-29)
   E. Announcement of His death (9:30-32)
   F. Necessity of humility (9:33-37)
   G. Necessity of proper judgment (9:38-41)
   H. Severity of hell (9:42-50)
   I. Essence of marriage (10:1-12)
   J. Necessity of simplicity (10:13-16)
   K. Warning against wealth (10:17-31)
   L. Announcement of His death (10:32-34)

M. Rebuke of selfish ambition (10:35-45)
N. Healing of blind Bartimaeus (10:46-52)
V. THE PRESENTATION AND REJECTION OF THE SERVANT (11:1—12:44)
  A. Triumphal Entry (11:1-11)
  B. Cursing of the fig tree (11:12-14)
  C. Cleansing of the temple (11:15-19)
  D. Instructions on prayer and faith (11:20-26)
  E. Questioning of His authority (11:27-33)
  F. Parable of the vineyard and husbandmen (12:1-12)
  G. Question about tribute (12:13-17)
  H. Question about the resurrection (12:18-27)
  I. Question about the law (12:28-34)
  J. Defense of the deity of the Messiah (12:35-40)
  K. The widow's mite (12:41-44)
VI. THE PROPHECY OF THE SERVANT (13:1-37)
  A. Destruction of the temple predicted (13:1-4)
  B. Signs of His coming outlined (13:5-13)
  C. Terror of the tribulation depicted (13:14-23)
  D. Second coming of Christ described (13:24-27)
  E. Parable of the fig tree related (13:28-33)
  F. Watchfulness admonished (13:34-37)
VII. THE PASSION OF THE SERVANT (14:1—15:47)
  A. Conspiracy against Christ (14:1-2)
  B. Anointing by Mary (14:3-9)
  C. Betrayal of Judas (14:10-11)
  D. Eating of Passover feast (14:12-25)
  E. Denial of Peter announced (14:26-31)
  F. Prayer in Gethsemane (14:32-42)
  G. Arrest of Jesus (14:43-52)
  H. Trial before Caiaphas (14:53-65)
  I. Denial of Peter (14:66-72)
  J. Trial before Pilate (15:1-15)
  K. Mockery of the soldiers (15:16-20)
  L. Crucifixion of Christ (15:21-41)
  M. Burial of Jesus (15:42-47)
VIII. THE RESURRECTION OF THE SERVANT (16:1-20)
  A. Announcement of His resurrection (16:1-8)
  B. Appearances of Jesus (16:9-14)
  C. Giving of the Great Commission (16:15-20)

Survey

(Since most of the content of Mark is found in Matthew, this survey will necessarily be briefer. Check with the parallel accounts in Matthew for further details.)

1:1-13

Mark introduced the servant ministry of Christ with the preparatory preaching of John the Baptist. The genealogy and birth of Christ are omitted because his Roman readers would not be interested in those accounts of a servant. John contrasted his water baptism with the future

Galilean commercial fisherman of today, sorting the day's catch at the village of Ein Gev, on the eastern side of the Sea of Galilee.

Spirit baptism of Christ. The baptism of Jesus revealed His eternal Sonship and the power of the Holy Spirit resting upon His life. His temptation was a Spirit-directed appointment, successful in spite of adverse circumstances: no food, the attack of Satan, and the presence of wild beasts (cf. Matt. 1-4).

1:14—2:22

Christ's active ministry began after the imprisonment of John by Herod. As a servant interested in the work of God, He recruited workers in ordinary occupations for spiritual responsibilities. The disciples left their casting and mending of nets to become fishers of men's souls. Casting out demons substantiated His authority over the evil supernatural world and illustrated the authority of His oral Biblical exposition in the synagogues. Healing was done both privately and publicly, both individually and corporately. Jesus' own prayer life is a real mark of His

101

humanity, an indication of His complete dependence upon the Father. The cleansing of the leper was designed as a specific sign to the priests of His authority over spiritual and physical defilement. The healing of the palsy demonstrated His intrinsic prerogative to forgive sin. Since this right belonged only to God, Jesus was claiming deity for Himself. His call of Levi revealed His compassion for sinners and His condemnation of hypocritical righteousness. The parables of the cloth and wineskins show that the new concepts of Christ's teaching could never be placed within the established system of Phariseeism.

2:23—3:35

He came into open conflict with the Pharisees when He defended His disciples' actions of grain plucking on the Sabbath and when He healed the man with the withered hand also on the Sabbath. This resulted in a joint conspiracy of the Pharisees and Herodians to murder Him. The twelve apostles were appointed for four reasons: to be with Him, to preach, to heal, and to cast out demons. Although His friends thought that He was insane and the religious leaders claimed that He was satanically controlled, Jesus continued to relate Himself to people on a spiritual basis.

4:1-34

The parable of the sower revealed to the disciples the determination

The town of Nazareth.

of Satan to prevent the Word of God from gaining entrance into the hearts of men and to show the hardness of those same hearts. The parable of the candle manifested the responsibility of believers to transmit the truth of God. The parable of unconscious growth proved that the fulfillment of God's program may be slow and imperceptible to the senses of man, but its climax is inevitable. The mustard seed assured the disciples that great things could come out of small beginnings.

4:35—5:43

The calming of the storm demonstrated Christ's eternal care over His own followers and His power over nature as its creator and governor. In spite of His word (4:35) and physical presence, they were afraid that they would sink; this manifested their lack of faith in Him. The casting of demons out of the maniac of Gadara showed how powerful the control of Satan is in the life of many. The reactions to the miracle showed the contrast between the selfish materialism of men and the compassionate concern of Christ. His power over disease and death can be seen in the healing of the woman with the issue of blood and the restoration of Jairus' daughter to natural life (cf. Matt. 9:18-26).

6:1—8:26

In spite of all the miraculous evidence put forth in the previous section (1:14—5:43), there was a growing opposition mounting up against the claims of Christ. His hometown of Narazeth simply treated Him as a mere human being. This passage (6:3) also reveals that several children were born to Joseph and Mary after the birth of Jesus. When Christ sent out the Twelve on a preaching mission, He anticipated for them the same type of opposition that He had been receiving. The murder of John by Herod out of personal and political expediency was a foregleam of Christ's trial and death under similar circumstances. The next two miracles (feeding the five thousand and walking on the water) revealed His compassionate concern for the needs of both the masses and His own. The tradition of the elders caused the Pharisees to repudiate the Lord and to criticize His disciples. In their hypocrisy they had replaced the commandments of God with human prejudices. They failed to see that genuine spiritual defilement originates within the heart. Christ healed the daughter of the Syrophenician woman in response to her intense faith even though His basic earthly ministry as the Messiah was to Israel ("children" refers to the Jews, whereas "the dogs" refers to the Gentiles). Both that miracle and the healing of the deaf and dumb man anticipated a future ministry to the Gentiles as a result of Jewish rejection. The opposition of the leaders did not keep Jesus from exercising compassion to the multitude (feeding of the four thousand).

Because of the adamant antagonism of the religious establishment, Jesus reiterated that no more miracles would be performed as public signs to the nation as a whole. The healing of the blind man confirmed His concern for the needy individual in the midst of universal hostility. This is the only miracle of healing that required two stages for completion: the first was the impartation of vision and the second was the correction of that eyesight (cf. Matt. 14-15).

8:27-38

After the opposition to His messianic claims had been firmly established, Jesus began a special instruction period for His disciples. His first challenge to them was about His true identity. Did they share the popular opinion of the multitudes that He was only a prophet or did they believe that He was more than that? In behalf of the others, Peter acknowledged Jesus to be the Christ. This correct evaluation was not to be preached since the nation had basically rejected His messianic claims. Christ then began to teach them about the necessity of His death and resurrection. The protest of Peter to this disclosure reflected the Satanic plot to keep Jesus from the cross. This provided Christ with an opportunity to teach His disciples about the essence of the Christian life and discipleship. Peter wanted Christ to save His life, but in losing His life in the will of God, Christ was able to save others. The death of selfish ambitions and the acceptance of the divine plan bring fulfillment and meaning to the life of any person.

9:1—10:52

The disciples wanted to see the kingdom, not the cross. The Transfiguration gave them a preview of the glory of Christ that will be manifested at His second coming. It also confirmed their earlier statement that Jesus was indeed the Christ, the Son of God. The glory of the mountain experience must be contrasted with the frustration in the valley. Here the disciples were unable to cast out a demon. After Jesus delivered the son, He taught His own about the importance of faith, prayer, and fasting. The ambitious, proud disciples were also in need of humility and sacrificial service to others. Their criticism of other preachers stemmed from their sense of superiority because they had been chosen to be Christ's select group of apostles. They needed to know about the severity of hell in order to preach out of a sense of urgency. Christ refused to arbitrate a Pharisaical debate over divorce; rather, He proclaimed the true essence of the marital union as God intended it. Whereas the disciples protested the presence of little children, Jesus exhorted the former to have a childlike simplicity of faith. Their awe of wealth was exposed through Christ's blunt treatment of the rich young ruler. Wealth can be used as a blessing to God and to man; but too often men become the pawns of riches. The third announcement of His coming death and resurrection again showed that riches and glory were not Christ's goals and should not be those of the disciples either. However, the desire of James and John to have the best thrones in the kingdom revealed their basic ignorance of Christ's spiritual teaching at this time. Christ wanted them to minister and to give just as He was about to do (cf. Matt. 16-20).

11:1—12:44

The Triumphal Entry into Jerusalem marked Jesus' official and final presentation of Himself to Israel as her rightful king. Although the event produced some rejoicing, the city did not fall on its knees before its God and King. The cursing of the fig tree illustrated the divine judgment that would fall upon Israel for her spiritual barrenness. The cleansing of the temple produced criticism and intensified the conspiracy to kill Christ. Christ was then challenged about the source of His authority. He claimed that His authority came from the same one who commissioned John the Baptist. Since the religious establishment repudiated the ministry of John, it was obvious that they would do the same to Him. In the parable of the vineyard, Christ pointed out that the religious leaders were like the husbandmen who had abused their stewardship responsibilities and who had killed the son, the rightful heir. This they planned to do to Him. These leaders then tried "to catch him in his words" (12:13). Christ avoided the charge of treason by showing the distinction between God and government. Conflict only comes when the state moves out of its divinely ordained sphere. He then devastated the liberalism of the Sadducees by a logical defense of the resurrection through the exposition of Scripture. Next, He reduced the commandments to the common denominator of love toward God and man. By showing that the Messiah had to be both human and divine, He substantiated His claims to deity. Finally, He pointed out that the widow's two mites were worth more in God's sight than all of the gifts of the wealthy because she gave sacrificially out of love and devotion (cf. Matt. 21-23).

13:1-37

Mark's analysis of the Olivet Discourse is much shorter than Matthew's. He includes the prediction that the Zerubbabel-Herod temple would be destroyed, the mention of signs that would precede His second advent, the terrible persecution that would befall those in the tribulation, and the heavenly signs that would announce Christ's descent. Jesus warned that men should watch and be sensitive to the times in which

The Garden of Gethsemane and Jerusalem's "Golden Gate" in the background.

they live. Since the exact time of His coming is unknown, men should be ready for His return at all times (cf. Matt. 24-25).

14:1-11

By this time the conspiracy to put Christ to death was certain; only the time and place of seizure needed to be decided. The leaders wanted to do it secretly to avoid a public uproar. The anointing of Jesus with costly perfume was regarded by many as a financial waste, but Jesus called the act "a good work on me" (14:6). Mary apparently understood the significance of Jesus' announcements about His death because He said "she is come beforehand to anoint my body to the burying" (14:8). The record of her action has become a perpetual "memorial of her" (14:9). Judas Iscariot, now thoroughly disenchanted with Jesus, betrayed Jesus by setting up the time and place of His arrest.

14:12-52

The night before His crucifixion, Jesus ate the Passover feast with His disciples in a room that had already been "furnished and prepared" (14:15) by its owner, perhaps by the mother or father of John Mark. Here Christ could fellowship with His own and teach them privately; both Judas and the religious leaders would have been unaware of these prior arrangements. At the feast Jesus informed the group that a traitor was in its midst; however, none of them knew that it was Judas. After Judas left to finalize the details of Jesus' arrest, Jesus instituted the ordinance of the Lord's Supper, a memorial of His death. The entire group voiced their allegiance to Christ in spite of His announcement of their cowardice and Peter's denial. From the upper room they walked to the Garden of Gethsemane where Jesus agonized over the problem of bearing human sin and guilt. His concern must be seen against the indifference of the tired disciples. After His third season of prayer, Jesus, identified with a kiss by Judas, was seized. In his fearful zeal Peter cut off the ear of the servant of the high priest and then fled along with the rest of the disciples. Christ criticized the soldiers for making the arrest at night instead of during the day in the temple. A young man, possibly Mark, tried to follow Jesus from the garden but fled when he was discovered.

14:53—15:47

At the evening trial before Caiaphas and the religious leaders, Jesus could only be charged with blasphemy because of His claim of equality with God. They found Him guilty of death and sarcastically mocked Him. It was during the events of this particular trial that Peter denied the Lord three times as Christ had predicted. In the morning the Sanhedrin agreed on their earlier decision and took Jesus to Pilate, the Roman governor of Judea. Pilate, recognizing the political innocence of Jesus, tried to free Jesus by giving the multitudes the choice of either Jesus or Barabbas. To his amazement, they asked for the release of Barabbas and the crucifixion of Jesus. Obliging the will of the multitude, Pilate delivered Jesus to the soldiers who mocked Him and led Him to Golgotha for His crucifixion. Hanging on the cross, Jesus endured more mockery from the multitude, the religious leaders, and the two thieves. The severity of His physical and spiritual sufferings caused an early death. After proper investigation over the certainty of Christ's death, the body of Jesus was entrusted to Joseph of Arimathaea for burial (cf. Matt. 26-27).

16:1-20

Mark devoted very little material to the postresurrection ministry of Christ. The announcement of His triumph over death was given to the women by an angel. They were charged to inform others about His resurrection. In the controversial long ending (16:9-20), His appearances to Mary Magdalene, to the two Emmaus travelers, and to the eleven disciples are described briefly. If the passage is genuine, then the unusual signs were to accompany the direct converts of the apostles. In this way, the preaching ministry of the apostles was divinely authenticated (cf. Matt. 28).

Increase Your Learning

By Doing

1. Since Mark is the gospel of action, underline or circle his favorite word which is translated in these ways: straightway, forthwith, immediately, and anon.

By Discussing

1. What are the characteristics of demon possession? How does a person become demon possessed? Can a believer be so controlled? Are Christians today able to cast out demons?
2. What are the values of prayer? Why did Jesus pray? Why should we pray when God has determined the future? Are all prayers answered?
3. Compare the traditions of the elders which Jesus criticized with many of the taboos of contemporary evangelicalism. In what ways are they similar? Different?
4. Relate the teachings of Christ about marriage and divorce to modern marital problems. Is divorce permissible? On what grounds? Is remarriage Scriptural?
5. Relate the inspiration and inerrancy of the original Biblical manuscripts with the errancy of copies. Should doctrine be based upon passages that are textually disputed?

By Reading

Cole, R. A. *The Gospel According to St. Mark.* Grand Rapids: Wm. B. Eerdmans Publishing Co., 1961.

English, E. Schuyler. *Studies in the Gospel According to Mark.* New York: Our Hope Press, 1943.

Swete, Henry Barclay. *The Gospel According to St. Mark.* Grand Rapids: Wm. B. Eerdmans Publishing Co., 1913.

Taylor, Vincent. *The Gospel According to St. Mark.* London: Macmillan, 1953.

Wuest, Kenneth. *Mark in the Greek New Testament.* Grand Rapids: Wm. B. Eerdmans Publishing Co., 1957.

6

LUKE

Writer

The third Gospel has been attributed to the pen of Luke, "the beloved physician" (Col. 4:14). Of all the writers of the entire Bible, he was probably the only one who was a Gentile. How do we know this? In listing his companions who were Jewish, "of the circumcision," Paul excluded Luke (Col. 4:11, 14). There is also a subtle hint of his Gentile background in his description of Judas' death and the subsequent purchase of a burial plot: "And it was known unto all the dwellers at Jerusalem; insomuch as that field is called in their proper tongue, Aceldama, that is to say, The field of blood" (Acts 1:19). Since the life history of Luke is directly involved in the problem of the authorship of Luke and Acts, the expression "in *their* proper tongue" takes on special significance. If Luke had been Jewish, he would have written "in *our* tongue"; the usage of "their" argues for a Gentile ancestry.

Several early Church Fathers, including Irenaeus, Tertullian, and Clement of Alexandria, ascribed the book to Luke. However, the real identity of the author can only be known through a thorough investigation of the content of Luke and Acts. Both of the books were written to the same person, Theophilus (Luke 1:3; Acts 1:1) and by the same writer (note the phrase: "The former treatise have I made," Acts 1:1). Actually, in order to determine the authorship of Luke, one must first solve the problem of the authorship of Acts. This can be done by a close observation of those passages where the author includes himself in the events by the use of the first person plural pronouns "we" and "us" (Acts 16:10-17; 20:5—28:31). The other narrative sections of Acts use the terms "they" and "them," showing that the author was not involved in those events. What then can be learned about the life of

Luke from these two books? In the Gospel prologue Luke indicates that he had not been an eyewitness of the earthly ministry of Jesus Christ (1:2). A sixth-century manuscript, Codex Bezae (D), has an interesting reading in Acts 11:28:

> And there was great rejoicing, and when we gathered together, one of their number, named Agabus spoke, indicating that a great famine was about to take place over the whole world.

Although this passage is not regarded to be genuine, it does reveal an early tradition that the author of Acts was a member of the church at Antioch in Syria where Paul and Barnabas labored (note the use of "we"). The first authentic "we" passage occurs within Paul's second missionary journey. After Paul had received the Macedonian vision at Troas, a city on the northwestern tip of modern Turkey, the text states: ". . . immediately we endeavored to go into Macedonia, assuredly gathering that the Lord had called us for to preach the gospel unto them" (Acts 16:10). Luke, the narrator, apparently joined the missionary team of Paul, Silas, and Timothy at Troas and journeyed with them to the European city of Philippi. When Paul and Silas were imprisoned later, they were charged with the crime of "being Jews" (16:20). Timothy and Luke were not jailed probably because they were Gentiles (the former was definitely half-Gentile; Acts 16:1). When the missionary team left for Thessalonica (16:40—17:1), Luke remained in Philippi, possibly to practice medicine or to oversee the young church (or both). At the conclusion of his third journey, Paul again traveled into Macedonia where Luke joined him once more at Philippi (20:1, 5-6). From this point on, Luke is the constant companion of Paul, possibly to minister to Paul's physical needs. He went with Paul from Philippi to Troas, Miletus, Tyre, Caesarea, and Jerusalem where Paul was arrested (20:6—21:17). When Paul was taken by the Romans from Jerusalem to Caesarea where he was imprisoned for two years, Luke went also. Luke was with Paul during the troubled voyage from Caesarea to Puteoli in Italy (27:1—28:13). Both the Acts narrative and the Epistles written by Paul during his two years of imprisonment at Rome reveal that Luke was there also (Acts 28:14-31; Col. 4:14; Philem. v. 24). It is generally agreed that Paul was released from this first Roman internment; however, Paul was later arrested and brought to a Roman jail for the second time. Since Luke was again with Paul during this second Roman imprisonment (II Tim. 4:11), it is safe to conclude that he also traveled with Paul during the interval between the two Roman imprisonments. Tradition is divided over the nature of Luke's death; some state that he died as a martyr, whereas others claim a natural death for him.

To establish that Luke was the real author of the "we" sections in Acts, the process of elimination must be followed. From an examination of the Epistles written during Paul's first imprisonment at Rome, these people were with him there: Aristarchus, Demas, Epaphras, Epaphroditus, Jesus called Justus, Luke, Mark, Onesimus, and Tychicus (Eph. 6:21; Phil. 2:25; Col. 4:7-14; Philem. vv. 10, 23-24). Since the author of Acts went with Paul to Rome, Epaphras and Epaphroditus would be ruled out because they arrived later (Phil. 4:18; Col. 4:12). Aristarchus (19:29), Mark (12:25), Timothy (16:1), and Tychicus (20:4) are eliminated because they are all mentioned in the third person in Acts. Onesimus, a converted runaway slave, came to Paul later and would be an unlikely candidate for authorship. Since Demas later deserted Paul (II Tim. 4:10), it is very doubtful that he would have composed these two books. Only Luke and Jesus called Justus remain as distinct possibilities. Since no early tradition ascribed the book to Justus and since it is known that Luke was later with Paul (II Tim. 4:11), it seems best to ascribe the third Gospel and Acts to Luke. Both of the books reveal the literary ability of an educated person such as a doctor. In fact, some see in Luke's account of the healing of the woman with an issue of blood the approach of a physician guarding the integrity of his professional peers (Mark 5:25-26; cf. Luke 8:43).

Origen regarded "the brother, whose praise is in the gospel throughout all the churches" (II Cor. 8:18) as a reference to Luke. Whether this is so is debatable, but Luke was beloved, both by Paul and by the Pauline constituency. Such a close friend and associate of the outstanding apostle would have been in an advantageous position to produce both the Gospel and the early history of the church with special emphasis placed upon the ministry of Paul. The early church would also have accepted the inspired, authoritative books from his hand because of the Pauline stamp of approval upon Luke's life and ministry.

Time and Place

The Gospel was obviously written before the second volume of the Lukan set. Since the chronicle of Paul's activities ends with his two-year imprisonment in Rome, it seems logical to conclude that Acts was completed by Luke at the end of that period, about A.D. 60. Any date shortly before 60 would therefore be satisfactory. Since Luke researched his Gospel and dealt with primary sources (Luke 1:1-4), it would appear that his best time to have done so would have been during Paul's two-year imprisonment at Caesarea (A.D. 56-58). Certainly if he did not write the Gospel at this time, he gathered the data for the composition which would have taken place during the voyage to Rome (Acts 27) or in the early months of Paul's first Roman imprisonment.

Purposes

The original design of the Gospel was to establish an individual,

Theophilus, in the Christian faith. Luke's purpose was put in these words: "That thou mightest know the certainty of those things, wherein thou hast been instructed" (1:4). The thrust of the book, therefore, was the edification of one who had already been saved, not for the evangelization of a lost sinner. Since his conversion, Theophilus had received oral instruction; now Luke wanted to put into his hands an inspired, authoritative account of the life and ministry of Jesus Christ.

Since "Theophilus" means "loved by God" or a "lover of God," some feel that Luke was writing to an unidentified person under that spiritual, symbolic name. Some have suggested that Paul was even this mystery person, but why would Luke be writing to Paul to give the latter certainty? Since every believer has been loved by God and in turn should be a lover of God, there may be the remote possibility that Luke was writing to a general audience of Christians under that unique title. However, it seems best to regard Theophilus as a real person with that name. Certainly all new converts can profit from the reading of this book.

Just as Matthew presented Christ as the King of the Jews and Mark represented Him as the Servant of Jehovah, it would appear that as a physician, Luke is interested in demonstrating that Christ was the perfect

Tiberius Caesar, the Roman emperor at the time of the death of Jesus.

man, the Son of Man. Luke does not minimize His deity or redemptive sufferings; rather, he focuses attention on the complete humanity of Jesus. He was the Son of Adam as well as the Son of God. A proper evaluation of the person of Jesus Christ must include both natures, divine and human.

Distinctive Features

Of the three synoptic writers, Luke has the most distinctive material. Over 50 percent of the content is found exclusively in this book whereas Matthew has about 40 percent exclusive material and Mark only 10 percent. In relationship to content, it should also be noted that in sheer length of reading material, Luke has written more (Luke-Acts) than any other New Testament writer, including Paul.

He has gained a reputation as an able historian through exactness. Note his procedure of exact dating (1:5; 2:1-2). Note also the exactness of political and geographical data as in the description of the beginning of John's ministry:

> Now in the fifteenth year of the reign of Tiberius Caesar, Pontius Pilate being governor of Judaea, and Herod being tetrarch of Galilee, and his brother Philip tetrarch of Ituraea, and of the region of Trachonitis, and Lysanias the tetrarch of Abilene, Annas and Caiaphas being the high priests, the word of God came unto John . . . (3:1-2).

This thorough investigation fulfilled his purpose of providing Theophilus with historical certainty.

As a physician, he would have naturally been interested in the miraculous births of John and Jesus. For that reason, he describes at great length the angelic announcements of those births to Zacharias and to Mary respectively (1:5-38). He also vividly depicts the births of both children with their attending circumstances (1:57—2:39). Only Luke includes these events, along with the visit of Mary to Elizabeth during the latter's pregnancy (1:39-56), the announcement of Christ's birth by the angels to the shepherds and the latters' worship of the child in the manger (2:8-20), the circumcision of the infant Jesus (2:21-24), the recognition of the infant Messiah by Simeon in the temple (2:25-35), and the thanksgiving of the aged prophetess Anna (2:36-38). In describing the dialogue between the twelve-year-old Jesus and the religious elders (2:41-52) Luke is the only Gospel writer to isolate any event from those thirty years between Christ's birth and His baptism. His interest in the human development of Jesus is aptly summarized: "And Jesus increased in wisdom and stature, and in favour with God and man" (2:52).

Some of the famous liturgical hymns of the church are based upon

113

five unique songs or poems of praise contained only in Luke's opening chapters: the song of Elizabeth voiced by her when her infant jumped within her womb at the coming of Mary (1:39-45);[1] the *Magnificat* or Mary's response to the song of Elizabeth (1:46-55); the *Benedictus* or the song of Zacharias praising God at the birth of John for the fulfillment of His covenants (1:67-79); the *Gloria in Excelsis* or the song of the angels rejoicing over the birth of Jesus (2:13-14); and the *Nunc Dimittis* or the praise of Simeon upon seeing the Messiah (2:28-32).

Luke stresses people. Special attention is given to names not found in the other Gospels: Zacharias, Elizabeth, Simeon, Anna, Zacchaeus, and Cleopas. The life-styles of people can be seen in the characters of Jesus' parables mentioned only here: the neighborly, involved Samaritan (10:30-37), the prodigal son and the self-righteous son (15:11-32), the clever steward (16:1-13), and the proud Pharisee and the skid row sinner (18:9-14).

The understanding relationship between physicians and women is well established. In his Gospel Luke elevates the role of the woman. He referred to women forty-three times, whereas they are mentioned only forty-nine times in Matthew and Mark combined. The birth of Jesus is analyzed from Mary's viewpoint while Matthew viewed it from Joseph's perspective. The early years also include references to Elizabeth and Anna (1:5-57; 2:36-38). Here are some other accounts that reveal the prominence of women: the healing of Peter's mother-in-law (4:38-39); the raising of the widow's son at Nain (7:11-18); the forgiveness of the sinful woman who washed His feet with tears (7:36-50); the naming of the women who supported financially the apostles and Jesus (8:1-3); the healing of the woman with the issue of blood and the raising of Jairus' daughter (8:40-56); the hospitality of Mary and Martha (10:38-42); the healing of a crippled woman (13:10-13); the search of the woman for her lost coin (15:8-10); the warning of Lot's wife (17:32); the two mites of the widow (21:1-4); the lament of the daughters of Jerusalem as He walked to Golgotha (23:27-31); the presence of the women at the cross (23:49) and at the burial of Jesus (23:55-56); and the resurrection reports to the women (24:1-12). The charge of male chauvinism certainly cannot be brought against Jesus or Luke.

Luke also emphasizes the prayer life of Jesus as a mark of His humanity. The Holy Spirit descended upon Jesus after His baptism while He was praying (3:21). After preaching and healing, He often

---

1. "Blessed" is a Greek perfect passive participle *eulogemene* (1:42). The force of this verbal idea is that Mary had been blessed by someone else, namely God. Elizabeth did not state that Mary was an innately blessed person. This concept is found in the Greek word *eulogetos,* used of the person of God (1:68; cf. Eph. 1:3).

went into solitary places to pray (5:16). Before He selected the twelve apostles, He spent all night in prayer (6:12-13). He prayed while in the presence of His disciples before asking them about His identity (9:18). His transfiguration occurred while He was praying (9:29). When the seventy returned from their preaching mission, He prayed and thanked the Father for spiritual illumination (10:21). His prayer life stimulated the disciples to ask for instructions in prayer (11:1). After informing Peter that Satan wanted to test him, Jesus encouraged Peter by stating that He had already prayed for the stability of his faith (22:31-32). He prayed three times in Gethsemane in anticipation of the cross experience (22:39-46). Two of the utterances on the cross were addressed to the Father in prayer (23:34, 46). In addition, Jesus gave the disciples the principles behind a model prayer (11:1-4), taught them a parable about importunity in prayer (11:5-13), and instructed them to pray always (18:1-8).

The empowering ministry of the Holy Spirit in the lives of individuals is noted throughout the book. Mary was overshadowed by the Spirit to conceive (1:35). Elizabeth (1:41), Zacharias (1:67), and Simeon (2:25) were filled with the Spirit in order to prophesy. John the Baptist was providentially prepared for his task as the messianic forerunner by the Spirit (1:15). The Spirit came upon Jesus at the baptism (3:22), led Christ into the wilderness to be tempted by Satan (4:1), and empowered Jesus for His preaching and healing ministries (4:18-19). After His resurrection, Jesus predicted that the apostles would carry out the Great Commission in the power of the Spirit (24:49). Luke's second book, The Acts, is a vivid chronicle of this accomplishment.

A unique section of parables (9:51—18:14) shows that Luke must have been infatuated with them. In fact, of the twenty-two parables in the book, the following seventeen[2] are found only in this Gospel: the two debtors (7:41-43), the good Samaritan (10:25-37), the friend asking for bread at midnight (11:5-8), the rich fool and his barns (12:16-21), the watchful servants (12:35-48), the barren fig tree (13:6-9), the chief seats at the wedding feast (14:7-11), the great supper and the excuses for not attending (14:15-24), the builder who did not finish (14:28-30), the king who sought counsel (14:31-32), the lost coin (15:8-10), the prodigal son (15:11-32), the clever steward (16:1-13), the unprofitable servants (17:7-10), the widow and the judge (18:1-8), the Pharisee and the publican (18:9-14), and the servants and the pounds (19:11-27).

Of the twenty miracles recorded in this book, six are peculiar to Luke:

---

2. If the story of the rich man and Lazarus is accepted as a parable, then the unique group of parables would be increased to eighteen.

the catch of fish (5:1-11), the raising of the widow's son at Nain (7:11-18), the healing of the woman with an eighteen-year-old spirit of infirmity (13:10-17), the healing of a man who had dropsy (14:1-6), the cleansing of the ten lepers (17:11-19), and the restoration of Malchus' ear cut off by Peter (22:50-51).

Method of Research

In his prologue (1:1-4), Luke indicated that many writers had written on certain aspects of Christ's earthly life before. This could possibly include the Gospels of Matthew and Mark, but he is referring probably to short narratives or gospelettes that were in circulation among the early Christians before any inspired Gospel was produced. Luke identified these writers as eyewitnesses of Christ's life and as ministers of the word, but he did not name them or call them apostles.

Although the Scriptures are God-breathed (II Tim. 3:16), the human concern and desire to write can be seen in his words: "It seemed good to me also . . . to write unto thee" (1:3). This desire came out of a sense of competence. He believed that he had "perfect understanding of all things from the very first." This means that he had checked out all of his recorded events in advance. He had sifted through the gospelettes, talked with eyewitnesses, traced down rumors, and separated fact from fiction.

Some have discounted Luke's laborious research by translating the Greek word *anothen* "from above" rather than "from the very first." This would mean that Luke's material was given to him by direct revelation or at least confirmed directly by God. It is true that *anothen* is so translated and understood in other passages (John 3:3, 31; 19:11; James 1:17; 3:15, 17). However, Luke used the word with the meaning "from the beginning" in a quotation of Paul's speech before Herod Agrippa II (Acts 26:5). It seems best to consider this a reference to Luke's knowledge of primary sources or to his plan to deal with matters about Jesus' birth and childhood (1:5—2:52).

The possible sources of Luke's research are multiple. It is conceivable that Luke could have talked with Mary, the mother of Jesus. Those things which she kept and pondered in her heart (1:29; 2:19, 33, 51) are here revealed. Since Luke and Mark were together in Rome (Col. 4:10, 14), Luke could have received some information from Mark especially if the Gospel was written in the early months of Paul's Roman imprisonment. Since the Gospels of Matthew and Mark were probably written before, Luke could have read them and incorporated some of their material into his Gospel. The many gospel narratives in circulation were known by him. He could have talked personally with some of the original seventy disciples (10:1), with some of the apostles in Jerusalem at the time he traveled with Paul and later during Paul's Caesarean imprisonment, with the certain women mentioned by him (8:2-3), and with Mnason, an old disciple (Acts 21:16).

Luke's method of research was probably typical of the other synoptic writers. All had general material at their disposal and had access to personal eyewitnesses. From this vast reservoir of content, they selected, arranged, and recorded the events for thematic effect under the superintendence of the Holy Spirit.

Outline

PROLOGUE (1:1-4)
I. THE PREPARATION OF THE SON OF MAN (1:5—2:52)
    A. Announcement of the birth of John (1:5-25)
    B. Announcement of the birth of Jesus (1:26-38)
    C. Visit of Mary to Elizabeth (1:39-45)
    D. Song of Mary (1:46-56)
    E. Birth of John (1:57-80)
    F. Birth of Jesus (2:1-7)
    G. Worship of the shepherds (2:8-20)
    H. Circumcision of Jesus (2:21-24)
    I. Praise of Simeon (2:25-35)
    J. Thanksgiving of Anna (2:36-38)
    K. Childhood of Jesus (2:39-52)
II. THE INTRODUCTION OF THE SON OF MAN (3:1—4:13)
    A. His forerunner (3:1-20)
    B. His baptism (3:21-22)
    C. His genealogy (3:23-38)
    D. His temptation (4:1-13)
III. THE MINISTRY OF THE SON OF MAN (4:14—9:50)
    A. Teaching at Nazareth (4:14-30)
    B. Casting out demons (4:31-37)
    C. Healing Peter's mother-in-law (4:38-44)
    D. Miraculous catch of fish (5:1-11)
    E. Cleansing a leper (5:12-16)
    F. Healing the palsied man (5:17-26)
    G. Recruiting Matthew (5:27-29)
    H. Defending His concern for sinners (5:30-39)
    I. Defending His disciples (6:1-5)
    J. Restoring the withered hand (6:6-11)
    K. Choosing the twelve apostles (6:12-19)
    L. Teaching the beatitudes (6:20-49)
    M. Healing the centurion's servant (7:1-10)
    N. Raising the widow's son at Nain (7:11-18)
    O. Eliminating the doubt of John (7:19-29)
    P. Criticizing the Pharisees (7:30-35)
    Q. Washing of His feet (7:36-40)
    R. Parable of the two debtors (7:41-50)
    S. Parable of the sower (8:1-15)
    T. Parable of the candle (8:16-18)
    U. Calming the storm (8:19-25)

    V. Casting out demons in Gadara (8:26-39)
    W. Raising of Jairus' daughter (8:40-56)
    X. Sending the apostles to preach (9:1-17)
    Y. Confession of Peter (9:18-22)
    Z. Explaining discipleship (9:23-26)
  AA. Transfiguration of Christ (9:27-36)
  BB. Delivering a possessed child (9:37-43)
  CC. Prediction of His death (9:44-45)
  DD. Teaching on humility (9:46-50)

IV. THE JOURNEY OF THE SON OF MAN TO JERUSALEM (9:51—19:28)
    A. Challenge to the disciples (9:51—13:21)
      1. Rejection of the Samaritans (9:51-56)
      2. Tests of discipleship (9:57-62)
      3. Mission of the seventy (10:1-24)
      4. Parable of the good Samaritan (10:25-37)
      5. Contrast between Mary and Martha (10:38-42)
      6. Model prayer (11:1-4)
      7. Parable of importunate friend (11:5-13)
      8. Blasphemy of the Pharisees (11:14-32)
      9. Parable of the candle (11:33-36)
     10. Woes upon the leaders (11:37-54)
     11. Warning against the leaven of the Pharisees (12:1-15)
     12. Parable of the rich fool (12:16-34)
     13. Parable of the watchful servants (12:35-41)
     14. Parable of the unprepared servant (12:42-48)
     15. Family divisions over Christ (12:49-59)
     16. Necessity of repentance (13:1-5)
     17. Parable of the barren fig tree (13:6-9)
     18. Healing of the infirm woman (13:10-17)
     19. Parables of the kingdom of God (13:18-21)
    B. Conflict with the religious leaders (13:22—16:31)
      1. Teaching on salvation (13:22-33)
      2. Lamenting the unbelief of Jerusalem (13:34-35)
      3. Healing of the man with dropsy (14:1-6)
      4. Parable of the chief seats (14:7-15)
      5. Parable of the supper and the excuses (14:16-24)
      6. Tests of discipleship (14:25-35)
      7. Parable of the lost sheep (15:1-7)
      8. Parable of the lost coin (15:8-10)
      9. Parable of the prodigal son (15:11-32)
     10. Parable of the clever steward (16:1-13)
     11. Lesson of the rich man and Lazarus (16:14-31)
    C. Instruction of the disciples (17:1—19:28)
      1. Importance of forgiveness (17:1-6)
      2. Parable of the unprofitable servants (17:7-10)
      3. Cleansing of ten lepers (17:11-19)
      4. Prediction of the Second Coming (17:20-37)
      5. Parable of the judge and the widow (18:1-8)
      6. Parable of the Pharisee and the publican (18:9-14)
      7. Concern for children (18:15-17)
      8. Challenge to the rich young ruler (18:18-30)

9. Repetition of His coming death (18:31-34)
10. Healing of the blind man (18:35-43)
11. Salvation of Zacchaeus (19:1-10)
12. Parable of the pounds (19:11-28)

V. THE PRESENTATION OF THE SON OF MAN (19:29-48)
  A. His triumphal entry (19:29-40)
  B. His lamentation over Jerusalem (19:41-44)
  C. His cleansing of the temple (19:45-48)

VI. THE REJECTION OF THE SON OF MAN (20:1—21:4)
  A. His authority questioned (20:1-8)
  B. Parable of the vineyard related (20:9-18)
  C. Question about taxes answered (20:19-26)
  D. Questions about resurrection discussed (20:27-38)
  E. His deity defended (20:39-47)
  F. Widow and the two mites commented on (21:1-4)

VII. THE PROPHECY OF THE SON OF MAN (21:5-38)
  A. Destruction of the temple predicted (21:5-6)
  B. Signs of His coming described (21:7-19)
  C. Destruction of Jerusalem predicted (21:20-24)
  D. His coming described (21:25-28)
  E. Parable of the fig tree related (21:29-33)
  F. Warnings given (21:34-38)

VIII. THE PASSION OF THE SON OF MAN (22:1—23:56)
  A. Betrayal of Judas (22:1-6)
  B. Observing of Passover (22:7-20)
  C. Announcement of His betrayal (22:21-23)
  D. Explanation of spiritual greatness (22:24-30)
  E. Prediction of Peter's denial (22:31-38)
  F. Prayer in Gethsemane (22:39-46)
  G. Arrest of Jesus (22:47-53)
  H. Denial of Peter (22:54-62)
  I. Trial before the council (22:63-71)
  J. Trial before Pilate (23:1-5)
  K. Trial before Herod (23:6-12)
  L. Second trial before Pilate (23:13-26)
  M. Crucifixion of Jesus (23:27-49)
  N. Burial of His body (23:50-56)

IX. THE RESURRECTION OF THE SON OF MAN (24:1-53)
  A. Announcement of angels to the women (24:1-12)
  B. Appearance to the two Emmaus travelers (24:13-35)
  C. Appearance to the ten (24:36-45)
  D. Giving of the Great Commission (24:46-48)
  E. Ascension of Christ (24:49-53)

Survey

(As with Mark, check with Matthew for further exposition of parallel accounts.)

1:1-80

Four hundred years of heavenly silence were broken when an angel, Gabriel, appeared and spoke to Zacharias announcing the birth and destiny of John, the forerunner of Christ (cf. Mal. 4:5). Zacharias' response of unbelief resulted in a divinely caused temporary dumbness. His wife later conceived as the angel predicted. In the sixth month of Elizabeth's pregnancy, the same angel informed Mary that she would be the mother of the Messiah, divinely conceived within her womb by the power of the Holy Spirit. In Him would be fulfilled the throne, house, and kingdom promises of the Davidic Covenant (II Sam. 7:11-16). When Mary visited Elizabeth, the fetus of John leaped within the latter's womb. Elizabeth, then filled with the Spirit, gave the first prophetic utterance since Malachi. She acknowledged Mary as one who had been blessed by God and as the human mother of her divine-human Messiah (meaning of "Lord"). In her response Mary recognized her sinfulness[3] and praised God for being faithful to the promises of the Abrahamic Covenant. When John was born, Zacharias was released from his dumbness and blessed God for His fulfillment of the Davidic and Abrahamic covenants.

2:1-52

The decree of Augustus ordered that all Roman subjects place their names on a census roll for the purpose of future taxation. The inconvenience of going to Bethlehem, the tribal center of Judah, was compounded by Mary's advanced pregnancy and imminent delivery. Since the inn was full of travelers, Joseph and Mary had to find crude accommodations in the animal shelter. The shepherds were the first to be informed of the birth of the Christ child and to see Him. The child was circumcised and named at the age of eight days; forty days after His birth, He was presented to the Lord and the offering, designated for the poor, was given for the ceremonial purification of Mary (cf. Lev. 12). At this time Simeon recognized the messianic deity of Jesus and announced to Mary her future grief over the coming sufferings of Christ. Anna also discerned the redemptive nature of His person. The next twelve years of Jesus' life were spent in Nazareth where He developed spiritually, mentally, physically, and socially. At the age of twelve, Jesus went with his parents[4] to the temple in Jerusalem for the Passover feast. At that time He revealed His divine-human character by His intelligence (asking and answering questions) and by His messianic consciousness: "Wist ye not that I must be about my Father's business?" (2:49). Jesus

---

3. The phrase "God my Saviour" (1:47) could only be spoken by a saved sinner because only sinners need a Savior. She also disavowed the "Mother of God" concept by the recognition of her "low estate" (1:48).
4. The Biblical writers use this terminology for Joseph and Mary. Although Joseph was not the paternal father of Jesus, he was His legal father according to Jewish custom.

The Judean town of Ain Karem, the traditionally cited birthplace of John the Baptist.

knew then that God was His real father, not Joseph. The next eighteen years were spent in a quiet development of His perfect humanity.

3:1—4:13

John's ministry was that of spiritual preparation. He demanded evidence of repentance which would secure remission of sins before he would baptize anyone. He showed no partiality, either to the Pharisees, the general populace, the publicans, the soldiers, or even Herod. His attack upon Herod's immorality and sinfulness caused his imprisonment. The baptism of Jesus marked His official identification as the Son of God. The genealogy demonstrated that He was also the Son of Man through Mary's ancestry.[5] The temptation proved that as man Jesus could be tempted but as God He could not respond. His sinlessness is directly involved in the union of the two natures within the single person of Christ.

---

5. The proper rendering of 3:23 should be "being (as was supposed the son of Joseph) the son of Heli. . . ." Heli was the father of Mary and the father-in-law of Joseph.

121

4:14—5:26

In the synagogue at Nazareth, Jesus claimed to be the predicted Messiah (cf. Isa. 61:1-2). His countrymen rejected His assertion and tried to kill Him when He pointed out that God had in the past blessed Gentiles because of Jewish disobedience. Their repudiation was totally unjustified because the authority of His person and the truthfulness of His words could be seen in the miracles which He performed: casting out demons, healing Peter's mother-in-law of a great fever, causing the unusual catch of fish, cleansing a leper, and healing a palsied man.

5:27—6:11

Christ justified His call of Levi and His association with sinners by manifesting His concern for the spiritually sick and sinful. He defended His disciples against Pharisaical criticism by explaining the real purpose of the Sabbath. His healing of the man with the withered hand on the Sabbath provoked the ire of the religious establishment, but doing good and saving lives were always permitted on that day by God.

6:12—7:29

The choosing of the twelve apostles was followed by an address in which Christ outlined the spiritual qualities that should mark the subjects of His kingdom. The healing of the centurion's servant and the raising of the widow's son demonstrated His authority over life and death, a prerogative of God only. He could heal whether absent or present; His word had equal power in both cases. The doubt of John was erased by the continued demonstration of Christ's miraculous credentials.

7:30—8:21

The religious leaders rejected the common ministries of John and Jesus and criticized those who accepted them. Jesus defended the loving actions of the immoral woman who washed His feet by the parable of the two debtors. Her great love matched the great forgiveness of her great sins; since the religious leaders did not think they had any sin, they naturally did not love. The parable of the sower revealed that Christ did not expect to have unanimous acceptance of His ministry. Spiritual relationships are based on doing God's word, not just hearing it.

8:22—9:50

The miracles of calming the storm, casting out the demons within the insane Gadarene, healing the woman with an issue of blood, and raising Jairus' daughter were designed to meet human needs, to establish the disciples in their conviction that Jesus was the Messiah, and to prepare them for their first preaching and healing mission. The feeding of the five thousand served to remind them that the joy of success in service should not replace one's obligation to serve the needs of others. Genuine discipleship must always be based upon the death of selfish ambitions, patterned after the death and resurrection of Christ. The Transfiguration demonstrated the necessity of Christ's death (an event criticized by the disciples), manifested His deity, and pledged the establishment of His kingdom.

9:51—10:24

The journey to Jerusalem to die had now begun (9:51; 18:31; 19:11, 28). On the way Jesus took time to instruct His disciples and to warn them against His opponents. The cry of the apostles for vengeance over the Samaritan disrespect was offset by His concern to save men, not to destroy them. He warned that the life of discipleship was not easy. Financial security, spiritual insensitivity, and improper priorities detract from genuine commitment. He cautioned the seventy about the unbelief of the cities.

10:25—11:13

The parable of the good Samaritan was given in answer to the lawyer's question. "And who is my neighbour?" (10:29). The neighbor was the Samaritan who showed mercy. Christ was "the Samaritan," the rejected one, who was showing mercy to the spiritual and physical needs of men whereas the religious leaders were totally indifferent. Eternal life (10:25-28), therefore, comes from loving Christ for rescuing man from his spiritual dilemma. The incident in the home of Mary and Martha showed

The Judean wilderness as viewed along the Jericho road, halfway between Jerusalem and Jericho.

that fellowship with Christ and receiving spiritual food from Him are better than mere service for Him. The famous Lord's Prayer is a prayer that Jesus taught His disciples to pray ("When ye pray, say"). The essence of the prayer, not the mere repetition of the words, was the real value of the model prayer. Such prayer should also involve persistence or importunity. Although Jesus instructed His own to ask the Father for the Holy Spirit (11:13), there is no indication that they ever did; later, He would ask in their behalf (John 14:16).

11:14—13:21

The accusation that Jesus was satanically energized was logically refuted by Him. Because of their blasphemous evaluation, Jesus announced that no more miracles would be done as public signs for Israel. The next sign would be that of His death and resurrection. Christ then pronounced woes upon the Pharisees and lawyers for their hypocritical traditionalism. In the parable of the rich fool and his barns, Jesus revealed that material possessions in themselves are not signs of divine blessing or earthly security. He then warned His disciples to watch for His coming and to work faithfully for Him in His absence. He assured them that families would be divided spiritually over Him. He warned the multitudes to be reconciled to Him and to repent before the judgment of God fell on them. The parable of the barren fig tree showed that for three years Christ had been looking for spiritual fruit from Israel and that if no fruit came in the fourth year, the nation would be judged. The healing of the infirm woman again revealed the vast differences between Christ and the leaders in their concern for the needs of the people.

13:22—16:31

As He continued to Jerusalem, Jesus expressed His great spiritual concern over the lost condition of the nation in His lamentation. He again came to open conflict with the Pharisees by healing a dropsied man on the Sabbath. In the two parables on the suppers, He pointed out that the Pharisees were like the men who thought so highly of themselves that they chose the best seats and who made all kinds of excuses for rejecting the invitations. He also cautioned the multitudes about counting the cost in becoming one of His disciples in the face of open hostility from the religious leaders. The three parables of the lost sheep, coin, and son were designed to refute their criticism of Him for eating with sinners (15:1) and to reveal the great joy in heaven when lost sinners are found or saved. The Pharisees can be seen in the elder brother with his angry self-righteousness. They were also like the clever steward who was about to be released from his responsibilities because he wasted his master's goods. In forming alliances with the Sadducees,

Herodians, and the Roman government itself, the Pharisees were looking out for their own interests. Christ then destroyed the Pharisaical notion that a man could be a lover of both God and money at the same time by telling the story of the rich man and Lazarus. The wealthy man went to Hades where he was in conscious torment, whereas the beggarly Lazarus was comforted. Some regard this account to be a parable, but if it is, it is the only parable in which a character is actually named. There is no reason to doubt that Jesus was speaking about a genuine historical experience.

17:1—19:28

Christ then tried to impress the disciples to cultivate the attitudes of ready forgiveness and sensitivity. They should not expect to be thanked or rewarded for everything they did. The cleansing of the ten lepers revealed the fact that many want what Christ can give them without returning any gratitude. He then informed the disciples that the conditions prior to His second coming would resemble the days of Noah and Lot. The parable of the judge and the widow taught that men should keep praying until they receive their requests. The parable of the Pharisee and the publican revealed that God does not honor the prayer of a proud person, but only that of a humble, needy soul. In blessing the little children, Jesus demonstrated that no one should think that he is above a ministry to the little ones. The interview with the rich young ruler revealed that often money can become one's idol. The ruler definitely loved it more than God or his fellowman. In response to another reference to His coming death and resurrection, the disciples again showed ignorance of the divine plan. Near Jericho, a blind man was healed out of divine compassion and in response to human faith. The salvation of Zacchaeus, a publican regarded as a sinner by the Pharisees, was a graphic example of the purpose of Christ's incarnation: "For the Son of man is come to seek and to save that which was lost" (19:10). Zacchaeus' attitude toward his goods evidenced genuine repentance (19:8; cf. Exod. 22:1). The parable of the pounds refuted the disciples' concept that Jesus would establish the kingdom upon His entrance into Jerusalem; rather, it showed that there would be some delay. It also taught the disciples that they were to be faithful in their varied responsibilities during Christ's absence.

19:29-48

The Triumphal Entry into Jerusalem marked Jesus' formal and final presentation of Himself to Israel as her king. His ride upon an unbroken colt demonstrated the type of authority He would exercise in the kingdom. The showy entry brought a rebuke from the Pharisees, but Jesus

The Dome of the Chain, an accessory building to the Dome of the Rock, at the Jerusalem temple site.

said that the dumb stones would praise Him if men did not. A second lamentation over Jerusalem was voiced because of the people's spiritual ignorance of the significance of the time period in which they were living. Their ignorance produced a rejection of Him which would lead to a divine judgment upon the city (accomplished in A.D. 70 by the Romans). This second cleansing of the temple symbolized the spiritual pollution of God's house by the religious leaders. He taught in the temple whereas they got rich through the sacrificial system.

20:1—21:4

Now that Christ was in Jerusalem, His authority to teach and to cleanse the temple was directly questioned. Jesus claimed to have the same authority as that behind the ministry of John the Baptist. Since the multitudes regarded John to be a holy prophet and martyr, the priests were trapped with their own question. In the parable of the vineyard, Christ identified the religious leaders as the husbandmen in charge of the vineyard (Israel) who rejected and beat the servants (Old Testament prophets and John) and who even killed the son (Christ) to gain what really belonged to the father and to the son. He then warned that the judgment of the father (God) would fall upon the husbandmen. This was no doubt a reference to their conspiracy to destroy Christ. In the questions about taxes and the resurrection, the leaders were trying

126

to get Christ to say something that would get Him in trouble with the civil authorities; however, He superbly answered them to their consternation. He then expounded a Davidic Psalm (Ps. 110) to show that the Messiah had to be both human and divine, a claim which Jesus made for Himself and which they rejected as blasphemy. His praise of the widow's giving showed that God is interested in the qualitative value of gifts, not the quantitative.

21:5-38

Jesus then announced that the temple would be completely devastated. The disciples then asked these prophetic questions: "Master, but when shall these things be? and what sign will there be when these things shall come to pass?" (21:7). In the Olivet Discourse, Jesus then outlined the signs that would precede His second advent to the earth: false messiahs, wars, earthquakes, famines, pestilences, persecution, siege of Jerusalem, flight of Jews, and astronomical phenomena. The parable of the fig tree showed that although the exact hour of His coming is unknown, the season can be discerned by sensitive, spiritual people. He also warned against indifference and secularism on the part of those who should be watching.

22:1-38

Luke then recorded in rapid succession the events that led up to the crucifixion. Judas, having become Satan-possessed, agreed to inform the priests about the time and place that Jesus could be seized secretly. In order not to be disturbed by the multitudes or the priests, Jesus arranged to eat the Passover feast with His disciples in a predetermined, prepared room, totally unknown to the disciples. The sign to Peter and John who were directed to prepare the meal in advance was to be a man bearing a water pitcher (normally a job for a woman) whom they were to follow. In the privacy of the room, Christ then ate the Passover feast with His own and subsequently instituted the memorial ordinance of the Lord's Supper. His announcement that a traitor was in their midst created confusion. No one knew of whom He spoke. In fact, they even debated among themselves as to which of them was the greatest of the Twelve. Christ rebuked them by stating that spiritual greatness can be seen in humble service to others, not in selfish praise of oneself. However, He assured them that they would all (Judas excluded) share in His fellowship and future rule. When Jesus informed Peter of Satan's request to test the apostle, Peter boasted of his allegiance; Christ then predicted his triple denial.

22:39—23:26

The group left the upper room and went to the Garden of Gethsemane where Jesus prayed and struggled with the complexities of His coming death. After His prayer period was over, Jesus was then seized by the soldiers who had been brought by Judas. While Jesus was being interrogated in the high priest's house, Peter denied Christ three times outside in the hall. After the questioning, Jesus was cruelly treated before He was taken to a "trial" before the entire Sanhedrin about 6 A.M. Here He was charged with blasphemy. However, when He was taken before Pilate, He was accused of two civil crimes: failure to pay taxes and treason in claiming to be a king. Pilate saw no political threat in Christ and sent Him away to Herod Antipas when he knew that Christ was from Galilee, the geographical jurisdiction of Herod. In deference to the murder of John, Christ remained silent before Herod whose soldiers mocked Him and sent Him back to Pilate who again testified to Jesus' civil innocence. However, under pressure from the Jewish leaders, he delivered Christ to be crucified.

23:27-56

While hanging on the cross, Jesus continued to be mocked by the people, the rulers, the soldiers, and the thieves. One of the thieves, repenting of his mockery, expressed faith in the messiahship of Jesus. Christ's death at 3 P.M. was preceded by three hours of darkness and the ripping of the temple veil. The body of Jesus was then removed by Joseph of Arimathaea, prepared for burial, and placed within the latter's tomb.

24:1-53

When the women came to the tomb early Sunday morning, they found that the stone had been rolled away and that the body of Jesus was gone. After they were informed by two angels that Christ had been resurrected, they returned to the city and told the eleven apostles about their experience. Since the apostles doubted the report, Peter went to the tomb himself, saw the empty burial clothes, and wondered about what was happening. That evening Jesus appeared to two disciples on the road to Emmaus and showed to them out of the Old Testament the necessity of His death and resurrection. These two then returned to Jerusalem and informed the apostles that they had seen Christ. The group that was with the eleven then reported that Christ had even been seen by Peter. At that instant Christ appeared in their midst and demonstrated that He had a real, material body (flesh and bones). They saw Him, heard Him, touched Him, and even saw Him eat. Christ then showed this group the necessity of His death and resurrection in fulfillment of prophetic Scripture. He commanded them to preach the gospel of repentance and remission of sins through His name to all the nations; however, He further instructed them that they should not begin until the descent of the Holy Spirit had occurred. Later they watched His ascension into heaven and returned to Jerusalem to await the coming of the Spirit.

Increase Your Learning

By Doing

1. Since Luke exalted the ministry of the Holy Spirit, circle the names of those people who were filled with the Spirit. Underline all references to the Spirit throughout the book.
2. Since Luke paid special attention to prayer and to women, circle or underline all references to them in your study Bible.

By Discussing

1. Relate the prominent position of women within this Gospel with the current women's liberation movement. In what ways are the two similar? Different?
2. The Roman Catholic Church has exalted Mary as the mother of God. Have evangelicals gone to the opposite extreme in ignoring her? How should she be regarded?
3. Compare Christ's tests of genuine discipleship with the commitment of convenience expressed today. Have Christians sacrificed? Do they count the cost?
4. Does the parable of the good Samaritan speak to the problem of the lack of involvement on the part of the modern believer? Do we really care about the needs of others?
5. Discuss the value of wealth and the way it is used. How can it be both a blessing and a curse?

By Reading

Geldenhuys, J. Norval. *Commentary on Luke.* Grand Rapids: Wm. B. Eerdmans Publishing Co., 1956.

Godet, F. *Commentary on the Gospel of St. Luke.* Edinburgh: T. & T. Clark, n.d.

Morgan, G. Campbell. *The Gospel According to Luke.* Old Tappan, N.J.: Fleming H. Revell Co., 1928.

Plummer, Alfred. *A Critical and Exegetical Commentary on the Gospel According to St. Luke.* Edinburgh: T. & T. Clark, 1922.

7

JOHN

Writer

Although the authorship is anonymous, the traditional position of the early Church Fathers, such as Irenaeus, Clement of Alexandria, Tertullian, Origen, and Hippolytus, ascribed the Fourth Gospel to John, the youngest of the twelve apostles. In recent years the theory that it was written by an obscure elder at Ephesus, also named John, has been embraced and propagated by some liberal scholars. This view is based upon a statement by Papias as quoted by Eusebius:

> If ever anyone came who had followed the presbyters, I inquired into the words of the presbyters, what Andrew or Peter or Philip or Thomas or James or John or Matthew, or any other of the Lord's disciples, had said, and what Aristion and the presbyter John, the Lord's disciples, were saying.[1]

The double mention of John has caused some to believe that there were two Johns: John the apostle and John the Ephesian elder. However, in both references in the quotation, John is designated as a presbyter or an elder, a title he used in his second and third Epistles. There is no justifiable reason to conclude that Papias was referring to two different people. In fact, the double reference to John and the difference in verb tenses ("had said" vs. "were saying") within the quotation may suggest that John was still alive at the time Papias wrote.

The internal content of the book supports Johannine authorship. First of all, the author must have been a Jew. He understood and quoted from the Old Testament (12:40; 13:18; 19:37). His knowledge of the

---

1. *Historia Ecclesiae,* III. xxxix. 4.

various Jewish religious feasts seemed to be very natural (2:23; 5:1; 6:4; 7:2; 10:22; 13:1). He was aware of the minute details within the Jewish customs: wedding feasts (2:1-10), ceremonial purification (3:25; 11:55), and manner of burial (11:38, 44; 19:40). He was acquainted with the Jewish expectation of the coming Messiah (1:19-28) and perceived the religious differences between the Jew and the Samaritan (4:9, 20). Second, he must have been a resident of Palestine because of his graphic geographical descriptions. His familiarity with Jerusalem and its surrounding area can be seen in his awareness that the pool of Bethesda had five porches (5:2), that Bethany was only fifteen furlongs away from Jerusalem (11:18), that Ephraim was near the wilderness (11:54), that the Garden of Gethsemane was on the other side of the brook Cedron (18:1), and that there was a paved area outside of the Praetorium (19:13). He was also acquainted with the region of Samaria because he located Jacob's well in Sychar (4:5-6), knew that the well was deep (4:11), and understood about the sacred mountain of Samaritan worship (4:20-21). His knowledge of Galilee can be seen in his descriptions of the cities in that area (1:44, 46; 2:1) and of the terrain (2:12). Third, the author clearly implies that he was an eyewitness of many of the events in Christ's earthly ministry. He had beheld His glory (1:14) which would include at least both the Transfiguration and the performance of miracles (2:11). He was at the Crucifixion where he observed that Christ's side was pierced and that His legs were not broken (19:33-35). He knew the number and size of the waterpots used in the creation of wine (2:6), the approximate value of the anointing perfume (12:5), the distance from shore of the apostles' boat (21:8), and the exact number of fish caught (21:11). Fourth, the author apparently identified himself as the disciple "whom Jesus loved," an expression used five times (13:23; 19:26; 20:2; 21:7, 20), and as the other disciple (18:15-16; 20:2; 21:2). He claimed to be the disciple about whom a rumor was spread that he would not die before Christ's return (21:20-25). Since the name of John is conspicuously absent in the book although he was one of the major apostles, it would seem very plausible to regard him as the anonymous disciple and author of this Gospel. In addition, the style and vocabulary of the three Johannine Epistles bear a striking resemblance to this book. His emphasis upon love is so noticeable that John has been characterized as the "Apostle of Love."

What can be learned about the life of John from the Scriptures? John's name is mentioned almost twice as many times as those of the other three Gospel biographers combined: Matthew, eight times; Mark, eight times; Luke, three times; and John, thirty-five times. Along with James, an elder brother who was also an apostle, he was the son of

Zebedee and Salome. Little is known about Zebedee except that he must have been a successful fisherman of Galilee because he employed hired servants in addition to the service of the two sons (Mark 1:19-20). Salome possibly was a sister or cousin to Mary, the mother of Jesus (Matt. 27:56; Mark 15:40; John 19:25). She was one of the women who assisted Jesus and the apostolic group financially (Matt. 27:55-56; Mark 15:40-41; Luke 8:3) and who observed the activities of the Crucifixion. John's family must have been one of means and influence since he was known personally by the high priest (18:15) and because he owned his own house (19:27).

John's own book reveals that he was a disciple of John the Baptist by whom he was personally introduced to Christ (1:35-40). John then followed Jesus on His first tour of Galilee (1:43). He attended the wedding feast in Cana where Jesus turned water into wine (2:1-2), accompanied Him to Capernaum and back to Jerusalem (2:12-13), traveled with Christ to Galilee through Samaria (4:4), and apparently returned to his occupation of fishing. Shortly after, Christ recruited him as a disciple and commissioned him to be one of the twelve apostles (Matt. 4:21-22; Mark 3:13-19). In the apostolic lists he always appears in the first group of four, along with Peter, Andrew, and his brother James (Matt. 10:1-4; Mark 3:16-19; Luke 6:13-16). He became a member of the special inner circle of three disciples who were with

Cana (Kafir Kanna) of Galilee, the traditional site of Jesus' first miracle recorded in John's Gospel, is a Christian village located northeast of Nazareth.

Christ at the raising of Jairus' daughter, on the Mount of Transfiguration, and in the Garden of Gethsemane (Mark 5:37; 9:2; 14:33). The other occasions in which he shared with the entire group of apostles in the ministry of Christ are too numerous to mention here. Many scholars believe that John was the other disciple who followed Jesus after His arrest and who went into the palace of the high priest because he knew the latter (18:15-16). Since the family of Zebedee was slightly wealthy, it is very conceivable that John could have been acquainted with the priest through frequent visits to Jerusalem. John, of course, was present at Golgotha for the Crucifixion and received the custody of Mary from Jesus (19:25-27). Along with Peter, he viewed the empty tomb and burial clothes (John 20:1-10); subsequently he saw the risen Lord. He was both taught and recommissioned as an apostle by Christ during His postresurrection ministry of forty days (Acts 1:1-8). He took an active part in the life of the early church and was looked upon as one of the pillars of the Jerusalem assembly, along with Peter and James, the half-brother of Jesus (Acts 3:1; 4:19; 8:14; Gal. 2:9). Tradition states that John became the leader of the Ephesian church in his later years and that he was banished to the island of Patmos in the Aegean Sea by the Roman emperor Domitian. Nerva, Domitian's successor, permitted John to return to Ephesus about A.D. 96. There he stayed until his death sometime during the reign of Trajan (A.D. 98-117). Through the years John, one of the "sons of thunder" (Mark 3:17) who was full of prejudice and vengeance (cf. Luke 9:49-56), was transformed into a gentle disciple of love.

Time and Place

Although some liberals date the book as early as A.D. 40 while others push it into the second century (A.D. 140-170), conservatives are agreed that the Gospel was written after the Synoptic Gospels and rather late in the first century, probably between 85 and 95. Tradition has placed its composition, at Ephesus where John spent his senior years. The earliest scrap of the New Testament is a papyrus fragment located in the John Rylands Library in Manchester, England, called P[52]. Since it contains only five verses of John (18:31-33, 37-38) and is dated about A.D. 125-35, this means that the Gospel had to be in circulation before the second century began. The tenth decade of the first century best fits the life history of John. It was probably written for Gentiles because the various feasts and geographical locations are described for the readers.

Purposes

The purposes for writing this Gospel are clearly seen in these two verses (20:30-31):

> And many other signs truly did Jesus in the presence of his disciples, which are not written in this book: But these are written, that ye might believe that Jesus is the Christ, the Son of God; and that believing ye might have life through his name.

The first was to convince his readers that Jesus was both divine and human. Living in a time when the truth of the Incarnation was being attacked by an increasing gnostic element within the church, John wanted to show that Jesus was not merely an appearance of God (similar to those in the Old Testament) or a man in whom dwelt the spirit of Christ. He intended to demonstrate that Jesus was both God and man and that within His single person was a perfect union of the two natures. The second purpose was based upon the first. He wanted his readers, convinced of Jesus' true identity, to believe on Him to receive the divine gift of eternal life. John's purposes then are both apologetic and evangelistic. Within the book is a theological defense of the hypostatic union (two natures in one person) and an invitation to the unconverted to become saved. Naturally, the Christian would receive profit from this book because it would indoctrinate him in Christology and would reinforce his initial faith.

Three key words are found in these verses: *signs, believe,* and *life*. The *signs* refer to miracles that have some special significance behind their performance. They were designed to reveal something about the person of Christ. Of the many miracles that Jesus performed, John selected eight to prove his point:

1. Turning water into wine (2:2-11)
2. Healing the nobleman's son (4:46-54)
3. Healing the impotent man (5:1-15)
4. Feeding the five thousand (6:1-14)
5. Walking on the water (6:15-21)
6. Healing the blind man (9:1-41)
7. Raising Lazarus from the dead (11:1-44)
8. Providing the catch of fish (21:6-11)

The first seven were done during His active ministry as an authentication of His claims, whereas the eighth took place during His postresurrection ministry. Around these miracles, John recorded a literary network of sermons, conversations, and his own editorial comments to give his book symmetry and unity. In some cases the miracle produced the sermon (feeding the five thousand provided the background for the sermon on the bread of life), while in others the sermon was illustrated by the miracle (His claim to be the light of the world was proved by giving sight to the man born blind). Just as the miracles produced faith on the part of those who witnessed them, so John trusted that the record of those miracles, sermons, and interviews would likewise create faith on the part of the readers of his Gospel.

Distinctive Features

John was the most selective of the Gospel writers. Over 90 percent of his content is found exclusively in this book. That statistic becomes even more amazing when one realizes that as the last author to write, he had at his disposal the other three Gospels. This graphically demonstrates that it was not his purpose to compose an exhaustive biography of the life of Christ. Totally aware of the entire scope of Jesus' ministry, John nevertheless selected only those miracles, sermons, and interviews that would best suit his literary intent. Of the eight recorded miracles, only two are found elsewhere: feeding the five thousand and walking on the water. Twenty-seven interviews are narrated, and the great majority of these are found only here. Although Jesus' preaching was full of parables, not one is recorded by John. The word "parable" is found in the English text (10:6), but here it is the translation of the Greek word *paroimia* rather than the typical word *parabolé*. The story of the good shepherd should be regarded as an allegory or an extended metaphor rather than a parable.

Many great sermons or topical discourses are found only in John: the new birth (3:1-13), the water of life (4:6-29), the defense of His deity (5:19-47), the bread of life (6:22-71), the light of the world (8:12-59), the good shepherd (10:1-30), and the Upper Room Discourse (13:1—16:33). Although not a sermon, Christ's prayer (17:1-26) is unique to this Gospel. Amazingly, John is silent about the famous Olivet Discourse (cf. Matt. 24-25), probably because he wrote after the destruction of Jerusalem and the dispersion of the Jews (A.D. 70).

Of all the Gospel writers, John places the most emphasis upon the deity of Christ through recording His actual claims about Himself. When Christ said: "Before Abraham was, I am" (8:58), the people knew that He was claiming the very name of God that was revealed to Moses at the burning bush (Exod. 3:14). This is why the people tried to stone Him for alleged blasphemy. Christ was and is the eternal *I AM*. In a series of assertions, He amplified that claim:

1. I am the bread of life (6:35).
2. I am the light of the world (8:12; 9:5).
3. I am the door (10:7).
4. I am the good shepherd (10:11, 14).
5. I am the resurrection and the life (11:25).
6. I am the way, the truth, and the life (14:6).
7. I am the true vine (15:1).

Other supporting statements include: "I and my Father are one" (10:30) and "he that hath seen me hath seen the Father" (14:9). No mere man would ever make such claims unless he were a liar or insane. Many liberals feel that John fabricated these bold assertions; however, there is no objective evidence that he did. Christ could make these statements because He was who He claimed to be, God manifest in human flesh.

John wrote in a very simple style. Of the four Gospels, this book is the easiest to read in the original Greek. John seems to center much of his narrative around Christ's various visits to Jerusalem to observe various feasts:

1. First Passover (2:23)
2. Unnamed feast (5:1)
3. Feast of Tabernacles (7:2)
4. Feast of Dedication (10:22)
5. Last Passover (13:1)

Outline

I. CHRIST AND INDIVIDUALS (chs. 1-4)
  A. Christ the Word (ch. 1)
    1. Prologue (1:1-14)
    2. Testimony of John the Baptist (1:15-34)
    3. Testimony of the disciples (1:35-51)
  B. Christ the creator (ch. 2)
    1. Changing water into wine (2:1-12)
    2. Cleansing the temple (2:13-25)
  C. Christ the Savior (ch. 3)
    1. Conversation with Nicodemus (3:1-21)
    2. Confession of John (3:22-36)
  D. Christ the water of life (ch. 4)
    1. Christ and the Samaritan woman (4:1-30)
    2. Christ and the disciples (4:31-38)
    3. Christ and the Samaritans (4:39-45)
    4. Christ healing the nobleman's son (4:46-54)
II. CHRIST AND THE MULTITUDES (chs. 5-12)
  A. Christ the judge (ch. 5)
    1. Healing of the lame man (5:1-18)
    2. Defense of His person (5:19-47)
  B. Christ the bread of life (ch. 6)
    1. Feeding the five thousand (6:1-14)
    2. Walking on the water (6:15-21)
    3. Sermon on the bread of life (6:22-59)
    4. Defection of His disciples (6:60-71)
  C. Christ the divider (ch. 7)
    1. Unbelief of His brethren (7:1-13)
    2. Division of the people (7:14-36)
    3. Prediction of the Spirit (7:37-39)
    4. Debate of the leaders (7:40-53)
  D. Christ the light of the world (chs. 8-9)
    1. Forgiveness of the adulteress (8:1-11)
    2. Sermon on the light of the world (8:12-59)
    3. Healing of the man born blind (9:1-41)

E. Christ the good shepherd (ch. 10)
   1. Sermon on the good shepherd (10:1-18)
   2. Opposition to His teaching (10:19-42)
F. Christ the resurrection and the life (ch. 11)
   1. Raising of Lazarus (11:1-46)
   2. Conspiracy to kill Jesus (11:47-57)
G. Christ the center of attraction (ch. 12)
   1. At the supper in Bethany (12:1-11)
   2. At the Triumphal Entry (12:12-19)
   3. At the anticipated cross (12:20-36)
   4. Rejected by the people (12:37-50)
III. CHRIST AND THE DISCIPLES (chs. 13-17)
  A. Christ the servant (ch. 13)
    1. Washing of the disciples' feet (13:1-20)
    2. Withdrawal of Judas (13:21-35)
    3. Denial of Peter predicted (13:36-38)
  B. Christ the comforter (ch. 14)
    1. Promise of heaven (14:1-6)
    2. Explanation of the Father (14:7-11)
    3. Promise of prayer (14:12-15)
    4. Promise of the Spirit (14:16-26)
    5. Promise of peace (14:27-31)
  C. Christ the vine (chs. 15-16)
    1. The disciples and Christ (15:1-17)
    2. The disciples and the world (15:18—16:4)
    3. The disciples and the Spirit (16:5-33)
  D. Christ the intercessor (ch. 17)
    1. Prayer for glorification (17:1-5)
    2. Prayer for preservation (17:6-16)
    3. Prayer for sanctification (17:17-19)
    4. Prayer for unification (17:20-23)
    5. Prayer for habitation (17:24-26)
IV. CHRIST AND HIS PASSION (chs. 18-21)
  A. Christ the sacrifice (chs. 18-19)
    1. His arrest (18:1-11)
    2. His religious trials (18:12-27)
    3. His civil trials (18:28—19:15)
    4. His crucifixion (19:16-37)
    5. His burial (19:38-42)
  B. Christ the victor (ch. 20)
    1. Appearance to Mary (20:1-18)
    2. Appearance to the ten (20:19-23)
    3. Appearance to Thomas (20:24-31)
  C. Christ the chief shepherd (ch. 21)
    1. Catch of fish (21:1-14)
    2. Challenge to Peter (21:15-17)
    3. Prediction of destinies (21:18-25)

Survey

1:1-14

The gist of the entire Gospel can be seen in the prologue. John first

137

identified the person of Christ: He was preexistent or eternal; He was a separate person from God the Father and enjoyed fellowship with the latter; He was God Himself; He was the creator, the source of both life and light; He was full of grace and truth; and He became incarnate. These claims John aptly demonstrated by the eight recorded miracles. As the creator, Jesus was able easily to turn water into wine, to multiply the bread and the fish, to walk on water, and to create a catch of fish. He proves that He is the life by healing the nobleman's son who was at the point of death, by restoring life to the lifeless limbs of the lame man at the pool of Bethesda, by raising Lazarus from the dead, and ultimately by raising Himself out of death and hades. He shows that He is the light of men by giving physical sight to a man born blind.

In embryonic form, the purposes of Christ's advent are set forth (1:9-12). Here can be seen His incarnation ("cometh into the world"), His lack of recognition during His thirty years of human development ("in the world . . . the world knew him not"), His presentation to Israel as her Messiah ("He came unto his own"), His rejection by Israel ("his own received him not"), and His invitation to the individual to believe on Him for salvation ("But as many as received him").

1:15-34

The testimony of John the Baptist is now given in support of the author's identification of Christ's person and work. John, older in the flesh by six months, recognized the preexistence of Jesus ("for he was before me"). He preached that Christ was the revealer of God, that He was the Lamb of God, the sin bearer, and that He was the Son of God, the Spirit baptizer. John saw himself only as a voice heralding the coming of the Lord.

1:35-51

Just as Andrew, Simon, Philip, and Nathanael came to believe that Jesus was the Son of God, the king of Israel, the Christ, the one "of whom Moses in the law, and the prophets, did write," so John trusts that the reader of these accounts will likewise believe in the deity of Christ to the saving commitment of his soul. This passage also teaches the importance of communicating faith in Christ to others who do not know Him.

2:1-12

Since Christ created the rivers and the first vineyards, it was a simple demonstration of His power to change the molecular composition of water into wine. This miracle accomplished two goals (2:11): the manifestation of His glory and the reinforcement of the disciples' faith. His statement to Mary (2:4) should not be regarded as abrupt rudeness;

rather, Jesus was showing her that the natural mother-son relationship that had existed for the past thirty years was now over because He had begun His messianic ministry. She must now approach Him as a sinner to her God and Savior, not as a mother to her son.

2:13-25

In fulfillment of Old Testament prophecy (Ps. 69:9; Mal. 3:1-3), Christ manifested His righteous indignation by cleansing the temple of religious racketeers at the outset of His ministry. In response to the Jews' request for a sign of His authority, Jesus replied: "Destroy this temple, and in three days I will raise it up." Just as the fulfillment of this prediction of Christ's death and resurrection brought faith to the disciples (2:22), so John trusts that the reader will put his faith in Him who made such a bold prediction.

3:1-36

The interview with Nicodemus revealed that all men of high moral, religious, economic, and social caliber like him need to experience a spiritual, second birth, in order to enter the kingdom of God. If Nicodemus had understood the full implications of the new covenant promised to Israel (Jer. 31:31-34; Ezek. 36:22-31), he would have known what Jesus was talking about. One of the literary problems in John is to distinguish between the narrative sections and the author's editorial comments. At what verse did Jesus' conversation with Nicodemus end and John's interpretation begin? Most see a break between 3:12 and 3:13 with another one coming between 3:30 and 3:31, isolating the confession of the Baptist from that of the apostle. John's comments clearly show the necessity of faith in Christ to secure personal salvation whereas lack of faith brings the judgment of God. John the Baptist was not jealous over the popularity of Jesus. He saw himself as the friend who was sent to prepare the bride (believing Jewish remnant) and to present her to the bridegroom (Christ). When John saw that his disciples were following Christ, he knew that his purpose had been fulfilled.

4:1-45

The contrasting interview with the immoral Samaritan woman showed that even persons of a low social, economic, and moral class can be saved by Christ. No doubt John recorded the interviews with Nicodemus and the Samaritan woman back to back in order to prove that all men and women, no matter where they are in the realm of human experience, need to and can be saved through a personal encounter with the Savior. In that Christ led her from thinking about natural issues to spiritual concerns, this paragraph provides a good illustration of a technique that can be employed in personal evangelism. To her Christ also revealed

139

Mount Gerizim and the village of Sychar. Gerizim is the holy mountain for the Samaritans and the Samaritan Passover is still celebrated each year on its summit.

some basic truths: the quenching water of everlasting life found in Him (4:14), the character of her past life (4:18), the nature of true worship (4:23-24), the spiritual essence of God (4:24), and His identity as the Christ (4:25-26). Her evaluation of Him (Jew, Sir, prophet, Christ) changed as her skepticism grew into conviction and witness. The disciples, more concerned about supper, had to be admonished about their spiritual responsibilities to be harvesters of men's souls.

4:46-54

The second recorded miracle, the healing of the nobleman's son who was at the point of death, demonstrated Christ's authority over life and death. As the source of life, He could give life to one who was about to die. It also proved the power of His word in that the son was healed the very moment Christ spoke miles away. Just as the nobleman and his family believed (4:53), so John hopes that the reading of the record of that miracle will likewise produce faith.

5:1-18

The third sign-miracle revealed that Christ could put life back into the lifeless limbs of the man who had been lame thirty-eight years. This miracle provides a good illustration of the fact that Christ healed both the cause and the after-effects of a physical malady; no therapy

140

was needed to recover the use of the atrophied legs. The religious leaders became hostile toward Jesus because He had broken their concept of Sabbatical restrictions. According to them, healing the man was the equivalent of work. They also wanted to kill Christ because He claimed that God was His own Father in a sense in which He is not the Father of anyone else (5:18).

5:19-47

Although Christ had not violated the divine intent of the Sabbath, it was true that He claimed equality with the Father. He further substantiated this claim with statements about His omnipotence, omnipresence, judgment, and honor. As the incarnate Son, He had been given authority not only to raise Himself from the dead, but also others, both saved and unsaved. Christ supported His own claim to deity by appealing to John the Baptist, His miracles, the Father, and the Old Testament as corroborative witnesses.

6:1-21

The fourth sign-miracle, the feeding of the five thousand, again demonstrated His creative power. Since Jesus created the first fish and wheat fields out of nothing, it was a simple task for Him to multiply five loaves and two fish. This miracle was both a test of the disciples' faith (6:6) and a proof of His real identity. He did not yield to the public pressure to make Him king because the public's motivation in doing so was strictly selfish (6:15; cf. 6:26). Through the fifth sign-miracle, the walking on the water, He illustrated His authority over the elements of nature; creation exists to serve the will of the creator. It further demonstrated His deity to the disciples who alone witnessed the event.

6:22-71

The next day Christ preached the sermon on the bread of life to the multitude who had shared in the multiplication of bread and fish. He charged them with following Him out of a selfish, materialistic desire (6:26-27). He challenged them to receive the *real* bread of life that was true (6:32), heavenly (6:33), satisfying (6:35), resurrection life (6:39), everlasting (6:40), and the Christ life (6:48). The sermon so disheartened some of His disciples that they forsook Him, a sign of their unbelief (6:64, 66). When questioned about their allegiance, Peter the spokesman affirmed their faith in Christ as the divine-human person, the source of eternal life.

7:1-53

Wherever Christ went, His presence produced a division of opinion

141

over Him. The Jews wanted to kill Him, and even His half-brothers did not believe in Him (7:5). Some people called Him a good man, whereas others regarded Him as a deceiver or a demoniac (7:12, 20). At the Feast of Tabernacles, the priests would fill pitchers of water from the pool of Siloam and then pour them out at the altar in symbolic remembrance of the time when God gave water out of the rock to Israel during the wilderness wanderings. Christ claimed to be the fulfillment of that ceremony, the one whom the rock typified (7:37-39; cf. I Cor. 10:4). He promised that living water in the person of the Holy Spirit would flow from the inner being of the believer. The religious leaders could not seize Jesus at this time because the arresting soldiers were too impressed by Christ; even Nicodemus pointed out their lack of impartiality in their judgment of Him.

8:1-11

The forced confrontation with the adulteress was a Pharisaical attempt to trick Christ in His speech. He repudiated their criticism of Him and her by forgiving the woman. In the account of this event only is it mentioned that Christ wrote something. What did He write in the sand? Some have conjectured that since the woman was taken in the very act of adultery He was asking for the identity of the adulterer.

8:12-59

This encounter was followed by His claim to be the light of the world. Christ accused His adversaries of using faulty human judgment (8:15), of ignorance of the Father (8:19), of perishing in their sins (8:21, 24), of being worldly (8:23), of being in bondage to sin (8:34), and of being the children of the devil (8:44). They reacted by charging Christ with an illegitimate birth (8:41), by calling Him a Samaritan demoniac (8:48), and by attempting to kill Him because of alleged blasphemy.

9:1-41

Jesus vindicated His claim to be the light of the world by healing the man who was born blind, this being the sixth miracle. Giving physical light proved that He was also the source of spiritual light. The healed man grew in his knowledge of his healer: Jesus (9:11); prophet (9:17); of God (9:33); and the Son of God (9:35, 38). Although he was put out of the synagogue for his testimony, Christ received him.

10:1-42

The healing of the blind man provided the occasion (10:20-21) for the discourse on the good shepherd. Christ identified Himself as the door of salvation and as the shepherd who gives His life for the sheep.

The religious leaders could be seen in the thieves and the hirelings. The porter was John the Baptist who opened Israel up to the ministry of Christ. Christ indicated that not all of the sheep would respond to His voice or ministry, only those who are genuinely saved. These would be joined to Gentile sheep to form a new flock, the Church (10:16). Christ then guaranteed eternal salvation or security for His sheep (10:27-29). His claim of equality of essence with the Father brought another charge of blasphemy against Him.

11:1-57

In the seventh sign-miracle Christ proved that He was the resurrection and the life by raising Lazarus from the dead. This miracle manifested Christ's glory (11:4, 40) and brought both a response of rejection and of belief from the observers. The religious council was so enraged by this deed that it intensified its conspiracy to kill Jesus.

12:1-50

The costly anointing of Jesus at the supper in Bethany marked Mary's recognition of Christ's coming death and burial. Judas saw it as a waste, but Jesus saw it as a memorial of Mary's love and faith. The next day at the Triumphal Entry, those who had witnessed the resurrection of Lazarus praised the kingship of Jesus as He rode into Jerusalem.

The Chapel of the Resurrection in Bethany. The structure commemorates Jesus' ministry to Mary, Martha, and Lazarus.

143

This rousing reception further antagonized the Pharisees. In the temple Jesus finally announced: "The hour is come, that the Son of man should be glorified" (12:23). He was aware that His time to die for the sins of the world had come; this was why He left heaven and became incarnate. John then concluded the first major section of his book (chs. 1-12) with this candid observation: "But though he had done so many miracles before them, yet they believed not on him" (12:37). In spite of the evidence of His holy, sinless life, His messages of truth, and His performance of miracles, the religious leaders and the nation as a whole persisted in their unbelief.

13:1-20

The next four chapters have been designated the Upper Room Discourse because the night before His crucifixion Christ met with His disciples in the upper room to set before them the new responsibilities and privileges that would be theirs as the result of His death, resurrection, and ascension and the subsequent descent of the Holy Spirit. However, before He could instruct them, He had to cope with their group argument over who was the greatest among them. By washing their feet, Jesus vividly showed that spiritual greatness does not come from pride or self-assertion, but through humility and service to others. His exchange of His garments for the servant's towel also portrayed His surrender of the outward manifestation of His divine being when He put on the clothing of humanity. This event further teaches that a Christian who has experienced the bath of regeneration only needs to have the cleansing of daily sins in order to have fellowship with Christ (13:8, 10-11).

13:21-38

When Jesus disclosed the presence of the traitor in their midst, the disciples did not look at Judas, for the latter's character was so hidden from them. When Judas left the room to make the final arrangements for Jesus' arrest, Christ again mentioned: "Now is the Son of man glorified" (13:31). Now, only to the eleven, Christ affixed an added meaning to the love commandment. Before they were to love one another as themselves, but now they were to love "as I have loved you" (13:34). In response to Peter's boast of courage, Jesus predicted his threefold denial of Him before the morning.

14:1-31

His announcement of His departure and separation from them brought anxiety to the disciples. This next section of teaching was given therefore to calm their troubled hearts. It begins and ends with the same words: "Let not your heart be troubled" (14:1; cf. 14:27). In between these two verses Christ revealed spiritual truths that if believed and applied to everyday life would bring peace to any bothered soul. He promised to prepare a place for them in heaven (14:2) and to return for them so that they would be with Him in that heavenly mansion (14:3). He assured them that He was the only way into God's presence (14:5-6). He revealed that the divine essence, shared by the three Persons of the Godhead including the Father, could be seen in Him (14:9). What is God like? Look at Jesus Christ! He encouraged them by stating that their spiritual power would be greater because of His ascension into heaven (14:12). Petitions were now to be asked in His name for the purpose of God's glorification (14:13). He informed them that love for Him should be the basis of future obedience (14:15). He told them that they would receive the permanent, indwelling presence of the Holy Spirit because He had so prayed (14:16-17). He promised that the Spirit would be their new teacher and that He would cause them to remember the events of Christ's earthly ministry (14:26). This prediction not only established their future oral ministry, but it anticipated and pre-authenticated the writing of the New Testament books (teach=Epistles; remembrance = Gospels). He also defined for them the basic essence of Christianity (14:20): "ye in me" (justification or acceptable spiritual position) and "I in you" (sanctification or necessary spiritual power). He ended this section with His guarantee of internal peace (14:27). The literary style of this section is built around questions or statements by four apostles (Peter, 13:36; Thomas, 14:5; Philip, 14:8; and Judas, 14:22) and Christ's respective responses.

15:1-17

The teaching of the next two chapters (chs. 15-16) and the intercessory prayer (ch. 17) were given on the way to the Garden of Gethsemane (14:31; cf. 18:1). Christ first of all depicted the new relationship that would exist between Him and the disciples in the metaphor of the vine and the branches. Their main purpose was to permit the life of Christ to flow through them in the production of fruit. They were to bear fruit, more fruit, and much fruit (15:2, 8). This could only be accomplished through a constant cleansing and pruning of their lives. If they failed to respond to divine care, then they would forfeit their position of fruit bearing. Christ was not here talking about the possible loss of salvation, but only about the privilege of service.

15:18—16:4

Jesus then warned them that the world's attitude toward them would not improve as the result of His death and resurrection. Rather, the world would hate, persecute, ostracize, and even kill them because of their identification with Christ. They were to react with a Spirit-directed witness of Christ.

145

16:5-33

Jesus next informed the disciples that the Holy Spirit could not come to them until He had gone into the Father's presence. The Spirit's role in the world would be to convict it of sin, righteousness, and judgment. Unable to reveal everything to the disciples at this time, Jesus promised that the Spirit would guide them into all truth, would reveal the future, and would glorify Christ. He then mentioned that sorrow over His death would be replaced by joy over His resurrection. He concluded with the promise of ultimate victory: "In the world ye shall have tribulation: but be of good cheer; I have overcome the world" (16:33).

17:1-26

This chapter contains the real Lord's Prayer, a prayer that Jesus Himself prayed, not a model prayer taught to others (cf. Matt. 6:9-15). In the first part, Christ prayed for Himself that He might be glorified at the cross and that His preincarnate glory might be restored to Him (17:1-5). In the second part, Christ prayed for the disciples (17:9) and for those who would believe through their oral and written word (17:20). This would include all of the believers of this age. He prayed for their spiritual preservation (17:11, 15), sanctification (17:17), unification (17:22), and habitation with Him (17:24).

18:1-27

With the prayer ended, Christ entered the Garden of Gethsemane where He was seized by the soldiers led by Judas. He repudiated Peter's act of violence and voluntarily submitted Himself to the will of God and to the actions of the soldiers. Christ then underwent three "trials" before Annas, Caiaphas, and the Sanhedrin. During the course of these trials, Peter denied the Lord three times as predicted.

18:28—19:15

Three civil trials before Pilate, Herod Antipas, and again Pilate quickly followed. Three times Pilate admitted Jesus' innocence (18:38; 19:4, 6) and in fact tried to release Jesus (19:12), but yielding to pressure from the Jews, delivered Christ to be crucified.

19:16-42

In his brief description of the Crucifixion, John noted two facts not found elsewhere. He observed that Christ's legs were not broken in order to hasten death and that Jesus was pierced in order to make sure that He was already dead. Both of these actions graphically fulfilled prophecy (Exod. 12:46; Zech. 12:10). The body of Jesus was then removed from the cross, anointed and clothed, and placed in the tomb by Nicodemus and Joseph of Arimathaea.

The site of Capernaum, on the northwest shore of the Sea of Galilee. Jesus' third postresurrection appearance to His disciples occurred on the shore of the Sea of Galilee.

20:1-31

The first evidences of the resurrection of Christ were the empty tomb and the empty grave clothes as witnessed by Mary Magdalene, Peter, and John. The clothes were not in an unwound heap; rather, the resurrection body of Jesus passed directly through them. Later, Jesus appeared to Mary and commissioned her to tell the disciples about His resurrection and ascension into heaven. That evening Jesus manifested Himself to the ten disciples who were hiding in the upper room. After showing them the crucifixion marks in His body, He recommissioned them to apostolic service. Since Thomas was not present, he doubted the testimonies of his companions. Eight days later Jesus again revealed Himself to the disciples, and this time Thomas saw the nail prints in His hands and the spear wound in His side. His faith response was "My Lord and my God" (20:28). The entire purpose of the Gospel of John was to get the reader to the point where he would also acknowledge Jesus to be his Lord and God.

21:1-17

Christ's third postresurrection appearance to His disciples occurred on the shore of the Sea of Galilee. After fishing all night without catching anything, the disciples were commanded by Christ to cast their nets once more; this time they caught so many that they had to drag the net to shore. This was the eighth sign-miracle in the book. Jesus then used the occasion to question Peter about his priorities. Did he love Christ more than he loved fishing? Three times Peter declared his love and three times Christ commissioned him to be a spiritual shepherd.

147

21:18-25

Christ then announced the details of Peter's martyrdom. At the same time He declared that it was conceivable that John could be still alive at the time of His coming. Rumors then circulated among the churches that John would not die; however, Christ had not said that. Since Christ could have come in the lifetime of John if that had been His will, believers today should expect Him to return in their lifetime. John closed his Gospel by stating that the deeds of Christ are innumerable.

Increase Your Learning

By Doing

1. Since John is the Gospel of faith, underline the words "faith," "believe" and other cognate words wherever you find them in the book.
2. In your Bible circle or underline the various names given to Christ and used by Him, including the great "I Am's."

By Discussing

1. Some Christians have argued that since Christ made water into wine they may drink wine with their meals. What do you think? Is their conclusion logical?
2. How involved in social welfare programs should Christians get? Relate this to the feeding of the five thousand by Christ and His subsequent refusal to do so.
3. How important to Biblical Christianity is a proper understanding of the deity of Christ? of His humanity? Can you believe in one without the other?
4. In Christ's day why did men reject Him? Do they do so today for the same reasons?
5. In our present world of skepticism, how could you present empirical and rationalistic evidence for the bodily resurrection of Christ?

By Reading

Godet, F. *Commentary on the Gospel of St. John.* Grand Rapids: Zondervan Publishing House, n.d.

Hendriksen, William. *New Testament Commentary.* Grand Rapids: Baker Book House, 1953.

Morris, Leon. *Studies in the Fourth Gospel.* Grand Rapids: Wm. B. Eerdmans Publishing Co., n.d.

Pink, Arthur. *Exposition on the Gospel of John.* Grand Rapids: Zondervan Publishing House, n.d.

Tasker, R. V. G. *The Gospel According to St. John.* Grand Rapids: Wm. B. Eerdmans Publishing Co., 1960.

Tenney, Merrill C. *John: The Gospel of Belief.* Grand Rapids: Wm. B. Eerdmans Publishing Co., 1948.

Westcott, Brooke Foss. *The Gospel According to St. John.* Grand Rapids: Wm. B. Eerdmans Publishing Co., 1954.

8

ACTS

Writer

The authorship of Acts was discussed previously (cf. Luke, pp. 109-11). The internal evidence of both books has corroborated the testimony of tradition that Luke, the beloved physician and companion of Paul, wrote them. The first verse of Acts refers to an earlier volume written to the same individual, Theophilus; only the Gospel of Luke could qualify as that "former treatise."

Some believe that the prologue to the Gospel (1:1-4) also serves as the prologue to Acts. This would mean that Luke's original plan was to write two volumes to give Theophilus "certainty of those things, wherein thou hast been instructed" (Luke 1:4). The first dealt with the person and earthly ministry of Jesus Christ, whereas the second treated the history and outreach of the early church. In the first was the record "of all that Jesus *began* both to do and teach" (Acts 1:1) and the second revealed what Christ *continued* to do and teach through the Holy Spirit in the lives of the apostles. The continuity in the two books can also be seen in the overlap of content between the closing verses of the Gospel (24:46-53) and the opening verses of Acts (1:1-12).

Since Luke researched the content of the Gospel, he doubtless used the same technique for Acts. He was acquainted firsthand with some of Paul's missionary activities (16:10-17; 20:5—28:31). During his traveling days with Paul, he would have had many opportunities to talk with Christians from such important cities as Jerusalem and Caesarea (cf. 21:8, 17). Much could be learned from men like Philip and Mnason (21:8, 16), from others in Paul's team (Silas, Timothy, Mark), and from the apostles themselves. It would have been very easy for Luke to

149

have compiled his historical data on the early church during the two years that Paul was interned in Caesarea (24:27).

Time and Place

Many liberals speculate that the author of Acts was dependent upon Josephus, a late first-century Jewish historian; therefore, they date the book very late, anywhere between A.D. 80 and A.D. 130. However, there is no objective, external testimony from church history for doing so. The historical movement of the book actually ends with Paul's first Roman imprisonment which lasted two years (28:16, 30). The book concludes rather abruptly especially since Paul was freed and traveled for a few more years in the Mediterranean area, visiting churches that he had earlier founded. The only logical position is that Luke finished the writing of The Acts during the two-year internment at Rome. This would give a date of A.D. 59-61, although some evangelicals date this imprisonment A.D. 58-60 or A.D. 61-63. It is difficult to arrive with absolute certainty at fixed dates for some of the New Testament events; however, it is safe to assume that the book was composed before these significant events: the burning of Rome (A.D. 64), the first imperial persecution of Christians (A.D. 64-67), the second Roman imprisonment of Paul (A.D. 64-67), the Jewish rebellion against the Romans (A.D. 66), and the destruction both of Jerusalem and the Jewish temple by the Romans (A.D. 70). Surely Luke would have incorporated these events into his book if he had written after their occurrences.

Purposes

The purpose—to confirm Theophilus in the faith—has already been mentioned (under *Writer,* p. 149). The Gospel indoctrinated him in the person and ministry of Jesus Christ; this book was designed to instruct him about the lives and activities of the apostles (1:1-2). Luke's method of instruction will be seen in the other purposes.

Luke wanted Theophilus to be aware of the geographical outreach of the gospel message. Christ's instructions to the apostles provided the general outline of his book, showing how the gospel was taken from Jerusalem to Rome: "But ye shall receive power, after that the Holy Ghost is come upon you: and ye shall be witnesses unto me both in Jerusalem, and in all Judaea, and in Samaria, and unto the uttermost part of the earth" (1:8).

Acts 1—7 (Jerusalem)
Acts 8 (Judea and Samaria)
Acts 9—28 ("Uttermost Part"—Syria, Phoenicia, Asia Minor, Greece, and Italy)

Luke emphasized the northern and western propagation of the gospel (into Asia Minor and Europe). Nothing is given on the apostolic thrust into the south (Africa) or the east (Babylon and Persia), although converts from those regions are mentioned (2:9-10; 8:27). In the early months the apostles restricted their ministry to the area around Jerusalem (chs. 1-7). Later, the gospel was carried into Judea and Samaria (8:1), Damascus in Syria (9:19), Lydda (9:32), Joppa (9:36), Caesarea (10:1), Phoenicia, Cyprus, and Antioch in Syria (11:19). Strong, lengthy missionary activity did not begin until the call of Paul and Barnabas (13:1-2). This first missionary tour led them to the island of Cyprus and to the central section of Asia Minor where they evangelized the cities of Antioch in Pisidia, Iconium, Lystra, and Derbe (chs. 13-14). Paul's second journey took him into the regions of Syria, Cilicia, and Mysia and to the European cities of Philippi, Thessalonica, Berea, Athens, and Corinth (15:36—18:22). In his third journey, Paul concentrated on the strategic city of Ephesus, but he also returned to the Greek mainland where he visited the churches established during the second trip (18:23—21:17). When as a Roman prisoner Paul finally arrived in Rome, the gospel had already preceded him to that great city (28:14-16).

In addition to tracing the geographical outreach of the gospel, Luke wanted to mark the numerical growth of Christianity from the small

A corner of the Roman forum at Salamis, on the island of Cyprus.

beginning in the upper room in Jerusalem to a multitude of people that filled the Roman empire. He did this by inserting statistics and summaries at strategic intervals: "and the same day there were added unto them about three thousand souls" (2:41); "and the Lord added to the church daily" (2:47); "the number of the men was about five thousand" (4:4); "and believers were the more added to the Lord, multitudes both of men and women" (5:14); "and the word of God increased; and the number of the disciples multiplied in Jerusalem greatly" (6:7); "then ... the churches ... were multiplied" (9:31); "and a great number believed" (11:21); "but the word of God grew and multiplied" (12:24); "and so were the churches ... increased in number daily" (16:5); and "so mightily grew the word of God and prevailed" (19:20). The reaction of the Thessalonian Jews to Paul's missionary team serves as a fitting evaluation and illustration of the numerical growth: "These that have turned the world upside down are come hither also" (17:6).

Luke also wanted to show that Christianity was not a political threat to Rome, but that it was basically spiritual in essence. Some have suggested that Luke researched the activities of the apostles, especially those of Paul, as part of Paul's defense before Caesar in Rome. This plausible view is supported by the closing verses of the book:

> And Paul dwelt two whole years in his own hired house, and received all that came in unto him, Preaching the kingdom of God, and teaching those things which concern the Lord Jesus Christ, with all confidence, no man forbidding him (28:30-31).

After Paul had been arrested in Jerusalem for an alleged violation of temple worship, he asked that his case be heard by Caesar himself. As a Roman citizen, he had this right. Apparently the Roman government did not find anything politically offensive in Paul because they did not forbid him to preach. They recognized that a person could be a member of the spiritual kingdom of God and a Roman citizen at the same time without any real conflicts.

Luke then desired to demonstrate that unbelieving Jews were the real persecutors of Christians and that frequently they stirred up the Gentile populace and the political authorities to accomplish their selfish, wicked ends. In other words, the Jews, not Paul, should have been on trial for civil disturbances. Just as they successfully forced Pilate to have Jesus crucified so, as Luke wanted to prove, they were trying to get the Romans to eliminate another one of their foes, namely Paul. It was the priests and Sadducees who imprisoned and threatened Peter and John because the latter preached the resurrection of Jesus, a truth they denied (4:1-3, 21). This same group later imprisoned, threatened, and beat the apostles (5:17-18, 40). They stoned Stephen to death for religious

152

reasons (7:54, 58). Through Saul, they drove Christian Jews out of Jerusalem (8:1-3). After Saul was converted, the Jews tried to kill him even though he was one of their former associates (9:23). James was killed and Peter imprisoned because Herod Agrippa I saw that it pleased the Jews (12:1-3). The Jews of Antioch in Pisidia stirred up "the devout and honourable women, and the chief men of the city" to persecute Paul and Barnabas and to expel them from the city (13:50). They repeated these actions in Iconium and Lystra, actually stoning Paul and leaving him for dead (14:1-2, 19). The Jews of Thessalonica forced him out of both Thessalonica and Berea by falsely accusing Paul before the authorities and the people (17:5-9, 13). When the Corinthian Jews "made insurrection with one accord against Paul" before Gallio, the deputy of Achaia, Gallio saw that their hatred was religiously, not politically, motivated (18:12). The Jews worked cleverly to stir up the idolatrous Ephesian silversmiths to persecute the Christians (19:33). The Jews later plotted against the life of Paul (20:3; 21:31; 23:12). Civil authorities constantly confirmed the political innocence of Paul in spite of false Jewish charges (17:2-7; 19:35-41; 26:31-32).

Paul wrote that the gospel was "the power of God unto salvation to every one that believeth; to the Jew first, and also to the Greek" (Rom. 1:16). Luke wrote to show that the apostles in spite of strong, frequent Jewish opposition, continued to preach to the Jew first. They were given many opportunities to believe, and yet they rejected the message of Christ through the apostles just as they had rejected the ministry of the Lord Himself (John 1:11). The early preaching of the apostles was limited to Jewish audiences. When the Christians were forced out of Jerusalem into Gentile regions, they initially witnessed only to Jews in those areas (8:4; cf. 11:19-20). Wherever Paul went, he constantly preached to Jews, both in and out of their synagogues, before he began a Gentile ministry (13:5, 14; 14:1; 16:13; 17:1, 10, 17; 18:4; 19:8; 28:17). Although God had worked in and through Israel from the time of Abraham to Christ, the church age is basically a Gentile period of blessing. Luke vindicated this change of divine operation by presenting the authenticated offer to the Jews of the Christian message, the rejection of that offer by them, and the outreach of the Gentiles. Paul's words in the synagogue at Antioch in Pisidia provide a fitting condensation of this purpose: "It was necessary that the word of God should first have been spoken to you: but seeing ye put it from you, and judge yourselves unworthy of everlasting life, lo, we turn to the Gentiles" (13:46). The book ends with this same conclusion and intention: "Be it known therefore unto you [Jews], that the salvation of God is sent unto the Gentiles, and that they will hear it" (28:28).

Distinctive Features

Acts is a book of firsts. It narrates the first election of a church officer (1:23-26), the first sermon of the new era (2:14-40), the first conversions (2:41), the first miracle (3:1-11), the first persecution (4:1-4), the first chastisement (5:1-11), the first deacons (6:1-7), the first sermon by a layman (7:2-53), the first Christian martyr (7:54-60), the first Gentile converts (10:44-48), the first time the name "Christian" is mentioned (11:26), the first apostolic martyr (12:2), the first call to missionary service (13:1-2), the first church debate or council (15:1-30), and the first preaching in Europe (16:12-13).

Acts must also be seen as a transitional book. It bridges the gap between the Gospels and the Epistles, between the ministry of Christ and the activities of the apostles. It is therefore an introductory book, full of historical background. Great care must be exercised lest one build his entire theological position of doctrine and practice upon what is found in its chapters. Doctrine must be primarily based upon the Epistles where apostolic teaching is spelled out in detail. Many events recorded in Acts were never intended to become a pattern for every generation of Christians to follow. For instance, no one should expect to be personally taught by the resurrected Christ as were the apostles (1:1-3). The phenomena of wind, cloven fiery tongues, and tongues-speaking should not be anticipated by the believer in the entrance of the Holy Spirit into his life (2:1-4). Christians do not have to sell their possessions as the early converts did (2:45; 4:34). Deliberate liars are not immediately struck dead today (5:1-11). Imprisoned Christians should not expect to be released by an angel (5:19; 12:7) or by an earthquake (16:26). Paul himself later experienced at least three other imprisonments in which no angel or earthquake came to his rescue. Should martyrs today expect to see the resurrected Christ as Stephen did (7:55)? Should soul winners expect to be transported from one geographic location to another by the Spirit as was Philip (8:39)? Should people expect to see the resurrected Christ before their conversion as did Paul (9:1-6)? Should unsaved men expect an angelic invitation informing them what evangelist to secure as did Cornelius (10:1-8)? The answers to these questions are obviously negative. In Acts God was doing a new thing; He was starting the church age which has lasted now for almost two thousand years. In the divine introduction were many unusual signs and miracles that were never designed to be sought after by later Christians. God practiced this same principle in earlier ages. When the law was given to Moses originally the event was accompanied by thunder, lightning, smoke, and an earthquake (Exod. 19:16-18); however, when the law was given the second time, these phenomena were not repeated (Exod. 34). Why? Because the age of the law had already begun. God nourished the chil-

154

dren with daily manna for forty years, but once the Israelites were in Canaan, the manna stopped. They were to work the land and to trust the Lord for its increase; they were not to expect a repetition of the manna provision.

The Holy Spirit is mentioned over fifty times in this book, more than in any other New Testament book. It is no wonder that some have dubbed it "The Acts of the Holy Spirit." Many important aspects of pneumatology can be drawn from Luke's narratives. His personality is demonstrated by the facts that He can be lied against (5:3), tempted (5:9), and resisted (7:51). His works are many and varied. Christ predicted that believers would be baptized in Him (1:5). By Him Christians are filled (2:4), comforted (9:31), commissioned to service (13:2), directed to the right fields of ministry (16:6-7), and appointed as pastors (20:28). He inspired the Old Testament (1:16; 28:25), caused the apostles to speak in tongues (2:4), witnessed to the death and resurrection of Christ (5:32), transported Philip (8:39), and guided the deliberations of church leaders (15:28). His entrance into the world and into the lives of believers is described in several ways: coming upon (1:8), poured out (2:17), promised (2:33), a gift (10:45), and being received (10:47).

Luke also emphasized prayer. Every chapter shows the result of earnest prayer and almost every chapter makes mention of it by name (1:14; 2:42; 3:1; 4:24; 6:4; 7:60; 8:15; 9:11; 10:2; 11:5; 12:5; 13:3; 14:23; 16:13; 20:36; 21:5; 22:17; 27:35; 28:15).

Acts is basically a book of mission and witness. Jesus charged: ". . . ye shall be witnesses unto me" (1:8). They were to evangelize the world, spreading the good news of Christ's person and redemptive work, including His vicarious death and bodily resurrection. It was agreed that Judas' replacement had to have seen the resurrected Christ (1:22). Peter proclaimed his witness to the Jewish pilgrims on the day of Pentecost (2:32), to the temple crowd who marveled over the healed lame man (3:15), to the antagonistic priests (5:32), and to the Gentile household of Cornelius (10:39-41). Paul witnessed to Christ's person and work in the synagogue at Antioch in Pisidia (13:31) and before Roman authorities (26:16, 22).

The concept of witness can also be seen in the twelve sermons dotted throughout the book. Four sermons of Peter are recorded: on the day of Pentecost (2:14-41), to the Jews at Solomon's porch in the temple (3:12-26), at Cornelius' house in Caesarea (10:34-43), and before the apostles and elders (15:7-11). Six sermons by Paul are condensed in the book: in the synagogue at Antioch in Pisidia (13:14-43); before the philosophers on Mars' Hill in Athens (17:22-31); his farewell address to the Ephesian elders at Miletus (20:17-38); and his defenses before

155

the hostile Jerusalem crowd (22:1-22), before the Roman governor Felix (24:10-21), and before Herod Agrippa II (26:1-24). James' concluding remarks at the Council in Jerusalem (15:13-21) and the extensive summary and commentary on the Old Testament by Stephen (7:2-53) complement the sermons by the two major apostles.

Not only the sermons but also the signs, or miracles, of the apostles are recorded. Paul wrote concerning himself: "Truly the signs of an apostle were wrought among you in all patience, in signs, and wonders, and mighty deeds" (II Cor. 12:12). The messages of the apostles were authenticated by divinely wrought miracles. Not all of their miracles were narrated by Luke, but a sufficient number is given to illustrate the typical apostolic ministry. Three instances of healing are attributed directly to Peter: healing of the lame man (3:1-11), strengthening the palsied Aeneas (9:32-35), and raising Dorcas from the dead (9:36-43). Five were performed by Paul: curing the cripple at Lystra (14:8-10), casting out the demonic spirit of divination at Philippi (16:16-18), restoring Eutychus, who had fallen (20:6-12), shaking the snake off his hand (28:1-6), and healing the feverous father of Publius at Melita (28:7-8). Miracles were also performed as demonstrations of chastisement and judgment: the deaths of Ananias and Sapphira (5:1-11), the sudden death of Herod Agrippa I (12:20-23), and the blindness of Elymas (13:6-12). In addition, there are general statements mentioning the healing of many people by Peter, Philip, Stephen, and Paul without giving any particulars (5:12-16; 6:8; 8:6; 19:11-20; 28:9) Also, many unusual supernatural phenomena occurred during the ministry of the early church: the bodily ascension of Jesus (1:9), the wind, fiery tongues, and glossolalia at the coming of the Spirit (2:1-4), the release of Peter from prison by an angel twice (5:19; 12:7), the transport of Philip (8:39), and the angelic visitation to Cornelius (10:1-6).

Acts contains four chapters in which unusual receptions of the Holy Spirit are narrated (2, 8, 10, 19). On the day of Pentecost (2:1-13), the Jewish apostles in Jerusalem were both baptized in the Spirit (2:2) and filled by Him (2:4). This event was accompanied by the sound of a rushing mighty wind, cloven fiery tongues appearing above them, and speaking in tongues. The tongues-speaking was in foreign languages and dialects understood by the unsaved Jewish audience without any interpretation. There is no mention that the apostles were praying for this experience nor that they laid hands on each other. Jesus had earlier prayed that they might receive the Spirit (John 14:16) and promised to send the Spirit to them after His death, resurrection, and ascension (John 16:7). The Spirit thus came on Pentecost in fulfillment of Christ's prayer and plan. This was the official beginning of our present church era, a nonrepeatable event similar to the first coming of Christ. When

156

The Roman theater at Caesarea.

the apostles in Jerusalem heard of the evangelistic success of Philip in Samaria, they sent Peter and John to the converts (8:5-25). After Peter and John prayed for the new believers and laid hands on them, they received the Holy Spirit. There is no mention of wind, fiery tongues, or tongues-speaking. There is no indication that the Samaritans prayed or laid hands on each other nor that Philip shared the apostolic power. This time interval between faith and the reception of the Holy Spirit demonstrated to the Samaritan converts that they had to be under the spiritual authority of Jewish apostles, appointed by Christ and stationed in Jerusalem. The third unusual reception occurred when Peter preached for the first time to a Gentile, Cornelius, in Caesarea (10:1-48). While Peter was preaching, Cornelius believed, received the Holy Spirit, and spoke in tongues. After this experience, he was baptized in water. Again, there is no indication that Cornelius prayed for this to happen to him. Also, Peter did not pray for or lay hands on him. This unusual reception was a sign to Peter and to the believing Jews that God could save Gentiles and that in this age, Jews and Gentiles share an equal spiritual position before God. The final unique reception occurred when Paul led twelve disciples of John the Baptist into more complete truth about Christ (19:1-7). In essence, they were Old Testament saints living in the New Testament era. They were looking for the coming of Christ

157

when He had already come. To confirm his message, Paul laid hands on them and they received the Spirit, externally attested by tongues-speaking. Again, there is no evidence that they prayed for this experience or that they laid hands on each other. In these four chapters the Spirit of God was being formally introduced to four classes of people: Jews, Samaritans, Gentiles, and Old Testament saints. In all four events, an apostle was vitally involved. These chapters were not designed to provide model experiences for all future generations of Christians to follow.

Acts is very important to the Bible student because it provides the historical background for many of the Epistles. No one should undertake the study of the following books until he has first examined the accounts in Acts where these churches were established or mentioned: Romans (28:14-31); I and II Corinthians (18:1-18); Galatians (13:3—14:28); Ephesians (19:1-41); Philippians (16:6-40); I and II Thessalonians (17:1-9); I Timothy (19:1-41; 20:17-38); and Titus (27:1-13).

Luke's reputation as an historian and geographer has been challenged, but the conclusions of archaeologists have always supported him. He was the only New Testament writer to mention any Roman emperors by name: Augustus (Luke 2:1) and Tiberius (Luke 3:1). In his identification of political leaders, he always used the terms properly even though the positions changed frequently. This would have required him to have primary information about various political offices in different parts of the Roman empire. Both Sergius Paulus (13:7) and Gallio (18:12) were correctly titled as *anthupatoi* (deputies or proconsuls), officials in charge of senatorial provinces. The magistrates at Philippi were *strategoi* (16:20, 22, 35, 36, 38). The "rulers of the city" of Thessalonica were properly called *politarchoi* (17:6, 8). He knew that the town clerk or scribe *(grammateus;* 19:35) at Ephesus had political authority over the people and responsibility toward Rome. He was aware that Felix the governor *(hegemon;* 23:24) held the same position in Judea that Pilate once had (Matt. 27:11), the ruler of an imperial province. "The chief man of the island" (28:7) of Malta was literally "the first man" *(ho protos),* a technical term for the ruling official. For these reasons, Luke must be known as a first-class ancient historian.

Luke structured his book in a simple fashion:

Missionary	Base	Mission	Chapters
Peter	Jerusalem	Jew	1-12
Paul	Antioch	Gentile	13-14 (first journey) 15-18 (second journey) 18-21 (third journey) 21-28 (in prison)

ACTS

Although called "The Acts of the Apostles," the book stresses the activities of only two of them, Peter and Paul. The first twelve chapters deal with the outreach of Peter toward the Jew from the church at Jerusalem. The closing chapters deal with Paul's ministry mainly to the Gentiles from his home church at Antioch in Syria. Paul's life is divided into two sections: his three missionary journeys (13:1—21:17) and his defenses of the Christian faith as a Roman prisoner (21:18—28:31).

Outline

I. THE WITNESS IN JERUSALEM (chs. 1-7)
    A. The ascension of Christ (1:1-11)
    B. The appointment of Matthias (1:12-26)
    C. The coming of the Holy Spirit (2:1-13)
    D. The message of Peter (2:14-41)
    E. The fellowship of the early church (2:42-47)
    F. The healing of the lame man (3:1-11)
    G. The message of Peter in the temple (3:12-26)
    H. The threat of the religious leaders (4:1-22)
    I. The reaction of the church (4:23-37)
    J. The chastisement of Ananias and Sapphira (5:1-11)
    K. The performing of various miracles (5:12-16)
    L. The persecution by the religious leaders (5:17-42)
    M. The appointment of deacons (6:1-7)
    N. The preaching of Stephen (6:8—7:53)
    O. The martyrdom of Stephen (7:54-60)
II. THE WITNESS IN JUDEA AND SAMARIA (chs. 8-12)
    A. The persecution of the Jerusalem church (8:1-4)
    B. The evangelization of Samaria (8:5-25)
    C. The conversion of the Ethiopian eunuch (8:26-40)
    D. The conversion of Saul (9:1-31)
    E. The healing of Aeneas (9:32-35)
    F. The raising of Dorcas (9:36-43)
    G. The conversion of Cornelius (10:1-48)
    H. Peter's report to the Jerusalem church (11:1-18)
    I. The ministry at Antioch (11:19-30)
    J. The martyrdom of James (12:1-4)
    K. The imprisonment of Peter (12:5-19)
    L. The death of Herod (12:20-25)
III. THE WITNESS TO THE UTTERMOST PART (chs. 13-28)
    A. Paul's first missionary journey (13:1—14:28)
        1. His commission (13:1-3)
        2. On Cyprus (13:4-13)
        3. At Antioch in Pisidia (13:14-52)
        4. At Iconium (14:1-5)
        5. At Lystra and Derbe (14:6-20)
        6. Return trip to Antioch (14:21-28)
    B. The council at Jerusalem (15:1-35)
        1. The problem (15:1)
        2. The deliberations (15:2-21)
        3. The solution (15:22-35)

C. Paul's second missionary journey (15:36—18:22)
 1. Dissension with Barnabas (15:36-41)
 2. Appointment of Timothy (16:1-5)
 3. At Philippi (16:6-40)
 4. At Thessalonica (17:1-9)
 5. At Berea (17:10-14)
 6. At Athens (17:15-34)
 7. At Corinth (18:1-18)
 8. Return trip to Antioch (18:19-22)
D. Paul's third missionary journey (18:23—21:17)
 1. Ministry of Apollos (18:24-28)
 2. At Ephesus (19:1-41)
 3. In Greece (20:1-5)
 4. At Troas (20:6-12)
 5. At Miletus (20:13-38)
 6. Return trip to Jerusalem (21:1-17)
E. Paul's imprisonment (21:18—28:31)
 1. His arrest in the temple (21:18-40)
 2. His defense before the multitude (22:1-30)
 3. His defense before the Sanhedrin (23:1-10)
 4. The conspiracy to kill Paul (23:11-22)
 5. His departure to Caesarea (23:23-35)
 6. His defense before Felix (24:1-27)
 7. His defense before Festus (25:1-27)
 8. His defense before Agrippa (26:1-32)
 9. His voyage to Italy (27:1-44)
 10. His ministry at Melita (28:1-10)
 11. His arrival at Rome (28:11-31)

Survey

1:1-11

For forty days after His resurrection, Jesus appeared to His disciples and taught them. Their witness to the world could not begin until the Holy Spirit had come upon them; therefore He commanded them to remain in Jerusalem. He would send the Holy Spirit to them as He had promised earlier (John 14:16-17, 26; 15:26-27; 16:7-14). The disciples thought that now that Christ had suffered He could establish the earthly kingdom; however, He cautioned them not to speculate about eschatology, but bear witness of Him throughout the world in the enabling ministry of the Holy Spirit. The disciples saw the Lord ascend into heaven and received the promise of the angels that He would return in like manner.

1:12-26

During the interval, the group of one hundred twenty disciples voted for Matthias over Joseph to fill the apostolic vacancy created by Judas' betrayal and death. Men have debated whether their action was justified. Should Paul have been the twelfth apostle? How could they make the decision apart from the ministry of the Spirit who had not yet come? Did they still have the indwelling presence of the Spirit given to them by Christ shortly after His resurrection (John 20:19-23). Regardless, Matthias was chosen and was recognized as a genuine apostle.

2:1-13

The descent of the Holy Spirit ten days after Christ's ascension on the day of Pentecost was marked by three unusual phenomena: the sound of a rushing mighty wind, fiery cloven tongues appearing over them, and speaking in tongues.[1] The Jewish pilgrims were amazed that the Galilean apostles could speak in their native languages and dialects (*glossa:* 2:4, 11, and *dialektos:* 2:6, 8). While some wondered, others attributed the tongues-speaking to drunkenness. At this time, the apostles were both baptized in the Spirit (1:5; cf. 2:2) and filled with the Spirit (1:8; cf. 2:4).

2:14-21

Peter explained that the descent of the Spirit was like that predicted by Joel. Joel's prophecy will be fulfilled in the last days of Israel's history, at the end of the great tribulation just prior to Christ's second advent to the earth to destroy the wicked nations and to establish His earthly kingdom (Joel 2:20—3:21). The signs written by Joel and quoted by Peter did not occur on the day of Pentecost. This is why Peter said "this is that" rather than "it is written" or "it is fulfilled." Peter's purpose was to show that the Old Testament predicted such an outpouring of the Spirit. Just as the Messiah one day will pour out the Spirit upon Israel, so He has poured out the Spirit upon the church in this age.

2:22-41

Peter then focused his message on the person of Christ. He stated that Christ had been divinely authenticated through His public display of miracles and healing. He then argued that their wicked crime of crucifixion and the subsequent resurrection of Jesus were both part of God's predetermined plan. God is definitely able to use the free-will actions of men, whether they be good or evil, to accomplish His ultimate goals: the glorification of Himself and the blessing of His people. He logically claimed that David in his psalm predicted the death and the resurrection of the Messiah. When Jesus died, His body was placed into Joseph's tomb and His soul went into hell *(Hades),* but His soul did not remain in hell nor did His body begin to decompose (2:31). Peter then concluded that the resurrected, ascended Christ had sent the Spirit into

---

1. For a further discussion, consult the author's book, *The Modern Tongues Movement* (Nutley, N.J.: Presbyterian and Reformed Publishing Co., 1967).

the world and into the apostles' lives in this dramatic fashion. What they saw and heard (2:33) was a sign to them of their error and sin in rejecting Christ. Convicted by the Spirit, they asked: "What shall we do?" Peter's answer has puzzled many (2:38). Did he mean that water baptism was essential to gain the remission of sins? An affirmative answer would contradict the clear teaching of Scripture elsewhere (Rom. 5:1; Eph. 2:8-9). The inward faith-repentance that secures the remission of sins will outwardly manifest itself in an open identification with Christ's redemptive work through water baptism. Baptism is a confession, the first work that faith produces. Three thousand received the word (repented and believed) and were baptized.

2:42-47

Although the early church increased rapidly in numbers, it maintained a strong spiritual quality. It was marked by doctrinal conformity, fellowship, constant observance of the communion ordinance, prayer, apostolic miracles, communal sharing of property, and joy. These Jewish believers continued to worship in the temple, but they also congregated "from house to house" (house-churches scattered throughout Jerusalem).

3:1-26

The healing of the lame man at the Beautiful Gate of the temple provided Peter another major opportunity to preach to a large Jewish multitude. He claimed that the miracle was caused through faith in the crucified, resurrected Christ, not through the human power and holiness of the apostles. His appeal was simple: "Repent ye therefore, and be converted, that your sins may be blotted out . . ." (3:19; note the omission of baptism as a prerequisite for salvation; cf. 2:38). They needed to repent (change their mind) of their rejection of Christ and to accept Him before His return in fulfillment of Old Testament prophecy.

4:1-31

There was a mixed reaction to Peter's message. Many believed, increasing the Jerusalem church from over three thousand to about five thousand (2:41; cf. 4:4).[2] However, the priests and Sadducees imprisoned Peter and John for the night. At their "trial" before the religious council the next day, the apostles again claimed that the miracle was wrought by the resurrected Christ, whom the leaders had rejected and in

---

2. Five thousand men were not saved as the result of this second sermon. The English "was" comes from the Greek *egenethe* ("came to be"). The 120 disciples (1:15) plus the 3000 Pentecostal converts (2:41) plus the daily converts (2:47) plus the converts of this second message caused the total number of believers to mushroom to 5000.

162

whom only could salvation be found. Unable to contradict the evidence of the healed man, they threatened the apostles about any further preaching; however, the latter refused to comply. Their release and return to the church caused a great prayer meeting in which they asked for boldness to preach and to heal in the face of such hostile opposition.

4:32—5:11

The unity of the early Christians ("of one heart and of one soul") could be seen in their attitudes toward material possessions. They sold their lands and houses, placed the sale money into apostolic care, and distributed to the needs of the group. In this financial demonstration of love for one another, no one suffered want. Some apparently had lost jobs and homes because of their new faith. The deception of Ananias and Sapphira must be seen against this display of general generosity. They lied to God the Holy Spirit (5:3; cf. 5:4) rather than to men when they deliberately plotted to keep back part of the sale price of their property. Their sudden deaths were not only a display of divine chastisement but also an indication of apostolic authority in retaining sin rather than remitting it (John 20:23). It further demonstrated that sin could not be tolerated within a church desirous of God's blessing and power.

5:12-42

The continuous ministry of healing by the apostles so vexed the Sadducees that they placed the former in prison. Released by an angel that night, the apostles were arrested a second time for preaching in the temple. Their trial or inquisition resembled that of Christ before the ruling elders. When the apostles reaffirmed their determination to preach the gospel, the council decided to kill them. Gamaliel, a Pharisaical doctor of the law, warned them against such hasty action. He argued that God's work could not be resisted and that man's work would eventually die out. He suggested that time alone would determine the source of the apostolic ministry. The leaders agreed not to kill the apostles, but they did beat and threaten them. The apostles reacted with joy and constant witnessing.

6:1-7

Increase of numbers often brings neglect of people. In the early church the material needs of Christian widows were supplied by the common treasury administered by the apostles. As the converts increased numerically, the needs of some widows were being neglected. There were too many widows and too few apostles. The apostles recognized that their first responsibilities were to preach and to pray. They asked that the church select seven qualified, spiritual men whom they might appoint to administer the widow welfare program.[3] After this was done, the church experienced another growth spurt.

6:8—7:60

Stephen, one of the appointed seven, extended his ministry into healing and preaching. He was so effective that the religious council brought false charges against him and arrested him. Their accusation of his message probably reflected a faulty interpretation of Jesus' prediction of the destruction of the temple (6:3-14; cf. Matt. 24:1-2). In his lengthy message, Stephen indicted both them and their ancestors for constantly rejecting the message of God's appointed servants and for resisting the ministry of the Holy Spirit. When they became enraged, the heavens opened and Stephen saw Jesus at the right hand of the Father. When he testified of his vision, they began to stone him. Just before he died, he uttered two short prayers, one for himself and one for his murderers.[4] The attitude in which he died no doubt troubled the conscience of Saul (who after his conversion became Paul the apostle).

8:1-4

The stoning of Stephen ignited a major persecution, led by Saul, against the church at Jerusalem. Although the apostles bravely stayed in Jerusalem, many scattered throughout Judea, Samaria, and such foreign regions as Phoenicia, Cyprus, and Syria. As they went, they preached the word but limited their early ministry to Jews in those areas (cf. 11:19).

8:5-40

Philip, a deacon-evangelist (6:5; 21:8), ministered in Samaria, preaching, healing, and casting out demons. The strange way in which his converts received the Spirit was discussed earlier. The ecclesiastical sin of simony (purchasing a church office through money) was condemned by Peter when he rebuked Simon, the converted (?) sorcerer. Philip's leaving Samaria to witness to the Ethiopian eunuch demonstrated that God was (and is) just as interested in individuals as in the masses. This account also shows that God will reveal truth about Jesus Christ to those who are genuine worshipers of God and who desire to

---

3. This action provides a pattern for church organization and administration. Officers are created to meet the specific needs of the congregation. Many believe that these seven represent the first board of deacons. Although the title for deacon (*diakonos*) is not found here, the concept can be seen in the words "ministration" (*diakonia*) and "to serve" (*diakonein*).
4. In these, he identified with Christ in His death. Compare "Lord Jesus, receive my spirit" (7:59) with "Father, into thy hands I commend my spirit" (Luke 23:46) and "Lord, lay not this sin to their charge" (7:60) with "Father, forgive them; for they know not what they do" (Luke 23:34).

The site of Jacob's well (center) and the surrounding Samaritan country-side, as viewed from the slopes of Mount Gerizim.

know the teaching of Scripture. After the conversion and baptism of the eunuch, Philip was supernaturally caught away. He later located at Caesarea (21:8).

9:1-31

On his way to Damascus to arrest Christians, Saul was struck blind and converted by the glorious revelation of Christ. Ananias, under divine instructions, went to the blind Saul, healed him of his blindness, laid hands on him, and baptized him. Immediately Paul began to witness in the synagogue at Damascus. When the enraged Jews plotted to kill him, Saul escaped and went to Jerusalem where the apostles received him because of Barnabas' testimony. Later, Paul returned to his hometown of Tarsus because of Jewish hostility at Jerusalem.

9:32-43

Peter meanwhile extended his ministry into Lydda where he healed the palsied Aeneas and into Joppa where he raised the benevolent Dorcas from the dead.

10:1—11:18

At this time Cornelius, a good but unsaved Roman soldier in Caesarea, was charged by an angel to send for Peter. God was preparing Peter for this opportunity to preach to a Gentile for the first time by giving a vision to him. At first Peter did not understand the significance of the vision, but later, after talking with Cornelius' emissaries and with Cornelius himself, he knew that God wanted him to preach to Gentiles

165

as well as to Jews. In his message Peter preached the necessity of faith in Christ to receive the remission of sins. The providentially prepared hearts of Cornelius and his friends responded. The unusual phenomenon of tongues-speaking that accompanied their conversion experience was discussed earlier (see p. 157). Back in Jerusalem, Peter was criticized for sharing the gospel with Gentiles until he explained the complex circumstances surrounding his visit to the house of Cornelius.

11:19-30

The ministry at Antioch in Syria among the Grecian Jews *(hellenistas)* or Greek Gentiles *(hellenas)* was so successful that Jerusalem sent Barnabas to assist in the work. Barnabas went to Tarsus to get Saul's help. Both of them then labored at Antioch for a year as teachers. Antioch became famous as the home church of Paul and as the place where believers were first called Christians. Later the church in Antioch sent Barnabas and Saul with a financial gift to the needy saints at Jerusalem.

12:1-25

About this time Herod Agrippa I killed the apostle James and imprisoned Peter. In response to prayer, Peter was released by an angel, contacted his praying friends, and then left the area (12:17). For his action Herod was judged by God with disease and death.

13:1-13

These next two chapters (chs. 13-14) contain the record of the first missionary journey of Paul and Barnabas in which the first serious

Antioch of Syria, the home base for Paul's missionary journeys. Its church sent delegates to the Jerusalem conference recorded in Acts.

A section of the Roman aqueduct that carried water to Pisidian Antioch. This city served as a center of civil and military affairs for the southern part of the province of Galatia.

attempt to reach Gentiles was made. It began with a specific call by the Holy Spirit to the ministering prophets and teachers at Antioch in Syria: "Separate me Barnabas and Saul for the work whereunto I have called them" (13:2). These leaders recognized the divine call and sent the two away with their blessing. Accompanied by John Mark, they sailed from the Syrian seaport of Seleucia to the city of Salamis on the island of Cyprus. After preaching in the synagogue, they traversed the length of the island, arriving at Paphos where Paul afflicted Elymas with blindness for the latter's opposition to the gospel message. When they left Cyprus for the south central section of modern Turkey, John Mark defected and returned to Jerusalem. Why did he do this? Perhaps the rigors of the travels were too much for him especially since he had no direct call; maybe his Jewish heritage reacted against the ministry to the Gentiles; or he may not have liked the increasing leadership strength exercised by Paul over his uncle Barnabas.

13:14-49

At Antioch in Pisidia Paul delivered a typical sermon that he would preach in a synagogue to both Jews and Gentile proselytes (13:16, 26, 43). In developing the past history of Israel, he referred to the messianic hope promised through Abraham and David; then he proceeded to prove how Jesus fulfilled those prophecies in His life, death, and resurrection.

167

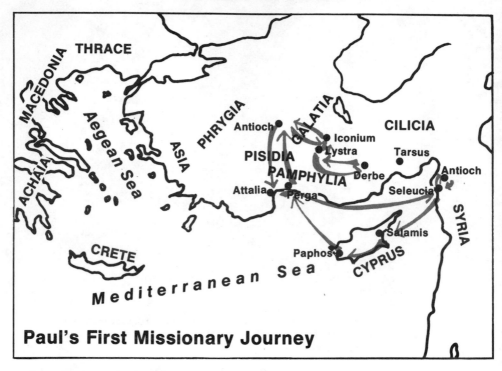

Paul's First Missionary Journey

Paul's Second Missionary Journey

Paul's Third Missionary Journey

Paul's Journey to Rome

His conclusion and invitation emphasized salvation by grace: ". . . through this man is preached unto you the forgiveness of sins: and by him all that believe are justified from all things, from which ye could not be justified by the law of Moses" (13:38-39). When Jewish hostility forced him out of the synagogue, Paul extended his ministry to the Gentiles of that region (13:45-49).

13:50—14:28

Forced to leave Antioch, they went to Iconium, preached and performed miracles, and were driven out by the combined efforts of the Jews, Gentiles, and rulers. At Lystra, after healing a cripple, Paul disavowed the worship of the idolatrous pagans by pointing them to the living God through the testimony of general revelation in nature. After being stoned almost to death, Paul continued on to Derbe. On their return trip through the same cities they had evangelized earlier, they instructed, comforted, and trained the converts to carry on an indigenous work in their absence. When they returned to Antioch in Syria for their first "missionary furlough" they explained how God "had opened the door of faith unto the Gentiles" (14:27).

15:1-35

The first doctrinal controversy in the early church centered on the necessity of circumcision for personal salvation. To settle the issue, a council was convened in Jerusalem. After major addresses by Peter, Paul, Barnabas, and James, the council decided that a Gentile convert did not have to be circumcised in order to have the same salvation possessed by a circumcised, Jewish Christian. In letters to the Gentile churches, they recorded their verdict; however, they did request that the Gentiles watch their diet and behavior for reasons of testimony to the Jews in their respective areas. Paul and Barnabas then returned to Antioch, accompanied by Silas.

15:36-41

Paul's second missionary journey (15:36—18:22) was conceived in this request of Barnabas: "Let us go again and visit our brethren in every city where we have preached the word of the Lord, and see how they do" (15:36). When they argued over the advisability of taking John Mark once again, Barnabas took him and sailed for Cyprus whereas Paul chose Silas and followed the land route into Syria and Cilicia. Since Paul had the recommendation of the church, he must have been right and Barnabas wrong. The latter's recorded ministry ends with this action.

16:1-40

After Timothy joined the team at Lystra, they advanced through the regions of Phrygia and Galatia to the Aegean port of Troas, having been forbidden of the Spirit to preach in the provinces of Asia and Bithynia. In a vision Paul was directed to go into the European region of Macedonia. Luke then joined the team and all four went to Philippi.[5] After some initial preaching and the unjust imprisonment and beating of Paul and Silas, a small nucleus of believers was established, meeting in the house of Lydia, the first convert in Europe.

17:1-34

Having left Luke in Philippi, the team traveled to Thessalonica where they labored for about a month. After a successful ministry, they were forced to leave when unbelieving Jews misrepresented them before the Gentile rulers of the city. The Thessalonian Jews followed Paul to Berea and pressured him out of this city also. The Berean brethren took Paul to Athens, and after their return, informed Silas and Timothy to join Paul in that city. Meanwhile, Paul preached both in the synagogue and on Mars' Hill before the pagan philosophers. In the condensed sermon recorded here, Paul declared that the unknown God whom they ignorantly worshiped had revealed Himself not only through nature but personally through Jesus Christ in His life, death, and resurrection. A few converts were won through his ministry there.

18:1-22

Paul's partners apparently joined him at Athens and were subsequently sent back to Macedonia (18:5; cf. I Thess. 3:1-6). Paul moved on to Corinth where he labored for eighteen months (18:11). At first, he worked as a tentmaker with Aquila and Priscilla to support himself and to maintain a reproach-free testimony (cf. I Cor. 9:1-18). Later he devoted all of his energy to a major ministry among Gentiles in spite of strong opposition. Paul and his team then returned to Antioch after short stops at Ephesus, Caesarea, and Jerusalem.

18:23—19:41

The third journey (18:23—21:17) began as an edification ministry in Galatia and Phrygia. Paul then went to the key city of the province of Asia, Ephesus, where he labored for three years, longer than in any other city (19:8, 10; 20:31). The first converts there were disciples of John the Baptist, won to that position by Apollos who subsequently became a Christian through the witness of Aquila and Priscilla. He preached in the synagogue for three months, separated the converts, and continued for two years in the school of Tyrannus. From this strategic

5. More information on chapters 16-19 can be found in the section entitled "Establishment of the Church" in the chapters on Philippians, I Thessalonians, I Corinthians, and Ephesians, pp. 256-57, 277-78, 200-01, 242-44.

spot all inhabitants of Asia heard the word. Many believe that the famous seven churches of Revelation (chs. 2-3) were started as a result of Paul's ministry in Ephesus. Many occultists were saved through Paul's ministry of healing and casting out of demons. There were so many converts that the "idol-making" industry began to suffer financially. The silversmiths, in their frustration, tried to rally the city behind their cause, but were unsuccessful.

20:1—21:17

Paul then revisited the churches of Macedonia and Greece that were founded during the second journey. He decided to return to Antioch via Macedonia and Asia. Several journeyed with him from Philippi to Troas, including Luke who was destined to accompany Paul from then on. A quick stop at Miletus enabled Paul to encourage the elders of Ephesus and to warn them against the rise of false teachers both from within and without the church. They then sailed for Caesarea with short stops at Coos, Rhodes, Patara, Tyre, and Ptolemais. Both at Tyre and Caesarea Paul was warned by believers speaking by the Holy Spirit not to go to Jerusalem. Many have debated whether Paul disobeyed the will of God by discounting this counsel and by going to Jerusalem. It is difficult to say whether Paul was right or wrong in his decision to do so.

21:18—22:30

To repudiate the false rumors about his ministry to Jews of the

Roman street and arch at Tyre.

The fortress of Antonia, as duplicated in the model of Herodian Jerusalem. The fortress was adjacent to the temple area. Roman troops were dispatched from here to rescue Paul from the mob.

dispersion, Paul agreed for the sake of testimony to purify himself ceremonially and to offer a sacrifice in the temple. When unsaved Jews of Asia (probably from Ephesus) saw him there, they falsely accused Paul of bringing a Gentile into the Jewish section of the temple. The Jews reacted by trying to kill him, but Paul was rescued and later bound by Roman soldiers. After explaining to the chief captain who he was, Paul was given opportunity to address the Jewish multitude. In his defense, or apology, Paul reiterated his conversion experience and call into the ministry. When he claimed that the resurrected Christ had commissioned him to preach to the Gentiles (22:21-22), the multitude became enraged. Paul was then taken into the castle and bound over for future investigation.

23:1—24:27

The next day Paul stood before the same religious council that "tried" Christ. He used psychology by identifying himself with the Pharisaical sect as over against the Sadducees. Such a fierce debate erupted that the Romans again removed him to the castle. When the soldiers heard of the plot to kill Paul, they transported him under heavy guard to the Roman governor Felix at Caesarea. About five days later, when the Jews brought formal charges against Paul, the apostle so ably defended himself that Felix delayed action on the case. For the next two years Paul was

173

interned at Caesarea. Although he heard Paul expound the gospel on several occasions, Felix refused to release him for two reasons: a desire to receive bribery money and a determination to please the Jews.

25:1—26:32

When Festus replaced Felix, he offered Paul a chance to be tried in Jerusalem, but Paul refused and asked to be tried by Caesar (his right as a Roman citizen). When Herod Agrippa II visited Festus, Paul was granted the opportunity to voice his defense before both of them. Again he centered his apology in his conversion experience at which time he saw the resurrected Christ and was commissioned by Him. Festus thought Paul was insane, but Agrippa wondered about the truth of the apostle's message. Both agreed that Paul was innocent and that he would have been released if he had not appealed to Caesar.

27:1—28:10

The voyage to Rome was marked by delay and difficulty. They sailed to Sidon, near Cyprus, on to Myra, and stopped at Crete. Against Paul's advice, the ship set sail and encountered a fierce storm. When the sailors and soldiers gave up hope of deliverance, Paul assured them that all lives would be spared. The ship finally wrecked near the island of Malta where Paul was delivered from the death of a poisonous snake bite by God. Paul then engaged in a ministry of healing on the island.

28:11-31

Three months later they sailed again, stopping at Syracuse, Rhegium,

St. Paul's Bay in Malta where Paul suffered shipwreck. On the large islet on the left, a statue of Paul commemorates the event of Acts 27.

and Puteoli. By land they then went to Rome where Paul underwent a special imprisonment (28:16). After Paul called for the Jewish leaders of Rome, he explained his imprisonment and declared the gospel to them. The book ends with a note about Paul's two years of house arrest in Rome with complete freedom to receive visitors and to proclaim the gospel.

Increase Your Learning

By Doing

1. In your Bibles circle the names of those places that Paul visited during his three journeys plus the voyage to Rome.
2. Draw your own map of the Mediterranean world, marking those regions and cities mentioned in Acts.
3. Make a list of all those who opposed the advance of the gospel. List the supporting verses.
4. Since Acts emphasizes prayer, the ministry of the Spirit, and the witness of Christians, underline all references to them in your Bible. Use three different colors to keep them separate.

By Discussing

1. Compare the sermons recorded in Acts with contemporary messages. Show their differences and similarities in style and content.
2. Is there any relationship between the problems of an integrated church today (black and white) and those of the early church (Jew and Gentile)? What lessons in this area can be learned from a study of Acts?
3. Should the financial practices of the Jerusalem church (2:45; 4:32-35) be regarded as a model for all Christians to follow? Can those who follow the communal life or communism find support for their life-styles and doctrines in the practices of the converts in Jerusalem?
4. Is the modern missionary enterprise (mission boards, deputation, etc.) contrary to or in harmony with the nature of Paul's missionary endeavors?
5. What principles of local church government can be gleaned from the organization of the early church?

By Reading

Blaiklock, E. M. *The Acts of the Apostles.* Grand Rapids: Wm. B. Eerdmans Publishing Co., 1963.

Bruce, F. F. *Commentary on Acts.* Grand Rapids: Wm. B. Eerdmans Publishing Co., 1954.

Ironside, H. A. *Lectures on the Book of Acts.* New York: Loizeaux Bros., 1943.

Morgan, G. Campbell. *The Acts of the Apostles.* Westwood, N.J.: Fleming H. Revell Co., 1924.

Rackham, Richard Belward. *The Acts of the Apostles.* London: Methuen and Co., 1951.

9

ROMANS

Writer

What can be said about this amazing life?![1] Almost the entire history of the apostolic church (Acts 9-28) can be equated with the personal history of Paul, the greatest of the apostles. He was born and raised in Tarsus, the chief city of Cilicia and one of the great learning centers of the Eastern World. Because his parents were Jews who possessed Roman citizenship, he inherited a unique status: he was both a Roman and a Jew. His Jewish heritage was flawless: "Circumcised the eighth day, of the stock of Israel, of the tribe of Benjamin, an Hebrew of the Hebrews" (Phil. 3:5). He was doubtless named "Saul" after the first king of united Israel. Most Romans had purchased their rights of citizenship, but Paul was born into his (Acts 22:25-29). Some believe that the Graeco-Roman name "Paul" was given to him by his parents because of the double world into which he was born. However, most evangelicals claim that Saul took the name "Paul" after his conversion, possibly after winning his first Gentile on his initial missionary journey, Sergius Paulus (Acts 13:7-12). Was it coincidental that Luke recorded the change of his name in the midst of the narrative account of the salvation experience of this Roman deputy?

Typical of Jewish male children, he learned a manual trade, tent-making (Acts 18:3). Probably at the age of thirteen, he was sent by his wealthy, Pharisaical father (Acts 23:6) to study in Jerusalem under the learned and respected Gamaliel, also a Pharisee and a doctor of the

---

1. For a comprehensive description of Paul's life and ministry, consult Merrill F. Unger, *Unger's Bible Dictionary* (Chicago: Moody Press, 1957), pp. 831-839.

Ruins of the ancient city wall of Tarsus.

law (Acts 22:3; cf. 5:34-39). In those training years he "profited in the Jews' religion above many my equals in mine own nation, being more exceedingly zealous of the traditions of my fathers" (Gal. 1:14). Within his peer group he showed the most promise of becoming an outstanding Pharisee.

He is first mentioned in Scripture as the young man in charge of the robes of those who stoned Stephen (Acts 7:58). From that point on he became a fanatical persecutor of Christians, both imprisoning them and putting them to death (Acts 22:4; 26:10-11; Gal. 1:13). Christians everywhere were deathly afraid of him (Acts 9:13, 26). Based upon attitudes and actions, Saul of Tarsus must have been considered the most unlikely candidate for salvation, and yet God sovereignly saved him when Jesus Christ manifested Himself to him on the road to Damascus (I Tim. 1:12-16; cf. Acts 9:1-16; Gal. 1:11-15; about A.D. 32). Through this supernatural revelation and others, Paul became both a witness of the resurrected Christ and a commissioned apostle (Acts 9:15-16; Gal. 1:11-12; I Cor. 15:8-10).

His early years of witness were spent mainly in Syria, Arabia, and Judea (A.D. 32-35; Acts 9:19-29; Gal. 1:17-21). He then went into relative seclusion at his hometown of Tarsus for about nine years (A.D. 35-44; Acts 9:30). Barnabas brought him from Tarsus to Antioch

177

in Syria to work in that growing church as a teacher (A.D. 44-47; Acts 11:25-30; 12:25). Antioch then became the home base for his three famous missionary journeys. The following chart will reveal the scope of those ventures:

Journey	Scripture	Time	Places Visited	Books Written
First	Acts 13:1— 14:28	A.D. 47-48	Seleucia, Cyprus (Salamis, Paphos) Perga, Antioch in Pisidia, Iconium, Lystra, Derbe	None
Second	Acts 15:36— 18:22	A.D. 49-52	Syria, Cilicia, Derbe, Lystra, Phrygia, Galatia, Mysia, Troas, Samothracia, Neapolis, Philippi, Thessalonica, Berea, Athens, Corinth, Ephesus, Caesarea, Jerusalem	I Thessalonians II Thessalonians
Third	Acts 18:23— 21:17	A.D. 52-56	Galatia, Phrygia, Ephesus, Macedonia, Greece, Philippi, Troas, Assos, Mitylene, Chios, Samos, Trogyllium, Miletus, Coos, Rhodes, Patara, Tyre, Ptolemais, Caesarea, Jerusalem	I Corinthians II Corinthians Romans

During the interval between the first and second journeys, Paul probably wrote Galatians and engaged in the deliberations of the council at Jerusalem (Acts 15).

At Jerusalem Paul was arrested and imprisoned, not only there but also at Caesarea for two years (A.D. 56-58; Acts 21:18—26:32; cf. 24:27). After a treacherous voyage, Paul arrived at Rome where he remained a prisoner for two more years (A.D. 58-61; Acts 27:1—28:31; cf. 28:30), during which time he wrote Ephesians, Philippians, Colossians, and Philemon. Although Scripture is silent on the subject, Paul was apparently released, enabling him to resume a limited itinerary, including Crete, Ephesus, and Macedonia (A.D. 61-64; I Tim. 1:3; Titus 1:5). During this freedom, he penned I Timothy and Titus. When the imperial persecution against Christianity began under Nero, Paul was arrested and taken to Rome where he was again imprisoned (A.D. 64-67). His last book, II Timothy, reflected his expectation of imminent martyrdom. Tradition states that he was beheaded about A.D. 67 in Rome and that his corpse was buried in subterranean labyrinths underneath the city.

Although critics have doubted the Pauline authorship of many of his Epistles, the Book of Romans has been accepted even by them as one of his genuine letters. Early Church Fathers, including Ignatius, Justin Martyr, Polycarp, Hippolytus, Marcion, and Irenaeus, definitely recognized the book as canonical and as written by the apostle. Internal evidence supports their judgment. The author claimed to be Paul (1:1). He regarded himself as a special apostle to the Gentiles (1:1; 11:13; 15:15-20; cf. Acts 9:15; Gal. 2:8). He was a Jew (9:3, 4). He was a pioneer missionary, laboring in untouched fields (15:15-20; cf. Acts 13-20). He planned to take a financial contribution to the poor at Jerusalem (15:25-26; cf. Acts 24:17; I Cor. 16:1-3; II Cor. 8-9). His apprehension over visiting Jerusalem corresponds with his fears expressed elsewhere (15:30-31; cf. Acts 20:22-23). His expressed purpose to visit the Roman church was also pointed out by his chronicler, Luke (1:10-15; 15:23-24; cf. Acts 19:21). This data in Romans can be found in other parts of Paul's letters and personal history. There can be no doubt that the author of this Epistle is none other than Paul the apostle.

City of Rome

The founding of the city in 753 B.C. is based more upon fanciful myth than objective history. Tradition states that it was started by Romulus, a son of Mars, who was preserved physically both by a wolf and a shepherd's wife after he was forced out of his house by wicked relatives. He became its first king and thus began that early monarchy. Later the city was named after him.

The city was located on swampy ground beside the Tiber, a river in Italy that flows into the Mediterranean Sea. The city itself was about fifteen miles from the sea. Over several years many hills or mounts were constructed and settled so that it came to be known as the "city of seven hills." These hills bear the following names: Palatine, Capitoline, Quirinal, Caelian, Aventine, Esquiline, and Viminal. Later these hills were enclosed by a stone wall.

By New Testament times the city had grown to a population well over a million (some have placed it as high as four million), the majority of which were slaves. As the center of the Roman empire, it attracted all kinds of people and religions. There were an estimated 420 temples there, dedicated not only to the gods of the Romans but also to the gods of the people that the Romans had conquered. The wealth of the city could also be seen in the magnificent buildings constructed throughout its borders. There was even a sizeable colony of Jews in Rome, probably brought there through the Palestinian conquests of Pompey.

Time and Place

When Paul wrote Romans, he was about to go to Jerusalem with the contribution of the Greek churches for the poor saints in the holy city (15:25-26). This means that he must have written this letter after the two Corinthian Epistles. Near the end of his three-year ministry at Ephesus during his third journey, he wrote First Corinthians in which he gave instructions for the collection (I Cor. 16:1-9). When he left Ephesus, he went into Macedonia (Acts 20:1; I Cor. 16:5). He apparently wrote Second Corinthians at this time because he informed the Corinthian church that he was bringing Macedonians with him and that he did not want the church to be unprepared at their arrival (II Cor. 9:1-5). Paul then moved from Macedonia into Greece or Achaia, the province in which Corinth was located, where he stayed for three months (Acts 20:1-3). Since his original purpose was to sail from Greece for Jerusalem via Syria (Acts 20:3), it must be that Paul wrote Romans during his brief stay at Corinth, probably about A.D. 55-56.

Third Journey Acts 18:23 - 21:17.

The Appian Way, near Rome.

This position is further supported by the fact that Paul commended to the Roman church Phebe, a deaconess in the church at Cenchrea, the seaport of Corinth (16:1-2). Since she is mentioned first in this long chapter of names, Phebe probably carried the letter from Paul to Rome. Paul also wrote: "Gaius mine host, and of the whole church, saluteth you. Erastus the chamberlain of the city saluteth you" (16:23). Since Gaius was a Corinthian convert (I Cor. 1:14) and since Erastus is later mentioned as a Corinthian inhabitant (II Tim. 4:20), Paul must have been in Corinth at the time of writing.

There is an alternate theory that suggests the place to be Philippi shortly before Paul sailed for Troas (Acts 20:5-6). It is true that Paul had to abandon his plans of sailing from Greece because of a Jewish plot against his life and that he subsequently returned to Macedonia before departing for Asia Minor and Jerusalem (Acts 20:3-4). However, his plan to go to Jerusalem fits more into his intended purpose to sail from Greece rather than into a pressured unintended change of plans. Also, the way in which he refers to the Greek collection (". . . of Macedonia and Achaia"; 15:26) implies that he was in Achaia at the time of writing, otherwise he would have reversed the order. The mention of Illyricum (15:19) does not mean that Paul had to be in the adjacent section of Macedonia at the time of writing; it only signified to the Roman church that he had gone as far north in his evangelism as he planned and that he now wanted to move westward toward Rome and Spain. Although the Philippi theory has a plausible ring to it, the traditional view of Corinth fits best into the existing evidence.

Purposes

If Galatians has been called the Magna Charta of freedom from legalism, then Romans must be regarded as the Constitution of Biblical Christianity. It was not designed as a tract for sinners, but as a doctrinal treatise to expound the complexities of the faith. These two verses (1:16-17) give the gist or essence of Paul's theme:

> For I am not ashamed of the gospel of Christ: for it is the power of God unto salvation to everyone that believeth; to the Jew first, and also to the Greek. For therein is the righteousness of God revealed from faith to faith: as it is written, The just shall live by faith.

The righteousness of God, as revealed in the gospel message, is based upon the faith principle from the beginning to the end. Sinners are not only saved or justified by faith in Christ, but justified men must also walk daily by faith. In his exposition Paul deals with the great doctrinal words of the evangelical Christian faith: gospel, resurrection, salvation, belief, faith, righteousness, wrath, judgment, repentance, sin, law, guilt, justification, redemption, propitiation, grace, imputation, peace, reconciliation, atonement, death, sanctification, adoption, glorification, hope, election, foreknowledge, predestination, and purpose. The following chart shows how Paul developed his general theme:

Plan of Redemption (chs. 1–8)	1:1–5:21 6:1–8:17 8:18-39	Justification (past penalty) Sanctification (present power) Glorification (future presence)
Israel (chs. 9–11)	9:1–11:36	
Application (chs. 12–15)	12:1-21 13:1-14 14:1–15:13	Church State Liberty
Conclusion (chs. 15–16)	15:14–16:27	

The first eight chapters manifest God's magnificent plan of redemption. First, Paul shows how a lost, guilty man can receive the righteousness of Christ, be given a justified standing before God, and thus forever be delivered from the penalty of sin. Then he reveals how a saved man can gain the sanctified life or victory over the power of the indwelling sin nature through the enabling ministry of the Holy Spirit. Finally, he demonstrates how the believer will eventually be delivered from the presence of sin through the change of his mortal, corruptible body into a glorified state.

A second general purpose in writing was to explain how the present plan of God in blessing mostly Gentiles could be harmonized with the unconditional covenant promises given to Israel. How could the Gentiles be absolutely sure that God would complete His announced program for them when He had not yet fulfilled the promises given to ancient Israel? Paul undertakes to answer this critical question in the second section (chs. 9-11).

Positional truth must be put into practice; therefore, Paul ended his teaching by showing how the righteousness of God could be applied to the daily walk of the believer. His triple thrust included the Christian's relationship to other Christians in the life of the local church (12:1-21), his attitudes toward the unsaved, especially government leaders, within society (13:1-14) and his deportment in those areas not specifically spelled out in Scripture (14:1—15:13).

Paul also wanted to inform the Roman Christians of his future plans to visit them after his trip of benevolence to Jerusalem was over (1:10-12; 15:22-32). Apparently he had tried to visit Rome several times before, but he had been prevented from doing so (1:13; 15:22).

In his closing remarks it was his desire to commend Phebe, his lady ambassador to Rome (16:1-2), and to send greetings to many of his spiritual acquaintances residing in Rome (16:3-16).

Some have wondered why Paul wrote such a lengthy letter to a church that he planned to visit in the near future. However, his Corinthian correspondence also was sent prior to a visit, involving an interval of time much shorter than that between the letter to the Romans and his trip to Rome. Actually, Paul was laying the groundwork for the western expansion of the gospel by establishing rapport with this strategic church. Perhaps he hoped that the Roman church would finance his proposed evangelization of Spain ("Whensoever I take my journey into Spain, I will come to you . . . and to be brought on my way thitherward by you" (15:24). Paul did have some apprehension over his reception in Jerusalem (15:31), knowing full well that his plans to go to Rome could be delayed indefinitely. Actually, this did occur, and he arrived at Rome as a prisoner some three years later. Since Rome was on the western edge of missionary expansion and had not yet had the benefit of direct apostolic teaching, either in oral or written form, there was a need for him to write in depth.

Distinctive Features

The Epistles are unique pieces of ancient literature. In the secular world of the New Testament era, the average letter contained about 1300 words, whereas the Epistles contained many more. The Pauline range extends from 335 words in Philemon to 7101 words in Romans. Thus, Romans is the longest of Paul's Epistles.

In fact, most of the New Testament books (twenty-one) are Epistles. In one sense, Revelation could even be classified among them since it was sent to the seven churches of Asia and includes seven "mini-letters" within the body of the text. This takes on significance when one realizes that there are no epistles found within the Old Testament canon.

The composition and sending of an epistle usually involved four people: author, secretary or amanuensis, messenger-mailman, and recipient. Because of his poor eyesight (Gal. 4:13-15; 6:11), Paul probably used amanuenses on several occasions. In all of his letters, he would write personally the closing lines in order to authenticate the contents of the book (I Cor. 16:21; Col. 4:18; II Thess. 3:17; Philem. v. 19). Some believe that Paul wrote the entire Book of Galatians under much physical hardship to himself, but others still contend that he wrote only the conclusion (Gal. 6:11-18). Tertius was the secretary employed for Romans (16:22); Peter used Silvanus for the composition of his First Epistle (I Peter 5:12).

The Book of Romans provides an excellent model for studying Paul's literary style. Usually his Epistles follow this format: an opening greeting or salutation, followed by a prayer of thanksgiving for the readers; an exposition of doctrinal truth, followed by specific applications to the lives of the readers; a conclusion with greetings, personal messages, and a bequest of grace.

The use of the first person plural pronouns (we, us, our) has stimulated some speculation. Did Paul use the editorial "we" in reference to only himself or did he include his associates (e.g., Silas, Luke) or did he refer to himself and to the amanuensis? Actually, one cannot have a firm opinion here because each use must be studied within its own context.

Christians should know where to find key doctrinal chapters or passages in the Scriptures, and Romans is a treasure house of those: the lost state of the heathen who have rejected and perverted the general revelation of God in nature (1:18-32); the faulty condition of man's conscience as a moral guide (2:1-16); total depravity, or the guilty standing of all sinners (3:9-20, 23); man's moral relationship to Adam (5:12-21); the believer's identification with Jesus Christ in His death and resurrection (6:1-11); the struggle of the two natures in the life of a Christian (7:7-25); the plan of redemption (8:28-39); the explanation of Israel's unbelief (9:1—11:36); the necessity of dedication (12:1-2); the relationship of the believer to government (13:1-7); and the principles of Christian liberty (14:1—15:3).

It should also be observed that Romans makes great use of the Old Testament. Paul initially declares that the gospel of God concerning the person and redemptive work of Christ was "promised afore by his prophets in the holy scriptures" (1:2). Of all the Old Testament quotations in Paul's writings, more than half of them are found in this book. No one could accuse Paul of destroying either the law or the prophets.

Unity of the Epistle

Some critics have attacked the integrity or unity of this Epistle by stating that all or parts of the last two chapters were not written by Paul and thus were not part of the original letter. According to them, there is no strong indication as to who made the addition or when it was done. This view is highly speculative. Actually, the content of 15:1-13 is necessary as a fitting conclusion to the principles of liberty deliberated earlier (14:1-23). Also, Paul's travel plans (15:14-33) correspond to other authoritative passages (Acts 19:21; 24:17; I Cor. 16:1-4; II Cor. 8-9). About three hundred extant Greek manuscripts of Romans include these chapters as part of the whole. There is no objective, manuscript proof for this theory of addition.

A slight abridgement of this critical view states that the closing chapter actually formed a part of a letter commending Phebe to the Ephesian church. Since it is known that Paul spent three years at Ephesus and that Aquila and Priscilla were pillars in that church (Acts 18:18-19, 24-27; cf. Rom. 16:3-5), they argue that Paul must have sent Phebe to Ephesus. The argument asks, how could Paul know so many people in Rome when he had not yet visited that city? However, it must be remembered that Aquila and Priscilla were originally from Rome and that they were forced to leave because of Claudius' decree (Acts 18:2). It is very likely that they returned to Rome after the death of Claudius and after their work in Corinth and Ephesus was over. Perhaps they went to Rome in anticipation of Paul's proposed trip to the capital. Since Paul traveled frequently among the churches and kept in constant communication with them, he would have known whether any of his friends and/or converts had gone to Rome. Thus, it would have been very natural to greet them.

Establishment of the Church

At the time Paul wrote, the church at Rome must have been in existence for some time. The fact that he had a desire for *many* years to visit it would confirm that statement (1:13; 15:23). Since the faith of the Roman Christians was "spoken of throughout the whole world" (1:8), years would have been needed to accomplish that outreach. Some have suggested that believers were among those Jews expelled from Rome by Claudius (A.D. 49; Acts 18:2). An early tradition states that they were driven out over rioting caused by a certain "Chrestus." Does this name refer to an unidentified Roman or to Jesus Christ? The latter is a distinct possibility.

The church was composed mainly of Gentile converts with a modest sprinkling of Jewish saints. The greeting list included Jewish, Roman, and Greek names (16:3-15). Paul clearly wrote: "For I speak to you Gentiles, inasmuch as I am the apostle of the Gentiles" (11:13). Other statements imply a large Gentile membership (1:5, 6, 13; 15:5, 6, 16, 18). He referred to the Jews as "my brethren, my kinsmen" (9:3), not as *ours,* which would have been the case if the readers were mostly Jewish. However, he does seemingly identify himself with some of his readers as being mutually Jewish (2:16-17; cf. 3:9; 4:1).

Although the real origin of this church is basically unknown, four strong possibilities have been suggested. The first is that Roman pilgrims, both Jews and Gentile proselytes, who were converted under Peter's preaching on the day of Pentecost returned to their city and founded the church (Acts 2:10). The second is that Aquila and Priscilla, upon their return to Rome, started the work through lay evangelism (Acts 18:2; cf. Rom. 16:3-5). The official position of the Roman Catholic Church is that the apostle Peter traveled to Rome and established the church there[2] during a lengthy ministry, perhaps twenty years or more. The fourth view is that the converts of Paul from Asia Minor and Greece won during his three journeys moved to Rome and congregated themselves into a local church because of their common faith.

This last view seems to be the most plausible for the following reasons. During the years A.D. 30-44, Peter's activities were confined mainly to Jews in Palestine (Acts 1-12). When Paul wrote Galatians (A.D. 48-49), it was generally recognized that God had called him to a ministry among the Gentiles and that Peter's labor was to the Jews (Gal. 2:7-9). On several occasions Peter was reluctant to associate himself with Gentiles (Acts 10; Gal. 2:11-14). Since the Roman church was predominantly Gentile, it would have been contrary to Peter's character and to his God-given sphere of ministry for him to have started it.

On the positive side, Paul openly declared his intention *not* to build on another man's foundation (Rom. 15:20). Now, if Peter or any other apostle had founded the Roman church, then why did Paul want to go to Rome? He stated: "For I long to see you, that I may impart unto you some spiritual gift, to the end ye may be established" (1:11). Why did Paul feel that he could give them something that Peter or any others could not? Did he believe that they had done a faulty or partial job? The only logical reason for his going was that his converts, so greeted by name (ch. 16), had founded the work and therefore he was the spiritual grandfather of the church. Since the church had never benefited from the direct, personal ministry of an apostle, he felt compelled to go.

When Paul greeted the Roman believers (Rom. 16), why did he omit Peter's name if the latter were there (A.D. 55-56)? Later, in the record of Paul arriving in Rome and staying for at least two years (A.D. 59-61), there is no mention that Peter was there. In the four Prison Epistles written at this time, Paul again did not refer to Peter. When Paul wrote II Timothy from Rome just before his martyrdom (A.D. 64-67), Peter's name is conspicuous by its absence. All of this inductive study adds up to the conclusion that the church was started indirectly by Paul through his converts.

---

2. This position contends that the authority supposedly invested in Peter (Matt. 16:17-18) was passed on to his successor after his death, that all popes have been in the line of apostolic succession, and that the Roman Catholic Church is the only true church in the world, the one established by Christ Himself.

Outline

SALUTATION AND THEME (1:1-17)
I. JUSTIFICATION (1:18—5:21)
    A. Its need (1:18—3:20)
        1. The guilt of the heathen (1:18-32)
        2. The guilt of the moralist (2:1-16)
        3. The guilt of the Jew (2:17—3:8)
        4. The guilt of the entire human race (3:9-20)
    B. Its provision (3:21-26)
    C. Its relationship to the law (3:27-31)
    D. Its illustrations (4:1-25)
    E. Its security (5:1-11)
    F. Its universal nature (5:12-21)
II. SANCTIFICATION (6:1—8:17)
    A. Its basis (6:1-14)
    B. Its principle (6:15-23)
    C. Its new relationship (7:1-25)
    D. Its power (8:1-17)
III. GLORIFICATION (8:18-39)
    A. Relationship to human sufferings (8:18-27)
    B. Relationship to divine purpose (8:28-39)
VI. ISRAEL'S DIVINE PURPOSE (9:1—11:36)
    A. Paul's concern for Israel (9:1-5)
    B. Her relationship to divine promise (9:6-13)
    C. Her relationship to divine justice (9.14-29)
    D. Her relationship to divine righteousness (9:30—10:21)
    E. Her relationship to divine election (11:1-10)
    F. Her relationship to Gentile blessing (11:11-22)
    G. Her future salvation (11:23-32)
    H. Paul's praise of divine wisdom (11:33-36)
V. APPLICATION OF RIGHTEOUSNESS (12:1—15:13)
    A. In the dedication of life (12:1-2)
    B. In the church (12:3-21)
    C. In the state (13:1-7)
    D. In society (13:8-14)
    E. In nonmoral issues (14:1—15:13)
VI. CONCLUSION (15:14—16:27)
    A. Paul's future plans (15:14-33)
    B. Paul's greetings (16:1-16)
    C. Paul's warning (16:17-27)

Survey

1:1-13

In his opening remarks, Paul identified himself in three ways: a servant, an apostle, and one separated unto the gospel. He declared that the gospel was promised in the Old Testament and that its message centered in the two natures of Jesus Christ as proven by His incarnation and resurrection. After greeting the Roman believers, Paul gave thanks for the universal testimony of their faith and revealed his desire to visit them.

1:14-17

The missionary heart of Paul can be seen in the famous three "I am's": "I am debtor . . . I am ready . . . I am not ashamed. . . ." He saw himself under moral obligation to proclaim the gospel to all classes of men. The cause-effect sequence of his motivation is revealed by the fourfold use of "for." Why was Paul ready to preach? *For* he was not ashamed of the gospel. Why was he not ashamed? *For* it is the power of God unto salvation. Why does it provide salvation? *For* in it the righteousness of God, received and nurtured by faith, is revealed. Why must the righteousness of God be received by faith? *For* all men stand condemned beneath the wrath of God.

1:18-32

In this next section (1:18—3:20), Paul demonstrated why the entire world is guilty before God. It is because all men have rejected some form of divine revelation. God's existence, power, intelligence, and deity can be known through nature (1:18-20; cf. Ps. 19:1),[3] but unsaved men held down the truth in unrighteousness, did not glorify God, were not thankful, became foolish, became idolatrous, and worshiped the creature instead of the creator. For this perversion they are without excuse. Divine retribution is seen in the thrice mention of "God gave them up" (1:24, 26, 28). Their hardened spiritual condition is illustrated in the closing verse of this section: "Who knowing the judgment of God, that they which commit such things are worthy of death, not only do the same, but have pleasure in them that do them."

2:1-16

The pagan moralist who criticizes the animistic heathen is just as guilty because he has rejected divine truth found in the image of God within himself. All men are moral personalities with an innate sense of oughtness, a sense of right and wrong as exhibited by the conscience. However, when they violate the moral law within their hearts, they blame their heredity or environment or rationalize their actions instead of repenting (2:15). These men will be divinely judged, without partiality, according to truth, their works, and the gospel (2:2, 6, 11, 16).

2:17—3:20

The Jew, who had the advantage of his religious and physical heritage plus the presence of oral and written divine revelation, is nevertheless no better in the sight of God because he likewise rejected His revelation. Thus, Paul proved "both Jews and Gentiles, that they are all under sin" (3:9). All men therefore are equal before God, equally guilty. They are

---

3. Called natural or general revelation by theologians.

all under the penalty, power, and presence of sin. Mankind is totally depraved. This means that all are as bad off as they can be, not that they are as bad as they can be. When men admit their guilt and inability to correct their spiritual condition, they are in a position to receive God's provision of righteousness.

3:21-31

Paul then argued that the reception of divine righteousness apart from human effort was even proved by the Old Testament (Gen. 15:6; Hab. 2:4). It can be received today through faith in Jesus Christ. This plan of salvation is for all men (heathen, Gentile, Jew) because all men are sinners and equally needy; God does not have two or three different plans to save different classes of men. It was because of Christ's redemptive death and resurrection, once anticipated but now fulfilled, that God could forgive sin and impute divine righteousness even in Old Testament times. God never gave the law that men might try to keep it and thereby gain eternal life; it was designed to reveal to men how sinful they were and how holy God was. When men saw that they were condemned by a broken law and cast themselves in faith upon a gracious, merciful God, then the purpose of the law was established in their lives.

4:1-25

To show that men have always been justified, or declared righteous, by faith, Paul selected two Old Testament characters. Abraham received the righteousness of God and the covenant promises on the basis of faith alone before the rite of circumcision was imposed upon him and before the law was given to Israel. Even after the law was given, David was justified by faith only. No works or law keeping has ever been added to the faith principle. Today, by faith only, men can receive God's righteousness "if we believe on him that raised up Jesus our Lord from the dead; who was delivered for our offences, and was raised again for our justification" (4:24-25).

5:1-11

Through justification by faith, a believer has an unalterable standing before God. He can rejoice in the fact that if God did so much for him when he was an ungodly sinner, He will do "much more" (5:9, 10) now that he is one of His children. Note the position enjoyed by every Christian: he is justified by faith, has peace with God, is standing in grace, experiences the presence of the love of God and the Holy Spirit in his heart, benefits from Christ's vicarious death, is justified by His blood, shall be saved from wrath through His resurrection life, is reconciled, and receives the Atonement.

5:12-21

Sin and death entered the world through Adam. All men spiritually lost are in Adam and are therefore condemned to both physical and spiritual death. Paul then contrasted this with the believer's position in Christ. In Christ one has the free gift of grace, justification, life, and righteousness. Men today in their spiritual standing are either in Adam, condemned, or in Christ, justified.

Having established how a guilty sinner could receive a justified standing before God, Paul then wanted his readers to know how they could put into daily practice their new position in Christ. Many believers who have been delivered from the penalty of sin have never enjoyed victory over the power of the indwelling sin nature or the sanctified life. To sanctify means to set apart. Initial sanctification is the act of God whereby He sets apart permanently the believing sinner from the world unto Himself (cf. I Cor. 1:2; 6:11; Heb. 10:14). This act entitles the believer to be called a saint, or a separated one.[4] His need now is progressive sanctification, the process by which he can be set apart from a sinful walk to a holy practice.

6:1-23

The problem that Paul dealt with in this next section (6:1—8:17) was: How can a saint become saintly? A secure spiritual standing should never issue in sinful license. Believers should know that they have been identified with Jesus Christ in His death and resurrection (cf. Gal. 2:20). When He died, they died in Him; when He arose, they arose in Him. Just as sin and death no longer have dominion over Him, neither do they over the believer. The Christian should believe to be true what is true (meaning of "reckon"). He should reckon himself as dead to sin and alive unto God and should yield himself completely to his new spiritual master. Christ's death not only removed the penalty of sin but also broke the power of the sin nature. Just as the believer was saved by faith in Christ's provision, so he may believe that His death has already destroyed the power of the indwelling sin principle. Human effort did not bring him justification nor will it produce sanctification. Once he was a slave to sin; now he should be a slave to righteousness.

7:1—8:17

The believer is not only free from the dominion of sin, but he is also released from any obligation to the Mosaic law through his new relationship with Christ. There was nothing wrong with the law; in fact, it was holy, just, and good (7:12). The law created an awareness of sin and a

---

4. "Saint" (*hagios*) and "to sanctify" (*hagiazo*) come from the same Greek stem or family of words.

sense of condemnation in the one who tried to keep it and failed. The problem was with man because in him there was no moral power to keep the law. This same dilemma exists in the life of the Christian who tries to please God daily in the energy of self; he only fails. Paul related this struggle between the two natures (old sin nature and new spiritual nature) from his own experience: "For the good that I would I do not: but the evil which I would not, that I do" (7:19). In this passage (7:15-25) note the excessive use of the first person singular personal pronoun (I, me) and the total absence of any mention of the Holy Spirit. When Paul could not satisfy the desires of the new nature in his own strength, he despaired; but then he learned the secret of spiritual success. Such desires could be fulfilled through the power of the indwelling Holy Spirit (8:1-17); note the frequent mention of the Spirit in this section.

8:18-27

A believer can possess the justified standing and enjoy a sanctified state, and yet suffer in a body subject to disease and destined to death. Until he receives the glorified, immortal, incorruptible body at the coming of Christ, he has not yet been delivered from the total effects of sin in his life. Glorification is the future aspect of the divine gift of salvation to us. When Christ returns, even creation will be delivered from the curse imposed upon it because of Adam's sin (Gen. 3:17-18; Isa. 11:1-9). Observe that the creation, the believer's body, and the indwelling Holy Spirit all groan in anticipation of the deliverance from physical suffering (8:22, 23, 26).

8:28-39

Paul saw glorification as the logical climax of God's eternal plan of redemption: foreknowledge, predestination, calling, justification, and glorification. The verbal tense[5] of the phrase "them he also glorified" is very significant. Since God "calleth those things which be not as though they were" (4:17), He views man's glorification as already accomplished because it is part of His unchanging decree, even though it is still future in time from man's perspective. This was why Paul could confidently assert: "And we know that all things work together for good to them that love God, to them who are the called according to his purpose" (8:28). Paul saw himself and all believers as constant objects of God's will. In a series of five questions and answers (8:31-39), Paul relates the argument that the free gift of salvation could never be taken away from the Christian because of the eternal extent of God's purpose, the fact that future sin cannot change the justified position of the believer,

---

5. Greek: aorist active indicative; signifies completed action in past time.

the reason that all condemnation has been removed through Christ's death, and the assurance that the child of God can never be separated from the love of God. In a word, the Christian is eternally secure.

Many view the next three chapters as parenthetically inserted between chapters 8 and 12; however, there is a logical connection between this section and the preceding eight chapters. In it Paul is anticipating a possible objection: How can the Gentiles know that they can trust God for the completion of His program for them (justification, sanctification, glorification) when His covenant promises to Israel have not yet been fulfilled? This was a fair question, and Paul proposed to resolve the difficulty.

9:1-13

First of all, Paul identified himself as a Jew with an intense spiritual burden for his fellow Jews in spite of the fact that the latter constantly persecuted him. He then listed a ninefold description of the Jewish nation that elevated her in spiritual privileges above any other people. However, Paul quickly observed: "For they are not all Israel, which are of Israel" (9:6). A true Israelite was one who was not only a physical descendant of Abraham (child of the flesh) but one who was also a spiritual child of Abraham through faith in Christ (child of the promise). Paul argued that the covenant promises were given only to the elect children of Abraham, i.e., his physical and spiritual posterity. These promises have always been kept. God's elective purposes were not determined by human choices, but by the divine will.

9:14-29

In the next few sections Paul carried on a rhetorical question-answer session with his readers. Throughout these paragraphs, he interrupted himself with questions introduced by phrases similar to this one: "What shall we say then?" (9:14; cf. 9:19, 30; 10:18, 19; 11:1, 7, 11, 19). First, he demonstrated that the sovereign actions of God were not unjust and were in perfect harmony with Old Testament declarations (9:14-18). God has a perfect right to do whatever He pleases because He is the Creator-God and man is His creature. Man has no right to question or to doubt His actions. His plan to set aside national Israel enabled Him to make Gentiles His "spiritual people" without violating the promises given to the elect remnant of Israel (9:19-29).

9:30—10:21

The reason why national Israel did not inherit the spiritual promises of the covenant was that she tried to gain the righteousness of God through works or human effort (9:32; 10:2-3). The righteousness demanded by the law can only be received through a believing confession

192

in the deity and redemptive work of Jesus Christ (10:4, 8-10). In a logical sequence of questions (10:13-15), Paul showed that men cannot call on Christ for salvation unless someone tells them about Him because "faith cometh by hearing, and hearing by the word of God" (10:17).

11:1-36

The question and answer: "Hath God cast away his people? . . . God hath not cast away his people which he foreknew" (11:1-2) are very important. Just as God has not cast away His elect, foreknown covenant nation even though her history was full of sin and unbelief, so God will not cast away an individual believer whom He has foreknown (cf. 8:29). Future conduct does not nullify God's unconditional promises and gifts. Even in the midst of this time of spiritual blessing upon Gentile peoples, there is a believing Jewish "remnant according to the election of grace" (11:1, 5). God sovereignly used the spiritual blindness of national Israel to accomplish the blessing of Gentiles (11:11), but one day Israel will again occupy the central position in God's redemptive program for the world (natural branches to be grafted back into the olive tree). The blindness of Israel is only partial (some Jews today are being saved) and temporary (until God's program for the church is completed; cf. 11:25). Then all Israel will be saved. In practice, the Jews of that generation were enemies, but in position, they were elect and beloved. Paul con-

A relief of the seven-branched candlestick, from a synagogue of New Testament times.

cluded: "For the gifts and calling of God are without repentance" (11:29). That means the eternal gift of salvation will never be taken back by God even though a believer may commit future sin. It also means that God will totally complete His program with Israel in spite of her present unfaithfulness. Paul ended this discourse on Israel by praising the wisdom of God for formulating such a gracious, intricate plan of redemption (11:33-36).

12:1-2

The admonition (12:1-2) forms the bridge between the doctrinal chapters (1-11) and the practical chapters (12-16).[6] Paul does not command; he beseeches. The connective "therefore" introduces a logical inference based upon the "mercies of God," the sovereign plan of God with its various gifts of salvation. The argument goes like this: If God has such an eternal, magnificent plan not only for individuals, but also for nations, then should not the believer yield himself completely to that God to run the daily details of his life? Only by so doing can he ever expect to know and to experience the will of God in his many involvements. If a Christian does not make this total dedication of life, then he will not be able to operate successfully in the areas mentioned in the next three chapters.

12:3-21

When a believer fully realizes that God was totally responsible for his salvation and commits his life to Him, then he will be in a frame of mind "not to think of himself more highly than he ought to think" (12:3). In the final analysis, all believers are sinners saved by divine grace. All believers are members of the spiritual body of Christ, the true church, and have been given differing functions to perform within that body. These functions are called gifts and are partially listed here: prophecy, ministry, teaching, exhortation, giving, ruling, and showing mercy. All believers in their relationships to one another in the body of Christ should manifest Christlike qualities in their deportment (12:9-21).

13:1-7

Since the power of government has been ordained of God and rulers have a ministry to perform for God, Paul charged that Christians should be obedient, submissive citizens. This passage elaborates upon Jesus' declaration: "Render therefore unto Caesar the things which are Caesar's" (Matt. 22:21). God established civil authority to be a terror or

---

6. Doctrine is practical and there is a doctrine of practice. However, since these terms are firmly fixed in the minds of most evangelicals, they are used here.

194

restraint to evil works, to punish evil doers, and to praise the good. As long as government operates in this realm, the believer must obey its dictates, not only to avoid punishment, but also to maintain a guiltless conscience for the sake of Christian testimony. This can be done by rendering tribute, custom, fear, and honor to those authorities who deserve it.

13:8-14

Believers also have responsibilities toward the unsaved within society. A person owes when he takes or borrows something without returning it; thus the Christian should not expect the world to give to him, but rather he should give to the world out of love. His testimony should be marked by spiritual alertness, moral purity, and an honest life. A Christ-filled life will not seek opportunities to gratify the desires of the sin nature.

14:1-12

Paul then gave guidelines as to how the justified person could apply the principles of righteousness to the area of Christian liberty. This deals with doubtful matters or nonmoral issues, those things which are neither forbidden in Scripture nor are morally impure in themselves. The attitudes in which they are done or not done and the effects caused by their doing do, however, involve moral choices. The problem at Rome dealt with the diet. Could a Christian eat meat taken from an animal that had been offered or dedicated to a pagan idol? Since the Roman believers differed on the issue, Paul developed three major principles that would solve the problem if observed with mutual love and respect.

The first was to recognize the existence of liberty in the area of nonmoral matters. Attitudes must not be critical. A believer ultimately is not responsible to another believer, but rather to his heavenly master. A Christian must have absolute conviction of heart that God has granted him permission to do a certain thing. In so doing he should be able to glorify and to thank Him. He should recognize that nothing is done in a spiritual vacuum, but that everything he does affects someone else. He should know that he will give account for his exercise of Christian liberty at the judgment seat of Christ.

14:13—15:3

The second was not to offend his brother in the exercise of his liberty. Instead of being critical of the other person's actions, the Christian should make sure that his life is above reproach. He should recognize that the source of moral defilement does not reside within the nonmoral matter itself, but in one's attitude toward it. Thus, he should not ask: "What's wrong with this?" Rather, he should ask: "What does my

195

brother think about this?" He should be careful not to weaken his brother's spiritual condition through his exercise of liberty. He should recognize that spirituality does not come from compliance to a list of Do's and Don'ts, but rather from a yielded life producing the fruit of the Holy Spirit. If there is a conflict between his liberty and his brother's opinion on the matter, he must be able to do it with a joyful spirit, free from any self-doubt or judgment. If he cannot do it in that way, he should not do it. The life of Christ should provide the perfect example of the proper use of rights. A believer should emulate Him by using his liberty for the edification of others, not for his own pleasure.

15:4-13

The third was to glorify God in his use of Christian liberty. Paul's conclusion was clear: "Wherefore receive ye one another, as Christ also received us to the glory of God" (15:7). When saved Jews and believing Gentiles join in harmonious praise of God, there will be less criticism of one another.

15:14-33

Paul then expressed his desire to the Roman church to visit them on his way to Spain. This he planned to do after he took the financial contribution of the Greek churches to the needy of the Jerusalem church. It was his goal to be a pioneer missionary and to evangelize the unreached regions of the world.

16:1-27

He then commended Phebe, the person who probably was Paul's courier, to the church. He then extended greetings to his many friends at Rome, including Aquila and Priscilla, whose home was the meeting place for the Roman Christians. He ended his greetings with a warning against false teachers, possibly the Judaizers who mixed law and grace (see Galatians). Paul then added the greetings of his co-workers to his blessing, including that of Tertius, his secretary. He ended the Epistle with a benediction exalting the gospel of salvation proclaimed by him.

Increase Your Learning

By Doing

1. In your Bibles underline the words "justify" and "righteousness" and their cognates wherever they are found in Romans.
2. From Romans make a list of the spiritual benefits received by the Christian at the very moment of salvation, and also after salvation.
3. In chapter 7 circle all references to the self; in chapter 8 circle all references to the Holy Spirit.

By Discussing

1. Is it fair for people who have never heard of Christ to go to hell? Are the heathen really lost? Can they be saved apart from the gospel message?
2. Can a Christian ever lose his salvation? Is he eternally secure no matter what he does after initial faith?
3. Can a person be a good Christian and anti-Semitic at the same time? What attitudes should exist between Gentile believers and Jews?
4. Apply the principles of Christian liberty to these controversial areas: movie attendance, card playing, mixed bathing, etc.

By Reading

Bruce, F. F. *The Epistle of Paul to the Romans.* Grand Rapids: Wm. B. Eerdmans Publishing Co., 1963.

Godet, F. *Commentary on Romans.* 2 vols. Grand Rapids: Zondervan Publishing House, 1956.

Murray, John. *The Epistle to the Romans.* 2 vols. Grand Rapids: Wm. B. Eerdmans Publishing Co., 1964.

Newell, William R. *Romans Verse by Verse.* Chicago: Moody Press, 1938.

Stifler, James. *The Epistle to the Romans.* Westwood, N.J.: Fleming H. Revell Co., 1897.

10

FIRST CORINTHIANS

Writer

Very little question is raised about the Pauline authorship of this book. Both at the beginning and end of the book, the author identified himself as Paul (1:1; 16:21). He claimed to be an apostle (1:1; 4:9; 9:1; 15:9) and to have seen the resurrected Christ (9:1; 15:8). Both of these assertions correspond to Paul's life history, recorded both by him elsewhere (Gal. 1:1, 12) and by Luke (Acts 9:1-16; 14:14). He looked upon Timothy in a spiritual father-son relationship (4:17; cf. I Tim. 1:2). He used himself and Apollos, both prominent in the establishment of the Corinthian church, as illustrations of the proper functions of ministers (1:12; 3:4-5; 4:6; cf. Acts 18:24-28). Finally, he disclosed that he had preached in Corinth (2:1-5) and that he had laid the foundation of the church (3:10). This could only refer to Paul's visit to Corinth during his second missionary journey (Acts 18:1-18). All of these points, added up together, make a strong case for Pauline authorship.

The writings of these Church Fathers confirm the early tradition that this book was canonical and written by Paul: Clement of Rome, Didache, Polycarp, Justin Martyr, Irenaeus, Ignatius, Clement of Alexandria, and Tertullian. A full description of Paul's life was discussed earlier (see pp. 176-79).

City of Corinth

A check of the map will show that Corinth was located on a narrow strip of land, called an isthmus, connecting the Peloponnesus with northern Greece. This isthmus also formed the land bridge between the

198

The Corinth Canal, near the site of ancient Corinth. The canal, completed in 1893, was partially excavated in ancient times under Nero with forced labor including Jewish captives.

Aegean and the Adriatic seas. Located forty miles west of Athens, Corinth was the capital of this southern province called Achaia. The Romans had destroyed the city in 146 B.C., but because its location was so important, they later rebuilt it under Julius Caesar in 46 B.C. By the time Paul arrived in the city (A.D. 50-52), the city had grown to a population of 500,000. Today only the ruins of the city remain.

In that day Corinth was the crossroads for travel and commerce, both north and south for the Greek peninsula and east and west from Rome to the Near East. It had two seaports, Cenchrea on the Aegean Sea to the east and Lechaeum on the edge of the Gulf of Corinth to the west. Commercial ships, instead of sailing around the dangerous southern tip of Greece, were portaged across the isthmus from one port to the other. This saved time and was less risky. Thus Corinth became a city of wealth and pleasure. People went there with money to spend and to indulge themselves in varied pleasures.

On the highest point in the city stood the pagan temple of Aphrodite, the goddess of love, full of religious prostitutes to serve the wishes of its devotees. These women also entertained in the night life of the city. Also located at Corinth was a stadium where athletic contests, next best to the Greek Olympics, were held every two years. Although Corinth was influenced by the philosophy of Athens, it never became a center of intellectual learning. The citizens and the tourists were too busy making and spending money to do much rationalistic speculation. Because it was a mercantile center, all kinds of people settled there: Romans, Greeks, and Jews. Corinth became a cosmopolitan city with all of the attending vices attached to that type of society.

Establishment of the Church

The founding of the Corinthian church was recorded by Luke in Acts (18:1-18). From Athens Paul had sent his associates Silas and Timothy back to the Macedonian churches at Philippi, Thessalonica, and Berea (Acts 17:15-16; cf. I Thess. 3:1-6), started earlier on this same second missionary journey. When Paul therefore left Athens for Corinth, he went alone. Cut off from his friends and supporting churches, Paul worked in tentmaking, a craft he had learned as a youth, to meet his financial needs. He found both work and lodging with a Jewish couple,[1] Aquila and Priscilla, who practiced this same craft and who had been expelled from Rome because of the anti-Semitic decree of Caesar Claudius. Perhaps through personal conversation with Paul and his subsequent synagogue preaching, this couple came to know Jesus Christ as their Messiah and Savior. During the week, Paul worked with his hands, but every Sabbath he was in the synagogue, logically proving from the Old Testament that the promised Messiah had to suffer death and to be raised from the dead and that Jesus was indeed that promised Savior (cf. Acts 17:2-3). Many in attendance, both Jews and Gentile proselytes to the Jewish religion, were convinced and believed. When Silas and Timothy joined Paul at Corinth with a good report of the faith and stedfastness of the Macedonian Christians, Paul was constrained to press the claims of Jesus Christ more strongly upon his synagogue listeners. When this occurred, the Jews resisted and blasphemed, forcing Paul to leave the synagogue with this declaration: "Your blood be upon your own heads; I am clean; from henceforth I will go unto the Gentiles" (18:6). It was also about this time that Paul wrote First Thessalonians, based upon the content of Timothy's report.

Paul then moved his ministry into the house of Justus which was adjacent to the Jewish synagogue. Soon after, the chief ruler of the synagogue, Crispus, along with his family, believed. From this new site,

---

1. It may be that only Aquila was a Jew and that his wife was a Gentile. Because of the marital union, she would have been forced to leave also.

a ministry to the pagan, idolatrous Corinthians was begun with much success. The opposition must have been intense at that time because Paul received special encouragement from God. He was informed that he would not suffer bodily harm and that many would be converted through his ministry. Paul then labored for eighteen months (A.D. 50-52) both as an evangelist and as a teacher of the new congregation.

In the midst of his ministry, the Jews brought charges against Paul before Gallio, the political deputy or proconsul of Achaia. Since the accusations were religious and not political in nature, Gallio refused to arbitrate the matter. In driving the Jews from the judgment seat, Gallio declared the innocence of Paul and recognized the troublesome character of the Jews. Later the Gentile proselytes to Judaism smote Sosthenes, the chief ruler of the synagogue, who probably was a Gentile himself and a recent convert to Christianity; again, Gallio reacted negatively.

Even after this burst of persecution, Paul remained a "good while" in Corinth. With Aquila and Priscilla he then left Corinth and set sail for Antioch in Syria via Ephesus.

Time and Place

Paul left Aquila and Priscilla at Ephesus and sailed for Caesarea (Acts 18.18-22). On his arrival he visited the Jerusalem church and then returned to his home church at Antioch. After spending "some time there, he departed, and went over all the country of Galatia and Phrygia in order, strengthening all the disciples" (18:23). Thus began his third missionary journey. During this period of Paul's absence from Ephesus, Apollos, an eloquent Jewish teacher of the doctrine of John the Baptist, came to that city and was led to a knowledge of Christ by Aquila and Priscilla. With his new faith Apollos traveled to Corinth in Achaia where he was received by the Corinthian believers and where he had a successful public ministry among the Jews (Acts 18:24-28).

While Apollos was in Corinth, Paul reached Ephesus where he would minister for the next three years (A.D. 52-55; Acts 19:1-10; 20:31). Many believe that Paul, either before or shortly after reaching Ephesus, wrote a short letter to the Corinthian church concerning the problem of fornication (I Cor. 5:9; to be discussed, p. 208-09). About this time, because of increasing factionalism in the Corinthian church, Apollos left that city and returned to Ephesus (I Cor. 1:12; 16:12). Some have suggested that Paul made a quick, personal visit to Corinth to arbitrate the controversy but was unsuccessful (II Cor. 2:1; 12:14).[2] Since

---

2. The argument goes like this: Paul's first visit to the city could not be characterized as a coming "in heaviness" (Acts 18:1-18; cf. II Cor. 2:1). Since Paul was in Ephesus when he wrote the first letter and in Macedonia

201

Corinth was only two hundred miles west across the Aegean Sea from Ephesus, travel and communication between the two cities was easy.

The situation at Corinth continued to deteriorate. Members of the household of Chloe brought a firsthand report of the divisions within the assembly (I Cor. 1:11).[3] They were followed by three members of the Corinthian church (Stephanas, Fortunatus, and Achaicus) who brought Paul a financial gift (16:17). Perhaps they also carried to Paul a letter from the church in which questions were asked about various doctrinal and moral issues (7:1). Thus, through personal conversations with Apollos, the Chloe household, and the three church emissaries plus the content of the letter, Paul learned about the troubled state of the Corinthian church. Unable to leave Ephesus at that time (16:3-9), Paul did the next best thing; he wrote this letter to resolve the many problems. It was probably written near the end of his ministry at Ephesus because he had already made plans for leaving the province of Asia (16:5-7). Thus, it was composed during the fall or winter of A.D. 55 because he said that he would stay at Ephesus until Pentecost (16:8).

Who took the letter from Paul to Corinth? It is difficult to be positive here. Some speculation has centered around Timothy, but would Paul have written "Now if Timotheus comes" (16:10) if he had planned to send the letter by him? Timothy did leave Ephesus for Macedonia (Acts 19:22) probably before Paul wrote the letter. It may be that Paul was informing the Corinthian church that Timothy might visit it after his ministry in Macedonia was over. Paul did want to send Apollos back to Corinth, but he refused to go (16:12). It may be that the return of the three church members afforded Paul the chance to send the Epistle back with them (16:12; cf. 16:17-18). This latter view seems to be the most plausible.

Purposes

The purposes are very clear. First, Paul wanted to correct the problems mentioned to him in the personal reports (chs. 1-6). He rebuked the existence of church factions and tried to bring unity out of division (1:10—4:21). He introduced this section with these words:

> Now I beseech you, brethren, by the name of our Lord Jesus Christ, that ye all speak the same thing, and that there be no divisions among you; but that ye be perfectly joined together in the same mind and in the same judgment. For it hath been declared

when he penned the second, the anticipated "third" visit implies a second that was not recorded in Acts (II Cor. 12:14).

3. It is not clear whether Chloe resided in Corinth or in Ephesus. They could have gone from Ephesus to Corinth, seen the situation, and returned to Ephesus. Or, they may have made a special trip from Corinth to Ephesus to inform Paul, and then returned to Corinth.

unto me of you, my brethren, by them which are of the house of Chloe, that there are contentions among you (1:10-11).

He then attempted to discipline *in absentia* the fornicators in their midst (5:1-13). This problem was introduced in this way: "It is reported commonly that there is fornication among you . . ." (5:1). Apparently, all visitors to Paul from Corinth brought news of this incest. He also tried to prevent warring church members from going to civil court against each other (6:1-8). To those who abused themselves sexually, he taught the sanctity of the believer's body (6:9-20).

Second, the rest of the book deals with the questions raised in the letter: "Now concerning the things whereof ye wrote unto me" (7:1). With that letter probably before him, Paul logically moved from one issue to another. He marked his movement and change of subject with the key introductory word "Now" (7:1, 25; 8:1; 11:2, 17; 12:1; 15:12; 16:1). He answered their questions concerning the necessity and the problems of marriage (7:1-24), the status of virgins and widows (7:25-40), the application of Christian liberty to the eating of meat sacrificed to idols (8:1—11:1), the conduct of women in the church (11:2-16), the order of the communion service (11:17-34), the nature and use of spiritual gifts, especially those of tongues speaking and prophecy (12:1—14:40), the necessity and nature of the resurrection body (15:1-58), and the financial collection for the poor saints at Jerusalem (16:1-4).

In addition, he wanted to announce to them his plans to visit Corinth after a tour of the Macedonian churches (16:5-18). He then closed by extending greetings to them from the Asian churches and brethren (16:19-24).

Lost Letter

In 5:9 Paul penned: "I wrote unto you in an epistle not to company with fornicators." Does this statement mean that Paul had sent a short letter to the Corinthian church before his composition of this First Epistle? If so, what happened to it and what did it contain? Was it an inspired letter or simply human correspondence? These are difficult questions with no easy answers, but there are two plausible alternatives. If Paul did write it, its theme was the relationship of Christians to fornicators. Apparently the Corinthians misunderstood Paul's teaching and thought that they should be separate from all immoral men. However, in this section (5:1-13) Paul corrected that notion by calling for separation only from professing believers who practiced fornication or other public sins; he did not mean that they should disassociate themselves from the unsaved fornicators. If this alternative is true, the content of the original letter was summarized and incorporated into this section (5:1-13); in which case, the church is not lacking any inscripturated

This diagram provides a synthetic view of the entire book:

Introduction	1:1-9	
Personal Reports	1:10—4:21	Divisions
	5:1-13	Fornication
	6:1-8	Lawsuits
	6:9-20	Body Purity
Letter	7:1-24	Marriage
	7:25-40	Virgins
	8:1—11:1	Christian liberty
	11:2-16	Women
	11:17-34	Lord's Supper
	12:1—14:40	Gifts
	15:1-58	Resurrection
	16:1-4	Collection
Conclusion	16:5-24	

book or truth. This "lost letter" may also have included Paul's plans for a return visit to Corinth (cf. II Cor. 1:15-16) and instructions for Corinthians' part in the collection for the Jerusalem saints (II Cor. 8:6, 10; 9:1-2). Even if this letter did exist and became lost, such a situation is by no means unique. After the council at Jerusalem was over, the church leaders wrote letters to the Gentile churches informing the latter of their decisions (Acts 15:20, 23-27); none of these letters has ever been found. However, the content of those letters was incorporated into Luke's record of those proceedings. The letter that the Corinthians wrote to Paul (7:1) is also lost, but the content of that letter is revealed in the answers given by Paul (7:1—16:4).

The second alternative is that 5:9 does not refer to a former letter, but to the Epistle Paul was presently writing. The verb "wrote" *(egrapsa)* would be regarded as an epistolary usage[4] of the Greek aorist tense (same word occurs in 5:11, translated "have written"). This means that Paul looked at his present discussion of fornication from the viewpoint of the Corinthian readers. At the time they would read it, his writing of it would be in the past. This is why he used a past verbal tense ("wrote") rather than the present ("write"). It is difficult to be positive here, but either alternative is an acceptable evangelical option.

Some liberals, who accept the thesis of a lost letter, actually believe

4. Consult H. E. Dana and Julius R. Mantey, *A Manual Grammar of the Greek New Testament* (New York: Macmillan, 1953), p. 198.

that parts of this lost letter can be seen in both Epistles (I Cor. 6:12-20; II Cor. 6:14—7:1). However, this theory rests merely upon subjective speculation, not upon objective, external or textual evidence for its support. The first passage deals with the believer's relationship to his own body, and the second warns against involvement with unbelievers rather than against involvement with professing believers who are guilty of sexual sins. They treat different subjects than that in the passage under discussion (5:1-13).

Outline

SALUTATION (1:1-9)

I. REPLY TO PERSONAL REPORT (1:10—6:20)
   A. Correction of church divisions (1:10—4:21)
      1. By a true concept of salvation (1:10-25)
      2. By an honest evaluation of their past (1:26-31)
      3. By an understanding of the ministry of the Holy Spirit (2:1-13)
      4. By a knowledge of carnality and spirituality (2:14—3:3)
      5. By an appreciation of the total ministry (3:4—4:21)
   B. Discipline of fornication (5:1-13)
   C. Criticism of lawsuits (6:1-8)
   D. Criticism of sexual abuse (6:9-20)

II. REPLY TO QUESTIONS IN THEIR LETTER (7:1—16:4)
   A. Concerning marriage (7:1-24)
   B. Concerning virgins (7:25-40)
   C. Concerning things sacrificed to idols (8:1—11:1)
      1. The problem (8:1-13)
      2. The rights of ministers (9:1-27)
      3. The lessons of the past (10:1-22)
      4. The principles of liberty (10:23—11:1)
   D. Concerning problems of worship (11:2-34)
      1. The veiling of women (11:2-16)
      2. The Lord's Supper (11:17-34)
   E. Concerning spiritual gifts (12:1—14:40)
      1. List of gifts (12:1-11)
      2. Need of gifts (12:12-31)
      3. Exercise of gifts (13:1-13)
      4. Contrast between prophecy and tongues (14:1-40)
   F. Concerning the resurrection (15:1-58)
      1. Part of the gospel (15:1-11)
      2. Necessity of Christ's resurrection (15:12-34)
      3. Nature of the resurrection body (15:35-50)
      4. Time of the resurrection (15:51-58)
   G. Concerning the collection (16:1-4)

CLOSING REMARKS AND GREETINGS (16:5-24)

Survey

1:1-9

Although the Corinthians were saturated with spiritual problems, Paul addressed them as sanctified ones or saints.[5] Their position in Christ had not changed even though their practice needed correction. They possessed a unity in Him that should have been manifested in their local church life but was not. He then thanked God that they had been endowed with all the spiritual gifts (cf. chs. 12-14) by the grace of Christ and that they expected His return. Before correction and criticism, he gave commendation.

1:10-17

On the basis of their same spiritual standing and hope, Paul appealed to them to strive for unity. The house of Chloe had informed him that there were divisions within the church, caused not by heretical doctrine but through the exaltation of human leaders: "Now this I say, that every one of you saith, I am of Paul; and I of Apollos; and I of Cephas; and I of Christ" (1:12). This does not mean that the Corinthians were divided into four groups following these four mentioned individuals. Later Paul wrote: "And these things, brethren, I have in a figure transferred to myself and to Apollos for your sakes . . ." (4:6). Paul chose not to identify the Corinthian leaders by name; rather he transferred the allegiance given to them to Christ, Peter, Apollos, and himself. In expressing thanks that he had not baptized more Corinthian converts,

---

5. *Hegiasmenois* ("to them that are sanctified") and *hagiois* ("saints") are based on the same Greek stem.

Fountainhead of Peirene at Corinth.

he did not deprecate the ordinance of water baptism, but rather he did not want men to exalt him for that personal involvement in their lives.

1:18-25

When men exalt other men, the former invariably exalt what the others know and/or their ability to communicate what they know. Paul tried to show that the wisdom of words, of the wise, and of the world was not responsible for their salvation, but that the gospel message of Christ's crucifixion saved them. To unsaved Jews who wanted a sign-miracle, this was a stumblingblock; to Greeks who wanted a philosophical presentation, this was foolishness; but to saved Jews and Gentiles, it manifested the power and wisdom of God.

1:26-31

Paul also reminded them that God did not save them because of who they were. He delighted to make "somebodies" out of "nobodies" so that the recipients of His creative grace would glory in Him, not in their station of life, either past, present, or future. To confound the wise, mighty, and noble, He chose the foolish, weak, base, and despised, and the things which are not. All spiritual possessions (wisdom, righteousness, sanctification, and redemption) have been made or imputed to us because of our position in Christ, not because of our human status.

2:1-8

Paul then reminded them of the methods employed by him when he evangelized them. His presentation was not marked by overwhelming human oratory or philosophical logic, but by human insufficiency and total dependence upon the Holy Spirit. Thus, their conversion by faith did not stand "in the wisdom of men, but in the power of God." In no way could they exalt the ability of Paul as the reason they accepted Christ.

2:9-13

Paul further explained that spiritual truth is only taught by the Holy Spirit to hearts that are open to Him. Mere human wisdom could not anticipate, let alone understand, divine truth. This truth must be revealed, and God has revealed it through the oral preaching and the inscripturated books of the apostles and prophets. This revelation was done and supervised *by His Spirit;* therefore, the believer has received the indwelling, teaching presence of the Holy Spirit in order to "know the things that are freely given to us of God." Paul was effective among the Corinthians because he spoke "not in the words which man's wisdom teacheth, but which the Holy Spirit teacheth." This passage therefore teaches that the divine works of revelation (2:10), inspiration (2:13), and illumination

(2:12) are accomplished by the Holy Spirit through men; thus He, not the human instrument, should be praised.

2:14—3:3

Paul then divided all men into three categories: natural, spiritual, and carnal. The natural man is the unsaved man who cannot perceive spiritual truth because he has no inner capacity to receive it; he is void of the indwelling presence of the Holy Spirit. The spiritual man is not only saved, but is yielded to the teaching ministry of this indwelling Spirit; thus he is in a position to receive all spiritual truth in which the Spirit chooses to instruct him. The carnal man is also saved, but he is not yielded to the Spirit; thus, because he is not in a position to be taught by Him, he will think and behave like an unsaved man. The church divisions at Corinth were no doubt caused by the presence of all three classes of men, especially the carnal Christians, within their ranks.

3:4-7

Following human leaders is an expression of carnality. Such actions fail to realize the real purpose of the ministry: "Who then is Paul, and who is Apollos, but ministers by whom ye believed, even as the Lord gave to every man?" (3:5). Ministers should not compete with each other, but they should complement each other. If anyone is saved and/or edified, it is because "God gave the increase"; no man can take the credit for that.

3:8—4:21

Paul reinforced this concept by equating the work of the ministry with the construction of a building. As the pioneer evangelist, he laid the foundation of the Corinthian church; those who ministered after him built upon that foundation. At the judgment seat of Christ, they will receive rewards or suffer the loss of rewards based upon the quality of their effort. All ministers have been given for the mutual benefit of all believers by Christ to whom they are ultimately responsible; therefore, Christians should not "think of men above that which is written, that no one of you be puffed up for one against another" (4:6). Paul then argued that whatever abilities men possess they have them because God gave them in the first place. How then can anyone boast of himself or another? With sanctified sarcasm, Paul tried to point out their erroneous thinking by contrasting their life-styles with the life-style of the apostles. He then warned them as a father would his son about resolving their differences before he visited them.

5:1-13

The second major problem brought to Paul via oral report centered in a church member guilty of a sexual sin not even practiced by unsaved

Gentiles. He apparently was having a known affair with his stepmother.[6] Instead of disciplining the fornicator, the church tolerated his presence in its midst. Paul exercised his apostolic authority and charged them to excommunicate the member. Deliverance to Satan of an erring brother was probably an extreme apostolic measure in harmony with divine chastisement (cf. I Tim. 1:20). Paul equated this type of open, unrepentant sin with leaven that would spread to other church members if not purged. He cautioned them against refraining from association with unsaved, wicked people because the latter need the witness of the former; however, he charged that believers should not keep company with professing Christians who are known for such wicked practices. It is the responsibility of the local church to judge its own members; God will judge the unsaved.

6:1-8

The divisions within the church had caused such deterioration that Christians were taking other believers before pagan civil magistrates to settle their differences. Since believers will judge the world and angels during the millennial kingdom and/or at the great white throne judgment, Paul argued that they should be able to solve their problems within the local church. He also suggested that it would be better to take wrong and to be defrauded than to expose the testimony of Christ and the church to public ridicule.

6:9-20

After positing that the unrighteous would not inherit the kingdom of God, Paul listed those men whose life-styles would prevent them from gaining the kingdom. However, God can take men with such sinful practice, as He did with some of the Corinthians, and transform them into saints with an acceptable spiritual position (washed, sanctified, justified). Many of the Corinthians, though, were abusing their bodies with improper diet or sexual relationships. Paul informed them that their bodies were now the temples of the Holy Spirit, that such sins were against their bodies, that they were now owned by God by right of spiritual redemption, and that they should glorify God with both their bodies and spirits.

7:1-9

Paul ended his reaction to the four problems brought to him orally (1:10—6:20) and began to answer the questions found in their letter to him (7:1). The first issue actually is related to the believer's understanding of the sanctity of his own body (6:9-20). Paul charged that

---

6. Not with his natural mother, because of the way in which Paul worded it: ". . . his father's wife."

209

premarital sexual affairs were wrong, that marriage was recommended in order to avoid sexual impurity, and that husbands and wives should understand their sexual responsibility to each other. His counsel to the unmarried and widows to remain single was given by permission, not of commandment. That meant that he did not speak as an apostle with divine authority, but rather as a spiritual brother giving his opinion.

7:10-24

The next section was addressed to married people. In it Paul set forth principles to govern separation, divorce, and reconciliation. Paul wanted the home to be maintained at all costs for the future salvation of the unsaved members of the household. Some have seen a difference between divine directives and human advice in two of Paul's admissions: "I command, yet not I, but the Lord" (7:10) and "But to the rest speak I, not the Lord" (7:12). The first meant that Paul voiced exactly what Christ had said on the subject (cf. Matt. 19:3-12), whereas the second meant that Christ had not orally spoken on the subject, but that Paul was speaking as a divinely authenticated apostle. He concluded that men should abide in that calling (slave, free, uncircumcision, etc.) wherein they were saved (7:20, 24). This principle could perhaps apply to the status of married life (a believer married to an unsaved partner).

7:25-40

Concerning virgins, Paul had not received any oral or written revelation from Christ; here he gave his judgment or advice after much thought on the subject (7:25; cf. 7:40). Because of the atmosphere of persecution at Corinth (7:26, 29), Paul recommended that the single remain single and that the widows remain unmarried. He further stated that the unmarried would be able to give more time and effort to the things of the Lord than the married person who also has obligations to his partner. He did recognize the acceptable option of marriage for the virgin and advised the widow, if she decided to remarry, to marry only a believer.

8:1-13

The problem of eating meat taken from animals sacrificed to idols also existed at Corinth (cf. Rom. 14). Perhaps the divisions in this church were caused partially by a difference of opinion in this area. In this controversial area of Christian liberty, Paul stated that men should be motivated by love, not by knowledge. Some believers knew that idols and gods did not actually exist because there is only one living God in the world; therefore, they could eat such meat with clear consciences. Other Christians still admitted the reality of pagan idolatry and could not eat such food with a pure conscience. The mere eating or noneating

210

was not the real spiritual issue; rather, Paul cautioned against offending the brother with a misuse of one's liberty. To eat with full knowledge that a brother is being spiritually hurt is to sin against Christ. Paul concluded that under such circumstances he would not eat.

9:1-27

As an illustration of not using one's rights, Paul referred to his own apostolic prerogative to be supported financially by the gifts of God's people. The Corinthians knew that Paul had been commissioned by the risen Christ to be an apostle through his spiritual ministry in their midst. Paul stated that both Barnabas and he had the same power to eat, to drink, to lead about a wife, and to stop manual labor as the other apostles. Both human logic and the Old Testament agreed that a minister should be supported materially; however, Paul chose not to exercise that right. He elected to work with his own hands as a tentmaker in Corinth so that none could accuse him of being in the ministry for what he could get out of it. Paul's motivation was clear: "For though I be free from all men, yet have I made myself servant unto all, that I might gain the more" (9:19). Paul wanted to win men to Christ, and to do that he adjusted his life-style and approach so that he would not offend the person he was trying to win. He also made sure that he had complete control of the desires of his body so that he would not forfeit the rewards of faithful service.

10:1—11:1

Paul concluded this section by referring to Old Testament examples of those who were severely chastised by God for sins of idolatry, fornication, tempting, murmuring, and pride. Apparently those who believed in the nonexistence of idols thought that they not only could eat meat sacrificed to idols but also participate in some of the pagan feasts. They had taken their liberty to an illogical, sinful extreme. Paul warned against such fellowship with demons and saw in it a provocation of God. He advised that expediency and edification should dictate whether one should exercise his liberty in all situations. In all such areas believers should seek to glorify God and to give no offense to either the unsaved or the saved. Liberty should not be used selfishly but benevolently.

11:2-16

Paul now moved from questions about personal life (7:1—11:1) to questions about the public worship service (11:2—14:40). The first dealt with the place of the Christian woman within the church. He introduced this section by outlining the order of authoritative headship within the divine plan: God, Christ, man, and woman. He argued that a man would dishonor Christ if he prayed or prophesied with his physical head covered and that a woman would dishonor her husband if she did these things with her head uncovered. The covering of the woman's head was a sign in that culture of the woman's subjection to her husband. The Christian woman probably reasoned that if she and her husband were spiritual equals in Christ, she need not wear the mark of subordination in spiritual activities within the church. However, the family headship of the man over the woman established at creation was not to be violated within the church. Just as there is an equality of spiritual essence within the three Persons of the divine Godhead, so there is also an order for the execution of the divine will. The same principle applies to the husband-wife relationship; there is an equality in Christ, but there is an order within the family and the church to do God's will properly.

11:17-34

The carnality visibly seen in the church divisions had even affected the public observance of the ordinance of the Lord's Supper. In the eating of the love feast that preceded the ordinance, those who had much food did not share with those who had none; in fact, some even became drunk while others hungered. Paul then outlined how the supper should be received by the believer. The eating of the bread and the drinking of the wine were to be done in remembrance of Christ's person and redemptive work and in anticipation of His return. Paul warned that their violations of this holy ordinance had brought physical sickness and premature death to many of the Corinthian church. He commanded that self-examination should precede the observance of the ordinance; if a believer does not confess and repent of his sin, then God must judge or chastise him in this life.

12:1-31

Another problem concerned ignorance over the nature and purpose of spiritual gifts.[7] Although there were more (Rom. 12:6-8; Eph. 4:11), Paul listed only nine: wisdom, knowledge, faith, healing, miracles, prophecy, discerning of spirits, tongues-speaking, and interpretation of tongues. Every believer received at least one of these gifts (12:7). These gifts were not chosen by men, but were sovereignly given (12:11, 18). By using the analogy of the one body with its many members, Paul demonstrated that believers should not all expect to have the same gift, that one gift should not be exalted above another, that all gifts should be used to complement the others, and that all should work together for the spiritual growth and health of the body, a symbol of the true church,

---

7. For a more thorough exposition of this subject, consult Robert G. Gromacki, *The Modern Tongues Movement* (Nutley, N.J.: Presbyterian and Reformed Publishing Co., 1967; revised, 1972).

composed of saved Jews and Gentiles and entered by the baptism in the Holy Spirit (12:12-31). These spiritual gifts then *(pneumatika* or *charismata)* were abilities given to the Christian out of the grace of God through the Spirit to be used for the spiritual profit of the entire church.

13:1-13

Paul then argued that unless the gifts were exercised in the attitude of love toward both God and Christian brethren, they were of no profit to anyone (13:1-3). In describing the qualities of love (13:4-8a), he repudiated their divisive spirit. Their exaltation of certain gifts no doubt contributed to the contentions among them. Paul predicted that the gifts of prophecy and knowledge would be rendered inoperative by the coming of "that which is perfect" and that tongues would cease even before that event.[8] Most evangelicals are divided over the meaning of "that which is perfect." It is seen as referring either to the completion of the canon (or written revelation) or to the second coming of Christ. If the former, then these gifts were definitely temporary and served only the needs of the apostolic church. If the latter, then the gifts of prophecy and knowledge would be permanently operative until Christ's return, whereas the gift of tongues would cease at some time before the event. Paul argued that the quality of love would go into eternity; therefore, it should be emphasized over the use of gifts.

14:1-40

The spectacular gift of tongues-speaking was at the center of the gift controversy. It apparently was misused and exalted out of proportion. Paul set forth several regulations to control the use of the gift in the public service of the church. Tongues had to be interpreted in order to have any profit for the entire congregation. Edification of the group was the main goal of any gift (14:3, 4, 5, 6, 12, 17, 26). Speaking in tongues was designed specifically as a sign to unbelieving Jews (14:21-22). There could be no more than three tongues-speakers in any service and they were to speak one at a time (14:27). A fourth person was to give the interpretation for all three tongues-speakers (14:27). If no interpreter were present, the tongues-speaker was to remain silent (14:28). Peace and order were to characterize the services (14:33, 40). Possibly the gift of tongues was not given to women (14:34), but this verse may refer to the interruption of the prophets by women questioners. Paul commended to them the gift of prophecy, but he warned them not to forbid tongues-speaking as long as the gift was sovereignly given.

---

8. The verbs translated "shall fail," "shall vanish away," and "shall be done away" (13:8, 10) are from the Greek *katargeo* and are all future passive indicatives. The verb "shall cease" is the future middle indicative of the Greek *pauo.*

15:1-58

The church was also involved in a doctrinal controversy over the resurrection. Paul stated that the bodily resurrection of Jesus Christ was an integral part of the gospel message and that no one could be saved apart from faith in a crucified, resurrected Christ (15:1-4). He alleged that Christ's resurrection was both historically and scientifically verified through His many postresurrection appearances (15:5-11). Some at Corinth apparently thought they could believe in the resurrection of Christ without believing in a future, general resurrection of the dead. Paul argued that Christ could not be separated from the stream of humanity. If there is no future resurrection, then Christ was not raised in the past; if that is true, then Paul saw himself as a false witness and the Corinthians as those still in their sins (15:12-19). However, Christ did rise from the dead, and that reality assures all men of a future resurrection (15:20-34). He stated that the resurrection body is related to the natural body, but not identical with it, that it is a spiritual, incorruptible, glorified body, and that it is of the same essence as Christ's resurrection body (15:35-50). Paul then disclosed the mystery[9] that not all believers would die before the coming of Christ, but that some would be alive when He returns. When He does return, the dead will receive a new body not subject to disease (incorruptible) or death (immortal) through resurrection, and the living will receive a new body through translation (15:51-58).

16:1-4

The final question dealt with the collection for the poor Jewish saints at Jerusalem. Paul advised the Corinthians to continue taking an offering every week so that he would not need to do it after he arrived at Corinth. He also suggested that some of their members could accompany him on his relief trip to Jerusalem.

16:5-24

Paul then closed the Epistle by announcing his travel plans, by informing them about Timothy and Apollos, by commending their three church ambassadors, and by extending greetings to them.

Increase Your Learning

By Doing

　　1. In your Bibles underline these verses to show the various changes in subject matter: 1:11; 5:1; 6:1, 9; 7:1, 8, 10, 25; 8:1; 11:2, 17; 12:1; 15:1; 16:1.

9. A Biblical mystery is that which was unknown or unrevealed in Old Testament times but which is revealed in the New Testament era for our understanding.

2. In the first three chapters underline these words: "wise," "wisdom" and "know."
3. Circle all references to the Spirit in chapter 2.
4. In chapter 6, underline the six references to "Know ye not."
5. Underline all references to "edification" in chapter 14.
6. In chapter 15 underline such words as these: "risen," "rose" and "resurrection."

By Discussing

1. Do evangelicals today have a tendency to exalt and to follow certain Bible teachers, pastors, authors, or evangelists? Is this encouraged in many circles?
2. Are many problems within the local church due to a lack of church discipline? What can be done about it?
3. In what ways have secular philosophies affected Christian belief and practice today? Has the new morality changed believers' attitudes toward sexual purity?
4. What kind of spiritual leadership responsibilities should the Christian woman expect to have in today's church?
5. Evaluate the charismatic, pentecostal movement. Are the adherents' practices in harmony with Pauline directives?

By Reading

Godet, F. *Commentary on St. Paul's First Epistle to the Corinthians.* 2 vols. Grand Rapids: Zondervan Publishing House, 1957.

Ironside, H. A. *Addresses on the First Epistle to the Corinthians.* New York: Loizeaux Bros., 1938.

Morris, Leon. *The First Epistle of Paul to the Corinthians.* Grand Rapids: Wm. B. Eerdmans Publishing Co., 1963.

Robertson, Archibald Thomas and Alfred Plummer. *A Critical and Exegetical Commentary of the First Epistle of St. Paul to the Corinthians.* Edinburgh: T. & T. Clark, 1914.

11

SECOND CORINTHIANS

Writer

Few have disputed the Pauline character or authorship of this book. The author definitely identified himself as Paul (1:1; 10:1). Many of the historical allusions within the book coincide with our knowledge of Paul's life contained elsewhere in Acts and in other Epistles. For instance, Timothy, Silas, and Titus were numbered among his associates (1:1, 19; 2:13; 7:6, 13-14; 8:6). His geographical movements and planned trips harmonize with Paul's itinerary (1:16; 2:12; 7:5). Some of his personal experiences, including that of his dramatic escape from Damascus, can be found in Acts (11:32-33; cf. Acts 9:24-25). It is true that much of the autobiographical data is not contained in Paul's other letters or in Acts, but this should not be construed as an argument against his authorship. Would a forger have included so much personal data not found elsewhere nor known by many if he wanted to pass off the book as a Pauline original? Only the one who in fact had experienced these events could report them publicly. The book opens with a typical Pauline greeting and blessing of grace and peace (1:2; cf. I Cor. 1:3; Gal. 1:3; Eph. 1:2). There do seem to be a few disguised references to the content of the First Epistle, showing some continuity between the two books (2:9; 12:21).

The testimony of the early church is sufficient to corroborate the internal evidence of the Epistle. These Church Fathers and canonical lists ascribed the book to Paul: Polycarp, Athenagoras, Cyprian, Tertullian, Clement of Alexander, Irenaeus, Marcion, and the Muratorian Canon.

Time and Place

Paul remained at Ephesus after the writing of First Corinthians to continue his ministry in that city and to await the results of his authoritative letter. Paul had hoped that the double thrust of the letter and of Timothy's visit (I Cor. 16:10-11) would solve the difficulties at Corinth, but apparently they did not. The intense church factions and growing opposition to Paul's apostolic authority persisted. Taking matters into his own hands, Paul probably made a quick trip across the Aegean Sea to Corinth to resolve the matters himself. Although this trip was unrecorded in Acts, the third trip anticipated in the Second Epistle (12:14; 13:1-2) presupposes a second trip made between the original journey to evangelize and the writing of Second Corinthians. This hasty visit ended in failure. Paul retreated once more to Ephesus with insults of his person and rejections of his authority ringing in his ears and burdening his heart (2:1; 12:14, 21; 13:1-2). False Jewish apostles had attacked Paul's integrity (chs. 10-11), and the sinning members were still unrepentant (12:21). Paul decided that he would not return to Corinth until the Corinthians adopted a different attitude toward him (1:23).

There is some speculation that Paul wrote a brief letter to Corinth at this time in criticism of the person who was against him (2:5-10; 7:12). Since there is no objective, manuscript evidence of the existence of this letter, it would be regarded as another lost letter, making two altogether (cf. I Cor. 5:9). Support for this lost letter is based upon Paul's statement: "For out of much affliction and anguish of heart I wrote unto you with many tears" (2:4; cf. 7:8). Could this tearful letter be identified with the First Epistle or is it an epistolary aorist reference to the Second Epistle itself? Most say not and conclude that this letter is now lost. Many liberals say that this letter was incorporated into our present Second Epistle as chapters ten through thirteen, but there is no objective support for such a position. At this time Titus did leave Paul for Corinth, and if such a letter did exist, he probably took it with him (7:8-13).

Because of intense pressure at Ephesus, Paul went to Troas where he expected to find Titus waiting for him (2:12-13), but his associate was not there. Burdened over his absence, Paul moved on to Macedonia, possibly to Philippi. Here Paul encountered more troubles (7:5), but he was comforted when Titus came with a glowing report from Corinth (7:6-16). Revival had broken out and the church was again warm and responsive toward Paul. He thus was prompted to write to inform them of his rejoicing over the repentance of the majority, his continued concern over the benevolent collection, and his sorrow over the constant opposition of the few. He therefore wrote from Macedonia about A.D. 55 in preparation of his visit to Achaia and to Corinth (cf. Acts 20:2).

Purposes

The purposes behind the writing of the book are inseparably connected

217

The temple of Apollo at Corinth. Erected in 590 B.C., the structure was an impressive tourist attraction even in New Testament times.

with the historical background of the Epistle. He thus wrote to present the purpose of his sufferings in Asia, notably Ephesus (1:3-11); to explain why he changed his plans for a return visit to Corinth (1:12—2:4); to give instructions about the discipline and the reconciliation of the offender (2:5-11); to express his joy over the revival (2:12-13; cf. 7:15-16); to set forth the superiority of the ministry of grace to that of law (2:14—6:10); to appeal for separation from false teachers (6:11—7:16); to urge the church to fulfill its collection responsibility (8:1—9:15); and to vindicate his apostleship against the charges of the false apostles (10:1—13:14).

Distinctive Features

This is the most autobiographical of all of Paul's Epistles. It gives an insight into the personal life and ministry of the apostle that none of the other letters give. Because of the false charges made against him, Paul was forced against his personal wishes to reveal events and secrets unknown to most of his converts. He prefaced his disclosures with these words:

> I say again, Let no man think me a fool; if otherwise, yet as a fool receive me, that I may boast myself a little. That which I speak, I speak it not after the Lord, but as it were foolishly, in this confidence of boasting (11:16-17).

Over and over again he inserted self-conscious explanations: "I speak as a fool" (11:21, 23) and "I must needs glory" (11:18, 30; 12:1, 5, 6). He concluded: "I am become a fool in glorying; ye have compelled me" (12:11). These expedient disclosures reveal that Paul suffered far more for the cause of Christ than any man would imagine. His sufferings became his main defense against the unjust charges. What had his enemies suffered for Christ? That was his countercharge.

The book also reveals the warm, human character of Paul. Many have pictured Paul as the methodical logician of Romans or Galatians. He was that, for his books do manifest a logical, argumentative style of writing. This Epistle, however, is emotional, full of tears and grief. It was written more with the heart than with the head. With the exception of Philemon, it is the most personal and the least doctrinal of Paul's Epistles. Greek students can testify to the change of writing style and vocabulary as they move from the first to the second letter in translation work. Second Corinthians is difficult to translate because Paul could hardly wait to get the words written to express the burden of his heart to the church.

This book carefully examines the character and the tactics of the false teachers that Paul encountered wherever he went. They were Jews (11:22), claiming to be the ministers of Christ (11:23). Paul, however, saw them differently; he characterized them as false apostles, as deceitful workers, and as Satan's ministers of righteousness (11:13-15). They apparently carried letters of commendation as their credentials so that they would be given opportunities of public ministry and provided financial support (3:1). They viciously criticized Paul's physical appearance and poor oratory (10:10; 11:6) and his refusal to accept money for spiritual service (11:7-12), and questioned the authenticity of his apostleship (11:5; 12:11-12). Paul saw them as proponents of "another" faith and thus subject to the divine anathema: "For if he that cometh preacheth another Jesus, whom we have not preached, or if ye receive another spirit, which ye have not received, or another gospel, which ye have not accepted, ye might well bear with him" (11:4; cf. Gal. 1:6-9).

The person and ministry of Satan are also emphasized in this Epistle. Paul identified him as Satan (2:11), the god of this world (4:4), the serpent (11:3), and as an angel of light (11:14). In relation to Christians, Satan tries to keep them from forgiving one another (2:10-11), attempts to deceive and to corrupt their minds (11:3), and is permitted by God to afflict them physically for their own spiritual protection (12:7-9). In relation to the unsaved, he blinds their minds so that they reject the gospel message (4:4) and uses a ministry of human self-righteousness to keep men from accepting the divine righteousness of Christ (11:15).

Some classic passages of doctrinal and practical truth are found within this book. The proper concept of the preaching ministry was exemplified by Paul (3:1—6:10). The intermediate state of the believer's body between death and resurrection is discussed at some length (5:1-9). The principles of giving in this age of grace by Christians are outlined clearly (8:1—9:15).

Outline

SALUTATION (1:1-2)
I. DEFENSE OF HIS CONDUCT (1:3—2:11)
  A. His sufferings (1:3-11)
  B. His past conduct (1:12-22)
  C. His future plans (1:23—2:4)
  D. His treatment of the offender (2:5-11)
II. DEFENSE OF HIS MINISTRY (2:12—7:16)
  A. Contrasted with legalism (2:12—3:18)
  B. Opposed by Satan (4:1-18)
  C. Examined by Christ (5:1-10)
  D. Motivated by love for Christ (5:11-19)
  E. Marked by lack of offense (5:20—6:10)
  F. Saturated with spiritual concern (6:11—7:4)
  G. Encouraged by joy over results (7:5-16)
III. DEFENSE OF THE COLLECTION (8:1—9:15)
  A. Example of the Macedonians (8:1-7)
  B. Example of Jesus Christ (8:8-15)
  C. Testimony of the church delegates (8:16—9:5)
  D. Blessings of giving (9:6-15)
IV. DEFENSE OF HIS APOSTLESHIP (10:1—12:13)
  A. His authority (10:1-18)
  B. His lack of financial support (11:1-15)
  C. His sufferings (11:16-33)
  D. His physical weakness (12:1-10)
  E. His miracles (12:11-13)
V. DEFENSE OF HIS PROPOSED VISIT (12:14—13:10)
CONCLUSION (13:11-14)

Survey

1:1-2

Paul opened this Epistle of defense by asserting that he was an apostle of Christ by the will of God; the defense of that claim will be seen throughout the Epistle. It was addressed not only to the church at Corinth but also to all the believers within the province of Achaia.

1:3-11

Paul first demonstrated that his sufferings and persecutions were not inconsistent with his position as apostle. In them he experienced the comfort of God which he could share with people in similar circumstances (1:3-4). Such sufferings were also endured by Paul for the spiritual benefit of the Corinthian church (1:6). The imminent sense of martyrdom in the Ephesian capital of Asia caused Paul to increase his trust in God and to lessen his confidence in himself (1:9). Paul's sufferings also burdened the Corinthians to pray for and to give to him (1:11). These troubles thus embellished his office of apostle.

1:12—2:1

Paul was attacked as a man of indecision, one who told the Corinthians that he would come to them but who hesitated and sent others in his place. Paul had originally planned to go from Ephesus to Corinth, into Macedonia, back to Corinth, and on to Jerusalem (1:15-16), but their attitudes toward him had changed his plans. He did not want to visit them with heaviness of heart or in a display of his apostolic authority (1:24; 2:1). Paul claimed to be a positive, secure person (1:17-20), one whose conscience was marked by simplicity and godly sincerity (1:12).

2:2-13

Paul was attacked as a man who held grudges, but he rejoiced over the repentance of the very man who had wronged him (2:2-3). When he originally ordered the discipline of this erring brother, he did it out of compassion and love for him and the congregation, not out of spite (2:4). Paul now wanted the congregation to forgive and to comfort the repentant offender, and in so doing they would echo his feelings (2:7-10). Holding grudges was a Satanic tool that Paul rejected.

2:14—3:5

Paul moved from the defense of his personal conduct to that of his ministry. He thanked God for a triumphant ministry even though there was a divided response to it; some rejected and remained in spiritual death, whereas others believed unto life everlasting (2:14-16). He took no credit nor blame for the results, but claimed to speak the word out of sincerity, not as his critics who corrupted it. He asserted that the integrity of his ministry should have been known by the Corinthians; they were his living epistles of commendation because they were saved and edified through his ministry.

3:6-18

He then demonstrated the superiority of his ministry by contrasting it with that of the Judaizers, those who taught that salvation was through faith and works, especially circumcision and obedience to the Mosaic law:

Judaizers	*Paul*
Old Testament	New Testament
Letter	Spirit
Kills	Gives Life
Ministration of death	Ministration of the Spirit
Condemnation	Righteousness
Glory	Exceeds in glory
Done away	Remains

221

Paul argued that the old was to give way to the new and that as long as men tried to gain the righteousness of God through conformity to the old, a special blindness would remain upon their hearts. When Jews embrace Christ, they are then released from that blindness and from any obligation to the old covenant.

4:1-18

The Judaizers accused Paul of being dishonest, of failing to preach a total message of faith and works. They said that Paul declared faith without circumcision lest the Corinthian Gentiles be repelled at the physical rite. Paul claimed that he was not dishonest, crafty, or deceitful and that he spoke the truth with clear conscience before both God and man (4:2). The Judaizers stated that they could not understand Paul's message; he countered by saying that his gospel was hidden to the lost who were blinded by Satan. Their spiritual blindness and darkness could only be removed through a divine work of illumination similar to the creation of physical light. In a series of paradoxes, Paul contrasted his outward sufferings and persecutions with the inner strength of his soul (4:7-10; cf. 4:16). He suffered that the Corinthians might benefit from his stand for the truth (4:15). He did not let earthly pressures detract from his hope of eternal glory.

5:1-13

The Judaizers charged that because Paul was afraid of physical suffering and death he fled from one city to another to avoid persecution. However, he rested in the hope of resurrection (4:14). He knew that if death should come he would have a new body, "a building of God, an house not made with hands, eternal in the heavens." This seems to refer to the intermediate state, the body which the soul or self has between death and resurrection. In fact, he looked forward to that day; he did not shrink from it. He saw that mortality would be "swallowed up of life" at death. Paul knew that as long as he was here on earth, he was absent from the resurrected Christ; he desired to be present with his Savior. He wanted his spiritual labor to be acceptable with Christ and he knew that his ministry would be evaluated at the judgment seat of Christ. At that time he would receive rewards or suffer the loss of rewards based upon the quality of his service (5:10; cf. I Cor. 3:12-15). The terror of the Lord, not of men, motivated Paul to preach with a proper heart, not in mere outward appearance.

5:14—6:10

Paul added that the quality and extent of Christ's love toward him

222

constrained him to turn his life completely over to Christ. Paul saw himself (and all believers) as a new creation in Christ, a reconciled sinner, a recipient of righteousness, and an ambassador for Christ. He discharged a ministry of reconciliation both toward unbelieving sinners (5:18-19) and sinning brethren (5:20). He defended himself as one "giving no offence in any thing, that the ministry be not blamed" (6:3). He was a model minister in ten troublesome situations in which he found himself (6:4-5), by nine spiritual qualities exhibited by him (6:6-7), and in eight paradoxical areas (6:8-10).

6:11—7:4

Paul was not indifferent toward the Corinthians as charged; rather, his life was marked by a genuine concern for their spiritual welfare. His cry expressed his emotional desire to effect a reconciliation between himself and them (6:11). He further commanded: "Be ye not unequally yoked together with unbelievers" (6:14). The principle of this imperative extended to all areas of their life experiences: religious, social, economic, and marital. In a series of five contrasts, he showed the logic behind his command (6:14-16). He added three more imperatives: come out, be separate, and touch not. Paul wanted them to make a clean break with all idolatry and false religious teaching in order to enjoy the full Father-son relationship. He concluded with this appeal: "Receive us; we have wronged no man, we have corrupted no man, we have defrauded no man" (7:2). He claimed that there was nothing wrong with him that should cause them to prolong the spiritual estrangement.

7:5-12

Paul then informed the church how he was troubled with outward persecution and inward fears (probably over the attitudes of the Corinthians toward him) when he came into Macedonia. The return of Titus, the rejoicing of Titus' heart over the revival, and his report of good attitudes toward Paul all brought comfort to the apostle's heart. He was glad that the previous letter had accomplished genuine repentance in their midst although he was apprehensive at the time he sent it. He clarified his purpose in sending it as genuine spiritual oversight (7:12).

8:1—9:5

In an attempt to renew interest in the collection for the poor Jewish saints at Jerusalem, he pointed to the example of the Macedonian churches (Philippi, Thessalonica, and Berea). In the midst of persecution and personal poverty, they gave liberally, even beyond their means, because they had first yielded themselves completely to Christ. Paul wanted the Corinthians to finish what they had begun (8:6; cf. I Cor. 16:1), to abound in the grace of giving, and to prove the sincerity of

223

their love. Paul recognized that within giving is a spiritual dimension and that men should measure their gifts by what Christ gave to us (8:9). Paul wanted their giving to be done willingly and in proportion to their possessions so that those in need might be supplied by the former's abundance. He hoped that their gifts would be a testimony to the other churches and to the messengers, Titus and the anonymous brother (possibly Luke) (8:16-19), and a confirmation of his own boasting over them (8:23-24). One year before, Achaia's plans to give had encouraged the Macedonians to do likewise. So that Paul and the Corinthian church might not be embarrassed, Paul sent the two messengers to Corinth before Paul and the Macedonian representatives arrived there to make sure that the Corinthian gift was already prepared.

9:6-15

Paul equated the principle of giving with that of sowing and reaping: the more you give or sow the more you reap, and the less you give or sow the less you reap. Purposeful and cheerful giving reaps the sufficient financial supply of God, the fruits of righteousness in the giver's life, and the thankful prayers in their behalf by the recipients of their gift. All giving is a modest expression of thanksgiving to God for His unspeakable gift of eternal life through Christ.

10:1-18

Some question Paul's apostleship in that his personal deportment and speech did not manifest that authoritative office. His enemies claimed that he was bold toward the Corinthians when he was absent from them, but mild mannered in their presence. Paul pointed to the meekness and gentleness of Christ as proper qualities of spiritual authority. Paul chose not to be bold or to seek revenge over his enemies lest he use fleshly tactics to accomplish his goals. He planned to use his authority for edification, not for destruction. He warned his enemies that he would say and do in person what he had written in the letters (10:9-11). He did not plan to lower himself to that level where men evaluated their ministries by those of others; he let his ministry speak for itself. His aspiration was toward pioneer evangelism, not to build upon another's work, which the Judaizers always did. Paul gloried in the Lord and sought only His commendation.

11:1-12

Paul had a holy jealousy for the Corinthian church; he did not want them to be corrupted through the spiritual flirtations and temptations of the false teachers who were being used by Satan just as he had worked through the serpent to beguile Eve. These Judaizers claimed that if Paul had been a genuine apostle he would have accepted the financial support of the Corinthians while in Corinth instead of working manually. He argued that he did it that way because he wanted to remove any charge of covetousness that some might conjure up against him (11:9, 12). He did take money from the Macedonian churches while he was in Corinth. Paul wondered how the Corinthians could question his motivation in this act of love toward them.

11:13-33

Paul's language was very strong in his evaluation of the spiritual character of these false teachers; he saw them as satanic emissaries. Contrary to his normal policy, Paul wanted the Corinthians to compare his person and ministry with those of the Judaizers. In revealing his ancestry and his persecutions, Paul showed that the false teachers finished a poor second to him. He stated that the churches did not go to the false teachers when they needed help; rather, they came to him (11:28).

12:1-13

He told them that he could have gloried in the visions and revelations given to him by Christ and in the experience of being caught up into the third heaven or paradise (he was the anonymous man). He hesitated to disclose such things "lest any man should think of me above that which he seeth me to be, or that he heareth of me" (12:6). In fact, to keep Paul from boasting about such experiences, God permitted Satan to afflict the apostle physically. Since it was God's will for him to keep the thorn in the flesh, Paul reasoned: "Most gladly therefore will I rather glory in my infirmities, that the power of Christ may rest upon me" (12:9). Paul saw his physical troubles as an authentication of his apostleship, not as a detraction (11:30-31; 12:5, 9-10). He expressed his disappointment that he had to stoop to such logic to convince the Corinthians who should have known that he was an apostle through the signs performed in their midst (12:11-12). His only error, as he saw it, was in not taking their money; for this wrong, he asked for their forgiveness (12:13).

12:14-21

In preparation of his third visit to them soon, Paul said that he would come as he had before, not seeking their money, but their love and edification. He conjectured: "And I will very gladly spend and be spent for you; though the more abundantly I love you, the less I be loved" (12:15). He expressed apprehension over their future attitudes and actions toward him (12:19-21).

13:1-14

He equated his three visits (two accomplished and one planned) with the testimony of two or three witnesses. Since they wanted a display of apostolic authority invested in him by Christ (which lack was used as an attack by the Judaizers), Paul promised to display it when he came the third time (13:1-4). Paul warned them to examine their own spiritual relationship: were they in the faith or were they reprobates? Paul wanted them to acknowledge his authority through this letter so that he would not need to use sharpness when he came to them. He concluded the Epistle with his typical salutation and benediction.

Increase Your Learning

By Doing

1. Make a list of all those things which Paul suffered for Christ. Underline all references to them in your Bibles.
2. Circle every mention of Satan and of the false teachers.
3. Underline all references to Christian financial giving.

By Discussing

1. If your Christian character and/or service were attacked, how would you react? What lessons or principles did you glean from Paul's defense?
2. What qualities should a church seek in a pastoral candidate? Compare inner attitudes with outward appearance.
3. In a public testimony meeting how much of one's private life should be disclosed?
4. Is tithing for today? What are the standards that should mark Christian giving?

By Reading

Hodge, Charles. *An Exposition of the Second Epistle to the Corinthians.* Grand Rapids Wm. B. Eerdmans Publishing Co., 1953.

Hughes, Philip Edgcumbe. *Paul's Second Epistle to the Corinthians.* Grand Rapids: Wm. B. Eerdmans Publishing Co., 1962.

Ironside, H. A. *Addresses on the Second Epistle to the Corinthians.* New York: Loizeaux Bros., 1939.

Tasker, R. V. G. *The Second Epistle of Paul to the Corinthians.* Grand Rapids: Wm. B. Eerdmans Publishing Co., 1958.

12

GALATIANS

Galatians has been called both the Magna Charta of Christian Liberty and the Christian Declaration of Independence. Out of its pages grew the Protestant Reformation for it was by study in Galatians that Luther's heart was opened to the truth of justification by faith alone.

Writer

Even critical liberals acknowledge the Pauline authorship of this book. There is nothing within the book or the writings of the Church Fathers that would cause anyone to question its authenticity. The author called himself Paul twice (1:1; 5:2). The many historical references can be harmonized with the events of Acts and of the other Epistles: his Pharisaical Jewish heritage (1:13-14; cf. Acts 22:3), his persecution of the church (1:13; cf. Acts 7:58; 8:1-3), his dramatic conversion on the way to Damascus (1:15-17; cf. Acts 9:1-25), his visit to Jerusalem (1:18; cf. Acts 11:30), his identification with Titus and Barnabas (2:1; cf. Acts 13:1-2; II Cor. 8:16), his home church at Antioch (2:11; cf. Acts 13:1), his physical problems (4:15; 6:11; cf. II Cor. 12:7-10), and persecutions (6:12, 17; cf. II Cor. 11:23-27).

Marcion placed Galatians first in his list of Paul's letters. These other Church Fathers regarded the book as canonical and as written by Paul: Polycarp, Justin Martyr, Origen, Irenaeus, Tertullian, and Clement of Alexandria.

Region of Galatia

Barbarians, about the fourth century B.C., migrated from north of the Black Sea westward into Macedonia, Greece, and France. Some tribes broke away and moved into north central Asia Minor. Here they were called *Galatai* by the Greeks and *Galla* by the Romans; thus the territory

A threshing floor near Konya (ancient Iconium).

came to be known as Galatia. The Romans looked upon them as allies, but when their leader Amyntas died, their region was annexed as a Roman province by Caesar Augustus in 25 B.C. He enlarged the province by adding part of Pontus to the northeast, part of Phrygia to the southwest, and most of Lycaonia to the south. The geographical limits were constantly changing, but in the New Testament era it was a large province bordered by other provinces as Asia (west), Cappadocia (east), Pamphylia and Cilicia (south), and Bithynia and Pontus (north). The southern and southwestern sections of the province were more densely populated because here the cities were connected by a network of Roman roads; thus southern Galatia became more important politically and economically. Within this region were the cities evangelized by Paul and Barnabas during their first missionary journey: Antioch in Pisidia, Iconium, Lystra, and Derbe.

The Galatians had adopted the mythological polytheism of the Greeks and the Romans. Just as the Cretans were known for their lying (Titus 1:12), so the Galatians were known nationally as an impulsive, changeable, and inconsistent people. This could be seen in their paradoxical desire to worship Paul at one moment and to stone him the next (Acts 14:11-19) and also in their quickness to receive the gospel and to abandon it (1:6).

GALATIANS

Establishment of the Galatian Churches

Paul with Barnabas evangelized the southern section of the Roman province of Galatia during his first missionary journey (Acts 13:14—14:26). After reaching the mainland from Cyprus, they moved quickly from Perga in Pamphylia to Antioch in Pisidia, a mountainous region which provided a refuge for thieves and Roman political enemies (cf. II Cor. 11:26). Antioch, a city founded by Seleucus I Nicator (312-280 B.C.), was a center of commerce on the trade route between Ephesus to the west and the Cilician Gates to the east. On the Sabbath they went into the synagogue where Paul was given the opportunity to preach to the congregation composed of Jews and Gentile proselytes (Acts 13:16, 26). In his sermon he identified the messianic hope of the Old Testament with Jesus Christ in His death and resurrection and proclaimed that forgiveness of sins and justification could be received only through faith in Him, not through legal obedience (Acts 13:38-39). After the Jews, apparently offended at his message, stormed out of the synagogue, the Gentiles present extended an invitation to Paul to preach the same sermon on the next Sabbath (Acts 13:42). Even as the result of this first proclamation, many Jews and Gentiles ("religious proselytes") were converted (Acts 13:43). When "almost the whole city" showed up at the synagogue to hear Paul the next Sabbath, the Jews were filled with jealousy because Paul had reached more Gentiles in one week than they had in several years of endeavor. When they attacked Paul, he countered with a stirring ultimatum:

A large section of the ancient aqueduct that brought water to Pisidian Antioch.

... It was necessary that the word of God should first have been spoken to you: but seeing ye put it from you, and judge yourselves unworthy of everlasting life, lo, we turn to the Gentiles. For so hath the Lord commanded us, saying, I have set thee to be a light of the Gentiles, that thou shouldest be for salvation unto the ends of the earth. And when the Gentiles heard this, they were glad, and glorified the word of the Lord: and as many as were ordained to eternal life believed (Acts 13:46-48).

From this point on in his ministry, Paul followed the policy of preaching to the Jew first and then to the Gentiles after Jewish opposition began. The ministry among the Gentiles met with great success (Acts 13:49, 52) but Paul and Barnabas were forced to leave when "the Jews stirred up the devout and honourable women, and the chief men of the city, and raised persecution against" them (Acts 13:50-51).

When they came to Iconium, they preached in the synagogue there; as a result, many Jews and Gentile proselytes believed in Christ. Again, the unbelieving Jews influenced the unbelieving Gentiles against the converts; in spite of this opposition, they stayed "a long time," preaching and performing miracles. Although the city was divided over their ministry, the unbelieving Jews and Gentiles plus their rulers determined to kill the apostles. When the latter learned of the plot, they fled to Lystra and Derbe (Acts 14:1-6).

These two cities were located in Lycaonia, a small landlocked province noted for its flat pasture land. The people there spoke a language composed of corrupt Greek mixed with Assyrian. Lystra was about eighteen miles southwest of Iconium; Derbe, a small town at the base of Mount Taurus, was sixteen miles east of Lystra.

At Lystra Paul healed a lame man, crippled through birth defects. When the pagans witnessed the miracle, they thought that the apostles were gods in the likeness of men (Barnabas as Jupiter and Paul as Mercury) and planned to offer animal sacrifices to them. Barnabas and Paul restrained the people from doing so through a brief sermon in which Paul admonished them to turn from their paganism to the living God of creation. Shortly after, Jews from Antioch and Iconium came to Lystra, stoned Paul, and dragged him out of the city. Paul, however, revived and went on to Derbe (Acts 14:6-20).

After preaching in Derbe, Paul and Barnabas retraced their steps through Lystra, Iconium, and Antioch teaching, comforting, and appointing leaders in the churches they had just started (Acts 14:21-23). They ended their journey by returning to Antioch (Acts 14:24-26).

Destination of the Letter

To what churches of Galatia (1:2; 3:1) did Paul write? This moot question has bothered commentators for generations. Although the answer does not affect the message of the book, it does determine the time of its composition. Two major views have been proposed. The first is that Paul wrote to churches within the old territory of north Galatia, a region that he evangelized during his second journey and revisited during his third (Acts 16:6; 18:23). The proponents argue that Luke used territorial, not Roman provincial, titles to describe the regions encompassed by Paul's itinerary (Acts 13:14; 14:6; 16:6; 18:23). However, it is difficult to determine the real meaning of Luke's words. Literally, he said that Paul went through "the Phrygian-Galatic country" (16:6) and later through "the Galatic-Phrygian country" (18:23).[1] This is a general designation and could refer to either the territory or province or both. The advocates add that since there is no mention of Paul's physical infirmity during the first journey (Acts 13-14), why would Paul refer to it in the letter (4:13)? However, Luke does not mention it in his accounts of the second or third journeys either. Many of Paul's persecutions and illnesses were not recorded by Luke or even by Paul himself (cf. II Cor. 11-12). They further suggest that Paul would have referred to his persecutions, including the stoning episode, if he had written to the south Galatian churches. But Paul did mention the marks *(stigmata)* that his body bore for his faith and testimony (6:17); also, it is conceivable that his eye problem (4:13-15) was caused or aggravated by the stoning incident.

In positive support for the second view that Paul wrote to those churches founded on the first journey, many have pointed out that Acts contains territorial designations whereas Paul chose to use provincial titles. In First Corinthians, Paul alluded to the churches of Galatia (16:1); in that same context, he referred to other regions by their provincial names: Macedonia (16:5), Achaia (16:15), and Asia (16:19). Thus, he most likely used "Galatia" as a provincial title also. It is also more likely that Paul wrote to churches whose establishment is recorded in Acts (chs. 13-14) than to churches about which we have little information. Caution must be exercised here because little is known about the founding of the Colossian church either. Judaizers, the enemies of Paul, would have invaded the densely populated areas of southern Galatia where Jews and synagogues were located rather than the sparsely settled northern sections. The reference to Barnabas, especially his defection at Antioch (2:1, 9; cf. 2:13), would only have significance to the southern Galatians because Barnabas was with Paul during the first journey, but not during the next two. Since there is no reference to the historic decision made at the council of Jerusalem (Acts 15), a decision that would have provided Paul with a clinching argument, the book

---

1. Note the reversal of order. Also notice that these proper names are adjectival rather than noun forms.

must have been written before that event occurred. In that case Paul could only have written to the south Galatian churches of Antioch, Iconium, Lystra, and Derbe. Although Peter was an unstable person at times, his defection at Antioch (2:11-14) would better fit into his life experiences before the council at Jerusalem than after. Finally, the several biographical references in the first two chapters correlate better with a south Galatian destination. The visit to Jerusalem in which he saw Peter and James (1:18-19; cf. Acts 9:26) occurred three years after his conversion (A.D. 32; cf. A.D. 35). The second visit to Jerusalem, which happened fourteen years after his conversion rather than after his first visit, probably was the famine visit rather than the trip to attend the council meeting (2:1; cf. Acts 11:30; A.D. 46). The council was a public, general meeting (Acts 15), whereas the visit of Paul, Barnabas, and Titus was private (2:2). The recognition of Paul's apostleship and message by the Jerusalem apostles certainly would have taken place before the council meeting. In the intervening years between the two Jerusalem visits, Paul spent nine in Tarsus (A.D. 35-44) and labored for two more in Syrian Antioch (A.D. 44-46).

Time and Place

Most of the older commentators favored the north Galatian theory. If they are correct, then the Epistle had to be written during Paul's third journey, probably from either Ephesus or Macedonia (A.D. 53-56).

Contemporary scholarship has embraced the south Galatian view. This would mean that the letter could have been written at any time after the completion of the first journey (A.D. 47-48). It has been dated from Corinth during the second journey (Zahn; A.D. 50-52), from Antioch just before the beginning of the third journey (Ramsey; A.D. 52), and from Macedonia or Greece during the third journey (Thiessen; A.D. 55-56). Most modern advocates of this theory place the writing of Galatians in Antioch just before the Jerusalem council (Gromacki, Tenney; A.D. 48-49). Consequently, after Paul and Barnabas returned to Antioch after their first journey, Peter visited them and the church at Antioch. There he fellowshiped with the Gentile Christians, withdrew from them, and was reproved publicly by Paul. Judaizers meanwhile had invaded the south Galatian churches, teaching the necessity of circumcision to gain and to maintain salvation and denying Paul's apostleship. When Paul received the report of this theological dilemma, he wrote Galatians prior to his attendance at the Jerusalem council.

Purposes

The purposes naturally grew out of the theological predicament of the churches. In the first two chapters Paul attempted to vindicate his apostleship and message which were under attack through answers to these questions: where did he get his apostolic authority and message, and who accepted him as an apostle? Through constant autobiographical references he demonstrated that his apostolic office was given directly by Christ and that it was recognized by the Jerusalem apostles. In so doing he made Galatians the second most autobiographical of his Epistles, next to Second Corinthians.

In the next two chapters (3-4), he logically explained and defended the doctrine of justification by faith. It was basically a counterattack against the false teaching that circumcision and legal obedience were necessary in addition to faith to secure a complete salvation.

The final two chapters (5-6) contain instructions for practical Christian living. The early section describes the Spirit-controlled life (5:1—6:10), whereas the closing paragraphs deal with warnings against the Judaizers (6:11-18).

The Judaizers were probably Judean Jews who penetrated the just-established Gentile churches of Galatia, warning them: "Except ye be circumcised after the manner of Moses, ye cannot be saved" (cf. Acts 15:1). They regarded the Gentile believers as "second class" spiritual citizens who needed to become Jewish in their approach to God. This proclamation would have appealed to the unsaved Galatian Jews who resisted and persecuted Paul (Acts 13:41, 45, 50-51; 14:1-5, 19). It is possible that these Judaizers accused Paul of preaching the necessity of circumcision to Jewish audiences, but not to Gentile crowds (cf. 5:11); thus they were saying that Paul was a coward and a spiritual compromiser. It is conceivable that some of the Galatians had succumbed to the influence of the Judaizers and that the former were even trying to convert their friends (6:13). To Paul, the situation was desperate. This is probably why he did not send his typical salutation of grace and peace, which would have included a prayer of thanksgiving for them. To impress the readers with his own urgent concern, Paul either wrote the entire letter himself or at least the closing section (6:11-18). In either case, he did not use an amanuensis or secretary in his normal fashion. The Galatians would have been emotionally moved when they saw the large letters of the Pauline script (6:11).[2] The severe spiritual tone of the letter can also be seen in Paul's condemnation of the false teachers (1:7, 9; 5:10, 12; 6:17).

It should also be observed that this is the only Epistle to be written

---

2. Literally: "Behold what large letters I have written to you by my own hand." The KJV "how large a letter" is misleading. The book was not lengthy, but the size of the Greek print was exceptionally large, due to Paul's poor eyesight (cf. 4:15).

by Paul to a group of churches. All others were sent to either individual churches or persons.

Outline

INTRODUCTION (1:1-5)
  I. HIS BIOGRAPHICAL ARGUMENT (1:6—2:21)
      A. His warning was against perverting the gospel (1:6-10)
      B. His apostleship was from God (1:11-17)
      C. His apostleship was not from man (1:18-24)
      D. His apostleship was recognized by other apostles (2:1-10)
      E. His message was maintained before Peter (2:11-14)
      F. His message was according to God's plan (2:15-21)
  II. HIS THEOLOGICAL ARGUMENT (3:1—4:31)
      A. The Holy Spirit was received by faith (3:1-5)
      B. Abraham was justified by faith (3:6-9)
      C. The law curses (3:10-14)
      D. The law cannot annul the promise (3:15-18)
      E. The purpose of the law is given (3:19-22)
      F. The condition under faith is superior (3:23—4:7)
      G. Legalism is no better than paganism (4:8-10)
      H. His original contact with the Galatians is described (4:11-18)
      I. The two covenants are contrasted (4:19-31)
  III. HIS PRACTICAL ARGUMENT (5:1—6:16)
      A. The danger of falling from grace (5:1-12)
      B. The law of love (5:13-15)
      C. The conflict between the Spirit and the flesh (5:16-26)
      D. The marks of spirituality (6:1-10)
      E. The warning against the Judaizers (6:11-16)
CONCLUSION (6:17-18)

Survey

1:1-5

Paul immediately denied any human origin for his apostleship. No group of apostles appointed him to that office ("of men"; cf. the choice of Matthias by apostolic vote; Acts 1:15-26). No individual laid hands on him and delegated to him apostolic authority ("by man"). Perhaps the Judaizers charged that Paul's assumed apostleship came through the ministry of Ananias (Acts 9:10-18) or through Barnabas who introduced Paul to the Jerusalem apostles and later involved him in the work at Antioch (Acts 9:26-28; 11:25-26). Paul's salvation and apostolic appointment were determined directly by Christ before his encounter with any of those men (Acts 9:1-9; cf. 9:15-16).

1:6-10

Paul then marveled at their spiritual gullibility in that they were so easily influenced by the Judaizers. These men troubled or confused the young converts with their impressive teaching of the law and perverted the real gospel in doing so. They actually preached another gospel (cf.

234

REFINERY

II Cor. 11:4). Here Paul employed a Greek word game. They preached another *(heteros:* another of a different kind) gospel which was not really another *(allos:* another of the same kind).[3] The difference between the message of Paul and that of the Judaizers was not in the presentation or emphasis,[4] but in its essence. The false teaching that both faith and works are necessary to gain justification actually redefines the concept of faith as used by Paul. Paul then pronounced an anathema, a curse, upon any who would preach another gospel than that preached by Paul and received originally by the Galatians.[5] The Judaizers charged that Paul was a religious salesman or man-pleaser in that he was afraid to preach the necessity of circumcision to adult, uncircumcised Gentiles; this Paul clearly denied (1:10).

1:11-24

Paul also denied any human origin for his message of justification by faith alone. He did not receive *via* letter the gospel content nor was he taught it by any apostle; rather, he received his commission and message in the same way as the other apostles. Christ revealed Himself to Paul as He did to the apostles during His forty days of postresurrection ministry. In support of this claim, he appealed to his preconversion life as a zealous, law-loving Pharisee. Paul wanted the Galatians to know that the Judaizers were no more zealous for the law in the present than he was in the past. In his zeal Paul persecuted Christians, and now the Judaizers were doing the same to him. It was the personal revelation of Christ and his subsequent conversion that caused Paul to preach Christ, not legal obedience, to the Gentiles. For three years after his conversion, Paul had no contact with the apostles in which to be ordained or taught by them. He later saw Peter and James, but only for fifteen days. For the next eleven years the churches of Judea rejoiced whenever they heard of Paul's ministry through secondhand reports. They could do this because he preached the same faith which once he destroyed and which they embraced, a message of justification by faith without circumcision.

2:1-10

Fourteen years after his conversion, Paul with Barnabas took Titus, an uncircumcised Gentile convert, to Jerusalem. There Paul explained

---

3. Illustration: A person who had just eaten a Delicious apple ate another fruit (pear: *heteros)* which was not another (McIntosh apple, etc.: *allos).*
4. In trying to win converts, some emphasize the love of God while others emphasize the holiness of God.
5. There are two different conditional clauses in these verses. Paul included himself and an angel in a theoretical possibility ("though"=*ean* with the subjunctive mood), whereas he did say that someone was actually preaching another gospel in their midst ("if"=*ei* with the indicative mood).

the message that he preached to the Gentiles and presented Titus as Exhibit A of the results. The apostles recognized that Titus was genuinely saved and did not force him to be circumcised. This action clearly destroyed the charge of the Judaizers that Paul preached a watered-down message. Paul also resisted an attempt of false brethren who tried to impose legalism upon his message. The Judaizers charged that Paul was afraid to stand for his beliefs, and yet he stood adamantly in the very center of Jewish Christianity. The apostles also recognized that Paul's apostleship was equal to theirs and that God had called Paul to a special ministry among the Gentiles just as Peter had been called to a unique ministry among the Jews. At no time did they question his apostleship or change his message.

2:11-21

Later Paul stood for his convictions in Antioch when he rebuked Peter publicly for failure to identify himself with believing Gentiles in the midst of Jewish Christians from Jerusalem. Since believing, uncircumcised Gentiles and believing, circumcised Jews share the same spiritual position in Christ, Peter by his actions denied that truth and manifested a false Jewish superiority. Even Barnabas and other Jewish believers followed Peter's example. Paul's rebuke was in the form of a theological argument which served as an appropriate conclusion to the autobiographical argument (chs. 1-2) and as a fitting introduction to the second major section of the Epistle (chs. 3-4). In it Paul demonstrated that no Jew or Gentile could be justified by the works of the law and that believers are under no present obligation to the Mosaic law, for they have a spiritual position in Christ. In fact, he concluded that Christ's death was meaningless if men could somehow secure divine righteousness (any portion of it) through human effort, including that of circumcision or conformity to the law.

3:1-5

The address and the question "O foolish Galatians, who hath bewitched you" begin the heart of Paul's theological argument. He first appealed to their salvation experience. Since they received the Holy Spirit by faith without works and subsequently were persecuted for that belief, why did they think that their present experience had to be perfected through human effort?

3:6-9

Since the Judaizers prided themselves on being physical descendants of Abraham (cf. II Cor. 11:22), Paul pointed out that Abraham received divine righteousness by faith before he was circumcised and before the Mosaic law was given (Gen. 15:6; cf. Gen. 17:9-14, 23-24). The real children of Abraham are those who have been justified in the same way that he was. He further argued that the Abrahamic covenant promise (3:8) extended to the justification of Gentiles by faith alone.

3:10-14

The law curses rather than saves. To avoid the curse, one had to keep every commandment every moment of every day. Since no man could do this, man was automatically under the curse of the law and thus could not gain a justified position through the keeping of it. Even Habakkuk, who prophesied after the Mosaic law was given, announced that justification was by faith alone (3:11; cf. Hab. 2:4). Since man could not remove himself from the curse of the law by his own effort, Christ redeemed man from the curse by bearing that curse (guilt and penalty) on the cross. In this way the promise given to Abraham could also be given to Gentiles through the son of Abraham, Jesus Christ.

3:15-18

Paul then anticipated this objection: Granted that God justified Abraham by faith, but did not God give the law 430 years later, and was not this law intended to replace the faith principle as the basis for righteousness? Paul then argued that the Abrahamic covenant, once confirmed, could not be rendered inoperative by the addition of the law. Also, the covenant promise was given to both Abraham and his seed (singular), namely Christ; from the logic of time, Christ came after the law.

3:19—4:7

If the law cannot give the Spirit (3:1-5), cannot give righteousness (3:6-9), has no blessing but a curse (3:10-14), and cannot change the original covenant (3:15-18), then why did God give the law? It was added to give sin the character of transgression, to create within man a sense of sin and moral guilt, and to drive men to place their faith in Christ. Just as children were under tutors or schoolmasters (paidagogos: a child guide) until they reached adulthood or sonship, so believers were under the authority of the law until the advent of Christ who through His redemptive work elevated men into spiritual sonship (adoption means to put into the position of sons). Justification by faith makes possible these spiritual possessions: children of God, baptism into Christ, clothed with Christ, oneness in Christ, spiritual children of Abraham, redemption, adoption, indwelling presence of the Holy Spirit, and heirs of God through Christ.

4:8-20

Paul then demonstrated that the standards of Mosaic legalism were no different in principle than the obligations within the pagan idolatrous system from which they had been saved. Such regulations enslaved them in the past, and Paul saw the teaching of the Judaizers as a new slave master. He feared that his evangelistic effort in Galatia had become fruitless. He wanted the Galatians to renew their confidence and love toward him, to remember how they treated him as an angel or as Christ in spite of his physical infirmity, and to recall their willingness to impart their own eyesight to him.[6] Paul appealed to them to change their attitudes toward him and to see the Judaizers as their real spiritual enemies.

4:21-31

In an allegory based upon a genuine historical event, Paul cleverly demonstrated that it was impossible to receive the promise of righteousness through both faith and works. Note these contrasts:

Abraham	
Sarah	Hagar
Freewoman	Bondmaid
Promise	Flesh
Jerusalem	Sinai
Free	Bondage
Born of Spirit	Born of flesh
Isaac	Ishmael

God promised Abraham that he would be the father of many nations. Both he and Sarah believed that promise, but when no son came, Abraham fathered Ishmael through Hagar. However, Ishmael did not receive the promise. Later Isaac was conceived out of the deadness of Sarah's womb. Just as Ishmael persecuted Isaac so the Judaizers were persecuting Paul. Paul also concluded that it was impossible to be born of two mothers at the same time; thus a man cannot be justified by both faith and works.

5:1-12

The last two chapters contain a practical appeal based upon the theological argument ("therefore" connects the two sections). He charged the Galatians to stand in the liberty from the law that Christ provided and not to get involved with the law either as a means of justification or sanctification. He admonished that if any believed that his initial faith was not sufficient but that he also had to be circumcised to gain justification, then Christ's death would no longer have any value for him (5:2, 4). To fall from grace did not mean to lose one's salvation, but rather to fall from God's standard of gaining salvation (grace) to

---

6. Paul's infirmity may have been poor eyesight. The Galatians, after their conversion, so loved Paul that they would have offered him their eyes *via* transplant if that had been possible.

the human standard (works). He explained that in Christ there is an equality of spiritual position between the circumcised Jew and the uncircumcised Gentile. He then warned them against the Judaizers who actually hindered the Galatians' obedience and expressed confidence that the believers would not be convinced by the false teachers. He equated the apostates with leaven and desired that God would judge them physically (5:10, 12). Some Judaizers even claimed that Paul preached the necessity of circumcision to Jewish audiences; Paul denied this by asking why he was persecuted by the Judaizers if this were so.

5:13-15

Not to be misunderstood, Paul explained that freedom from the Mosaic laws did not mean freedom from God's moral laws, or lawlessness. Liberty should not be construed as license to do as one pleases; rather one has become free to love one another. This essence of the Mosaic law is binding upon all believers.

5:16-26

Just as human effort could not gain justification, neither can it achieve sanctification. Within every believer is the conflict between the flesh (sin nature) and the Holy Spirit (new nature). When the Christian is walking and is being led by the Spirit, then the ninefold fruit (singular) of the Spirit will be grown or developed through the man's personality. If the believer is not yielded to the Spirit, he will manifest the works of the flesh, the very sins that mark the habitual life-style of the unbeliever.

6:1-10

Paul then outlined basic qualities of a genuine spiritual person. Such a person will attempt to restore his sinning brother in a spirit of humility and self-protection (6:1). He will bear the prayer burdens of others (6:2). He will not have a high opinion of himself (6:3). He will examine the quality of his own Christian service, rejoicing in the satisfaction that it was done for God's glory, not for human recognition (6:4). He knows that he will bear the responsibility for his own spiritual tasks (6:5).[7] He will support financially the ministry of his spiritual teachers (6:6). He is aware of the principle of sowing and reaping as it applies both to giving and to living. He does not grow weary in Christian service, knowing that results will follow faithfulness. He will do good to all men, unsaved and saved, especially the latter.

6:11-18

Paul ended his book with a final warning against the Judaizers. In his

---

7. There is no contradiction here (6:2; cf. 6:5). Paul used two different Greek words, translated as "burden" (bare: 6:2; cf. phortion: 6:5).

concern Paul penned at least this conclusion with large-size letters, so written because of his poor eyesight. He charged that the Judaizers who claimed that Paul was afraid to preach the whole gospel including the necessity of circumcision were themselves afraid to preach justification by faith only because they knew that they would be persecuted by their own Jewish friends. He further stated that even the Judaizers could not keep the regulations they were trying to impose upon the Galatians. They gloried in their converts' willingness to submit themselves to the former, but Paul gloried only in the cross. Paul again stated that spiritual position was the real issue before God, not circumcision. He again appealed to the scars of his persecutions as evidence that he stood for his apostleship and message.

Increase Your Learning

By Doing

1. To identify the argument from Paul's personal life, circle or underline all references to "I" or "me" in the first two chapters.
2. Underline all references to justification, to circumcision, and to the law throughout the book.
3. In the last two chapters underline all references to the flesh and to the Spirit.

By Discussing

1. Identify the modern equivalents of the Judaizers. In what ways do they preach another gospel?
2. Discuss how God's servants can be separated from their mothers' wombs. How do heredity and environment affect divine preparation?
3. When should erring believers be reproved publicly? Can this be done both orally and in the written page?
4. Is it wrong to desire the enemies of the gospel to be cut off? Does this mean that they are beyond salvation?
5. Why do believers not get spiritually involved in the lives of other Christians today? Are they afraid of being misunderstood?

By Reading

Burton, Ernest D. *A Critical and Exegetical Commentary on St. Paul's Epistle to the Galatians.* Edinburgh: T. & T. Clark, 1920.

Ironside, H. A. *Expository Messages on the Epistle to the Galatians.* New York: Loizeaux Bros., 1941.

Lightfoot, J. B. *Saint Paul's Epistle to the Galatians.* Grand Rapids: Zondervan Publishing House, 1957.

Ridderbos, Herman N. *The Epistle of Paul to the Churches of Galatia.* Grand Rapids: Wm. B. Eerdmans Publishing Co., 1961.

Tenney, Merrill C. *Galatians: The Charter of Christian Liberty.* Grand Rapids: Wm. B. Eerdmans Publishing Co., 1951.

13

EPHESIANS

Writer

From the content of the book, there is no reason to question the Pauline authorship of this Epistle. The writer identified himself as Paul (1:1; 3.1). In addition, he mentioned that he was both an apostle and a prisoner, titles that he claimed in other Epistles and that harmonize with Paul's life history. His frank estimation of his low estate was seen elsewhere (3:8; cf. I Cor. 15:9-10). He seemed to identify himself as a Jew in contrast with his Gentile readers ("you," 2:1, 12-13; "us," 2:3-5). The Pauline style of writing is very evident throughout this book. After the initial greeting comes the exposition of doctrinal truth followed by practical appeals and closing with personal matters. The book bears such a close affinity to Colossians in vocabulary and content as to argue for the same author and the same time of composition. It has been said that of the 155 verses in Ephesians, the content of 78 of them is repeated in Colossians with some differences. This is why the two books are called the "Twin Epistles."

The early Church Fathers recognized the strong internal evidence and agreed that the Epistle was written by the apostle Paul. Some of those who stated this conclusion are: Ignatius, Polycarp, Irenaeus, Clement of Alexandria, Tertullian, Marcion, Clement of Rome, Ignatius, and Hippolytus. Ephesians was also listed within the Muratorian Canon.

City of Ephesus

The city was colonized in the eleventh century B.C. by the Athenians. In subsequent generations it was conquered by the Persians, the Macedonians, and the Romans. Destroyed by fire in 356 B.C., it was immedi-

241

ately rebuilt because of the pride of its inhabitants and the importance of its strategic location. Located on the banks of the Cayster, it was both the chief port and capital of the province of Asia. In New Testament times it was famous as a political, commercial, and religious center. It boasted a twenty-five-thousand-seat theater, a race course, and the temple of Diana, known as one of the seven wonders of the ancient world.

Both the city and its province attracted a large number of the diaspora Jews (Acts 2:9; 6:9; 19:8, 10) who were very zealous and prejudiced about racial and religious differences. These were the Jews who caused the Jerusalem Jews to riot against Paul in the temple (Acts 21:27-32).

This city enjoyed the ministry of several apostolic leaders. Paul labored there for three years; his companions, including Aquila, Priscilla, Apollos, and Timothy, were involved in the work; and tradition states that the apostle John spent his last years in Ephesus and died in that city.

Today the ancient city lies in ruins. There is a small Turkish town called Ayasaluk located nearby.

Establishment of the Church

Paul had wanted to go into the province of Asia during his second missionary journey, but the Holy Spirit prohibited him (Acts 16:6). After founding works at Philippi, Thessalonica, Berea, Athens, and Corinth, Paul on his way back to Syrian Antioch made a brief stop at Ephesus (Acts 18:18-19). During his week there, he had an opportunity to preach to the Jews in the synagogue. They wanted Paul to stay for a longer period, but he had to leave; he assured them, however, that he would return if it were God's will (Acts 18:19-21).

Aquila and Priscilla, who had accompanied Paul from Corinth to Ephesus, remained at Ephesus after Paul sailed. When Apollos, an orator, expositor, and evangelist of the teachings of John the Baptist, came to Ephesus, the couple explained the truth about Christ to him, and he was converted. Apollos then left for a ministry in Corinth (Acts 18:24-28).

Meanwhile Paul had started out from Antioch on his third journey through Galatia and Phrygia on his way to Asia. After his arrival in Ephesus, his first converts were twelve disciples of John the Baptist, probably so influenced through the ministry of Apollos (Acts 19:1-7). Accepting an earlier invitation, Paul preached in the local synagogue for the next three months. When public opposition developed, Paul withdrew from the synagogue, taking the converts with him, and continued his ministry for the next two years in the school of Tyrannus. This work was so effective "that all they which dwelt in Asia heard the word of the Lord Jesus, both Jews and Greeks" (Acts 19:10). It is very plausible that all of the seven churches of Asia (Ephesus, Smyrna,

Pergamos, Thyatira, Sardis, Philadelphia, and Laodicea; cf. Rev. 2–3) were founded at this time either directly by Paul or indirectly through Paul's associates or converts.

God authenticated the ministry of Paul in an unusual way so "that from his body were brought unto the sick handkerchiefs or aprons, and the diseases departed from them, and the evil spirits went out of them" (Acts 19:12). There is no indication that this type of miracle was performed by God through Paul elsewhere or that it was intended to become a pattern for other apostles or believers to follow or to expect. Human attempts to counterfeit these miracles failed. As a result of this miraculous display, many Jews, Greeks, and followers of the occult were saved. Luke recorded: "So mightily grew the word of God and prevailed" (Acts 19:20). Paul himself wrote: "For a great door and effectual is opened unto me, and there are many adversaries" (1 Cor. 16:9).

Opposition came from pagan silversmiths who made their living through the manufacture of miniature statues of Diana and of replicas of her temple (Acts 19:23-41). Paul had already planned to leave Ephesus, to visit Macedonia and Achaia, to return to Jerusalem, and then to sail for Rome; he sent an advance team, but stayed on in Asia "for a season" (Acts 19:21-22). It was at this time that Demetrius, enraged over the decline of shrine sales, provoked a mob to seize Paul's companions, Gaius and Aristarchus, and to take them before the pagan Ephesians in the theater. Paul wanted to join his friends in their hour of

The stage area of the theater at Ephesus. The theater had a seating capacity of twenty-five thousand.

need, but the believers restrained him from doing so. When it looked as though the two companions would be executed, the town clerk (or mayor) warned the assembly that their actions would be investigated by Rome, declared that legal channels were open to the silversmiths, and dismissed the assembly.

When the uproar was over, Paul left Ephesus for Macedonia, ending a ministry of about three years in that city (Acts 20:31), the longest period of time that he spent in any city on his three missionary journeys. Later at Miletus, on his trip to Jerusalem, he counseled the Ephesian elders about their responsibilities to teach the believers and to warn them against the advent of false teachers (Acts 20:17-38). This was his last contact with the church until the writing of this Epistle.

Destination of the Letter

To whom did Paul write? The opening verse reads: ". . . to the saints which are at Ephesus, and to the faithful in Christ Jesus" (1:1). However, there is a slight problem with the text here. The words "at Ephesus" (en Epheso) are not found in three major Greek manuscripts: a Chester Beatty papyrus, dated about A.D. 200 (P 46); Codex Sinaiticus, dated in the fourth century (ℵ); and Codex Vaticanus, likewise dated from the fourth century (B).[1] Because of this omission, many believe that Paul wrote this book as an encyclical letter to the seven churches of the province of Asia. This means that the Epistle was first sent to the leading church of that area, Ephesus, and that after it was read and perhaps copied, it was sent on to Smyrna. There the procedure was repeated, and the letter moved on to Pergamos. The letter thus made the circuit of the seven churches, ending up at Laodicea. In his conclusion to Colossians, Paul charged: "And when this epistle is read among you, cause that it be read also in the church of the Laodiceans; and that ye likewise read the epistle from Laodicea" (Col. 4:16). Some have identified the Laodicean letter as the encyclical letter, known to us as Ephesians. Although no positive identification can be made, this position appears plausible. For further support that this was a general letter, it has been pointed out there are no personal greetings contained within the letter and that there is no treatment of specific local church problems. This is strange in light of the fact that Paul spent a lengthy three years in Ephesus. Also, the unusual use of the word "heard" (1:15; 3:2; 4:21) seems to indicate that both Paul and his readers had only an indirect knowledge of each other's affairs. It is true that Paul was unknown personally to many within the province of Asia (Col. 2:1), but he knew very well the believers at Ephesus. This position, accepted by several evangelicals, does have one major problem: There are no Greek manu-

---

1. The symbols are the designations of textual critics.

scripts that include the name of any other city in the space normally occupied by "at Ephesus." If the Epistle did make the rounds of the seven churches and if the churches were to insert their own geographical location into the blank space, then why has not at least one manuscript been found bearing the name of Smyrna or Thyatira or Philadelphia, etc.?

The great majority of Greek manuscripts do include the words "at Ephesus." The early Church Fathers wrote that the Epistle was sent to Ephesus. The omission of personal references may be attributed to Paul's purpose in writing and/or to the purity of the Ephesian church (cf. Rev. 2:1-7).

Even if the letter was designed as an encyclical Epistle, it would appear that the book was first sent to Ephesus and that it probably returned to Ephesus, the mother church of Asia, after it moved through the church circuit. In that way, it gained the title of Ephesians. In any case, the content or teaching of the Epistle is not affected by the problem of destination.

Time and Place

During Paul's third missionary journey, a burden to visit Rome developed within him (Acts 19:21; Rom. 15:24-25). However, he first had to discharge a responsibility of taking a financial offering to the Jerusalem church. In spite of warnings against going to the holy city (Acts 21:4, 10-13), Paul arrived in Jerusalem, purified himself ceremonially, and entered the temple to offer a sacrifice as a testimony to the Jews (Acts 21:18-26; cf. I Cor. 9:20-22). There he was seized by the Jews and almost killed. Roman soldiers "rescued" him, chained him, and held him in custody until an investigation could be made. To maintain his physical safety, Paul was transported to Caesarea where he spent two years in prison (Acts 23:23-25; 24:27). Both at this time and during his subsequent voyage to Rome, he was assured by God that he would have the desired opportunity to witness in Rome (Acts 23:11; 27:24). Finally, Paul arrived at Rome where he spent the next two years as a prisoner under house arrest (Acts 28:16-31). Here Paul was able to receive visitors and to preach without any restrictions imposed upon him.

It was at this time (A.D. 59-61) that the four Prison or Captivity Epistles were written (Ephesians, Philippians, Colossians, and Philemon). All four make mention of Paul's bonds (Eph. 3:1; 4:1; 6:20; Phil. 1:12-13; Col. 1:24; 4:18; Philem. v. 1). Their common origin at this time and from this place can also be seen in the listing of his companions, of whom some are mentioned more than once: Tychicus (Eph. 6:21; Col. 4:7; Timothy (Phil. 1:1; 2:19; Col. 1:1; Philem. v. 1); Epaphroditus (Phil. 2:25); Onesimus (Col. 4:9 Philem. v. 10); Aristarchus (Col. 4:10; Philem. v. 24); Mark (Col. 4:10; Philem. v. 24); Jesus Justus (Col.

4:11); Epaphras (Col. 4:12; Philem. v. 23); Luke (Col. 4:14; Philem. v. 24); and Demas (Col. 4:14; Philem. v. 24).

Although no one denies that these four books were written from prison, the location of that prison has been questioned. The traditional view held by most evangelicals is that Paul was in Rome. However, some have argued for either Caesarea or Ephesus as the place of origin. It is true that Paul spent two years in Caesarea, but were all of these companions with him at that time? In fact, were the churches of Philippi and Colosse aware that he was in Caesarea before they sent Epaphroditus and Epaphras respectively? Since Philip the evangelist lived in Caesarea (Acts 21:8), it would have been strange for Paul to have omitted his name if these books had been written from that coastal city. There is no indication from the Biblical record (Acts) that Paul expected to be released from his Caesarean imprisonment, but these books express a hope of deliverance (Phil. 1:24-27; Philem. v. 22).

In recent years Ephesus has gained increasing support as the place of origin. Before either his Caesarean or Roman imprisonments, Paul did indicate that he had been "in prison more frequent" (II Cor. 11:23), but this phrase probably referred to short prison stays, similar to the one at Philippi (Acts 16:19-40). In Corinth he mentioned his fellow prisoners (Rom. 16:7). He did confess that he was under the sentence of death in Asia, which included the city of Ephesus (II Cor. 1:8-10). Supporters argue that it would have been much easier for the churches of Philippi and Colosse to have communicated with Paul if he had been in Ephesus rather than in Rome. However, Paul's imprisonment at Rome did last for two years, and no doubt many of the churches, if not all, knew that Paul had appealed to Caesar at Rome. Access to and from Rome was easy in that day, so until more positive evidence is forthcoming, the traditional view that Paul was in Rome when he wrote the four Prison Epistles must stand.

Since Tychicus was about to conduct Onesimus back to Philemon and to Colosse, Paul entrusted the Epistle into the care of Tychicus to be delivered to the church at Ephesus and/or to the other churches of Asia (Eph. 6:21; Col. 4:7-9). Apparently Tychicus carried from Paul three of these Prison Epistles: Ephesians, Colossians, and Philemon. Since Colosse was only about one hundred miles east of Ephesus, this would have been a simple task. Tychicus later must have rejoined Paul because just before the apostle's martyrdom during his second imprisonment at Rome, Paul sent Tychicus back to Ephesus (II Tim. 4:12), quite possibly his home town and church.

Purposes

The book divides naturally into three sections which manifest his three major purposes in writing. The first two sections are divided by this key verse: "I therefore, the prisoner of the Lord, beseech you that ye walk worthy of the vocation wherewith ye are called" (4:1). The third is separated from the second in this manner: "Finally, my brethren, be strong in the Lord, and in the power of his might" (6:10). This chart shows the contrasts of the three sections:

Calling	Conduct	Conflict
Doctrine	Duty	Defense
Wealth	Walk	Warfare
Position	Practice	Power
1:1—3:21	4:1—6:9	6:10-24

In the first section, Paul expounds the nature of the universal church, the body of Christ, by showing its sovereign calling, its composition of saved Jews and Gentiles, and its eternal purpose. In the second section, he exhorts the members of this universal Church to proper conduct toward each other, the world, God, and members of their own earthly families. The third division contains an appeal to the believer to be prepared for spiritual conflict as he attempts to put into practice his blessed spiritual position.

Distinctive Features

The theme of Ephesians is the Church; however, Paul was not emphasizing the organization of the local church, but the organism of the universal Church. This was the Church which Christ predicted would be built upon His person and redemptive work (cf. Matt. 16:18-21). Paul entitled it the Church (1:22; 3:10, 21), his [Christ's] body (2:16; 4:4), the household of God (2:19), the building (2:21), an holy temple in the Lord (2:21), an habitation of God (2:22), the mystery (3:3), the mystery of Christ (3:4), the whole family in heaven and earth (3:15), the saints (4:12), the body of Christ (4:12), the whole body (4:16), dear children (5:1), children of light (5:8), members of his body, of his flesh, and of his bones (5:30), and the mystery of the gospel (6:19).

Both Ephesians and Colossians stress the relationship between Christ, the head, and the Church, the body. However, in Ephesians the emphasis is more upon the body; and in Colossians it is upon the head of the body, Christ.

Certain key words or phrases were used rather frequently in this book: in (ninety times), grace (thirteen), spirit or spiritual (thirteen), body (eight), walk (eight), heavenlies (five), and mystery (five).

Pneumatology is stressed in the book. The personality of the Holy Spirit is seen in the facts that He is holy (1:13), that He has wisdom and can reveal truth (1:17; 3:5), and that He can be grieved (4:30). He is called the Holy Spirit of promise (1:13), one Spirit (2:18), the Spirit (2:22), his Spirit (3:16), and the holy Spirit of God (4:30). His works are many: at the moment of faith believers were sealed with Him (1:13); He is the earnest of their inheritance (1:14); by Him believers have access to the Father (2:18); the church is being built through Him (2:22); spiritual truth has been revealed by Him (3:5); believers are strengthened internally by Him (3:16), should be filled with Him (5:18), and should pray in Him (6:18); and the Spirit provides one piece of the Christian armor, the word of God (6:17).

Some classic passages of Scripture are found in Ephesians. Their content should be familiar to all evangelical believers: the purpose of God in salvation (1:3-14), the lost condition of the unsaved man (2:1-3), salvation by grace alone (2:4-10), the Church as a mystery (3:1-12), the love relationship between Christ and the Church (5:22-33), and the spiritual armor of the Christian (6:10-18).

Outline

INTRODUCTION (1:1-2)
I. THE WEALTH OF THE CHURCH (1:3—3:21)
    A. The plan of God (1:3-14)
        1. The Father (1:3-6)
        2. The Son (1:7-12)
        3. The Spirit (1:13-14)
    B. The prayer of Paul (1:15-23)
    C. The people of the Church (2:1-22)
        1. Sinners made alive (2:1-10)
        2. Jews and Gentiles made one (2:11-22)
    D. The purpose of the Church (3:1-12)
    E. The prayer of Paul (3:13-21)
II. THE WALK OF THE CHURCH (4:1—6:9)
    A. In unity (4:1-6)
    B. In diversity (4:7-16)
    C. In holiness (4:17—5:17)
    D. In the Spirit (5:18-21)
    E. In domestic affairs (5:22—6:9)
        1. Wives (5:22-24)
        2. Husbands (5:25-33)
        3. Children (6:1-3)
        4. Parents (6:4)
        5. Servants (6:5-8)
        6. Masters (6:9)
III. THE WARFARE OF THE CHURCH 6:10-20)
    A. The need for armor (6:10-13)
    B. The nature of the armor (6:14-17)
    C. The purpose of prayer (6:18-20)
CONCLUSION (6:21-24)

Survey

1:1-6

After his typical greeting, Paul eulogized God: "Blessed[2] be the God and Father of our Lord Jesus Christ, who hath blessed us with all spiritual blessings in heavenly places in Christ" (1:3). All believers have already been blessed with the positional spiritual blessings that Paul is about to enumerate. They share equally in these blessings because they are all the same *in Christ*. The first three stress the work of the Father in their behalf. First, in his own interest[3] from eternity past He chose believing sinners to be holy and without blame before Him. Second, He determined beforehand that those whom He had chosen would in eternity future stand before Him fully conformed to the image of Jesus Christ (cf. Rom. 8:28-30). Third, He made believers acceptable in the beloved, who is Christ; sinners do not make themselves acceptable (cf. I Cor. 1:30). Paul concluded this section with a brief doxology: "To the praise of the glory of his grace." This phrase is repeated three times in praise to the triune God: the Father (1:6), the Son (1:12), and the Spirit (1:14).

1:7-11

The second group of blessings emphasizes the work of the Father through the Son. First, as a present possession in Christ believers have redemption through His blood. Second, they have the forgiveness of sins according to (not out of) the riches of His grace. Regardless of the quantity or quality of a man's sins, there is enough divine grace to forgive them. Third, through Christ God has revealed the redemptive program of the ages which believers are able to understand. Fourth, in Christ believers were obtained as an inheritance.[4] This magnificent plan has been executed according to (note the three uses of this phrase: 1:5, 9, 11) the divine will.

1:12-14

The third listing of blessings deals with the special ministry of the Holy Spirit. All Christians at the moment of saving faith[5] were sealed with the Spirit. The indwelling presence of the Spirit is the sign of divine owner-

---

2. The Greek word for "blessed" is *eulogetos*. Since God is blessed in His essence, He is able to bless others. He has not been blessed (*eulogemenos*) by others.
3. Greek: *exelexato*, aorist middle indicative. The middle voice indicates God's self interest; salvation is basically theocentric, not anthropocentric.
4. Greek: *eklerothemen*, aorist passive indicative. The meaning is not that we have gained something, but that God has gained us for His inheritance.
5. Chronologically, believing and sealing occur simultaneously. Logically, sealing follows believing.

Magnificent ruins line Marble Street at Ephesus.

ship (cf. I Cor. 6:19). He is also the earnest, the down payment or guarantee, that all that God has promised the believer will possess.

1:15-23

Paul then prayed that his readers might understand what he had just revealed to them. He prayed that God would give them divine enlightenment to perceive three things (indicated by the threefold use of "what"; 1:18 [twice], 19). He wanted them to know the hope of the divine calling, that is, God's purpose in His choice of them; to know the riches of the glory of God's inheritance in the saints; and to understand the greatness of God's power which raised Christ from physical death and effected His ascension. Only after Christ's death, resurrection, and ascension could He assume the position of the spiritual head of His spiritual body, the Church.

2:1-10

The first chapter outlined God's plan for the Church; the second describes the people who make up the spiritual body.[6] All members of the true Church once shared this same lost condition. All were dead in trespasses and sins; they were world conformists; they were energized by Satan; they obeyed the rule of the sin nature; and they all deserved the

---

6. Some see 2:1-3 as a continuation of Paul's prayer. He wanted them to know the power which raised Christ from physical death and them from spiritual death. Note the connective "and" (2:1).

250

wrath of God. However, God manifested His mercy, love, and grace when He quickened them, raised them up, and made them to sit *together* with Christ in the heavenlies. The spiritual position of the believer is identified with the physical position of Christ. The believer is in Christ, and Christ in heaven; thus the believer positionally is already in heaven. The purpose of God's plan of redemption is to manifest His grace throughout eternity. Thus salvation in its initial acceptance by faith and in its resultant standing has its source only in God.[7] Once the believer walked in sin; now he is to walk in good works.

2:11-22

Generally, the true Church is composed of believing sinners; specifically, it is made of Jews and Gentiles formed into one new spiritual entity. In Old Testament times believing Gentiles still maintained their racial identity, distinct from believing Israelites. In Christ, however, there is neither Jew nor Gentile (cf. Gal. 3:28); racial identities are erased. The Gentiles are described in several ways: uncircumcision, without Christ, aliens, strangers, hopeless, Godless, and far off. The Jews are designated as the circumcision and "them that were nigh." Christ's death not only removed the sin barrier but also the law which separated the Jew from the Gentile. The true Church is one new man, one body, the houschold of God, built upon the foundation laid by the apostles and prophets, namely the person and redemptive work of Christ (cf. I Cor. 3:10-11). Both Jews and Gentiles have a spiritual sameness in Christ.

3:1-12

Paul called the church "the dispensation of the grace of God" and "the mystery of Christ." As a mystery, it was a truth unknown and unrevealed in past ages, but now manifested for the understanding of believers. The church mystery is: "That the Gentiles should be fellow-heirs, and of the same body, and partakers of his promise in Christ by the gospel" (3:6). God purposed that through His program for the Church His manifold wisdom would be revealed to man. The plan of salvation not only displays divine grace, but also divine intelligence. Only God could merge His program for the Church into His program for Israel and for the ages.

3:13-21

Paul then ended this doctrinal section with a prayer and a benediction.

---

7. The phrase "are ye saved" (2:8) is the translation of *este sesosmenoi,* a perfect passive participle in periphrastic construction. Paul's emphasis is that a believer's standing is maintained by grace, not by works. No human works can gain salvation or keep salvation.

251

He prayed that the readers might be strengthened spiritually, that Christ would be at home in their lives, that they would perceive the fourfold dimension of Christ's love, and that they might be filled with the fullness of God. In the benediction Paul expressed his desire that the Church bring glory to God because He had done more than anyone could ask or think.

4:1-16

The second major section (4:1—6:9) contains an appeal to Christians to put into practice their spiritual position in Christ. The "vocation [calling] wherewith ye are called" had just been discussed (chs. 1-3); now believers are instructed to walk worthy of it. First of all, they are to walk in unity. Paul listed seven unities that all believers share: body, Spirit, hope, Lord, faith, baptism, and Father. The practical manifestation of this unity requires sincere effort, however. Within this unity of position there is a diversity of practice as far as believers' responsibilities are concerned (4:7). The ascended Christ, as the Head of the Church, has given gifted men (apostles, prophets, evangelists, and pastor-teachers) to perfect saints so that the saints, also gifted by Christ, might do the work of the ministry. When all believers fulfill their God-given responsibilities, the body of Christ will be edified. The purposes of both gifts and gifted men are to develop spiritual maturity within the Church, to ground the believers in doctrinal stability, and to grow and to increase itself through the love and involvement of all the believing members.

4:17-32

Second, Paul charged them to walk "not as other Gentiles walk, in the vanity of their mind" (4:17). Here Paul dealt with basic moral values that should characterize the life of every believer. Their life should be the opposite of that unsaved man who is marked by a darkened understanding, lifelessness, ignorance, blindness, uncleanness, and deceit. In a series of contrasts, Paul admonished them to put off the old man and to put on the new man: truth instead of lies; work instead of stealing; giving instead of stealing; edifying speech instead of corrupt communication; and forgiveness instead of bitterness. These should be true of the believer because of Christ's nature (4:20), the unity of the believers (4:25), and the forgiveness of God through Christ.

5:1-17

Paul then charged them to walk in love (5:2), to walk as children of light (5:8), and to walk circumspectly (5:15). The standards for the earthly walk are all divine or heavenly. They are to walk as ones whom Christ loved and for whom He gave Himself, as saints, and as those aware of the will of God. In a series of imperatives (5:3, 6, 7, 11) he commanded them not to get involved in the sinful and heretical practices of the lost.

5:18-21

Between Paul's treatment of the general walk of the believer (4:1—5:17) and his specific walk (5:22—6:9), he commanded: "And be not drunk with wine wherein is excess; but be filled with the Spirit." The believer in his walk should be Spirit-intoxicated. This means that the Spirit should have total control of his life—his emotions, thoughts, and ambitions. The three participles (speaking to yourselves, giving thanks, and submitting yourselves) reveal the three signs or effects of the Spirit-filled life—joy, thanksgiving, and submission.

5:22—6:9

Only as a believer is Spirit-filled can he fulfill his obligations within the family. Wives are to be submissive to their husbands, the family heads, in the same way they are submissive to Christ, the Church Head. Husbands are to love their wives as Christ loved the Church. The relationship between the husband and the wife should reflect the love relationship that exists between Christ and His Church. Children are to obey and to honor their parents; parents are to bring up children in the nurture and admonition of the Lord. Slaves are to serve their masters as unto the Lord and masters are to treat their slaves as they would want their heavenly Master to treat them.

6:10-18

Paul cautioned the believer that his attempts to put into practice his spiritual position would be done in the midst of spiritual warfare. To understand the attacks of Satan, the believer must put on spiritual armor. The foe of the Christian is not human, but demonic. This armor is defensive in character because the battle will be brought to the believer. It is the believer's responsibility to repel the attacks and to stand his ground. There are six pieces or features of this spiritual armor: girdle of truth, breastplate of righteousness, sandals of peace, shield of faith, helmet of salvation, and the sword of the Spirit, the Word of God. In putting on the armor and in withstanding the attacks, the believer must constantly be praying for himself and for other saints.

6:19-24

Paul ended his Epistle with a request that the Ephesians pray for him that he might boldly preach the word during his Roman imprisonment. He informed them that Tychicus would make known the apostle's personal affairs. He concluded with a typical Pauline benediction.

Increase Your Learning

By Doing

1. Underline the word "grace" wherever it is found in this book.
2. Circle all descriptive titles of the Church in the Epistle.
3. Underline all prepositional phrases beginning with "in" that pertain to Christ.
4. Underline the word "walk" wherever found.

By Discussing

1. Can sovereign election be harmonized with human responsibility? Does the unsaved man really have a free will?
2. Why is the unity of the Spirit not kept today? What can be done to eliminate black and white racial distinctions in the body of Christ?
3. Why are believers not Spirit-filled today? Is this a crisis or a growth experience?
4. Why are some Christian families breaking down today? What can be done to correct the problem?
5. How does Satan attack the believer? Identify some of his wiles.

By Reading

Eadie, John. *Commentary on the Epistle to the Ephesians.* Grand Rapids: Zondervan Publishing House, n.d.

Foulkes, Francis. *The Epistle of Paul to the Ephesians.* Grand Rapids: Wm. B. Eerdmans Publishing Co., 1963.

Ironside, H. A. *In The Heavenlies.* New York: Loizeaux Bros., 1937.

Paxson, Ruth. *Wealth, Walk, and Warfare of the Christian.* Old Tappan, N.J.: Fleming H. Revell Co., 1939.

Simpson, E. K., and Bruce, F. F. *Commentary on the Epistles to the Ephesians and the Colossians.* (NIC). Grand Rapids: Wm. B. Eerdmans Publishing Co., 1957.

14

PHILIPPIANS

Writer

The content of the Epistle strongly supports the traditional view that Paul wrote this book. First of all, he calls himself "Paul" (1:1). Not only is Timothy closely associated with him in the ministry, but Paul regarded him as his son (1:1; 2:19-23; cf. I Tim. 1:2). The reference to Timothy is significant because he was on the missionary team that originally evangelized Philippi along with Paul (Acts 16). The biographical background of the author (3:4-6) harmonizes with the details of Paul's life as recorded in the other Pauline letters and in Acts. The historical background for the writing of the letter fits into Paul's known life. He was in prison, probably in Rome (1:7, 13), but he expected to be released and to revisit Philippi (1:25, 27; 2:24; cf. I Tim. 1:3).

The acceptance of the book as part of the Biblical canon and the recognition of authorship by Paul can be seen in the listing of the Muratorian Canon and in the writings of these early Church Fathers: Ignatius, Clement of Rome, Polycarp, Irenaeus, Clement of Alexandria, Tertullian, and Marcion. There is no solid reason to reject the Pauline authorship of Philippians.

City of Philippi

The city was located on a fertile plain about nine miles from the Aegean Sea, northwest of the island of Thasos. Neapolis served as its seaport. In New Testament times it was regarded as "the chief city of that part of Macedonia, and a colony" (Acts 16:12), but Thessalonica was actually the capital of the Roman province. Its inhabitants were Roman citizens who had the rights not only to vote but also to govern themselves. It is probable that they were quite anti-Semitic since no Jewish synagogue was constructed in the city although large numbers of

Jews were found in other Greek cities (Thessalonica, Berea, Athens, and Corinth).

Its history is interesting. Originally, it was a Phoenician mining town because of its proximity to gold mines located in the mountains and on the island of Thasos. Later Philip of Macedon, the father of Alexander the Great, took the city from the empire of Thrace and renamed it after himself.[1] Still later, a crucial battle between the coalition of Octavius and Antony and that of Brutus and Cassius was fought there. The former won, thus ending the Roman republic in 42 B.C. As a Roman colony, the city grew in prominence because it was on the main road from Rome to the province of Asia.

Today the city lies in ruins. The site has been excavated by archaeologists who have uncovered a marketplace, the foundation of a large arched gateway, and an amphitheater dating back to Roman times.

Establishment of the Church

Soon after Paul and Silas started out on the former's second missionary journey, they recruited Timothy to assist them (Acts 15:36—16:5). Forbidden by the Spirit to preach in Asia and Bithynia, they came to the coastal city of Troas. There "a vision appeared to Paul in the night; There stood a man of Macedonia, and prayed him, saying, Come over into Macedonia, and help us" (Acts 16:9). The missionary team, joined by Luke, sensed that God wanted them to evangelize Macedonia and left for Neapolis the next day. This was the first time that the gospel moved into Europe.

At Philippi on the Sabbath, they ministered to a group of women (probably Jewesses and Gentile proselytes) by the river since there was no synagogue in the city. Lydia, a merchant woman of Thyatira, and her household believed and were baptized (Acts 16:12-15). Lydia's house then became the base of missionary operations in that city and the meeting place of the young church (Acts 16:15; cf. 16:40).

The next significant event occurred when Paul cast out of a slave girl a demonic spirit that enabled the girl to tell fortunes. Her enraged masters seized Paul and Silas,[2] dragged them to the city's rulers, and brought this false accusation against them: "These men, being Jews, do exceedingly trouble our city, and teach customs, which are not lawful for us to receive, neither to observe, being Romans" (Acts 16:20-21). Because of the Roman antagonism toward Jews, the multitude beat them and cast them into prison.

At midnight they prayed and sang, communicating their faith to the

---

1. The Greek word for Philippi means "lover of horses."
2. Probably the reason Luke and Timothy were not seized was because the former was a pure Gentile and the latter was half Greek.

At the site of Philippi, the
chief city of Macedonia,
where Paul established a
Christian colony.

other prisoners. An earthquake shook the prison's foundations, opened
the doors, and loosed the chains from the walls. The jailor, fearful that
the prisoners under his care had fled, was about to commit suicide when
Paul stopped him. Paul then led the jailor and his household to a saving
knowledge of Christ. At his release the next day, Paul revealed that
both he and Silas had Roman citizenship and had been beaten wrongfully. They then went to Lydia's house, ministered to the believers, and
left for Thessalonica, leaving Luke behind.[3] The young church at Philippi
probably had a strange membership consisting of a converted business
woman, a demonic soothsayer, a jailor, and perhaps some prisoners.

Close contact between Paul and the Philippian church was maintained
after this initial contact. The church sent gifts on two separate occasions
to Paul during his ministry in Thessalonica (4:14-16; cf. Acts 17:1-9).
Silas was probably sent by Paul from Athens to do some additional work
there (Acts 17:15-16; I Thess. 3:1-6; cf. Acts 18:5). During his third
journey, Paul went into the province of Macedonia with an obvious
stop at Philippi (Acts 20:1), and after three months in Corinth, he
revisited Macedonia and Philippi before he left for Jerusalem (Acts
20:2-6). On this final contact Luke rejoined Paul and accompanied him
until the apostle's martyrdom.[4]

3. The first "we" section (Acts 16:10-40) ended here; the narrative reverted
to the third person plural "they"; therefore, the author, Luke, must have
stayed in Philippi.
4. Note the resumption of the "we-us" narrative (Acts 20:5-6) and the
continued usage of it throughout the rest of Acts.

Time and Place

The complicated background behind the writing of this Epistle can best be illustrated through a series of five directional arrows:[5]

| Paul
in
Rome | 1 ———————→
←——————— 2
3 ———————→
←——————— 4
5 ———————→ | Church
in
Philippi |

News of Paul's imprisonment in Rome had come to the Philippian church by some unknown means, and it created a great deal of concern and anxiety (arrow 1). To get firsthand information on Paul's predicament, the church authorized Epaphroditus to go to Rome to confer with Paul and to present him a monetary gift for his financial needs (4:10, 14-18; arrow 2). When Epaphroditus saw that Paul's material needs were much greater than the size of the Philippian gift, he stayed on in Rome, working to raise more money for Paul (2:25, 30). In doing this, Epaphroditus became very ill and almost died (2:27, 30). Word of his severe sickness somehow reached Philippi and caused a new concern for the church (2:26; arrow 3). The fact that the church knew about his illness then reached Epaphroditus in Rome and became a burden to him (2:26; arrow 4). During the time period covered by the third and fourth communications, God had healed Epaphroditus totally or at least sufficiently so that he was well enough to return to Philippi (2:27). Paul determined then to send Epaphroditus back to Philippi so that the church might rejoice at his return (2:28). The apostle thus used this occasion to write this Epistle and to send it to Philippi by way of Epaphroditus (arrow 5). It probably was written near the end of Paul's two years of imprisonment at Rome (A.D. 59-61) because Paul was confident about an imminent acquittal or release (1:25; 2:24).

There has been some thought that Paul wrote this letter from an imprisonment in Ephesus. Some plausible arguments have been set forth for this position. First, Paul planned to send Timothy to Philippi, and he did just that from Ephesus (2:19-23; cf. Acts 19:22), but why did Paul not mention Erastus in the Epistle if these two sendings of Timothy are identical? Second, it is possible that there was a Praetorium guard[6] stationed at Ephesus (1:13) and that "Caesar's household" referred to imperial civil servants (4:22) located in Ephesus, but the natural use of those phrases argue for a Roman setting. Third, it is argued that

---

5. The number of each arrow, enclosed in parentheses, appears after appropriate remarks.

6. A better translation for *en to holo praitorio* is "among the whole praetorium guard" (soldiers) rather than 'in all the palace" (a building).

Luke is not mentioned in Philippians although he was in Rome with Paul and was listed both in Colossians and Philemon. Since Luke was not with Paul in Ephesus (Acts 19), that city seems to be more likely as the place of origin. However, Luke was not mentioned in Ephesians either. Also, if Paul did write from Ephesus, why did he not include the names of those who were with him in that city (e.g., Gaius and Aristarchus, Acts 19:29)? Fourth, the Ephesian proponents say that too much time would have been involved in the five exchanges of communication; however, it only required a month to travel from Rome to Philippi. These exchanges could have taken place within a six-month period, well within the two-year limits of Paul's Roman imprisonment. Until more objective evidence is forthcoming, the traditional view that Paul wrote from Rome must stand.

Purposes

Paul learned about the spiritual needs of the church through conversations with Epaphroditus and with those who came to Rome with the report of the church's concern over the illness of Epaphroditus. First, Paul wanted to relieve their anxiety over the circumstances of his imprisonment (1:1-30). They thought that the apostle's ministry had been brought to an abrupt stop, but Paul assured them that God was using the episode for the advancement of the gospel. Second, there apparently was a growing disunity among the members because Paul appealed to them to manifest humility and unity (2:1-8). Third, he wanted to inform them of a possible imminent visit by Timothy to them (2:18-24). Fourth, he attempted to explain the reasons behind Epaphroditus' sickness and healing (2:25-30). Fifth, he desired to warn them against the deceitful tactics and doctrines of the Judaizers (3:1—4:1). Sixth, he admonished two women, Euodias and Syntyche, to maintain spiritual unity (4:2-3). Seventh, he prescribed truth that would give them mental and emotional stability to replace their anxiety (4:4-9). Eighth, he wanted to thank them for their financial assistance (4:10-20). Finally, he expressed greetings to all of them (4:21-23).

Distinctive Features

The intimate relationship that existed between Paul and the Philippian church can be seen in his frequent use of the first person singular, personal pronoun. There are over one hundred occurrences in these four short chapters of such words as "I," "me," and "my." In fact, the word "I" can be found fifty-two times. This does not mean that Paul lacked humility; rather, it shows the natural person-to-person rapport between him and them. Thus, of all the Epistles written to churches, Philippians is the most personal.

259

Within the book is a strong emphasis upon the word "gospel," found nine times in various constructions: "fellowship in the gospel" (1:5); "defence and confirmation of the gospel" (1:7); "furtherance of the gospel" (1:12); "defence of the gospel" (1:17); "conversation be as it becometh the gospel of Christ" (1:27a); "faith of the gospel" (1:27b); "laboured with me in the gospel" (4:3); and "beginning of the gospel" (4:15).

This book has a traditional reputation of being the epistle of joy. Various forms of the words "joy" and "rejoice" are found eighteen times in the book. This theme can be seen in the key verse of the book: "Rejoice in the Lord alway: and again I say, Rejoice" (4:4).

One of the greatest Christological passages occurs within this book (2:5-11) as an example or illustration to the Philippians of genuine humility and obedience. It speaks to Christ's eternal deity, incarnation, humiliation, death, resurrection, and exaltation via ascension. Theologians have called it the Kenosis passage based upon the Greek text underlying the phrase: "But made himself of no reputation" (2:7). The three Greek words of this phrase *(alla heauton ekenosen)* are literally translated: "But himself he emptied." The Kenosis theory takes its name from a transliteration of the Greek *ekenosen*. The question raised is: Of what did Christ empty Himself when He became man? Did He empty Himself of His divine attributes? If He did, then He was less than God when He walked upon the earth. But He was just as much God when He was in the womb of Mary or when He hung on the cross as He was when He created the worlds. Rather, Christ surrendered the independent exercise of His divine attributes when He became incarnate. He had them, but He did not always use them. He learned, hungered, and grew weary; these are characteristics of His human nature. However, He did use His attributes at times under the control of the Holy Spirit. He forgave sin, created food, gave life to the dead, and walked on the water. The Kenosis also involved the veiling of the outward display of His deity, namely His glory, in human flesh. No halo was upon His head nor did a glow radiate from His face. Only on the Mount of Transfiguration (Matt. 17:1-13) was His glory permitted to shine through His flesh. He also emptied Himself of the prerogative of sovereignty to be served in order to assume the attitude of a servant to serve others.

The book also provides an insight into Paul's motivations: "For to me to live is Christ, and to die is gain" (1:21). Just as people think "golf" when the name Arnold Palmer is mentioned, so believers thought "Christ" when Paul's name was spoken. Paul wanted Christ to be magnified in his body whether through living or dying for Him. He later elaborated upon His goals:

That I may know him, and the power of his resurrection, and the fellowship of his sufferings, being made conformable unto his death (3:10).

I press toward the mark for the prize of the high calling of God in Christ Jesus (3:14).

Paul never conceived of retirement in the Christian life or from the gospel ministry. His goals were ever forward and upward. Such goals have frequently been used to challenge the lives of Christians in all generations.

Outline

I. REJOICING IN OPPORTUNITIES TO SERVE CHRIST (1:1-19)
   A. Ministry of writing (1:1-2)
   B. Ministry of prayer (1:3-5, 8-11)
   C. Ministry of the Spirit (1:6)
   D. Ministry of defense (1:7)
   E. Ministry of witnessing (1:12-13)
   F. Ministry of stimulation (1:14-18)
   G. Ministry of intercession by the Philippians (1:19)
II. REJOICING IN WAYS TO GLORIFY CHRIST (1:20-30)
   A. For Paul (1:20-26)
   B. For the Philippians (1:27-30)
III. REJOICING IN THE SELFLESSNESS OF CHRIST (2:1-11)
   A. Need of the Philippians (2:1-4)
   B. Example of Christ (2:5-11)
IV. REJOICING IN THE PURPOSE OF CHRIST (2:12-16)
   A. Man's responsibilities (2:12, 14)
   B. God's responsibility (2:13)
   C. God's goals for the believer (2:15-16)
V. REJOICING IN THE SELFLESSNESS OF CHRISTIANS (2:17-30)
   A. Paul (2:17-18)
   B. Timothy (2:19-24)
   C. Epaphroditus (2:25-30)
VI. REJOICING IN THE CROSS OF CHRIST (3:1-9)
   A. True or false circumcision (3:1-3)
   B. His or their confidence (3:4-6)
   C. Divine or human righteousness (3:7-9)
VII. REJOICING IN THE CALLING OF CHRIST (3:10-16)
   A. Paul's ambitions (3:10-14)
   B. Philippians' aim (3:15-16)
VIII. REJOICING IN THE COMING OF CHRIST (3:17—4:3)
   A. Become imitators of Paul (3:17)
   B. Beware of false teachers (3:18-19)
   C. Look up to heaven (3:20-21)
   D. Stand in the Lord (4:1-3)
IX. REJOICING IN THE PROVISION OF CHRIST (4:4-19)
   A. Provision of peace (4:4-9)
   B. Provision of money (4:10-19)
CONCLUSION (4:20-23)

Survey

1:1-19

In the first chapter Paul wanted to assure the Philippians that his ministry had not ceased simply because he was in prison. He wrote: "But I would ye should understand, brethren, that the things which happened unto me have fallen out rather unto the furtherance of the gospel" (1:12). How could this be? This imprisonment gave Paul time to write four canonical books. During his second Roman imprisonment, he wrote Second Timothy; thus five of his thirteen books were written during a time of restricted movement. In prison Paul could still carry on a ministry of intercessory prayer; although he could not physically be in Philippi, he could pray and God could answer prayer in Philippi. Paul also wanted to assure the Philippians that the work of God within the lives of believers is not stopped by prison walls (1:6). He looked upon the defense of the gospel as being just as necessary as the propagation of the gospel; they are the positive and negative sides of declaring the whole counsel of God (cf. Acts 20:17-38). In prison Paul maintained a personal witness to the praetorium guard, the soldiers assigned to his house arrest, and to Caesar's household (1:13; 4:22). Just as God used Paul's imprisonment to save the Philippian jailor and his family, so God was using this experience to save soldiers and servants at Rome. Paul's steadfast stand also encouraged other preachers to take up the slack and to evangelize in his absence (1:14-18). Finally, the trial of Paul stimulated the Philippians to undertake a new ministry of prayer in behalf of the apostle (1:19). Often Christians do not pray fervently until one of their loved ones is in desperate need.

1:20-26

Although Paul did not expect to be martyred at this time (1:19; 2:24), he did not fear death if it should come. He saw in it another opportunity to glorify Christ; dying for Christ is just as effective as living for Him. He knew that death would bring him personal gain because it would usher him into the presence of Christ; however, he recognized that prolonged life on earth would be of benefit to the Philippians and to other believers under his apostolic care.

1:27-30

He then admonished them to stand in unity in the midst of persecution and not to be afraid of their persecutors. Such an experience proved their possession of salvation and the lost condition of their oppressors. He argued that suffering must of necessity follow faith and that they should follow the example which he set both at Philippi which they observed and at Rome of which they heard.

2:1-11

Paul used the Philippians' concern over his happiness as a basis of appeal. To make him rejoice they should be marked by spiritual unity, by lack of a selfish competitive spirit, by humility, and by a genuine concern for others. These qualities can be produced not through self effort, but only through yieldedness to the indwelling Christ: "Let this mind be in you, which was also in Christ Jesus" (2:5). Christ manifested these attitudes when He became incarnate to die on the cross. He and the Father shared the divine oneness both in essence and in program. He emptied Himself of glory, whereas some believers were after an empty (vain) glory. By adopting the attitude of servanthood, He was able to minister to others. He did not look upon the glories of His eternal being; rather, He looked upon the spiritual needs of mankind. Because of His condescension, humiliation, and obedience, God exalted Him to a position higher than He had ever had before. The way up is the way down; humiliation must always precede exaltation.

2:12-16

Paul then charged them to cooperate with God in the public manifestation of their salvation. They were to work out their salvation which they possessed, not to work for a salvation not yet obtained. In so doing, they needed to recognize that God was energizing them or working in them to accomplish His will.

2:17-30

Paul then gave them three examples of men who were working out their salvation and who were manifesting the selfless mind of Christ. Paul first mentioned himself as one who was willing to sacrifice himself for the faith of the Philippians just as Christ sacrificed Himself for them Timothy was one likeminded with Paul; he would look on the needs of the Philippians rather than upon his own desires. Epaphroditus was another who did not regard his own life, but rather expended himself to meet the needs of Paul.

3:1-9

In the third chapter Paul warned against the inroads of the Judaizers (3:2, 18-19). He characterized them in eight ways: dogs (cf. Isa. 56:10-11), evil workers (cf. Matt. 7:21-23), the concision, enemies of the cross, destined for destruction, worshipers of their belly, earthly minded, and those who glory in what they should be ashamed of. In contrast, he set himself as an example of all true believers, designated in four ways: the genuine circumcision (cf. Rom. 2:29), worshipers of God in spirit, rejoicing in Christ, and having no confidence in self.

263

Paul then mentioned seven ways (3:5-6) in which his life could have given him confidence more than other men. Paul was the most moral and religious man who ever lived; if anyone could have earned heaven through human effort, it would have been Paul. He pointed out, however, that what he regarded once as gain, he had to esteem as loss or dung to win Christ and to receive the righteousness of Christ. The phrase "and be found in him" must be contrasted with "in the flesh." In Christ, a believing sinner achieves a justified standing.

3:10-19

Justification logically leads to sanctification. "And be found in him" leads to "that I may know him." Paul was not apathetic, but ambitious in his daily spiritual pursuits. He wanted to know three things: the person of his Savior, the power of His resurrection which could give him victory over sin, and the passion of the cross which exemplified total obedience to the will of God. Paul knew that he was not yet the man God wanted him to be nor that he had done all that God wanted him to do. He determined to forget his past victories and failures and to achieve in his life experience all that God had purposed for him when He called him into salvation and service. He wanted the Philippians to follow his example, not that of the false teachers.

3:20—4:3

The Judaizers were earthly minded, but Paul was heavenly minded because his citizenship and his Savior were in heaven. The coming of Christ would give him glorification because his mortal, corruptible body would be changed to have the same nature as Christ's resurrection body. Based on God's provision for justification (3:1-9), sanctification (3:10-19), and glorification (3:20-21), Paul again appealed for unity.

4:4-9

In the final chapter Paul rejoiced before the Philippians for God's provision of peace, contentment, and money. Although the church was anxious about Paul, he was experiencing the peace of God that gave him mental and emotional stability even in prison. Four prerequisites for freedom from worry are: constant rejoicing, a gentle spirit, an awareness of God's presence, and prayerful commitment. Once the peace of God has been given, it can be maintained through positive, wholesome thinking. Paul wanted the Philippians to share the same peace that he enjoyed (4:9).

4:10-19

Paul then rejoiced because the Philippians had renewed their financial interest in him, although they had wanted to before but had had no opportunity to do so. He informed them that he had learned the lesson of contentment, regardless of his financial condition. He noted that some spiritual lessons can only be learned in times of need and that others can only be learned in times of abundance. He knew that God would enable him to get by with whatever provision was made. He thanked them for previous gifts, indicating that their gifts would also bring them rewards through his work. He then thanked them for their sacrificial gifts sent through Epaphroditus and assured them that God would make up any need they suffered in sending it.

4:20-23

He closed the book with a doxology (4:20), praising God for what He was doing both for him and the Philippians. He then sent greetings from himself, his associates, the Roman Christians, and especially some of Caesar's household. A typical benediction concludes the book.

Increase Your Learning

By Doing

1. Underline "rejoice" and all related words wherever found.
2. Underline the word "gospel" wherever found.
3. Mark all references to unity or oneness wherever found.
4. Circle all of Paul's references to himself (I, me, my).

By Discussing

1. How can an invalid have a ministry for Christ? a blind person? What avenues of service are available to the average Christian today?
2. What is the difference between holy ambition and self-assertion? Between humility and shyness? Between involvement in and interference with the lives of others?
3. Why do Christians still glory in their past, in the achievements of their unsaved life, when Paul counted them but loss?
4. Why are believers apathetic today? What can be done or said to stir them out of their complacency?
5. Why are so many Christians suffering mental and nervous breakdowns? Are such experiences part of the abundant life that Jesus promised?
6. How can contentment over one's financial condition be harmonized with a desire for pay increases or a high standard of living?

By Reading

Lightfoot, J. B. *Saint Paul's Epistle to the Philippians.* Grand Rapids: Zondervan Publishing House, 1953.

Martin, Ralph P. *The Epistle of Paul to the Philippians.* Grand Rapids: Wm. B. Eerdmans Publishing Co., 1959.

Moule, H. C. G. *The Epistle of Paul the Apostle to the Philippians.* Cambridge: University Press, 1895.

Tenney, Merrill C. *Philippians: The Gospel at Work.* Grand Rapids: Wm. B. Eerdmans Publishing Co., 1956.

15

COLOSSIANS

Writer

All evidence definitely points to Paul as the author. He named himself as Paul three times (1:1, 23; 4:18). He identified himself both as an apostle and a minister (1:1, 23, 25). He ended the Epistle with his typical handwritten salutation (4:18; cf. II Thess. 3:17). His associates at the writing of Colossians (1:1; 4:9-14) are also mentioned in Philemon (vv. 1, 10, 23-24): Timothy, Onesimus, Aristarchus, Mark, Epaphras, Luke, and Demas. In both of these books, he addressed Archippus (Col. 4:17; Philem. v. 2). These features argue for a single author of both books at the same time from the same place.

Some have argued against Pauline authorship by stating that the style and vocabulary in this book are different from the style and vocabulary in his other Epistles. The nature of the subject matter often determines the literary style and the choice of words, however. Actually, there is a great similarity of content between Ephesians and Colossians. Others feel that the nature of the heresy was too advanced for the sixth and seventh decades of the first century and that it reflects a second-century error; however, the book refutes an incipient Gnosticism, not a mature expression. Some critics believe that the theological concepts of Christ's person and work are also advanced, but His sovereign deity is expressed elsewhere by Paul (cf. Phil. 2:5-11).

Early church tradition supported the Pauline authorship of Colossians. The Muratorian Canon and these historical Fathers recognized it as canonical: Justin Martyr, Irenaeus, Clement of Alexandria, Tertullian, Origen, and Marcion.

City of Colosse

The city was situated on a rocky ridge overlooking the valley of the Lycus River that ran through this mountainous district. It was located about one hundred miles east of Ephesus and about twelve miles north of Laodicea. In the fifth century B.C. during the Persian wars, it was a very important city, but as her companion cities Laodicea and Hierapolis grew, she declined. In New Testament times she ranked third behind the other two. However, the city did retain some mercantile value because it was one of the stops on the trade route to the east and because glossy black wool was provided through the sheep industry in the adjoining hills. The city was destroyed by an earthquake during the reign of Nero, but it was quickly rebuilt. Today, the ancient site lies in ruins with a modern town, Chronas, located nearby.

Establishment of the Church

The evangelization of Colosse is not specifically mentioned in the Book of Acts. During Paul's three years of ministry in Ephesus, Luke recorded "that all they which dwelt in Asia heard the word of the Lord Jesus, both Jews and Greeks" (Acts 19:10). Most scholars feel that it was at this time the church at Colosse was founded. Paul, though, probably did not go to Colosse himself. He wrote: "For I would that ye knew what great conflict I have for you, and for them at Laodicea, and for as many as have not seen my face in the flesh" (2:1). This verse suggests that both the Laodicean and the Colossian churches had not experienced his direct, personal ministry. How then were the churches started? There are two strong alternatives. The first is that one of Paul's associates, possibly Timothy, went into the region of Laodicea and Colosse during the apostle's stay at Ephesus. Perhaps this is why the name of Timothy is included in the introductory greeting (1:1). The second is that residents of Laodicea and Colosse, perhaps Epaphras (1:7-8; 4:12-13), Nymphas (4:15) and/or Philemon (Philem. vv. 1-2), journeyed to Ephesus, were saved directly through Paul's ministry, returned to their hometowns, and started churches there. Paul had led Philemon to Christ (Philem. v. 19) and since Paul knew several by name in Colosse and Laodicea (Epaphras, Nymphas, Philemon, Apphia, and Archippus), this view looms as a strong possibility. The converts of these initial converts had never had the privilege of seeing Paul, and yet they looked to him for apostolic direction. In a sense, he was their "spiritual grandfather." This is why Paul's knowledge of their spiritual condition was secondhand (1:4, 8).

The membership was composed largely, if not exclusively, of Gentiles. Paul identified them as "being dead in your sins and the uncircumcision of your flesh" (2:13; cf. Eph. 2:1). The title "uncircumcision" is a

267

designation for Gentiles (cf. Rom. 2:24-27; Eph. 2:11). It is hermeneutically possible that the phrases "among the Gentiles" and "in you" were meant to be synonymous. The phrase, "And you, that were sometime alienated and enemies in your mind" (1:21), sounds like Paul's description of lost Gentiles elsewhere (Eph. 2:11-12; 4:17-18).

Nature of the Heresy

The false teaching at Colosse consisted of a mixture or merger of Jewish legalism, Greek or incipient Gnostic philosophy, and possibly Oriental mysticism. Because of these diverse elements, some have thought that Paul was dealing with two or three different groups of false teachers; however, the characteristics are so interwoven throughout the book as to suggest one group of heretics with multiple errors in their teaching. Were these teachers Jewish or Gentile? It is difficult to say with certainty; neither answer affects the content of the heresy. Thus it is safe to identify the false teaching as either Judaistic Gnosticism or Gnostic Judaism. Many Jews lived in that area because their ancestors were forced to migrate there under the Seleucidae ruler, Antiochus III. The descendants eventually strayed away from orthodox Judaism and sucumbed to the influence of Greek philosophy. The heresy at Colosse did have a strong Jewish ritualistic character, whereas second-century Gnosticism manifested more the philosophical element. It is also difficult to determine whether these heretics were within the church membership or attacked the church from without. Paul warned against both sources (Acts 20:29-30). Since the church was young and did have some adequate leadership, it would seem that the heresy came as an outside threat.

What were its teachings? It taught that spiritual knowledge was available only to those with superior intellects, thus creating a spiritual caste system. Faith was treated with contempt; advanced Gnosticism even taught that salvation was received by knowledge. Adherents believed that they could understand divine mysteries totally unknown and unavailable to the typical Christian.

Another influence of Greek philosophy was in its teaching that all matter was innately evil and that the soul or mind was intrinsically good. This logically led to a denial of the creation of the material world by God and to a denial of the incarnation of Jesus Christ. The latter involved a repudiation of His humanity, His physical death, and His physical resurrection.

To explain the existence of the material world, the heresy taught that a series of angelic emanations created it. According to them, God created an angel who created another angel who in turn created another angel *ad infinitum*. The last angel in this series then created the world. This angelic cosmogony thus denied the direct creation and supervision of the world by God. This conviction resulted in some practical theological error. It stressed the transcendance of God to the exclusion of His immanence. Since God did not create the world in the past, He does not work in the world in the present. This would rule out the value of prayer or the possibility of miracles. It led to a false worship of angels. If the world resulted from angelic emanations, then the person in the world had to work his way back to God through this series. Thus he would have to know who those angels were and how many there were in order to give each his proper respect.

Christ was reduced by most Gnostics into a creature, perhaps the highest being that God created. This was an attack upon the Trinity and upon the eternal, sovereign deity of Jesus Christ.

In daily living, the heresy led to asceticism and legalism. If matter is evil, then the body is evil. The heresy taught that to destroy the desires of the body to satisfy the needs of the soul, a rigid code of behavior, including circumcision, dietary laws, and observances of feasts, had to be followed.

The dangers of the heresy were quite obvious to Paul. His refutation of them will be seen in the survey.

Time and Place

During Paul's absence from Asia, this Judaistic-Gnostic heresy began to infiltrate the area. The leaders of the Colossian church were apparently unable to cope with it so they sent Epaphras to Rome to consult with Paul. Quite possibly, Epaphras was the founder and pastor of the church; when he left, Archippus assumed the pastoral responsibility (1:7; 4:17). Epaphras informed Paul of the Colossians' faith (1:4-5), their love for Paul (1:8), and the heretical threat. Unable to go to Colosse because of his imprisonment, Paul penned this Epistle and sent it to the church through Tychicus and Onesimus (4:7-9). For some unknown reason Epaphras was imprisoned along with Paul by the Roman government (Philem. v. 23). Since Epaphras could not return to Colosse at this time to correct the situation with the apostolic authority of the Epistle, the task was assigned to Tychicus. However, Paul assured the church that Epaphras was laboring "fervently for you in prayers, that ye may stand perfect and complete in all the will of God" (4:12). Thus, within eight years of the establishment of the church, Paul had to write to this young, immature, threatened church to warn them against the errors of the heresy (2:8, 16, 20).

Purposes

Paul wrote, therefore, to express his prayerful interest in the spiritual development of the Colossian believers (1:1-12), to set forth the sovereign headship of Jesus Christ over creation and the Church (1:13-

29), to warn them against the moral and doctrinal errors of the heresy (2:1-23), to exhort them to a life of holiness (3:1—4:6), to explain the mission of Tychicus and Onesimus (4:7-9), to send greetings from his associates (4:10-15), and to command the exchange of correspondence with the Laodicean church (4:16-18).

Distinctive Features

The close resemblance to Ephesians both in content and vocabulary must again be mentioned. So much of Colossians is repeated in Ephesians that the two books must have been written at the same time from the same place with similar themes. Here are some related contrasts:

Colossians	*Ephesians*
Completeness in Christ	Oneness in Christ
Christ in the body of the believer is a mystery	Jew and Gentile as one in the body of Christ is a mystery
Christ as the *Head* of the body is emphasized	The Church as the *Body* of Christ is emphasized

This book contains a classic passage on the preeminence of Jesus Christ (1:14-22). It actually develops grammatically as a relative clause ("in whom," *en ho*) within the apostle's prayer (1:9-14). The listed descriptive titles of Him are unique: the image of the invisible God, the firstborn of every creature, the head of the body, the beginning, and the firstborn from the dead. His role as creator of the universe is explained through four prepositional phrases: sphere of creation (literally, "in him," *en auto;* 1:16); agent of creation ("by him," *di autou;* 1:16); goal of creation ("for him," *eis auton;* 1:16); and prior to creation ("before all things," *pro panton;* 1:17). Paul also called Him the sustainer of creation ("by him all things consist"). Both in the natural and in the spiritual creations, Christ is sovereign and should have the preeminence.

Colossians contains the most severe warning against unguided human intellect or non-Biblical philosophy: "Beware lest any man spoil you through philosophy and vain deceit, after the tradition of men, after the rudiments of the world, and not after Christ" (2:8). The Greek word for "philosophy" *(philosophia)* means "love of wisdom." In Christ are "hid all the treasures of wisdom [*sophias*] and knowledge" (2:3); therefore, a genuine love for wisdom should lead to a perfect love for Christ. However, there are many systems that go under the guide of "philosophy" that are really governed by human or world standards, by humanism or antisupernaturalism, rather than by divine revelation centered in the

270

person of Christ. Christians need to distinguish between true and false philosophies.

Outline

Survey

1:1-8

Paul's refutation of the heresy will be seen through a positive presentation of the truth rather than through a repudiation of it point by point. He initially declared that his apostleship came from the will of God and that the Colossian believers had received grace and peace from both the Father and the Son, thus denying the allegation that God had no direct contact with mortal man. He then gave thanks for their faith, love, and hope; but note the obvious omission of wisdom, the very thing the heretics exalted. These three spiritual realities were produced by hearing "the word of truth of the gospel" (1:5) and "the grace of God in truth" (1:6), not through Gnostic mysteries.

1:9-13

Paul then prayed that the believers "might be filled with the knowledge of his will in all wisdom and spiritual understanding" (1:9). His use of the very terms employed by the heretics probably startled his readers; however, Paul demonstrated that such knowledge was available to all of the believers, not just to a privileged few, and that this knowledge was not an end in itself but should issue in a worthy walk before Christ. The fourfold description of this walk was marked by the phrases introduced

271

by these four participles: being fruitful, increasing, being strengthened, and giving thanks. The Father deserved thanks for three works: He "made us meet to be partakers of the inheritance of the saints in light"; He "delivered us from the power of darkness"; and He "translated us into the kingdom of his dear Son."[1]

1:14-19

After mentioning the Son, Paul expounded the nature of the person of Jesus Christ and His relationships both to the natural, material creation and to the supernatural, spiritual creation. As the image of the invisible God, He had revealed God to man; all that God is, He is (John 1:18; 10:30; 14:9). He was the firstborn[2] or sovereign of the material world because He made and sustains it. Through His death and resurrection He became the sovereign head of His spiritual creation, the Church. Christ was personally responsible for both material and spiritual realities, not a series of angelic emanations. Both in the natural world and in the Church, He (not angels) deserves the preeminence, because the fullness of deity is within Him.

1:20-23

Paul then emphasized that peace and reconciliation could be secured only through "the blood of his cross" and "the body of his flesh through death." These are material entities, things that the heretics claimed to be innately evil. Paul also placed their past spiritual alienation and enmity in their minds, the immaterial part of man that the heretics exalted and claimed to be intrinsically good. Paul's teaching thus was diametrically opposed to theirs. He warned that yielding to the heresy could result in the loss of future reward and could possibly manifest the fact that they were not really saved in the first place.

1:24—2:3

Paul then claimed that he was a minister of the dispensation of God which had been given to him and that he could reveal a spiritual mystery unknown to past generations. The mystery was that Christ, in His spiritual presence, was indwelling every believer. Based on that fact, Paul warned, and taught, and desired to present "every man" perfect to Christ. Thus the charge of the heretics that perfection was available to

1. Literally, "the son of the love of him."
2. In Near Eastern families, the firstborn (*prototokos*) received the birthright and subsequent family headship. It became a title of authority and respect. Paul did not claim that Christ Himself was a creature, the first and highest creature, as charged by the sect Jehovah's Witnesses. The phrases following in the text disprove that. Besides, Paul could have used the Greek word *protoktistos* if he wanted to show that Christ was the first creature of God's creation.

only a select few was wrong. Since all of the treasures of divine wisdom are in Christ (2:3) and Christ is in every believer (1:27), then every believer has access to the divine reservoir of spiritual truth.

2:4-8

Paul then warned the readers against the enticing words and the human, worldly philosophy and vain deceit of the heretics. He wanted them to remain steadfast, to walk by faith, to be established doctrinally, and to be thankful for what God had provided in Christ.

2:9-15

Paul then argued that the believer's position in Christ released him from ritualistic, legalistic obligations so imposed by the Judaistic Gnostics. Every Christian is complete or positionally perfect in Christ; each has experienced spiritual circumcision; each died, was buried, and rose again in Christ as pictured by baptism; each has been quickened; and every one has been judicially forgiven of all his trespasses. Christ's death blotted out and removed "the handwriting of ordinances" (the law with its regulations and curses); His resurrection and ascension have set believers free from them.

2:16 23

Based on Christ's accomplishments, Paul issued two imperatives. First, "Let no man therefore judge you. . . ." The legalistic regulations of diet and feast observances in the Old Testament were designed as shadows or types to point to the substance or the antitype, namely Christ. Embrace the body, not the shadow, was Paul's cry. Second, "Let no man beguile you. . . ." Paul claimed that the worship of angels stemmed from a hypocritical humility, ignorant speculation, carnal pride, and a devaluation of Christ's sovereign headship. Paul then asked a rhetorical question of his readers: How could they subject themselves to ascetic prohibitions when they were dead to them through Christ?

3:1-17

The alternative to a legalistic, ascetic life is a Christ- and heaven-centered mind and heart. He explained the correct principles of Christian living through a series of nine imperatives: Mortify (3:5); put off (3:8); lie not one to another (3:9); put on (3:12); put on love (3:14); let the peace of God rule (3:15); be ye thankful (3:15); let the word of Christ dwell in you (3:16); and do all in the name of the Lord Jesus (3:17). These commands are based on the facts that their present practice should not manifest past experiences (3:6-7), that they positionally have put off the old man and have put on the new (3:9-10), that they are the elect of God (3:12), that they have been forgiven (3:13), that they have been called into one body (3:15), and that they should be thankful for all that God had done for them (3:17).

3:18—4:6

Paul then gave specific illustrations as to how these general principles could be put into practice in domestic, family situations. He used direct address and pointed imperatives: Wives, obey; Husbands, love and be not bitter; Children, obey; Fathers or Parents, provoke not; Servants, obey and do heartily; and Masters, give. He concluded the instructional section of this Epistle with four commands for all of the church members: continue in prayer; watch in prayer with thanksgiving; walk in wisdom; and let your speech be always with grace. He requested their prayer for him and his ministry in prison.

4:7-18

Finally, he informed them that Tychicus would give them an oral report of his personal state and that Tychicus was his authoritative representative to deal with the heresy and to comfort them. He also mentioned that Onesimus, a native Colossian, would assist Tychicus. He then sent greetings to them from Aristarchus, Marcus, and Jesus Justus, three Jewish co-workers (4:10-11). He continued with more greetings from Epaphras, Luke, and Demas (4:12-14). Paul notified them that he wanted to be remembered to the believers at Laodicea, to Nymphas, and to the latter's house-church (possibly in Hierapolis). He charged them to exchange their Epistle with the one from Laodicea (possibly Ephesians). He asked the church to influence Archippus to fulfill his ministry and concluded with his typical salutation.

Increase Your Learning

By Doing

1. Circle all words that refer to wisdom, knowledge, and understanding.
2. Make a list of all of Christ's titles.
3. Underline all of the imperatives in chapters 3 and 4.

By Discussing

1. Has Christ lost His preeminence in the world and in the church today? Why?
2. How much humanistic philosophy should a Christian study or read? Could he take philosophy courses at a secular university without being tainted?
3. Is a brilliant mind an asset or a danger to the believer? How can reason and faith be harmonized?
4. How would you refute the claim by Jehovah's Witnesses that Christ was the son of God but not God the Son?
5. It has been said that some people are so heavenly minded that

they are no earthly good. Is this possible? Could a person be so earthly minded that he would be no good to heaven?

By Reading

Carson, Herbert M. *The Epistles of Paul to the Colossians and Philemon.* Grand Rapids: Wm. B. Eerdmans Publishing Co., 1960.

Ironside, H. A. *Lectures on the Epistle to the Colossians.* New York: Loizeaux Bros., 1929.

Lightfoot, J. B. *St. Paul's Epistles to the Colossians and Philemon.* Grand Rapids: Zondervan Publishing House, n.d.

16

FIRST THESSALONIANS

Writer

The author doubtless was Paul. He called himself by that name twice (1:1; 2:18). His associates at the time of composition were Silas and Timothy, the very men who assisted Paul in the evangelization of Thessalonica (1:1; cf. Acts 17:1-9). The geographical movements of the author from Philippi to Thessalonica to Athens to Corinth (2:2; 3:1, 6; cf. Acts 16-18) correspond to Paul's recorded journey. The typical Pauline style of an opening salutation, blessing, prayer of thanksgiving, followed by a major section on doctrine and practice, and ending with a personal greeting and benediction can be traced in the book. Distinctive Pauline words and phrases (e.g. faith, love, and hope; 5:8; cf. Col. 1:4-5) are dotted throughout the Epistle.

Several Church Fathers recognized these features and acknowledged the Epistle to be from Paul. Among them were Marcion, Irenaeus, Tertullian, and Clement of Alexandria. It was also listed with the Pauline letters in the Muratorian Canon.

City of Thessalonica

The city was founded in 315 B.C. by Cassander who named it after his wife, the stepsister of Alexander the Great. When Rome organized Macedonia into a province in 146 B.C., Thessalonica was made its capital. It soon grew into the second largest city of that area, next only to Philippi which was about one hundred miles to the northeast. As a free city, it had its own government, ruled by politarchs (Acts 17:6).

It had a commercially strategic location. Situated at the head of the Thermaic Gulf, it was able to serve as a seaport for the rich agricultural plains of Macedonia. It was also the largest city on the Via Egnatia, the main highway between Rome and the region north of the Aegean Sea. In commerce with the Orient, it almost rivaled Corinth and Ephesus. Its mercantile importance no doubt attracted a good number of Jews since there was an active synagogue in the city.

Today the city still stands, bearing the name Salonika and having a population of over 200,000.

Establishment of the Church

After overnight stops at Amphipolis and Apollonia, Paul with Silas and Timothy came to Thessalonica from Philippi (Acts 17:1; A.D. 50). For three Sabbaths Paul had the opportunity to preach in the Jewish synagogue. His logical reasoning had a double thrust: first, the Old Testament predicted that the Messiah or Christ had to suffer, to die, and to rise again; second, Jesus of Nazareth fulfilled in His life, death, and resurrection those prophecies (Acts 17:2-3). As a result, some of the Jews, and "of the devout Greeks a great multitude, and of the chief women not a few" believed and identified themselves with the missionary team (Acts 17:4). During those three weeks and shortly after Paul's synagogue ministry was over, a great number of pagan idol worshipers also were converted (I Thess. 1:9).[1]

The unbelieving Jews, full of rage and jealousy, then hired a mob to stir up the unbelieving Gentiles and to assault the house of Jason, possibly the meeting place of the Christians and the lodging site of the missionary team. When they did not find Paul and his companions there, they dragged Jason and some of the Thessalonian believers before the politarchs. They brought several false charges of insurrection and treason against the Christians.[2] The rulers and the inhabitants were troubled over the accusations, but when they investigated the situation, they released Jason and his friends.[3] Because of the persecution, the team was conducted out of town secretly by night, and they journeyed on to Berea (Acts 17:5-10).

The ministry at Thessalonica lasted approximately one month, although some have argued for a longer stay. Such advocates state that

---

1. It cannot be said of synagogue Jews and Greek proselytes that they turned from idols.
2. The unbelievers may have misunderstood the concept of Christ's return to the earth, the overthrow of the wicked, and the establishment of Christ's kingdom as an imminent threat to the Roman empire.
3. The "security" was probably a guarantee of no political trouble by the believers rather than a pledge that Paul and his associates would leave; otherwise, Paul would not have jeopardized Jason by trying to return (cf. I Thess. 2:18). However, it could have contained the pledge that the missionary team would leave immediately, thus easing the present situation.

Paul must have stayed long enough to receive two financial gifts from Philippi (Phil. 4:16), to have worked with his hands to set a precedent (2:9; II Thess. 3:6-13), and to have evangelized such a large number of pagans. However, these events could have been achieved during an intensive ministry of one month. Paul did work night and day. The overwhelming success of his ministry no doubt provoked the unbelieving Jews to envy and worried the political authorities. Some key converts out of Thessalonica were later associated with Paul in the ministry: Demas (II Tim. 4:10), Secundus (Acts 20:4), Gaius (Acts 19:29),[4] and Aristarchus (Acts 19:29; 20:4; 27:2).

Time and Place

Forced out of Thessalonica, Paul and his team went to Berea where many Jews and Greek proselytes believed through his synagogue ministry. When the unbelieving Jews of Thessalonica heard that Paul was preaching in Berea, they came to that city, stirred up the people, and forced him out of that city also. The Berean Christians personally conducted Paul out of Macedonia to Athens in Achaia; Silas and Timothy remained in Berea to establish the work. At Athens Paul told the believers that when they returned to Berea they should charge Silas and Timothy to rejoin him in Athens (Acts 17:10-15). While Paul waited for them, he preached in the synagogue, in the marketplace, and on Mars' Hill (Acts 17:16-34). After the two associates came to Athens, Paul became burdened over the spiritual condition of the Thessalonians so he sent Timothy back to establish and to comfort them in the midst of their

---

4. Not the same as another Gaius (Acts 20:4). Lystra was in Galatia, not Macedonia.

A close-up view of the Corinth Canal.

persecutions (3:1-5). At this time Silas was also sent to Macedonia, probably to Philippi or Berea.

Paul then moved alone to Corinth (Acts 18:1). Soon afterwards Silas and Timothy joined him there (Acts 18:5). Timothy brought back a glorious report that the Thessalonian believers loved Paul exceedingly, that they wanted to see him again, and that they were standing firm in their faith in spite of the persecutions (3:6-9). Full of joy, Paul penned this Epistle to commend them for their faith and to explain his absence and deportment (chs. 1-3). Timothy, however, did report that there were some moral, practical, and doctrinal deficiencies in the church. Unable to return to Thessalonica to correct the problems himself, Paul in the last part of the letter determined to "perfect that which is lacking in your faith" (3:10). The apostle thus wrote this letter from Corinth during his second missionary journey (A.D. 51). The letter carrier is unknown, possibly Timothy.

Purposes

Paul wrote to commend them for their exemplary living under persecution (1:1-10), to defend his conduct at Thessalonica against criticism that had developed in his absence (2:1-16), to explain his absence from them (2:17-20), to explain why he sent Timothy to them (3:1-13), to give instructions on sexual purity (4:1-8), to admonish them to proper manifestations of brotherly love (4:9-12), to correct misconceptions about the relationship of the Christian dead to living believers at the return of Christ (4:13-18), to define the character of the Day of the Lord and to show the believers' relationship to it (5:1-11), to outline their obligations to their spiritual leaders (5:12-13), and to command them about various spiritual duties (5:14-28).

Distinctive Features

The major theme of the Epistle is the second coming of Jesus Christ. Every chapter contains at least one reference to that great truth (1:3, 10; 2:19; 3:13; 4:13-18; 5:23). The classic passage on the rapture of the church is found here: "Then we which are alive and remain *shall be caught up* together with them in the clouds, to meet the Lord in the air: and so shall we ever be with the Lord" (4:17, italics mine). The term "rapture" is based upon the Latin equivalent of the Greek word translated "shall be caught up." This passage (4:13-18), the Olivet Discourse (Matt. 24-25), the defense of the resurrection (I Cor. 15), and the Book of Revelation, contain the great prophetic sections of the New Testament. The dominance of this theme demonstrates the fact that eschatological truths were among the basic fundamental doctrines taught to new converts (Acts 17:7; I Thess. 5:1-2; II Thess. 2:5).

The exaltation of the deity and lordship of Jesus Christ is clearly seen in the book. These titles were ascribed to Him: Lord Jesus Christ (1:1 [twice], 3; 2:19; 3:11, 13; 5:9, 23, 28); Lord Jesus (2:15; 4:1, 2); Lord (1:6, 8; 3:8; 12; 4:6, 15 [twice], 16, 17 [twice]; 5:2, 12, 27); Christ Jesus (2:14; 5:18); Christ (2:6; 3:2; 4:16); Jesus (1:10; 4:14 [twice]); and His Son (1:10). This corresponds to the content of Paul's synagogue ministry at Thessalonica (cf. Acts 17:3).

Outline

SALUTATION (1:1)
  I. THE NATURE OF THE CHURCH (1:2-10)
    A. The character of the church (1:2-3)
    B. The example of the church (1:4-7)
    C. The reputation of the church (1:8-10)
  II. PAUL'S RELATIONSHIP TO THE CHURCH (2:1—3:13)
    A. His behavior in the church (2:1-12)
    B. His reception by the church (2:13-16)
    C. His concern for the church (2:17—3:10)
    D. His prayer for the church (3:11-13)
  III. THE PROBLEM OF THE CHURCH (4:1—5:22)
    A. Sexual purity (4:1-8)
    B. Social conduct (4:9-12)
    C. State of the Christian dead (4:13-18)
    D. Times and seasons (5:1-11)
    E. Church officers (5:12-13)
    F. Church responsibilities (5:14-22)
CONCLUSION (5:23-28)

Survey

1:1-10

Immediately Paul gave thanks for their work which faith produced, for their labor which love for Christ prompted, and for their patient endurance in trials which hope in Christ's imminent return inspired. The faith, love, and hope trio is emphasized not only in the Thessalonian correspondence (1:3; 5:8; II Thess. 1:3-4) but also elsewhere in Paul's writings (cf. I Cor. 13:13; Col. 1:4-5). The apostle knew positively that the Thessalonians were elected by God to salvation by the manner in which they received him and his message (1:5; cf. 2:13); by the exemplary lives they lived, having received the gospel outwardly with much affliction and inwardly with joy produced by the Holy Spirit (1: 6-7); by the quick spread of their testimony elsewhere (1:8); and by the report given to him by others concerning the Thessalonians' conversion experience (1:9). The majority of the members were pagans who had turned to God from idols ("work of faith") to serve God ("labour of love") and to await the imminent appearing of Christ ("patience of hope"). Theirs was a faith in a living Person who died, rose, and ascended, and who could come at any moment.[5]

---

5. The literal translation of v. 10b is: "Jesus, the one who delivers us out of

2:1-12

In the next section Paul defended his integrity against the criticisms of those unbelieving Jews who questioned his motives. In so doing, he outlined the characteristics of the model servant of God. Paul was not afraid of persecution, as some charged, for after he was beaten in Philippi, he boldly preached at Thessalonica in the midst of his adversaries (2:1-2). In a series of negatives, he claimed that his methods were not out of deceit, uncleanness, guile, men-pleasing, flattery, or covetousness, nor of seeking glory of men. Rather, he asserted that he pleased God who was the judge of his heart, that he treated them both as a nursing mother and a father, that he imparted his soul as well as the gospel, that he worked with his hands to support himself financially lest anyone think that he was after their money, and that his behavior was above reproach.

2:13-20

Paul reminded them that they received his message as the authoritative word of God and that they were persecuted by their countrymen just as the Judean Christians were persecuted by their fellow Jews. He then gave a sixfold description of the Jewish nation to show that the persecution of Paul by the Thessalonian Jews was identical to that received by Jesus Christ. He told them that he tried to return to their city at least twice, probably from Berea, and that Satan hindered him, no doubt through the antagonism of the Macedonian Jews. He then testified that their genuine salvation would be his cause to rejoice at the coming of Christ.

3:1-13

The third chapter was discussed under **Time and Place** (pp. 278-79). Here Paul explained his purpose in sending Timothy, his joy over Timothy's report, his prayer for a future visit to see them and to correct their doctrinal and moral deficiencies, and his prayer for their love and stability.

4:1-8

The pagan Thessalonians brought into their Christian experience some faulty misconceptions about love, courtship, and marriage. To correct them, Paul used such terms as: beseech, exhort, received of us how ye ought to walk and to please God, abound, and commandments (4:1-2). Paul's authoritative words on the subject came "by the Lord Jesus." He then logically demonstrated that sexual purity was part of the will of

the wrath, the coming one." This is not the wrath of Hades or of the lake of fire; a believer *was* delivered from this wrath at conversion. Christ's imminent coming *will* deliver the believer from the divine wrath of the Great Tribulation (cf. 5:9).

God for a sanctified life, that purity protects the holiness and honor of the involved parties,[6] and that purity or virginity was contrary to the philosophy of a godless world. He argued that abuse of sexual purity defrauded the other person, that it would bring the judgment of God, and that such sin was ultimately against God who placed His Spirit within the believer's body.

4:9-12

Paul acknowledged that all believers were divinely taught to love one another (cf. I John 3:14) and that the Thessalonians were doing just that, but he admonished them to "increase more and more." Specifically, they needed to manifest their love by not being an annoyance to others and by working industriously in order to maintain a testimony to the unsaved and to have no material needs. Apparently some of the believers, in a practical misapplication of the belief that Christ could come at any moment, had stopped working and had become a problem to the others (cf. II Thess. 3:6-14).

4:13-18

In the interval between the establishment of the church and Timothy's return visit, some of the believers had died, either through natural causes or persecution. The living Christians were concerned over the relationship of their departed loved ones to themselves and to the return of Christ. Paul acknowledged that sorrow was appropriate, but that it should be of a different kind than that of a hopeless world. The believer should realize that the departed Christian is with Christ and that he will return when Christ comes for the true Church. His coming will be announced in a threefold fashion: a shout, the voice of the archangel, and the trump of God. At that instant the spirit of the departed believer will return to be united with a resurrected body; then the living Christians will be translated into immortal, incorruptible bodies; both groups will be caught up to meet Christ in the air; and they will be with Him forever. Death dissolves physical relationships, but it does not sever the spiritual union of believers.

5:1-11

In a series of contrasts, Paul proved that believers would not go into the Day of the Lord, namely the tribulation in which the wrath of God would be poured out:

---

6. The vessel may refer to the body of the woman who becomes the wife (cf. I Peter 3:7) or to the body of the man (II Cor. 4:7). It is difficult to be dogmatic in one's choice; however, by maintaining the purity of the one body, the other would also be kept pure.

Ye — They
You — Them
Light — Darkness
Day — Night
Us — Others

The hope that the believer has is that Christ will save or deliver him from the wrath of the Day of the Lord, a period of time that will surprise the unsaved. The nature of the child of God is just the opposite to the character of the unsaved man who is suited for the Day of the Lord.

5:12-22

Paul then charged the believers to know their spiritual leaders personally, to understand the latter's responsibilities, and to esteem them highly (5:12-13). In a series of six imperatives (5:14-15), he exhorted them about proper relationships to both the saved and the unsaved at Thessalonica. Another list of eight commands followed (5:16-22), outlining their responsibilities to their own spiritual development and to the exercise of spiritual gifts in their midst.

5:23-28

He then prayed that their total being[7] would be preserved blameless until the coming of Christ (5:23). He assured them that God would preserve them (5:24). He ended with a typical request for prayer in his behalf, a greeting, a charge, and a benediction.

Increase Your Learning

By Doing

1. Underline all verses that contain a reference to the second coming of Christ.
2. Circle the word "brethren" wherever found.
3. Underline every name ascribed to Christ wherever found.

By Discussing

1. What kind of a reputation does your church have in your community? Outside of your area? What can be done to increase your sphere of influence?
2. Is it possible to turn to God without turning from idols? Is a person who does not do so a genuine convert?
3. Should sex education be part of the Christian home? the church? Are Christian young people brainwashed by the philosophy of the new morality or situation ethics?

---

7. This verse with its reference to "spirit and soul and body" is the main support for trichotomy, the doctrine that man is a tripartite being. In contrast, dichotomy teaches that man is only material and immaterial and that the terms "spirit and soul" should be treated as synonyms.

4. How would you define the Christian work ethic? Should sluggards be given material help?
5. Should the time of the rapture be made a basis of personal fellowship? of ecclesiastical affiliation? Can a person be dogmatic about the time of Christ's return?

By Reading

Frame, James Everett. *A Critical and Exegetical Commentary on the Epistles of St. Paul to the Thessalonians.* Edinburgh: T. & T. Clark, 1912.

Hendriksen, William. *Exposition of I and II Thessalonians.* Grand Rapids: Baker Book House, 1955.

Milligan, George. *St. Paul's Epistles to the Thessalonians.* Grand Rapids: Wm. B. Eerdmans Publishing Co., 1952.

Morris, Leon. *The Epistles of Paul to the Thessalonians.* Grand Rapids: Wm. B. Eerdmans Publishing Co., 1957.

————. *The First and Second Epistles to the Thessalonians.* Grand Rapids: Wm. B. Eerdmans Publishing Co., 1964.

17

SECOND THESSALONIANS

Writer

In spite of the close relationship between the two Thessalonian letters, some liberals have questioned the Pauline authorship of the Second Epistle. First of all, they have claimed that the apostle would not have written two letters with so many similarities within such a short time of each other. However, in the second letter Paul did not deal with every subject discussed in the first (e.g., sexual purity, state of the Christian dead). The similarities are only partial; certainly the author of both should be granted permission to repeat some truths for further clarification and emphasis. Second, they point out that the teaching on the Second Coming is somewhat different in the two Epistles. However, in the first letter he emphasized the relationship of His coming to believers, both dead and living; whereas in the second he characterized the relationship of His advent to "them that know not· God, and that obey not the gospel of our Lord Jesus Christ" (1:8) and to the destruction of the antichrist (2:8). Third, they state that the extended section on the man of sin (2:1-12) is not mentioned in the first letter. The inconsistent reasoning of the critics can be clearly seen in this charge. They try to build a case for their position from the abundance of similarities on the one hand and from the uniqueness of a passage on the other. Actually, the Thessalonians' misconceptions about the Day of the Lord necessitated such an exposition of the key concept of that period. Fourth, they feel that the tone of the two Epistles is very different; to them the first is warm and commendatory, while the second is cold and severe. However,

285

the personal warmth that existed between Paul and the church was still there (1:1-4; cf. I Thess. 1:1-3). Paul did manifest his apostolic authority in the second to discredit the false teaching and to repeat his commands to the disorderly.[1]

On the positive side, he did call himself "Paul" twice (1:1; 3:17). He again associated himself with Silas and Timothy (1:1; cf. I Thess. 1:1). The opening salutations and prayers of thanksgiving found in both Epistles are almost identical. Paul's familiar trio of faith, love, and hope is again seen (1:3-4; cf. I Thess. 1:3; 5:8). Some problems, introduced in the first letter, are developed further in the second: lack of work (I Thess. 4:9-12; cf. 3:6-14) and the Day of the Lord (I Thess. 5:1-11; cf. 1:5—2:12).

Not only was this book listed among the Pauline Epistles in the Muratorian Canon, but it was also recognized as a Pauline original by these Church Fathers: Irenaeus, Tertullian, Clement of Alexandria, and Marcion.

Time and Place

Very little time, perhaps a month or two, elapsed between the writing of the two Epistles. Paul heard (3:11) that the disorderly had not followed his exhortation to return to work (I Thess. 4:10-12). Either the messenger who took the First Epistle to Thessalonica or else a recent visitor to that city[2] brought back this report. Paul was also told about a doctrinal discrepancy that was disrupting the church: "That ye be not soon shaken in mind, or be troubled, neither by spirit, nor by word, nor by letter as from us, as that the day of Christ [Lord][3] is at hand. Let no man deceive you by any means..." (2:2-3a). In the First Epistle Paul had charged: "Quench not the Spirit. Despise not prophesyings" (5:19-20). Apparently some teachers, either from within or without the church, had preached that the persecutions which the Thessalonians were receiving proved that they were in the Day of the Lord. Also, there was a forged letter, purported to be from Paul (note "as from us"), that declared that believers would go into the Day of the Lord or the Tribulation. Since Paul had·preached and written differently, the church membership was confused. Since these problems were very real and personal, Paul deemed it necessary to write another Epistle to them to clarify their misunderstandings. Thus the Second Epistle was written also

---

1. Compare this with the change of tone between First and Second Corinthians. Persistent rebellion caused a change in Paul's apostolic attitude and approach.

2. Another possibility is that a Thessalonian church member (or members) informed Paul.

3. Strong textual evidence favors "day of the Lord" rather than "day of Christ."

from Corinth (A.D. 51), one to three months after the sending of the first letter.

Purposes

First, Paul wanted them to know that he continued to thank God for their increasing faith, love, and patience (1:1-4). Second, he wanted to assure them that Christ's second advent would not only deliver them from their persecutions but that it would also cause the destruction of the unsaved (1:5-12). Third, he attempted to calm their anxiety caused by the false teaching that they were actually in the Day of the Lord (2:1-12). Fourth, he exhorted them to obey his commands, whether oral (by himself or Timothy) or in the two Epistles (2:13—3:5). Fifth, he wanted to give further instructions about the discipline of the disorderly (3:6-15). Finally, he gave them a sign whereby they could distinguish his correspondence from forgeries (3:16-18).

Distinctive Features

The dominant theme of the First Epistle, the return of Christ, was carried over into the second letter. Each chapter has at least one reference to it (1:7-10; 2:1, 8; 3:5). The first passage contains a graphic description of the judgment aspect of His return.

In his discussion of the Day of the Lord, Paul revealed more truth about the person and work of the coming antichrist. He entitled him as the man of sin, the son of perdition, and that Wicked one. Through Satanic enablement, he will perform "all power and signs and lying wonders" (2:9) to deceive men and to cause them to worship him as God. He will not only oppose the real God but any other object of worship. From the temple in Jerusalem he will rule as God. He eventually will be destroyed by the coming of Christ to the earth.

Will men who have rejected Christ in this church age have a second chance to accept Him? This question, raised quite often in prophetic conferences, is difficult to answer. If there is any passage that seems to give the answer, it is found in this book:

> And with all deceivableness of unrighteousness in them that perish; because they *received not* the love of the truth, that they might be saved. And for this cause God shall send them strong delusion, that they should believe a lie: That they all might be damned who *believed not* the truth, but *had pleasure* in unrighteousness (2:10-12; italics mine).

The answer revolves around the three italicized verbs. When did they not receive and believe? When did they have pleasure in unrighteousness? It does not say whether the action took place during the church age or after the rapture. Either position could suit the context; for that reason, no one should be dogmatic in his answer.

The use of "traditions" (Greek, *paradoseis)* is unique (2:15; 3:6). The verbal equivalent of this noun is found elsewhere, translated as "delivered" (Luke 1:2; I Cor. 15:3). Paul delivered or communicated in two forms that truth which he himself received from Christ: his oral teaching and his written Epistles. He did not regard them as man-made traditions, but as authoritative pronouncements from God (I Thess. 2:13; 5:27; cf. II Thess. 3:14); thus obedience or disobedience toward his letters was actually directed at God rather than at him. This demonstrates that the apostles wrote with a conscious recognition of divinely invested authority.

Paul's exaltation of the person of Christ, as seen in the first letter, is also emphasized in the second. He identified Him mainly as the Lord Jesus Christ (1:1, 2, 8, 12 [twice]; 2:1, 14, 16; 3:6, 12, 18), as the Lord Jesus (1:7), as Christ (3:5), and as the Lord (1:9; 2:8, 13; 3:1, 3, 4, 5, 16). Once He is named as the Lord of peace (3:16).

Outline

SALUTATION (1:1-2)
    I. THE THESSALONIANS AND PERSECUTION (1:3-12)
        A. Paul's thanksgiving (1:3-5)
        B. Paul's encouragement (1:6-12)
    II. THE THESSALONIANS AND THE PAROUSIA (2:1—3:5)
        A. He quiets their anxieties (2:1-2)
        B. He explains the apostasy (2:3-12)
        C. He encourages them to stedfastness (2:13-17)
        D. He exhorts them to prayer (3:1-5)
    III. THE THESSALONIANS AND DISCIPLINE (3:6-15)
        A. His example (3:6-9)
        B. His command (3:10-15)
CONCLUSION (3:16-18)

Survey

1:1-4

In his opening remarks Paul gave thanks for their growing faith, abounding love, and patient endurance in the midst of their persecutions and tribulations. This referred to the time period between Timothy's ministry (I Thess. 3:1-6) and the writing of the Second Epistle. He told them that he continued to use them as an illustration of the model church.

1:5-12

He assured them that God was not unfair in permitting them to experience these tribulations and that their behavior demonstrated that they were worthy of the kingdom of God. He then explained that their persecutors would go into the Great Tribulation (1:6) and that Christ would take vengeance on them at His coming to the earth. Not only would they be killed physically, but they also would be punished with everlasting separation from God. He further stated that in that day Christ would be glorified in them and admired by them. He then prayed that God would continue to work out His will in their submissive lives and that He would be glorified in them now in the midst of their persecutions.

2:1-2

Through various means,[4] the believers had become mentally and emotionally disturbed over the possibility that they might be in the Day of the Lord. They believed that Christ could come at any moment, but some had equated their persecutions with those to be committed in the Great Tribulation. They wondered whether they had missed the Rapture because they had not been watching or whether they were wrong about the time of the Rapture.

2:3-12

Paul informed them that they could not be in the Day of the Lord because two major events of that day had not yet occurred: the moral, doctrinal apostasy[5] and the revelation of the man of sin. He pointed out that the antichrist would set himself up in the temple at Jerusalem as an object of worship; since this had not happened, they could not possibly be in the Day of the Lord. He wanted them to remember his original teaching on this subject.[6] He acknowledged that the program of sin was already active in the world, but he argued that the man of sin could not be revealed until the Holy Spirit removed His restraining influence. He claimed that the world would be deceived by his Satanic miracles, that they would believe the lie[7] that he, a man, was actually divine, and that he would be destroyed at Christ's second coming.

2:13—3:4

Paul then gave thanks for their spiritual standing as seen in contrast to the deceived world. They were chosen to salvation from the beginning; they were set apart by the Spirit for His convicting, quickening ministry; they believed the truth when God efficaciously called them through Paul's preaching; and they were destined to share Christ's glory (2:13-14). He then encouraged them to stand and to hold the doctrinal

---

4. A prophetic utterance (tongues-speaking?), a sermon, and a forged letter.
5. The basic meaning of "falling away" (Greek *apostasia;* English transliteration is "apostasy") is "departure." Some believe that the word refers to the departure of the church into heaven.
6. This demonstrates that eschatological truths, including the truth regarding the antichrist, were taught to new converts by the apostle.
7. The Greek text has "the lie" rather than "a lie."

positions that he had taught them, to be comforted by God, and to pray for his ministry at Corinth that was performed in the midst of constant peril.

3:5-15

Whereas in the first letter Paul exhorted (4:10), in the second he commanded concerning the disorderly brother (3:6, 10, 12). He advised the church to withdraw fellowship from a professing believer who refused to work. He cited himself as an example of one who believed in the imminent coming of Christ and who at the same time gave himself to secular work. He pointed out that as an apostle he did not need to work but he chose to do so to provide an example for the Thessalonians. If the disorderly did not obey the Second Epistle, Paul charged the church to have no company with him—not to count him as an enemy, but to admonish him as a brother.

3:16-18

Paul closed the short Epistle with the prayer that they would be conscious of God's presence, peace, and grace. He then indicated that he signed off each of his Epistles with his distinctive signature; this would guard them against any future forged letters.

Increase Your Learning

By Doing

1. Circle the designation "brethren" wherever found in the book.
2. Underline all verses that refer to the return of Christ.
3. Circle all names assigned to Christ in this book.

By Discussing

1. How can the vengeance of God and His grace and longsuffering be harmonized? Are they contradictory?
2. What trends do you detect in modern society that would create an atmosphere ripe for the coming of the antichrist?
3. Why are men more willing to believe a lie than the truth? Are Christians susceptible to this error?
4. Discuss the differences between ecclesiastical and Scriptural traditions. Are they ever the same?

By Reading

(See books under First Thessalonians.)

18

FIRST TIMOTHY

Authorship of the Pastoral Epistles

The books of First Timothy, Second Timothy, and Titus have been called the Pastoral Epistles because in them Paul gave instructions to his young associates as to how they should maintain the spiritual oversight or pastoral care of their respective churches. Timothy and Titus were not pastors *per se;* rather, they were apostolic representatives sent to Ephesus and Crete respectively to supervise the proper organization and function of the churches under the trained leadership of pastors and deacons. In the personal charges given to them, however, are principles applicable to local church leaders of all generations.

Of all the thirteen Pauline Epistles, the authorship of these three has been questioned most severely by modern critics. This has been done in spite of the strong testimony of the Church Fathers. These accepted the books as canonical and as written by Paul: Ignatius, Polycarp, Justin Martyr, Clement of Alexandria, Tertullian, and Irenaeus. They were also listed in the Pauline section of the Muratorian Canon. The Fathers' decisions reflect the internal witness of the books. All three books begin with the claim that the writer was Paul the apostle (I Tim. 1:1; cf. 2:7; II Tim. 1:1; Titus 1:1). The author's analysis of his spiritual past agrees with the Book of Acts (I Tim. 1:11-15). His identification of Timothy and Titus as his "sons" in the faith is definitely a Pauline designation (I Tim. 1:2, 18; II Tim. 1:2; 2:1; Titus 1:4).

Some who have rejected Pauline authorship view the Pastorals as pseudonymous[1] writings, written either by a second-century opponent

---

1. Pseudonym means "false name." This does not refer to an author writing under a fictitious pen name (e.g., Samuel Clemens writing as Mark Twain).

of Gnosticism or by a follower of Paul who incorporated genuine Pauline material after the martyrdom of the apostle.[2] However, this position is highly subjective. Who determines what is authentic? Why are the genuine passages mostly found in Second Timothy? Why did the pseudonymous writer compose three books? Could he not have achieved his purpose by writing merely one? Would not the writing of three pseudonymous books be more suspect than the writing of one? Actually, pseudonymous writings were rejected by the early church, not accepted. Although it may have been an acceptable literary style of the pagan world, it did not meet the standard of honesty and authenticity required of canonical books. Paul warned against such forgeries carrying his name (II Thess. 2:3). Authorship by an apostle or by an authoritative associate of an apostle was deemed necessary as the basis of acceptance by the church.

The arguments set forth against Pauline authorship are many. First, the rejection of these books by some second-century Church Fathers (Basilides, Tatian, and Marcion) has caused some to doubt. However, these men were Gnostic heretics who disagreed with some of the content of these letters. When Paul stated that the law was good (I Tim. 1:8) and that Timothy should avoid "profane and vain babblings, and oppositions of science falsely so called" (I Tim. 6:20), he mentioned concepts contrary to the philosophy of Marcion.[3] It is no wonder that they rejected them.

Second, critics believe that there are some discrepancies between the historical data in the Pastorals and that recorded in Acts and found in the recognized Pauline writings. However, this charge is based upon the assumption that Paul experienced only one Roman imprisonment. Paul's release from his first internment at Rome, a subsequent ministry of two or three years, and a second imprisonment at Rome can easily account for the difference in historical data. Paul did expect to be released from his first imprisonment (Phil. 1:25; Philem. v. 22) and he apparently was released. Some Church Fathers (Clement of Rome, Eusebius) mentioned a Pauline ministry in the West, possibly as far as Spain (cf. Rom. 15:24). This could have been accomplished in the interval between the two imprisonments. The Pastorals describe the historical movements of Paul after the history of Acts was recorded (A.D. 30-61; cf. A.D. 61-64).

Rather, it refers to a writer who uses the name of a real person, living or dead. This writer may firmly believe that he has written what the "real person" would have penned had the latter been around to do so.

2. These passages have been suggested as being authentic: I Tim. 1:13-15; II Tim. 1:4-5, 16-18; 3:10-15; 4:1-2a, 5b-22; Titus 3:12-15.

3. The latter phrase "oppositions of science falsely so called" is based upon the Greek *antithesis tes pseudonumou gnoseos*. Note the use of "antithesis" and "gnosis," terms emphasized by Marcion.

In these closing years Paul visited Ephesus (I Tim. 1:3), Crete (Titus 1:5), Nicopolis (Titus 3:12), Corinth (II Tim. 4:20), Miletus (II Tim. 4:20), and Troas (II Tim. 4:13), and was finally taken to Rome (II Tim. 1:17).

Third, some have claimed that the local church organization as described in the Pastorals is too advanced for the actual time of Paul's ministry. However, the appointment and the assigned responsibilities of the bishop-pastor-elder were an integral part of Paul's ministry of edification (Acts 14:23; 15:2-6; 20:17-28) and of Peter's admonitions (I Peter 5:1-4). The concept of the function of the deacon developed very early in the church (Acts 6:1-6; cf. Phil. 1:1). Women always played an important role in church life (Acts 9:36-39; 16:14-15; Rom. 16:1). The care of a designated group of widows is what prompted the creation of the diaconate initially (Acts 6:1-6). Proper order within worship services had developed before the writing of the Pastorals (I Cor. 11-14).

Fourth, critics believe that the false teaching attacked by the Pastorals is the Gnostic heresy of the second century. They point out that abstinence from marriage and a vegetarian diet (I Tim. 4:3) were common characteristics of advanced Gnosticism. However, the heresy faced by the Pastorals still had a strong Jewish influence (I Tim. 1:3-10; Titus 1:10, 14; 3:9). This corresponds more to the incipient Judaistic Gnosticism refuted in Colossians than to the mature philosophical Gnosticism of the second century.

The fifth proposed argument is that the style, vocabulary, and doctrinal outlook in the Pastorals are radically different from that in the other Pauline Epistles. It is a fact that there are 175 words in the Pastorals that are not found elsewhere in the New Testament.[4] However, the difference in subject matter would account for most of this. A man's style normally changes with increasing age and experience. Actually, this is an argument in reverse for Pauline authorship. Would a forger have incorporated so many unique words if he were trying to pass the books off as Pauline originals? Would he have dared to call the beloved apostle Paul the "chief" of sinners?

The arguments proposed against the Pauline authorship of the Pastorals are not as strong as they appear initially. Evangelical answers are readily available. Until better evidence is forthcoming, it must be concluded that both the external and the internal evidence supports the Pauline authorship of these books.

Life of Timothy

A native of Lystra, Timothy was the son of a Greek father and a Jewish mother (Acts 16:1). In his early youth he was influenced by the

---

4. These words are called *hapax legomena,* "words spoken only once."

godly lives of his grandmother Lois and his mother Eunice (II Tim. 1:5; 3:15). He apparently was converted to Christ by Paul during the latter's first missionary journey (I Tim. 1:2, 18; cf. Acts 14:6-23).[5] Because of his spiritual gifts and rapid Christian maturity, he was selected by Paul during the latter's second journey to become an associate in the missionary enterprise (Acts 16:1-3). At that time he was circumcised[6] and ordained (Acts 16:3; I Tim. 4:14; II Tim. 4:5).

He shared in the establishment of the works at Philippi, Thessalonica, and Berea (Acts 16:1—17:14). When he rejoined Paul at Athens, he was sent back to Thessalonica to continue the edification of that church (Acts 17:14-16; cf. I Thess. 3:1-2). He later returned to Paul at Corinth and assisted the apostle in the founding of that church (Acts 18:5). The Biblical record is silent as to whether Timothy traveled with Paul from Corinth to Ephesus to Caesarea to Jerusalem to Antioch and finally back to Ephesus (Acts 18:18—19:1). However, he did work with Paul at Ephesus (Acts 19:22). Paul then sent him into the provinces of Macedonia and Achaia to minister to the churches in those areas and to prepare the way for a proposed visit by Paul (Acts 19:22; cf. I Cor. 4:17; 16:10). Before Paul left Ephesus, Timothy rejoined him in that city (II Cor. 1:1, 19; Rom. 16:21).[7] He then traveled with Paul from Ephesus to Macedonia to Achaia back to Macedonia and on to the province of Asia (Acts 20:1-5). Again, the Biblical record is silent about the presence of Timothy with Paul on the latter's trip to Jerusalem, his arrest at the holy city, his two-year imprisonment at Caesarea, and his voyage to Rome (Acts 21:1—28:16). However, since Timothy was with Paul at Rome (Phil. 1:1; 2:19; Col. 1:1; Philem. v. 1), he probably also was with him during those silent years. If he was not, then he must have rejoined Paul at Rome in the early months of the apostle's imprisonment. From Rome he may have been sent to Philippi (Phil. 2:19-24), although Paul's release may have stopped that desire from being fulfilled. After Paul's release, he journeyed with the apostle to Ephesus where he was left to care for the church (I Tim. 1:3). He was not with Paul when the latter was arrested and quickly taken to Rome. However, Paul requested that he come to Rome (II Tim. 4:9). It is difficult to say

5. Paul's constant mention of Timothy as his son doubtless refers to the latter's conversion as well as the close relationship which developed between them.
6. The circumcision of Timothy was not a contradiction of Paul's teaching (cf. Gal. 5:2-3). He was circumcised not to gain justification but to increase his effectiveness as a witness to Jewish audiences who knew his racial background (cf. I Cor. 9:19-20).
7. Timothy was gone when Paul wrote First Corinthians, but he was with the apostle when the Second Epistle was written. Note the respective omission and inclusion of his name in the salutations.

whether Timothy did go to Rome and whether he arrived before the apostle's martyrdom. If Paul wrote Hebrews,[8] there is some speculation that Timothy went to Rome, was imprisoned, and was later released (Heb. 13:23-24). Tradition states that Timothy was martyred during the reign of either Domitian or Nerva.

Time and Place

After Paul was acquitted by the Emperor and released from his first Roman imprisonment (A.D. 61), he resumed his missionary activities, accompanied by Timothy, Titus, Luke, and possibly some others. Contrary to his earlier thinking, he was able to return to Ephesus; there he left Timothy in charge while he moved on to Macedonia (I Tim. 1:3; cf. Acts 20:25, 37-38). Paul expected to rejoin Timothy at Ephesus, but he was not sure about the time of his arrival (3:14; 4:13). Thinking that he might be delayed longer than he had expected, Paul thus wrote to Timothy to encourage and to instruct him in his many tasks: "But if I tarry long, that thou mayest know how thou oughtest to behave thyself in the house of God, which is the church of the living God, the pillar and ground of the truth" (3:15). The book therefore was written from Macedonia about A.D. 62, although some have suggested either A.D. 63 or 64.

Purposes

Because Paul's approach was very methodical, the purposes in writing are clearly discernible. He wanted to charge Timothy to oppose the false, legalistic teachers (1:1-20), to outline the nature and purposes of prayer in the public worship service (2:1-8), to discuss the spiritual responsibilities of women (2:9-15), to list the qualifications of the bishop-pastor-elder (3:1-7) and of the deacons (3:8-13), to explain his plans for rejoining Timothy (3:14-16), and to give guidance to Timothy about the latter's personal conduct (4:1—6:21). In these last three chapters Paul charged his young associate to warn the church about the future moral and doctrinal apostasy (4:1-6), to develop spiritual maturity for his own benefit and that of his congregation (4:7-16), to provide financial care for the elderly Christian widows within the church (5:1-16), to exercise wisdom in the ordination, support, and discipline of elders (5:17-25), to counsel the Christian slaves about their relationships to their masters (6:1-2), to withdraw himself from false, greedy teachers (6:3-10), to avoid their errors and to develop a positive Christian life (6:11-16), to admonish the wealthy believers to be good stew-

---

8. The speculation could stand even if Hebrews were written by one other than Paul after the martyrdom of the apostle.

ards of God's money (6:17-20), and to avoid philosophical speculation (6:20-21).

Outline

SALUTATION (1:1-2)
 I. CHARGE TO TIMOTHY (1:3-20)
    A. Rebuke the false teachers of the law (1:3-11)
    B. Heed the example of Paul (1:12-20)
 II. CONDUCT OF THE LOCAL CHURCH (2:1—3:16)
    A. Priority of prayer (2:1-8)
    B. Place of women (2:9-15)
    C. Qualifications of the bishop (3:1-7)
    D. Qualifications of the deacons (3:8-13)
    E. Purpose of the church (3:14-16)
 III. CONDUCT OF TIMOTHY (4:1—6:21)
    A. In relation to apostasy (4:1-5)
    B. In relation to himself (4:6-16)
    C. In relation to widows (5:1-16)
    D. In relation to elders (5:17-25)
    E. In relation to slaves (6:1-2)
    F. In relation to greedy teachers (6:3-10)
    G. In relation to his ministry (6:11-16)
    H. In relation to the rich (6:17-19)
    I. In relation to false science (6:20-21)

Survey

1:1-10

Paul had personally warned the Ephesian church about the rise of false teachers that would occur during his absence from them (Acts 20:29-31), and it happened. After Paul's release from Rome, he journeyed to Ephesus, left Timothy there, and went on to Macedonia. Right at the beginning of this Epistle, he reminded Timothy why he was left at Ephesus. The apostle wanted him to charge those who desired to be teachers of the law "that they teach no other doctrine neither give heed to fables and endless genealogies" (1:3-4). Paul claimed that such teachers were ignorant of the real purpose of the law. The law had a good, lawful use if one employed it to control lawlessness and to bring a sense of guilt and condemnation to those who violated it. The law was not designed to save a sinner or to sanctify a righteous person; men are saved by trusting Christ and then they walk by faith under the control of the Holy Spirit.

1:11-20

Paul then cited himself as one who loved the law, taught it, and tried to keep it to gain a righteous standing before God. However, his zeal for the law caused him to become "a blasphemer, and a persecutor, and injurious" (1:13). His love for the law made him into a hater of Christ and Christians. He then admitted: ". . . but I obtained mercy, because I did it ignorantly in unbelief" (1:13). The false teachers at Ephesus were in the same spiritual plight: ". . . understanding neither what they say, nor whereof they affirm" (1:7). Paul argued that if God could save him, the chief of sinners, He could save anyone else, even the Ephesian false teachers. Paul saw in his conversion "a pattern to them which hereafter believe on him to life everlasting" (1:16). He expressed thanks that Christ enabled him and called him into the ministry because he had been faithful.[9] He reiterated his charge to Timothy to fulfill the expectations of his ministry (1:18-20).

2:1-8

In the next two chapters Paul discussed the order of the local church. He exhorted that four types of prayer should be made for all men. Specifically, they were to pray for all men, including civil authorities, for two basic reasons. First, ". . . that we may lead a quiet and peaceable life in all godliness and honesty" (2:2). A peaceful environment would assist in the pursuit of the holy life. Second, they were to pray for all men because God wanted "all men to be saved, and to come unto the knowledge of the truth" (2:4). Since Christ was the only mediator between God and man, they were to testify to that fact in their civil deportment, witness, and prayers. Even after Paul had been held in prison for four years in Caesarea and Rome by Roman officials, he wanted Christians to pray for them that the government might not oppress the advance of Christianity.

2:9-15

He then exhorted that Christian women should be marked by the inner adornment of the soul, not by the outward dress of the body. Their lives should express modesty and good works. In the organizational structure of the local church, the woman was not to have an administrative, authoritative teaching position over the man. The priority of man's creation and the curse placed upon the woman after her sin (Gen. 2:21-23; 3:16; cf. I Cor. 11:2-16) established the authoritative headship of man over the woman both in the home and in the church. The woman, however, has been saved from spiritual uselessness[10] in that she can have an authoritative, teaching position over the children within

---

9. Paul's faithfulness may refer to the time between his conversion (Acts 9) and his formal call to the missionary ministry (Acts 13).

10. The phrase "she shall be saved in childbearing" has caused many interpretations. Some believe that the curse and the guilt of the woman have been removed by *the* childbearing of Mary, or the incarnation of Jesus Christ. It must be noted that "saved" does not always mean deliverance from hell (cf. 4:16).

her family and in the church. She can also teach other women (cf. Titus 2:3-5).

3:1-7

The main church leader was designated by three terms,[11] used interchangeably of the same person: bishop, pastor, and elder (Acts 20:17, 28; I Tim. 3:1-2; Titus 1:5, 7; I Peter 5:1-2). He was to be blameless in four areas: personal life (3:2-3), family supervision (3:4-5), spiritual development (3:6), and reputation before the unsaved (3:7). He was to be an experienced, tested man.

3:8-13

The deacons were also to be blameless in their personal lives (3:8), in their orthodoxy (3:9), and in their family supervision (3:12). The character of their wives apparently was also to be considered as one of the bases for their selection (3:11). They were to be proved or examined before they could begin the privileged responsibilities of the office of deacon (3:10, 13).

3:14-16

Paul then informed Timothy that he expected to rejoin the latter at Ephesus; however, in anticipation of a delay, he wanted to give Timothy written instructions about his ministerial conduct in the church. Paul identified the local church, the visible functioning unit of the universal church, as the "pillar and ground of the truth" (3:15). The local church was to be the guardian and the propagator of the mystery of godliness. It was her job to proclaim the truth of Christ's incarnation, His earthly life, His death, resurrection, and ascension, and the necessity of believing faith.

4:1-5

The last three chapters emphasize Timothy's walk and work within the church. Paul wanted Timothy, as a good minister, to warn the church against the future moral and doctrinal apostasy. This defection from *the* faith, not from personal faith, would be characterized by six features: deception by evil spirits, commitment to demonic doctrines, hypocritical lies, seared consciences or amoral values, rejection of the institution of marriage, and a vegetarian diet. Paul explained that the eating of meat was perfectly acceptable if done with thanksgiving.

4:6-16

Paul remarked that a good minister would be "nourished up in the

---

11. The term "bishop" comes from *episcopos,* meaning "oversight." The term "pastor" comes from *poimene,* meaning "to feed or to shepherd." The term "elder" comes from *presbuteros,* meaning "to preside."

words of faith and of good doctrine" (4:6). Both his life and his knowledge should reflect spiritual maturity (4:16). In a series of ten imperatives, Paul gave guidelines so that Timothy would achieve the above goals: refuse, exercise, let no man despise, be thou an example, give attendance, neglect not, meditate, give thyself wholly, take heed, and continue. Only in so doing could Timothy guarantee that both he and the congregation would be delivered from the moral and the doctrinal errors that would mark the coming apostasy (4:16).

5:1-2

Paul wanted Timothy to conduct himself within the church in the same way as he would within a family. He was to treat a man older than himself as a father, an older woman as a mother, younger men as his brothers, and younger women as his sisters in all sexual purity.

5:3-16

Widows were to be honored. Widows who had believing relatives were to be supported financially by those relatives. In order for a widow to be cared for by the church membership, she had to meet eight qualifications (5:9-10). Younger widows were encouraged to remarry and to be blameless in their social conduct (5:11-15). Paul explained that the church should not undertake a financial responsibility that should rightfully be borne by the family (5:16).

5:17-25

Paul instructed Timothy that elders who ruled and taught well should be given double remuneration. Both testaments taught that spiritual work should be rewarded with material pay.[12] Accusations against elders had to be brought with two or three witnesses; those who brought false complaints were to be publicly rebuked. In the ordination of elders, Timothy was not to show personal preference or to ordain men without proper investigation of the person's background. Although a church leader was to abstain from wine (3:3, 8), Paul advised Timothy to take some for medicinal reasons. He then warned that both the sins and good works of the elders would be made manifest at the judgment seat of Christ.

6:1-2

Timothy was to exhort Christian slaves to honor their unsaved masters as a testimony for God and the gospel. He was also to teach other Christian slaves not to despise their Christian owners, but to obey them.

---

12. Note how Paul equated the Gospel of Luke (Luke 10:7) with the writing of Moses (Deut. 25:4). Both were regarded as authoritative and as Scripture (use of singular rather than plural to show the unity of the testaments).

No doubt some Christian slaves had become bitter because their Christian masters had not set them free.

6:3-10

The apostle then admonished Timothy to withdraw himself from those who taught contrary to the words of Christ and to godly doctrine. Apparently, these false teachers measured their spirituality by the size of the financial gifts received through their teaching (6:5). Paul stated that Timothy should be content with the basic necessities of life (6:6-8). He further claimed that those teachers who desire to be rich, marked by a love for money, will err from the faith and will be stricken with emotional regrets (6:9-10).

6:11-16

Although Timothy was young, Paul called him a "man of God." As such, he was to flee the greedy ambitions of the false teachers, to follow the godly life, to fight for the truth, and to keep the charge of Paul until the return of Jesus Christ. At all times the young associate was to be aware of the fact that he was performing his ministry both before God and Christ.

6:17-19

Timothy was then commanded to warn the wealthy Christians not to be proud nor self-sufficient, but to trust in God. The rich were to recognize that their money was a divine gift of stewardship entrusted to them. With it they were to do good, to be rich in good works, to give, to share, and to invest in heavenly values.

6:20-21

Finally, Paul reiterated his charge to Timothy to "keep that which is committed to thy trust" (6:20; cf. II Tim. 1:14) and to avoid erroneous philosophical speculation that ruined the ministries of some others.

Increase Your Learning

By Doing

1. Underline those verses that begin with: "This is a faithful [true] saying" (1:15; 3:1; 4:9).
2. Underline all verses that refer to the call of Timothy into the ministry.
3. Circle all imperatives in chapter 4.
4. Circle the famous three F's of chapter 6: "flee," "follow," and "fight."

By Discussing

1. Are any men incapable of being saved? What about a Catholic pope or an atheist like Madalyn Murray O'Hair?

2. Should women teach a Sunday school class of men? Of mixed adults? Do women missionaries violate the Pauline directives?
3. If a pastor or a deacon has a wayward child, should he leave the ministry? Does a man have to be married and to have children in order to become a pastor?
4. Can the rise of Satan-demon worship and the rejection of traditional marriage norms in contemporary America be the fulfillment of Paul's prophecy (4:1-5)?
5. Can a man minister to others and fail to minister to himself? In what ways?
6. Have churches failed in their financial care of senior citizens? Should churches construct nursing homes and retirement centers?
7. How much salary should a minister receive? Can churches pay too much as well as too little?

By Reading

Guthrie, Donald. *The Pastoral Epistles.* Grand Rapids: Wm. B. Eerdmans Publishing Co., 1957.

Hendriksen, William. *Exposition of the Pastoral Epistles.* Grand Rapids: Baker Book House, 1957.

Kent, Homer A., Jr. *The Pastoral Epistles: Studies in I and II Timothy and Titus.* Chicago: Moody Press, 1958.

Simpson, E. K. *The Pastoral Epistles.* Grand Rapids: Wm. B. Eerdmans Publishing Co., 1954.

Wuest, Kenneth S. *The Pastorals in the Greek New Testament.* Grand Rapids: Wm. B. Eerdmans Publishing Co., 1952.

19

SECOND TIMOTHY

Time and Place

Within three years after his release from his Roman imprisonment, Paul was arrested and taken back to Rome. The cause of his arrest is unknown. Some have suggested that Nero blamed the burning of Rome upon the Christians since they believed and taught a destruction of the world by fire (cf. II Peter 3:10-14). Since Paul was known to Nero as one of the leaders of this new religion, he was naturally apprehended. Others feel that Alexander the coppersmith brought formal charges against the apostle either at Ephesus or at Rome (II Tim. 4:14). If this is the same Alexander mentioned elsewhere (Acts 19:33; I Tim. 1:20), then he may have been a Judaizer, a false teacher of the law, whom Paul severely disciplined. In his anger toward Paul, he may have stirred up old charges of political insurrection against the apostle. The place of arrest is also unknown, perhaps Nicopolis or Troas. The latter is a good possibility since he left important personal possessions (cloak, books, parchments; 4:13) in that city. If he underwent a quick, hostile seizure in Troas, then it is very likely that he was rushed off to Rome without an opportunity to contact his friends or to gather his things.

Before he wrote this Epistle, Paul had already given one defense[1] of his theological and political position in the Roman court (4:16). By that time many of his associates had already left him for good purposes or had deserted him (4:10-12; cf. 4:16). No verdict was reached at this first trial, but Paul knew that his martyrdom was imminent (4:17; cf. 4:6-8).

---

1. The word "answer" is based upon the Greek *apologia,* meaning "a reasoned defense." Paul gave such defenses earlier before the Jewish multitude at Jerusalem (Acts 22:1) and before Festus and Herod Agrippa II (Acts 26:1-2).

SECOND TIMOTHY

Out of a concern for Timothy and a desire to see him before his death, Paul wrote to his young associate who was probably still at Ephesus to rejoin him at Rome. Thus, this book was Paul's last, written from a Roman prison shortly before his martyrdom (A.D. 64-67).

Purposes

In this communication Paul wanted to encourage Timothy not to be afraid but to discharge unashamedly his ministry (1:1-18); to exhort him to suffer for Christ, not to deny Him (2:1-13); to charge the Ephesian congregation not to be divisive (2:14-26); to inform Timothy about the moral character of the coming apostates (3:1-5); to cause him to turn away from such apostate teachers (3:5-9); to present to him Paul's own example of stedfastness in the midst of persecutions (3:10-13); to recommend that he continue to develop spiritual maturity based upon the Scriptures (3:14-17); to charge him to preach the Word of God in spite of men's desires for religious novelty (4:1-4); to urge him to complete his ministry (4:5); to inform Timothy of his imminent martyrdom (4:6-8); to ask Timothy to come to Rome, bringing Mark and his personal possessions (4:9-13); to warn him about Alexander (4:14-15); to inform him about the results of the first trial (4:16-18); to send greetings to some of his friends at Ephesus (4:19-20); and to send greetings to Timothy from the brethren at Rome (4:21-22).

Nero was the Roman emperor at the time of Paul's imprisonment, trial, and martyrdom.

Distinctive Features

The second chapter contains a series of metaphors that describes the ideal Christian. Paul either identified Timothy with these or else wanted his associate to manifest these qualities. They are: sonship, which shows intimate relationship between two believers (2:1); strength, or spiritual fortitude (2:1); teacher (2:2); soldier (2:3); athlete (2:5); husbandman (2:6); sufferer (2:9-13); student, or workman of God (2:15); separatist (2:16, 22-23); a vessel of honor (2:20-21); and a servant (2:24).

The classic statement on the divine origin and purpose of Scripture is found in this book:

> And that from a child thou hast known the holy scriptures, which are able to make thee wise unto salvation through faith which is in Christ Jesus. *All scripture is given by inspiration of God,* and is profitable for doctrine, for reproof, for correction, for instruction in righteousness: That the man of God may be perfect; thoroughly furnished unto all good works (3:15-17; italics mine).

The italicized words are the English translation of only three Greek words *pasa graphe theopneustos.* All Scripture is literally "God-breathed" or "breathed out by God." This does not mean that God breathed into the writings of men and thus they became Scripture; rather, at the moment of writing, the words composed by men were the actual words of God. Since God is truth, He only speaks the truth; thus the Scripture as God's written word is true, inerrant, and authoritative. Since God is living, His Word is living; the Scriptures thus have life-giving and life-edifying properties. They are profitable for the reproof of doctrinal error, for the correction of moral imperfection, and for the positive teaching of doctrinal and moral truths.

In this book Paul used the expression "in Christ Jesus" in seven distinctive contexts. In Him there is the promise of life (1:1); God's purpose and grace given to us before the world began (1:9); faith and love (1:13); grace that supplies strength (2:1); salvation (2:10); persecution for godly living (3:12); and salvation through faith (3:15).

The book of course contains Paul's evaluation of his ministry and the classic contemplation of his imminent death:

> For I am now ready to be offered, and the time of my departure is at hand. I have fought a good fight, I have finished my course, I have kept the faith: Henceforth there is laid up for me a crown of righteousness, which the Lord, the righteous judge, shall give me at that day: and not to me only, but unto all them also that love his appearing (4:6-8).

Paul had already presented his body to Christ to live for Him (Rom. 12:1); now he was willing to make the double sacrifice by presenting his body to die for Him (4:6; cf. Phil. 2:17). He looked upon death not as the end but as a departure from earth to be with Christ in heaven (4:6; cf. Phil. 1:23). Earlier he had written that he had not yet achieved the full purpose for which Christ had saved him (Phil. 3:12-14), but now he saw his ministry as completed. For him there were no regrets, only an expectation of reward.

Outline

SALUTATION (1:1-2)

I. BE FAITHFUL TO GOD AND TO PAUL (1:3-18)
   A. Exhortations
      1. Stir up the gift of God (1:6)
      2. Be not ashamed (1:8)
      3. Share the afflictions of the gospel (1:8)
      4. Hold fast the truth (1:13)
      5. Keep your ministry (1:14)
   B. Reasons for the exhortations
      1. Nature of God's Spirit (1:7)
      2. Purpose of salvation (1:9)
      3. Achievements of Christ (1:10)
      4. Purpose of the ministry (1:11)
      5. Defections of many (1:15)

II. BE FAITHFUL TO YOURSELF (2:1-26)
   A. In relation to your personal life (2:1-13)
   B. In relation to your public life (2:14-26)

III. BE FAITHFUL TO THE MINISTRY (3:1—4:15)
   A. Reason for the ministry (3:1-13)
   B. Duties of the minister (3:14—4:15; also 3:5-13)
      1. Turn away from apostate teachers (3:5-9)
      2. Be prepared to suffer (3:10-13)
      3. Continue in the Word (3:14-17)
      4. Preach the Word (4:1-4)
      5. Complete your ministry (4:5-8)
      6. Come to me (4:9-15)

IV. THE LORD HAS BEEN FAITHFUL TO PAUL (4:16-18)
CONCLUSION (4:19-22)

Survey

1:1-18

After his greeting, Paul stated that he was praying for Timothy constantly, desiring to see him and to relieve him of his sorrow over Paul's seizure. It is very plausible that Timothy witnessed Paul's sudden arrest at Ephesus and that he was prevented from accompanying the apostle to Rome (1:4; cf. 1:15, 18; 4:14-15). Paul then used Timothy's family spiritual heritage as a reminder and encouragement to stir up[2] his spiritual gift or ministry of teaching that Paul had authoritatively

---

2. Literally, to fan the flame of burning coals that are about to go out.

imparted unto him.[3] Timothy was apparently fearful of his life (and Paul's), so Paul explained that the Holy Spirit does not produce anxiety, but stability within the believer's life. He charged Timothy not to be ashamed of the ministry or of Paul, but to be involved in persecutions because of God's eternal purpose which was being worked out in their lives. A Christian need not fear death, because Christ destroyed death through His resurrection. Paul then expressed three major convictions of his life: "I am appointed"; "I am not ashamed"; "I am persuaded." Following his example, Paul challenged Timothy to hold fast the truth and to keep or guard his ministry. This was especially important since the defection in the province of Asia (where Timothy was) was intense. Paul then cited the family of Onesiphorus who ministered to Paul's needs and who was not ashamed of Paul's imprisonment either at Ephesus or in Rome.

2:1-26

Paul continued to encourage his young associate with a series of directives: be strong (2:1); commit (2:2); endure hardness (2:3); consider (2:7); remember (2:8); put them in remembrance (2:14); study (2:15); shun (2:16); flee (2:22); follow (2:22); and avoid (2:23). He wanted Timothy to continue his multiplication ministry of teaching,[4] to endure the difficulties of the ministry, not to get involved in the worldly ways of making a living, to strive for excellence in his ministry and to endure suffering for the spiritual benefit of others. He wanted Timothy to avoid profitless discussions (2:14-16), to avoid the sinful practices that doctrinal perversions produce (2:17-19), to be pure in doctrine and life (2:20-22), and to express such qualities as the servant of the Lord that would attract the deceived to the Lord (2:23-26).

3:1-13

Paul reminded Timothy that conditions both in the world and in the church would deteriorate. He then listed twenty characteristics of the apostates (3:2-5). Timothy was to withdraw from such people because these were the types who perverted local churches and who resisted the genuine spokesmen for God (3:5-9). Paul then admonished him to follow the apostle's example (set forth in nine ways), to live godly, and to suffer persecutions at the hands of evil men.

---

3. Apostles had divine authority and ability to confer spiritual gifts upon whomever they willed. This was one sign of the divine authentication of their ministry (Rom. 1:11; Heb. 2:3-4).
4. Note the fourfold sequence of teaching: Paul to Timothy to faithful men to others.

3:14—4:8

He wanted Timothy both to continue in the Word and to preach it (3:14; 4:2). The reasons for doing so were numerous: the character of Paul as his teacher (3:14); the ability of Scripture to prepare men for salvation (3:15); the authority of the Word (3:16a); the necessity of the Word to a mature life (3:16b-17); the evaluation of his ministry at the judgment seat of Christ (4:1); and the tendency of men to prefer religious novelty (4:3-4). In a series of commands, Paul finally charged his associate to complete his ministry: preach, be instant, reprove, rebuke, exhort, watch, endure, do, and make full proof of his ministry. The reason was clear: Paul's ministry was over; therefore, Timothy had to take over (4:6-8).

4:9-22

Paul then charged Timothy to come to Rome. This would require an act of love and spiritual courage. Paul then mentioned that only Luke was with him; others either had defected (Demas) or had been sent by Paul to various cities (Tychicus). He wanted Timothy to bring Mark, his cloak, parchments, and his books when he came. He then warned him about Alexander and informed him of the results of the first trial. He concluded by sending greetings and by pronouncing a benediction.

Increase Your Learning

By Doing
1. Circle all direct commands given to Timothy within the book.
2. Underline the various metaphors used of the ideal servant in chapter 2.
3. For one week, glean illustrations from a newspaper of the twenty characteristics of the last days (3:1-5).
4. Make a map and show the movements of Paul and his associates that are mentioned in this book.

By Discussing
1. Are ministers today failing to stir up their gifts? What causes them to do so?
2. Why do Christians not strive for excellence in spiritual matters? In what ways can they become entangled with the affairs of this life?
3. Can God use unclean vessels? How can a person be sure that he is a vessel to honor?
4. Are evangelical sermons fulfilling the purposes of Paul's directives to Timothy? What does it mean to preach the Word?
5. What is verbal plenary inspiration? Can a person become a Christian without believing in it? Should it be the basis of personal or ecclesiastical fellowship?

By Reading
(See books under First Timothy.)

20

TITUS

Life of Titus

Unlike Timothy, Titus was a full Greek by ancestry. Since Paul called him "mine own son after the common faith" (1:4), he was probably converted under the apostle's ministry, perhaps at Syrian Antioch. When Paul and Barnabas went to Jerusalem to discuss the requirements of salvation with the apostles, they took Titus along as a graphic exhibit of a Gentile who was saved by faith in Christ without the rite of physical circumcision (Gal. 2:1-3). Apparently Titus' life and character must have manifested spiritual depth at that time or else Paul would not have brought him. Although his name is not mentioned in the Book of Acts, Titus was with Paul during the latter's third missionary journey. Paul sent him to Corinth from Ephesus to deal with the delicate problems there. Titus had a genuine spiritual concern for the Corinthian church (II Cor. 8:16-17); Paul recognized this fact and so identified Titus as his "partner and fellowhelper concerning you" (II Cor. 8:23). When Paul left Ephesus, he was very concerned when he did not meet Titus at Troas (II Cor. 2:12-13); however, when he moved on to Macedonia, Titus joined him (II Cor. 7:5-16). Titus gave Paul a report that the Corinthians had received his ministry and that the church had been reconciled to Paul. With that news Paul wrote Second Corinthians and sent it back to the church via Titus. Titus was also given some of the responsibility to gather the financial collection for the poor Jerusalem saints (II Cor. 8:16-23).

The Bible is silent as to whether Titus was with Paul during either the latter's Caesarean or first Roman imprisonments. However, he did travel with Paul during some of the months of Paul's release-interval between the two Roman imprisonments. Paul took him to Crete and left him there in charge of the work (1:5). Later Paul wanted Titus to rejoin him at Nicopolis (3:12). It is difficult to say whether Titus did just that, but he was with Paul in Rome for the second imprisonment. Perhaps he was with Paul when the apostle was arrested and subsequently journeyed with him to Rome. In his last book Paul remarked that Titus had left Rome for Dalmatia (II Tim. 4:10). Tradition states that Titus in his senior years was the overseer of the Christian work on Crete and that he died naturally on that island.

Island of Crete

Crete is a very large island in the Mediterranean Sea, about 150 miles long and varying from 6 to 35 miles wide. Located southeast of Greece, it had experienced a great civilization in its past. Since the island was very mountainous, the people depended upon the sea for their living, both through fishing and merchant shipping. The ship that was supposed to take Paul to Rome sailed along its southern coast and actually harbored there (Acts 27:7-21).

On the day of Pentecost, Cretans who were in Jerusalem to worship God heard Peter's message (Acts 2:11). If some of them were converted, they may have carried the Christian message back to the island with them. This passage also indicates that there was a Jewish, monotheistic influence on the island long before Paul arrived there.

The typical Cretans, however, were known as "liars, evil beasts, slow bellies" (1:12), so depicted by one of their own poets, Epimenides. Many of the classical writers wrote of the untruthfulness of the Cretans. In fact, the Greek verb *kretizein*, meaning "to act as a Cretan," became synonymous with the concept "to play the liar." Such was the national, environmental heritage of most of the Cretan believers with whom Titus had to cope.

Time and Place

During his voyage to Rome, Paul had briefly stopped at Crete (Acts 27:7-21). Perhaps this contact created within him a desire to return to the island to evangelize it. When he was released from his imprisonment, he journeyed to Crete and established several small works in the major cities of the island. When he sailed away, he left Titus behind to "set in order the things that are wanting, and to ordain elders in every city" (1:5). Titus was thus given the task of completing the organization of the local church. Since Paul knew that the work at Crete was difficult because of the background of the Cretan believers and the threat of Jewish legalists, he wrote this book to give Titus some instructions in the performance of his task. It may be that Zenas and Apollos were going to the island, so Paul used that occasion to send the letter via them; however, if those two were already on the island assisting Titus, then the messenger of the letter is unknown. The letter was probably written shortly after First Timothy (A.D. 62), from Macedonia, Nicopolis, or Ephesus.

Purposes

Generally, the book was written to urge Titus to finish the organization of the work begun by Paul (1:5). Specifically, the apostle wrote to list the qualifications of the elders whom Titus was to ordain (1:5-9), to warn against the perverting influence of the Jewish legalists (1:10-16), to give instructions concerning proper Christian domestic behavior (2:1-10), to demonstrate that a correct knowledge of the doctrine of the grace of God should issue in good works rather than looseness of living (2:11-15), to give guidelines for proper relationships to the unsaved, especially the civil rulers (3:1-8), to point out the right order in church discipline (3:9-11), to inform Titus of Paul's future plans for his associate (3:12-13), and to send greetings (3:14-15).

Distinctive Features

Some have sensed a contradiction between Paul and James over the relationship of faith or grace to works. However, the Book of Titus demonstrates clearly that Paul emphasized works just as much as James. In this book, which contains a classic description of the grace of God (2:11-14; 3:4-7), there are six references to "good works." The false teachers were "unto every good work reprobate" (1:16). Titus was to be "a pattern of good works" (2:7). Christ died to redeem a people "zealous of good works" (2:14). The believers were "to be ready to every good work" (3:1), to be "careful to maintain good works" (3:8), and to "learn to maintain good works for necessary uses" (3:14). To Paul, good works came after saving faith (2:14; 3:8) and were a visible sign of genuine salvation (1:16). James would have heartily agreed with his evaluation of the false teachers: "They profess that they know God; but in works they deny him" (1:16). A related theme can be seen in the use of the word "sound." Both the elders and Titus were to preach sound doctrine supported by sound speech (1:9; 2:1, 8). The believers were to be sound in faith (2:2).

Within this brief letter are references to many of the major doctrines of the Christian faith: election (1:1), eternal life (1:2; 3:7), the savior-hood and deity of Christ (1:3-4; 2:13), inspiration (2:5), grace of God (2:11), universal nature of salvation (2:11), the second coming of Christ (2:13), substitutionary atonement (2:14), total depravity (3:3), love and mercy of God (3:4-5), regeneration (3:5), cleansing (3:5), person and work of the Holy Spirit (3:5), justification (3:7), and heirship (3:7).

Outline

Survey

1:1-4

The opening salutation contains a wealth of theological truth. Paul recognized that God had proposed to give men eternal life even before the beginning of the world and that God had personally elected him to salvation. He also knew that the message of God had been committed to him; for this reason, he could identify himself both as a servant and an apostle. His responsibility was to lead God's elect into saving faith and to "the acknowledging of the truth which is after godliness" (1:1). This latter phrase introduces the theme of the letter: Apprehension of spiritual truth should issue in godly living. This is what Paul wanted Titus to communicate.

1:5-9

Titus was given two main responsibilities by Paul: to eliminate the moral and doctrinal deficiencies of the believers and to provide trained leadership for the churches (1:5). The second purpose is discussed in the remaining part of the first chapter, whereas the first purpose is treated in the following two chapters. The elder-bishop had to be blameless in his marital, family, personal, and social relationships (cf. I Tim. 3:1-7). He had to be trained doctrinally so that he could use that truth

311

"to exhort and to convince the gainsayers." He needed ability to point out what was wrong and what was right.

1:10-16

The reason for the need of trained leaders was the invasion of the house-churches by false teachers. Paul labeled them as unruly, vain talkers, deceivers (1:10), money hungry (1:11), defiled, unbelieving, possessing a defiled mind and conscience (1:15), abominable, disobedient, and reprobate (1:16). Their error was in teaching things which they ought not (1:11), namely Jewish fables and human commandments (1:14). The false teachers were both Jews and Cretan Gentiles (1:10, 12). Since Titus could not be everywhere at one time, the presence of trained elders in each house-church would prevent the false teachers from having an opportunity to preach and to take money from the believers.

2:1-10

Sound doctrine should issue in good works, so Paul charged Titus to admonish the various groups within the membership with that general principle. The aged men were given six specific goals (2:2). Aged women were to manifest holy behavior in three ways (2:3). The aged women had a responsibility to teach the young women eight ways by which the latter could keep from blaspheming the Word of God (2:4-5). Sobermindedness was to mark the young men (2:6). Titus himself was to provide the Cretan believers with "a pattern of good works" in life, doctrine, and speech so that his opponents could not discredit his ministry by pointing out flaws in his life (2:7-8). Christian slaves were directed in five ways to adorn divine doctrine (2:9-10).

2:11-15

Paul knew that a proper understanding of divine grace could correct the wrong behavior of the Cretan believers. He stated that the grace of God which saves also teaches. Negatively, it teaches that Christians should deny ungodliness and worldly lusts; positively, it teaches that believers should live in right relations to self, others, and God. If a person sincerely looks toward the cross, he will also be looking up for the coming of his Savior. Christ died not only to remove the penalty of past sins, but to keep believers from future sins, zealous of good works. Such concepts Titus was directed to preach.

3:1-8

In a series of five infinitives, Paul commanded Titus to remind the believers of their responsibilities toward civil authorities and the unsaved (3:1-2). The reason why Christians should not be critical of the behavior of the unsaved is that they were once like that when they were lost (3:3).

Just as God saved them apart from moral reformation, so He could save the Cretan unbelievers (3:4-7). Their responsibility before the unsaved was to manifest a life of good works.

3:9-11

Paul then instructed Titus to avoid four types of dialogue that were spiritually unprofitable. After warnings, discipline was to be exercised on those heretics who succumbed to the false teachings.

3:12-15

In his closing remarks, Paul told Titus that he planned to send a replacement to Crete, either Artemas or Tychicus. When that emissary came, Titus was to join Paul at Nicopolis for the winter, bringing along Zenas and Apollos. Paul then sent Titus greetings from the apostle's associates and asked Titus to greet his friends on Crete.

Increase Your Learning

By Doing

1. Circle the five references to "sound" in the book.
2. Underline the phrase "good works" wherever found.
3. Make a list of the responsibilities of the various church members.

By Discussing

1. Should a person become a pastor without formal theological training? Is Bible knowledge a prerequisite to church leadership?
2. Do Christians from varying nationality backgrounds reflect various emotional temperaments in their spiritual experiences? If so, can they be changed?
3. Analyze this statement: "Now that I am saved, I can do anything that I please without being lost."
4. Are Christians sometimes more concerned about the conduct of the unsaved than in their lost condition? Why is this so?

By Reading

(See books under First Timothy.)

21

PHILEMON

Writer

Of the four Prison Epistles, this is the only one written directly to an individual. Pauline authorship is self-evident through the repetition of his name (1, 9, 19). The listed associates were with Paul during his Roman confinement (1, 23-24). He identified himself twice as "a prisoner of Jesus Christ" (1, 9) and as "the aged" (9); both of these appellatives would fit into Paul's life history at this time. Its similarity to Colossians (1-2, 23-24; cf. Col. 4:10-17) argues for a simultaneous writing from the same place by the same author. The book was listed within the Pauline section of the Muratorian Fragment and was acknowledged both as canonical and as written by Paul by these early Church Fathers: Ignatius, Tertullian, Origen, Eusebius, and Marcion.

Time and Place

Onesimus, a slave of Philemon who lived in Colosse, had stolen some of his master's goods and fled to Rome (18-19). In the imperial city Onesimus somehow came into contact with Paul who led the slave into a saving knowledge of Christ during the apostle's captivity (10). For a while Onesimus stayed in Rome and ministered to Paul's material needs, perhaps as a house servant or chef (11, 13). Paul, however, knew that the slave had to be returned to his legal master (13-14). Since Tychicus was returning to the province of Asia with the letters to the Ephesians and Colossians (Eph. 6:21-22; Col. 4:7-8), Paul decided to send Onesimus back to Philemon with his letter messenger. The letter was thus composed to explain the situation to Philemon and to instruct the master as to how the runaway slave, now a Christian, should be received. This personal letter, then, was written from Rome during Paul's first imprisonment (A.D. 60).

Some current liberal thinkers believe that the book was actually sent to Archippus, the real owner of Onesimus. To them, Philemon was the general overseer of the Christian work in Laodicea, Hierapolis, and Colosse with his residence in Colosse. Paul sent the letter and the slave first to Philemon who in turn brought them to Archippus. It was planned that Philemon would exert pressure on his understudy and that Archippus would comply with Paul's request. In so doing, they equate the Book of Philemon with the "epistle from Laodicea" (Col. 4:16). Also, the fulfillment of Archippus' ministry would be in the release of Onesimus (Col. 4:17). Although this novel approach appears plausible in places, it has not received acceptance by evangelical scholarship. Since Philemon was mentioned first, the book must have been written to him. If it had been written to Archippus, the text would have read "to the church in *his* house rather than *"your* house." Also, the simple explanation of Archippus' ministry is the general ministry (perhaps the pastorate), not a specific task to set a designated slave free.

Purposes

In this intimate letter Paul thus wrote to commend Philemon for his Christian compassion toward the needs of fellow believers (1-7); to effect the forgiveness and restoration of Onesimus by Philemon (8-21); to announce plans of a future visit, based upon his hopes of an imminent release (22); and to send greetings from many of Paul's associates who were probably known to Philemon (23-25).

Distinctive Features

The finest human illustration of the theological concepts of forgiveness and imputation permeates this book. Paul earlier wrote: "And be ye kind one to another, tenderhearted, forgiving one another, even as God for Christ's sake hath forgiven you" (Eph. 4:32). Human forgiveness should reflect divine forgiveness. To the spiritually sensitive, the personages of Paul, Philemon, and Onesimus symbolize respectively Christ, the Father, and the converted sinner. When Paul besought Philemon to receive the slave forever as Paul himself (12, 15, 17), the truth that God accepts believing sinners in the beloved one, Christ, takes on flesh. Paul also wrote: "If he hath wronged thee, or oweth thee ought, put that on mine account . . . I will repay it" (17, 18). This is the language of imputation (cf. II Cor. 5:19-21). The debt of the sinner (sin, guilt, and penalty) was paid by Christ's redemptive death. The person who paid the debt is also the one in whom the believer finds an acceptable standing.

Although the Bible nowhere attacks directly the institution of human slavery, principles for the humane treatment of slaves are found everywhere (Eph. 6:5-9; Col. 3:22—4:1; I Tim. 6:1-2; I Peter 2:18-25). They were to be treated as people, not property. In this personal letter, however, there is a hint of a principle which if properly applied would lead a Christian master to release his slaves, especially those who were Christian. Paul wanted Philemon to receive Onesimus "not now as a servant [slave], but above a servant, a brother beloved" (16). He later added: "Having confidence in thy obedience I wrote unto thee, knowing that thou wilt also do more than I say" (21). The words *more than I say* provide the clue. Do they not contain Paul's hope and prayer that Philemon would not only forgive Onesimus, but that he would also release him from the yoke of human bondage? The principle is clear: If God our heavenly master freed us who were slaves to sin, should we not also release men from human slavery if it is within our power to do so?

Outline

I. GREETINGS (1-3)
II. THANKSGIVING AND PRAYER (4-7)
III. THE APPEAL OF PAUL (8-20)
    A. The basis of the appeal (8-9)
    B. The object of the appeal (10-14)
    C. The purpose of the separation (15-16)
    D. The nature of the appeal (17-20)
IV. THE CONFIDENCE OF PAUL (21-22)
    A. In Philemon's obedience (21)
    B. In his release (22)
V. CLOSING GREETINGS (23-24)
VI. BENEDICTION (25)

Survey

1-3

Paul and his associate Timothy sent this letter not only to Philemon, but also to Apphia, probably his wife, to Archippus, presumably his son, and to the assembly of believers that met in his house, possibly at Colosse. Thus, everyone would be aware of Onesimus' conversion and of Paul's request to Philemon concerning the runaway slave. In a sense Philemon's decision would not be entirely private.

4-7

Paul then gave public thanks for Philemon's love, faith, compassion, and kindness that were manifested both toward Christ and the believers. The apostle's anticipated request was disguised within his prayer that "the communication of thy faith may become effectual by the acknowledging of every good thing which is in you in Christ Jesus" (6).

8-21

Paul could have exercised his apostolic authority by issuing a command to Philemon, but he chose to beseech him on the basis of love, age, and his imprisonment which no doubt caused Philemon some concern (8-9). He probably startled his friend when he named Onesimus as the object of his appeal. He proceeded to identify the converted slave in many ways: my son, whom I have begotten in my bonds, once unprofitable but now profitable, mine own bowels (cf. 7), and a brother beloved. The apostle informed Philemon that Onesimus had been profitable through his household ministry and that he had wanted to keep the slave in Rome, but he sent him back because he did not want to impose his desire upon Philemon (11-14). He then conjectured that God had used the slave's theft and flight as the impersonal means to secure his eternal salvation (15). Paul next expressed his wish that Philemon would receive the slave as a brother beloved and even as the apostle (16-17). Paul offered to pay any debts owed to Philemon by the runaway. He used the fact that Philemon's salvation was gained through Paul's ministry as his "collateral" or foundation for the future payment (18-19). Both Philemon and Onesimus had one thing in common: both had been saved through Paul. Paul wanted Philemon to refresh his bowels, namely Onesimus (20; cf. 7, 12) just as he had expressed compassion toward others. The apostle then expressed his confidence that Philemon would obey his requests and even go beyond them.

22-25

Paul concluded by asking Philemon to prepare a lodging for him because the apostle believed that he would be released from his Roman captivity as a direct result of his friend's prayers (22). Greetings were then extended to Philemon from Epaphras, the Colossian messenger who had also been imprisoned, Mark, Aristarchus, Demas, and Luke. A simple benediction ended the short letter.

Increase Your Learning

By Doing

1. Circle the word "I" wherever found.
2. Make a list of the various ways in which Onesimus was described by Paul.

By Discussing

1. Can slavery ever be justified? Were Christians of the first century right in owning slaves? believers in the Old Testament? How does the Civil War conflict enter into this discussion?
2. Discuss Paul's use of tact and diplomacy in his approach to Philemon.

3. Ask for testimonies of those who were saved as a direct result of a geographical move (15).
4. Why are men not willing to forgive when they themselves have been forgiven by God? What is the difference between conditional and unconditional forgiveness?
5. How can God use the prayers of believers to affect the decisions of civil authorities? Cite some familiar illustrations.

By Reading

Gaebelein, Frank. *Philemon: the Gospel of Emancipation*. New York: Our Hope Press, 1948.

Moule, H. C. G. *Colossians and Philemon Studies*. London: Pickering and Inglis, n.d.

(See other books under Colossians.)

22

HEBREWS

Writer

Who wrote Hebrews? This question has puzzled believers for generations. The book is actually anonymous,[1] but although the name was not indicated, the writer was definitely known to his readers. Even though there is frequent quotation of the Old Testament,[2] not once did the author refer to any Biblical writer by name. In order to remain consistent within his literary style, the author perhaps chose to remain anonymous. In this way his readers would be motivated by the impact of his message rather than by the influence of his personality or position.

Scholars have suggested several names as possibilities for the authorship of this book. Among them are Apollos, Barnabas, Luke, Priscilla, Silas, and, of course, Paul. Generally, the debate centers around Paul: Did he or did he not write the book? Quite often, more effort is spent in the denial of Pauline authorship than in the positive affirmation of arguments for a substitute writer. Even the early church had problems over the authenticity of the book. The Eastern church accepted it as an original Pauline, canonical book, whereas the Western church denied its Pauline authorship and excluded it from the canon, mainly because of the uncertain authorship.

What, then, are the arguments used against the view that Paul wrote the book? Since Paul opened all thirteen of his Epistles with a salutation including his name, the absence both of his name and the salutation is first cited (cf. II Thess. 3:17). The critics also claim that the literary

---

1. This is not unique, because many Biblical books do not contain the name of the author; e.g., I, II, III John; the Gospels; and Esther.
2. Second only to Revelation in the New Testament.

319

style which undergirds Hebrews is substantially different from that in acknowledged Pauline writings. Since Paul was the self-acknowledged Apostle to the Gentiles (Acts 9:15; Gal. 2:7), would he have written such a lengthy treatise to a Jewish assembly? Paul claimed that his message and apostleship were given to him directly by Christ (Gal. 1:1, 11-12), but this writer was dependent upon others for his knowledge of salvation: "How shall we escape, if we neglect so great salvation; which at the first began to be spoken by the Lord, and was confirmed unto us by them that heard him?" (2:3). Like Luke, he seemed to identify himself as a second generation Christian (cf. Luke 1:1-2). The central theme of the book, the high priesthood of Christ, is not found anywhere in Paul's writings. The quotations of the Old Testament are all taken from the Septuagint, whereas Paul generally quoted from both the Greek translation and the Hebrew Old Testament. Timothy's release probably took place after the writing of Second Timothy or after Paul's martyrdom (13:23; cf. II Tim. 4:9, 21). Since the book was probably written just before the destruction of the Jerusalem temple (A.D. 70) or in the latter third of the first century, the author's expectation of a release from imprisonment does not fit into the political atmosphere of Paul's second Roman captivity (10:34; 13:23; cf. II Tim. 4:6). Honest inquiry must admit that these arguments considered together do appear impressive.

On the other side, what are the proofs cited to support the Pauline authorship of this book? The author was in prison, and Paul suffered many imprisonments (10:34; cf. II Cor. 11:23). This one does not have to be equated with his second Roman captivity. In all previous confinements he did expect to be released (13:23; cf. Phil. 2:23-24; Philem. v. 22). Contrary to critical analysis, there are several doctrinal affinities between Hebrews and Paul's writings: the preeminence of Christ (1:1-3; cf. Col. 1:14-19); the authentication of apostles by divine gifts and miracles (2:3-4; cf. I Cor. 12-14; II Cor. 12:12); the humiliation of Christ (2:9-18; cf. Phil. 2:5-11); the use of Israel's wanderings as examples to contemporary believers (3:7—4:8; cf. I Cor. 10:1-11); the temporary nature of the old covenant (8:1-13; cf. II Cor. 3:6-18); and the emphasis of the faith principle (11:1-40; cf. Rom. 1:17). In fact, Habakkuk's declaration that the just shall live by faith (Hab. 2:4) is quoted three times in the New Testament (Heb. 10:38; cf. Rom. 1:17; Gal. 3:11). This quotation seems to have been a distinctive Pauline trait. The close companionship of Timothy is also cited (13:23). Although Paul saw himself as an apostle to the Gentiles, he preached to the Jews first wherever he went (Rom. 1:16), often visited the Jerusalem church, and had a deep spiritual concern for Israel (Rom. 9:1-5; 10:1-4). His Pharisaical training under Gamaliel in Jerusalem would have provided him with a thorough knowledge of the history and the rites of the Jewish sacrificial system (Acts 22:30). Few others would have had the background to compose such a book heavy with allusions to Exodus and Leviticus. The closing section bears a great resemblance to Pauline concerns. He requested prayer in his behalf (13:18; cf. Eph. 6:19), desired a good conscience (13:18; cf. Acts 24:16; II Tim. 1:3), identified the Father as the God of peace (13:20; cf. Rom. 15:33; Phil. 4:9; I Thess. 5:23), and pronounced a benediction of grace (13:25; cf. Philem. v. 25). Some have even suggested that Peter's allusion to Paul's writings included a specific reference to Hebrews (II Peter 3:15-16).[3]

What conclusions can be drawn from this debate? In the final analysis, only God knows for sure who the author was. Although the book is nameless, this fact does not detract from the authenticity or inspired authority of its contents. If the book was not written by Paul, then it must have been composed by a close associate of the apostle with or without his direct supervision.

Recipients of the Letter

To whom did the author write? The answer to this important question will help solve many of the interpretative problems within the book. Were they saved? Unsaved? Did the author think that they were saved but in reality they were not? Where did they live?

First of all, he regarded his readers as believers. He addressed them as "brethren" (3:1, 12) and as "beloved" (6:9). To him, they were "partakers of the heavenly calling" (3:1) and "partakers of Christ" (3:14). The warnings given to them would only apply to genuine believers (3:12-13). Unbelievers are already possessed with an evil heart of unbelief; nowhere are they commanded to exhort each other.

Second, they were immature (5:11-14). They had been saved a long time, but they had not grown spiritually. They were unable to receive the meat of Biblical teaching because they were on a milk diet. They did not have enough knowledge or experience to make adult distinctions between right and wrong choices. The writer saw them as spiritual "babes."

Third, they were wavering in their faith. After their conversion, they had endured persecutions, identified themselves with other oppressed believers, seen their material possessions destroyed, and had compassion over the author's imprisonment (10:32-34). However, their present conduct did not manifest that initial freshness and joy any more. They

---

3. Since Peter was an apostle to the Jews, he probably wrote to Jewish Christians (I Peter 1:1; cf. Acts 2:9-11; 8:1-4). The phrase "written unto you" (II Peter 3:15) thus would refer to a letter written to Jewish Christians. Only Hebrews would qualify.

grew tired of their persecutions and failed to trust God as they once did (10:35-38).

Fourth, they were apparently well known to the author. He planned to visit them after his release from prison (13:23). In the hope of his restoration to them (13:19), there is a hint that he had been with them at least on one occasion before.

Fifth, the readers either resided in Rome or in Palestine. In his closing salutation, he wrote: "They of Italy salute you" (13:24). Does this mean that the author was in Italy, perhaps Rome, and that the Italian believers wanted to send greetings? Or, does it mean that Italian believers, outside of their homeland, wanted to be remembered to their Christian friends back in Italy?[4] Evangelical opinion is divided over the issue. Advocates of a Roman destination point out that the readers were known for their financial generosity (6:10) whereas the church at Jerusalem was marked by poverty (Acts 11:27-30; Rom. 15:26). However, the Jerusalem believers did unselfishly share their material possessions (Acts 2:44-45; 4:32-37). Even the Macedonian churches were known paradoxically for both their poverty and liberality (II Cor. 8:1-2). If the readers' knowledge of the sacrificial rites came from a past participation in temple worship at Jerusalem, then they were probably residents of the environs around the holy city; however, as loyal pilgrims to the annual feasts of Passover, Pentecost, or Tabernacles (cf. Acts 2:10), they could have gained their facts through that experience. If their knowledge was based solely upon a study of the Old Testament, then they probably resided outside of Palestine. In conclusion, no one can really be dogmatic about the exact destination.

Time and Place

As indicated before, the readers had been saved for a rather long period of time (5:12). They had been verbally assaulted and had suffered the loss of personal property for their faith, but they had not yet been beaten or killed (12:3-4). However, the threat of such severe persecution now loomed in their immediate future. It may be that the imminent Jewish-Roman war prompted this threat. As Jewish Christians, they faced a personal dilemma. Should they identify themselves racially with their fellow Jews in possible combat against the Romans and thus gain the favor of their countrymen? Or, should they remain identified with the Jewish-Gentile Christian assembly and assume a neutral position politically, especially since Christ predicted the destruction of Jerusalem with its temple because of her rejection of Him (Matt. 23:37—24:1-2)? This latter action would incur the wrath of their fellow Jews. They thus

---

4. Grammatically, the preposition *apo*, translated "of," seems to support the second view.

faced this question: Shall we go on with Christ and His people even though it means persecution and possible death, or shall we go back to be identified with Jewish national and religious life again and thus avoid this persecution? Some had already made their decision and had defected from the Christian assembly (10:25). The majority had not yet made up their minds. The author, aware of the situation, wrote to admonish them not to take this drastic step of disobedience but to endure patiently and faithfully the persecutions while they anticipated both the imminent coming of Christ and the destruction of Jerusalem with its temple (10:22-25).

There is good evidence that the book was written just a few years before the destruction of Jerusalem (A.D. 70), perhaps about A.D. 67-68. It had to be composed during the lifetime of second generation Christians who themselves had been saved for some while (2:3-4; 5:11-14). Timothy was still alive (13:23). The author used present verbal tenses and participles to describe the ritual service of the priests (8:4, 13; 19:4,

The Arch of Titus, in Rome, was erected to commemorate the victory of Titus over the Jewish revolt. One panel of the arch depicts Roman soldiers carrying out booty from the temple at Jerusalem.

5, 9; 10:1, 8, 11; 13:10, 11). This would seem to indicate that the temple was still standing. However, some have pointed out that the use of the present tense was only a literary device and it was employed by Church Fathers writing after A.D. 70. They further claim that the author was comparing the priestly ministry of Christ with that of the Mosaic tabernacle, not that of the Zerubbabel-Herod temple. The natural reading of the text, though, seems to refer to a comparison of simultaneous ministries on earth and in heaven. If the book had been written after A.D. 70, certainly the author would have referred to the destruction of the temple as his capstone argument. His silence argues for the earlier date.

Purposes

The main purpose was to demonstrate the superiority of the person and work of Christ to the Old Testament sacrificial system (1:1—10:18). Once the author had made that point, he was then able to combat the imminent danger of defection (2:1-4; 10:19-25), to provoke his readers to growth into Christian maturity (5:11-14; 10:32-39), to comfort them in their persecutions (11:1—12:13), to warn them about the severity of divine chastisement (6:3-12; 10:26-31; 12:3-13), to alert them to the dangers of false teaching (13:9), and to request prayer for himself (13:18-25).

Distinctive Features

This book contains the classic presentation of the doctrine of the priesthood of Christ. Although other books emphasize the value of Christ's death, the emphasis here is upon Christ as the priest who made the sacrifice of Himself. In addition, the book reveals an area of Christ's ministry untouched in other volumes: His present priestly ministry of intercession. Paul mentioned that Christ was at the right hand of God, making intercession for believers (Rom. 8:34); the Book of Hebrews describes the nature of that intercession:

> But this man, because he continueth ever, hath an unchangeable priesthood. Wherefore he is able also to save them to the uttermost that come unto God by him, seeing he ever liveth to make intercession for them (7:24-25).

The key passage on the exposition of divine chastisement is also found here (12:3-12). A believer should not despise the chastening of God, but he should endure it and profit spiritually from it. Chastisement is a sign of divine love and sonship; lack of it may indicate an illegitimate relationship or an unregenerate heart. It should produce reverence, submission, peace, righteousness, and encouragement in the believer's life.

The book also contains the "Faith Hall of Fame" (11:1-40). The Old Testament characters of Abel, Enoch, Noah, Abraham, Isaac, Jacob,

324

Joseph, Moses, Joshua, Rahab, and others are cited as examples of men and women who believed that "he [God] is, and that he is a rewarder of them that diligently seek him" (11:6). These endured the persecutions of the world because they trusted God. The famous definition or description of faith is set forth here: "Now faith is the substance of things hoped for, the evidence of things not seen" (11:1). Whenever evangelical Christians think of the subject of faith, their minds automatically turn to Hebrews 11.

The book is full of warnings, inserted at various intervals within the presentation of the author's theme (2:1-4; 3:7-9; 4:1-13; 5:11—6:20; 10:26-31; 12:14-17; 12:18-29). The writer did not want to wait until his conclusion to apply the truths to the lives of his readers. These warnings were signaled by the sevenfold use of "lest" (2:1; 3:12, 13; 4:11; 12:3, 13, 15).

The author involved himself in the commands he directed toward his readers by making use of the Greek hortatory subjunctive. These are all introduced by the words "Let us. . . ." Here is a listing of the thirteen instances:

1. Let us therefore fear (4:1).
2. Let us labour therefore to enter into that rest (4:11).
3. Let us hold fast our profession (4:14).
4. Let us therefore come boldly unto the throne of grace (4:16).
5. Let us go on unto perfection (6:1).
6. Let us draw near with a true heart in full assurance of faith (10:22).
7. Let us hold fast the profession of our faith without wavering (10:23).
8. Let us consider one another to provoke unto love and to good works (10:24).
9. Let us lay aside every weight (12:1).
10. Let us run with patience the race that is set before us (12:1).
11. Let us have grace (12:28).
12. Let us go forth therefore unto him without the camp (13:13).
13. Let us offer the sacrifice of praise to God continually (13:15).

This type of command was not as direct or harsh as a regular imperative.[5] The author thus spoke to himself as well as to his readers.

The key word of the book is "better." The word is used thirteen times to show the superiority of the believer's position in Christ (1:4; 6:9; 7:7, 19, 22; 8:6 [twice]; 9:23; 10:34; 11:16, 35, 40). In Christ the believer has a better hope, covenant, promises, substance, country, and resurrection.

Outline

I. CHRIST IS BETTER THAN THE PROPHETS (1:1-3)

---

5. Compare "Let us fear" with "Fear ye." The second is more direct.

A. Declaration in the Son (1:1-2a)
B. Deity of the Son (1:2b-3)
II. Christ Is Better than the Angels (1:4—2:18)
    A. In His divine nature (1:4-14)
        Warning (2:1-4)
    B. In His human nature (2:5-9)
    C. In His redemptive nature (2:10-18)
III. Christ Is Better than Moses and Joshua (3:1—4:13)
    A. More glory than Moses (3:1-6)
        Warning (3:7—4:7)
    B. More rest than Joshua (4:8-13)
IV. Christ Is Better than Aaron and the Levitical Priesthood (4:14—10:18)
    A. A better position (4:14-16)
    B. A better order (5:1—7:28)
        1. Qualifications of the two orders (5:1-10)
            Warning (5:11—6:20)
        2. Contrasts of the two orders (7:1-28)
    C. A better covenant (8:1-13)
    D. A better sanctuary (9:1-11)
    E. A better sacrifice (9:12—10:18)
V. Application of the Argument (10:19—13:25)
    A. Be faithful to God (10:19-25)
        Warning (10:26-31)
    B. Endure and believe God (10:32-39)
    C. Illustrations of those who believed and endured (11:1—12:2)
    D. Understand divine chastisement (12:3-13)
        Warning (12:14-29)
    E. Concluding exhortations (13:1-25)
        1. Social obligations (13:1-6)
        2. Church obligations (13:7-17)
        3. Personal obligations (13:18-25)

Survey

1:1-3

In the opening verses of this book, which begins more like a treatise than a letter, the author set forth three contrasts between two modes of divine revelation:

In time past . . .	In these last days
Unto the fathers . . .	Unto us
By the prophets . . .	By His Son

Visions, dreams, and theophanies marked Old Testament history. Whereas the prophets said: "Thus saith the Lord," Christ said: "I say unto you." In seven ways He was better than the prophets: heir of all things, creator of the time-space universe,[6] brightness of God's glory, express image of

---

6. Literally, "through whom he also made the ages." "Ages" is a time word, whereas "worlds" is a space word (cf. John 1:1-3).

His person, sustainer of the world, purger of our sins, and the One seated beside the Father.

1:4—2:18

In a series of seven direct quotations from the Old Testament (1:4-14), the author demonstrated that Christ was better than the angels because of His deity. He was the Son (1:5), the incarnate firstbegotten (1:6a), the object of angelic worship (1:6b), God (1:8a), the righteous ruler (1:8b), the immutable creator (1:10-12), and the seated one (1:13). Angels ministered both to Him (1:7) and to those who would be saved (1:14). Why did he have to show the superiority of Christ to the angels? In his *first warning* (2:1-4), he pointed out the difference between that "spoken by the angels" and that "spoken by the Lord." Angels had a part in the giving of the law to Moses (cf. Gal. 3:19). Since those who disobeyed the Mosaic law were punished physically, is it not logical that those who disobey the word of Christ (and He is better than the angels) will receive a greater chastisement? The superiority of Christ can further be seen through His humanity (2:5-9). When God originally made man, He gave to man, not to angels, dominion over the created world; however, man lost that dominion through his sin. Christ became man and through His death and resurrection regained for man that lost dominion which He will exercise in the millennial kingdom. In a third way, Christ was better than the angels because of His saviorhood (2:10-18). Christ did not become an angel to die for angelic sin (2:16); He received a human nature (flesh and blood, seed of Abraham) in order to die for human sin. In so doing, He destroyed the most powerful angel, the devil, the one who had the power to keep men in the realm of death short of resurrection. Christ tasted death for every man and thus could bring many sons into glory (2:9-10). By becoming lower than the angels, He has lifted men to a spiritual position higher than the angels.

3:1-19

Christ was not only better than the spiritual agents in the giving of the law (angels), but also the human agent (Moses). Christ has more glory because as the Son He is the builder of His spiritual house, whereas Moses was merely a servant in God's house. The *second warning* (3:7-19) centered around the decision made by Israel when they came to Kadesh-Barnea under Moses' leadership. Instead of going into the land and claiming the land promised to the Patriarchal Fathers, they feared for their lives when they heard the spies' report that there were giants in the land dwelling in walled cities. They did not believe that the God who had redeemed them out of Egypt and who had nourished them from

Mount Sinai, the traditional site where the "Law of Moses" was given to ancient Israel.

Egypt to Kadesh could overcome their enemies. Because of their unbelief, God chastised them with forty years of wilderness wanderings, during which time an entire adult generation died. The readers had come to a spiritual Kadesh. Would they go on with Christ who had redeemed them, certain that some would lose their lives at the hands of their persecutors? Or, would they fail to trust Him and thus bring divine chastisement into their lives? The author admonished them not to repeat the same mistake: "Harden not your hearts, as in the provocation, in the day of temptation in the wilderness" (3:8).

4:1-13

The *third warning* centered around Christ's superiority to Joshua.[7] Although Joshua led Israel into Canaan, he did not establish a permanent rest (cessation of conflict) for the people. Christ, however, can provide a rest in which the believer can find the total provision of God through complete obedience to the will of God. In Canaan, some of the Israelites lost their lives in battle; in the rest of Christ, it is entirely possible that martyrdom will come, but it is better to die in the will of God (in the land) than outside of it (in the wilderness).

4:14-16

The next section (4:14—10:18) contains the heart of the author's

7. "Jesus" is the Greek equivalent of the Hebrew "Joshua" (4:8).

argument. In it he demonstrates that Christ is better than the Aaronic high priesthood and the Levitical priestly order in five different ways. First, He has a better position. On one day of the year, the Day of Atonement, the high priest could go into the Holy of Holies, the inner sanctuary of both the tabernacle and the temple. On the other hand, Christ "is passed into the heavens," the heavenly Holy of Holies, and is there every day of the year. Since the high priest was the representative of men before God, it is self-evident that Christ can do more for His people because of His permanent presence before the Father. Because of who Christ is, the believer can know that He has a sympathetic high priest (4:15); because of where He is, the Christian can go to Him by faith and "obtain mercy, and find grace to help in time of need" (4:16).

5:1-10

To be a priest, one had to be human and appointed of God. The priests of Israel were able to have compassion on the sinning nation because they committed the same sins and offered sacrifices not only for the nation but for themselves as well. Christ qualified for the priesthood by becoming human and by being appointed to the priestly order of Melchisedec. In Gethsemane Christ's emotions were manifested, and there He yielded Himself completely to the will of God. As a high priest, He offered Himself as a sacrifice for the sins of the people, but not for Himself because He was without sin (cf. 4:15).

5:11—6:20

The reference to Melchisedec introduced the *fourth warning*. Because of the readers' immaturity, the author was not able to disclose certain spiritual truths. He admonished them to go on to perfection or spiritual adulthood and to leave the elementary doctrines of the Christian faith (6:1). In a series of four participles, he characterized their spiritual status: They were once spiritually enlightened (II Cor. 4:3-6); they tasted the heavenly gift;[8] they became partakers of the Holy Spirit (Rom. 8:9); and they also tasted the Word of God and the coming world powers. He then warned that if such people fell away,[9] they could not be renewed to repentance. At Kadesh-Barnea, after Israel made its crisis decision not to go on, God announced that the adult generation would die in the wilderness. The stunned people changed their minds the next day and decided to go into Canaan, but it was too late. Their decision was irreversible. The author warned that they had reached

---

8. They tasted it in the same degree that Christ tasted death (2:9). This same word indicates not a mere sampling, but a total eating.
9. The phrase "if they shall fall away" is the translation of one Greek word, an aorist participle *parapesontas*. The KJV translators regarded it as a conditional use of the participle.

their spiritual Kadesh. A decision not to go on would bring the severe chastisement of premature physical death.[10] The author knew that his readers had not yet made that final decision. They were still ministering to the saints as they once did. As long as they continued to bear some fruit for God, He was willing to use them, but if the time ever came that they stopped producing fruit, then chastisement would fall upon them (6:7-12; cf. John 15:1-11).

7:1-28

Melchisedec provided a perfect type of Christ (7:1-3). Christ is able to be both a king and a priest as he was. The order of Melchisedec was better than the order of Levi because Levi, genetically present in his great grandfather Abraham, gave tithes to the mysterious king-priest and the latter in turn blessed Levi through Abraham. The principle is clear: "And without all contradiction the less is blessed of the better" (7:7). The author further argued that if the Levitical order had been designed to be permanent, then David would have never declared the advent of a priest after the order of Melchisedec (7:11-22). Death ended the priestly functions of the Levites, but Christ through His resurrection has an unending priesthood (7:24). Since there is no break in the continuity of His priesthood, His order is necessarily better.

8:1-13

In the opening five verses the author gave a summary of his discussion of the priesthood so far (cf. 4:14—7:28). He pointed out that Christ is a high priest in the true heavenly tabernacle which provided a pattern for the construction of the earthly Mosaic tabernacle. He concluded: "But now hath he obtained a more excellent ministry, by how much also he is the mediator of a better covenant, which was established upon better promises" (8:6). Note the three contrasts in that verse. His priesthood is superior because it is based upon a better covenant, the new covenant (cf. Jer. 31:31-37). He then argued that if God had planned for the ritualistic Mosaic covenant to be permanent, He would never have promised a new covenant years later. The old was to be replaced by the new.

9:1-11

The fourth superiority was revealed in the comparison of sanctuaries. The earthly tabernacle was divided into two sections: the first with the lampstand and table of showbread and the second or the Holiest of all. Since the high priest could go into the second area only once a year, it

---

10. This passage does not teach the loss of salvation. If it did, then it would also teach that salvation could not be regained.

signified "that the way into the holiest of all was not yet made manifest, while as the first tabernacle was yet standing" (9:8). Christ, however, was a "high priest of good things to come, by a greater and more perfect tabernacle . . ." (9:11). His constant presence before the Father guarantees the believer eternal access into the heavenly Holy of Holies.

9:12—10:18

The superiority of Christ's sacrifice of Himself provides the fifth contrast. The author argued that if animal blood could produce outward, ceremonial purification, "How much more shall the blood of Christ, who through the eternal Spirit offered himself without spot to God, purge your conscience from dead works to serve the living God?" (9:13-14). Since Christ was the mediator of a new testament, He had to die before man could receive the promise of an eternal inheritance. Just as animal blood purified the earthly tabernacle (9:21), so Christ's blood purified the heavenly sanctuary (9:23). The Levitical priests offered their sacrifices often (9:25), but Christ only offered Himself once (9:28). This section also mentions the three appearings of Christ: His present appearance in heaven as our intercessor (9:24); His past appearance to die on the cross (9:26); and His future appearing to save (9:28). The Old Testament sacrifices were a shadow of the very image, the sacrifice of Christ. The former could never remove the guilt of the sinful conscience; otherwise the sacrifices would not have been repeated. Christ, however, secured the positional sanctification of the believer through the offering of His body once for all (10:10). The priests' work was never done (10:11), but Christ sat down after He offered the one sacrifice of Himself. His work was finished (cf. John 19:30).

10:19-31

The author has finished his argument for the superiority of Jesus Christ and one's spiritual position in Him. Based on the fact that the believer has access into the heavenly Holy of Holies and since Christ is there as our high priest (10:19-21), the author then gave his readers three exhortations: "Let us draw near with a true heart in full assurance of faith"; "Let us hold fast the profession of our faith without wavering"; and "Let us consider one another to provoke unto love and to good works" (10:22-24). Because of the defection of some and the imminence of the destruction of Jerusalem, they needed to unite, not to separate (10:25). He then gave a *fifth warning* (10:26-31). Under the Old Testament there was no sacrifice provision for open, deliberate sin; rather, the rebel was put to death by men. He then warned that if they defect after receiving "the knowledge of the truth" (10:26; cf. 1:1—10:18), they would receive a "sorer punishment" at the hands of God.

331

11:40

He then asked them to remember their immediate postconversion lives in which they trusted God and endured the persecutions of men. Their present need was to recapture that faith and patience (10:32-39). To encourage them he cited Old Testament characters who went through the same experiences. Abel was murdered by his brother because the former offered "a more excellent sacrifice" (11:4). Because they accepted the sacrifice of Christ, they may also lose their lives at the hands of their Jewish kinsmen. Enoch was translated into the presence of God, and it may be that they would likewise be raptured by Christ's coming before physical death would overtake them (11:5). Noah believed and endured the reproaches of men for 120 years; they needed to realize that judgment would soon overtake their oppressors as it overtook his (11:7). Abraham believed God, obeyed, and "went out, not knowing whither he went" (11:8). Paradoxically, the "land of promise" was also "a strange country" to him, because although he was where God could bless him, he knew that he was a pilgrim and he looked for that heavenly country and city. Abraham was even willing to sacrifice Isaac as a testimony to his faith because he knew that if God could bring life out of the deadness of Sarah's womb, He could also raise Isaac from the dead. As both physical and spiritual children of Abraham, the readers, so the author hinted, might be called upon to offer their sons in martyrdom. Would they respond as Abraham had? After citing the faith of Isaac, Jacob, and Joseph (11:20-22), he pointed to Moses as one "choosing rather to suffer affliction with the people of God, than to enjoy the pleasures of sin for a season" (11:25). Moses could have avoided persecution by hiding his identity as a Hebrew, but this he refused to do. The readers could avoid persecution also if they refused to be identified with the Christian church. Many other examples are mentioned (11:30-38). Just as they "obtained a good report through faith" (11:39), so the author wanted his readers to do likewise.

12:1-2

Since historical precedent had been established for their anticipated experiences, the author admonished them: "Let us lay aside every weight, and the sin which doth so easily beset us, and let us run with patience the race that is set before us" (12:1). The sin was the lack of faith. In their effort they should look to Christ as the supreme example of one who endured in order to receive the joy. Their endurance in persecutions could never compare with His endurance of human mockery and of the wrath of God upon the cross. He did it for them; now they can do it for Him.

12:3-13

He reminded them that chastisement was a sign of spiritual sonship and that it should not be despised. In fact, if deliberate disobedience does not bring such discipline, it may be an indication that the person is not related to Christ (12:8). Instead of feeling sorry for themselves, they should look at Christ and what He suffered for them (12:3). No one had died yet for his faith (12:4). God chastised them for their profit if they would only learn the lessons of the experience.

12:14-29

The *sixth* and *final warning* is now given. Do not be like Esau who sold his birthright (basis of future spiritual blessings) for a moment of physical relief from his distress. Later, when he changed his mind, he found out that the decision of his father could not be reversed. The question was obvious: Would they exchange future spiritual blessing for a moment of relief from physical persecutions? Such a sin would not be against a legalistic system (12:18-21) but against God's program of grace described in ten ways (12:22-24). The warning concludes: "See that ye refuse not him that speaketh. For if they escaped not who refused him that spake on earth, much more shall not we escape, if we turn away from him that speaketh from heaven" (12:25). Breaking the law brought human punishment; disobeying the voice of Christ would bring divine chastisement. The Jewish nation was about to be destroyed, but the believers had a spiritual kingdom that could not be moved (12:28). He then exhorted: "Let us have grace, whereby we may serve God acceptably with reverence and godly fear: For our God is a consuming fire" (12:28-29).

13:1-6

In closing his book, the author gave a rapid series of commands dealing with the readers' obligations to others. Brotherly love (13:1), hospitality (13:2), compassion (13:3), sexual purity (13:4), and contentment (13:5) were to mark their lives. These charges were to be obeyed with the awareness of Christ's presence and help and with a fearlessness toward their persecutors (13:5-6).

13:7-17

He then admonished them to follow the faith-example of their spiritual overseers (13:7) and to obey them (13:17). Since Christ is constant in His character (13:8), they were to reflect a stability in their doctrinal position (13:9). Since Christ died without the gate of Jerusalem, they were to be identified with Him and not with those Jews who crucified Him. There may be a hint here to Jerusalem Christians to leave the city and not to defend it against an imminent Roman threat. They should put their hope in the heavenly city, not in the earthly one (13:10-14). He admonished them to offer spiritual sacrifices of thanksgiving and generosity instead of returning to the sacrificial system of the temple (13:15-16).

13:18-25

He then requested prayer for himself that he might have a good conscience and an honest life and that he might be restored to their fellowship (13:18-19). After his benediction (13:20-21), he exhorted them to obey his warnings and commands (13:22). He then informed them of Timothy's release, sent greetings to them, and closed with a brief blessing (13:23-25).

Increase Your Learning

By Doing

1. Underline all exhortations that begin with the words "Let us. . . ."
2. Circle the word "lest" wherever found.
3. Underline every reference to Christ's priesthood and to His blood sacrifice.
4. Underline the word "faith" and circle the names of the heroes of faith in chapter 11.

By Discussing

1. Does God still reveal Himself and His will today through visions and dreams? Defend your answer.
2. How do angels minister to humans? Are there really guardian angels?
3. What are the causes of spiritual immaturity? What can be done to correct the situation? What is the difference between immaturity and carnality?
4. In what ways does God chastise? Can a Christian really get away with sin?
5. Why do believers not trust God more? Why are they impatient? What is the solution to this problem?

By Reading

Bruce, F. F. *The Epistle to the Hebrews*. Grand Rapids: Wm. B. Eerdmans Publishing Co., 1964.

English, E. Schuyler. *Studies in the Epistle to the Hebrews*. Findlay, Ohio: Dunham Publishing Co., 1955.

Hewitt, Thomas. *The Epistle to the Hebrews*. Grand Rapids: Wm. B. Eerdmans Publishing Co., 1960.

Newell, William R. *Hebrews Verse by Verse*. Chicago: Moody Press, 1947.

Westcott, Brooke Foss. *The Epistle to the Hebrews*. Grand Rapids: Wm. B. Eerdmans Publishing Co., n.d.

23

JAMES

Writer

The book opens with these words: "James, a servant of God and of the Lord Jesus Christ" (1:1). The name "James" is based upon the Greek transliteration *(Iakobos)* of the Hebrew "Jacob." But which "James" is this? There are four men who bear the name of James in the New Testament. First, there is the father of one of the apostles, Judas, not Iscariot (Luke 6:16); however, his life is too obscure to be considered for the authorship of this book. Second, there is James, the son of Alphaeus (Matt. 10:3), probably also known as James the less (Mark 15:40). If he had been the author, he doubtless would have mentioned his apostleship. Also, outside of his listing with the other eleven apostles, his life lacked renown. Third, there is another apostle, James the son of Zebedee and the brother of the beloved John (Matt. 4:21). As a member of the inner circle of three disciples, he was well known and held in high esteem. However, since he was martyred rather early in the history of the early church (A.D. 44; Acts 12:2), it is very unlikely that he could have written this book. If he had, he certainly would have identified himself as an apostle and/or as the brother of John. The most plausible possibility is that James, the brother of Jesus, wrote the Epistle (Matt. 13:55; Gal. 1:19). Although "James" was a common name, only a person of prominence could have used it without any further identification.[1] It was so used of the brother of the Lord several times (Acts 12:17; 15:13; 21:18; Gal. 2:9, 12; Jude 1). Writing much later, Jude identified

---

1. Compare "The Lord is risen indeed, and hath appeared to Simon" (Luke 24:34). Two apostles bore the name of Simon (Matt. 10:2, 4), but it is clear that this is a reference to the prominent Simon Peter.

335

himself as "the brother of James" (Jude 1). His readers must have known that his blood brother was also the Jerusalem overseer and the writer of this early canonical book (cf. Mark 6:3). Further proof of this position can be seen in the striking similarity between the vocabulary of the book and the speech that James gave at the Council of Jerusalem: "Greeting" *(chairein,* 1:1; cf. Acts 15:23); forms of the verb "to visit" *(episkeptomai,* 1:27; cf. Acts 15:14) and "to turn" *(epistrepho,* 5:19-20; cf. Acts 15:19); and the equation of the phrase "that worthy name by which ye are called" (2:7) with "upon whom my name is called" (Acts 15:17).

What was the exact relationship of James to Christ? Those who argue for the perpetual virginity of Mary claim that James was either a cousin or a stepbrother, a child of Joseph by a former marriage. They believe that either view best explains the arrogant, sarcastic unbelief of Christ's relatives (John 7:3-5)[2] and the commitment of Mary to John the apostle rather than to them at the cross (John 19:25-27). However, the natural reading of the text suggests that Mary was the real mother, not only of Jesus, but also of his brothers and sisters (Matt. 12:46-50; 13:55; Mark 6:3; John 2:12; 7:3, 10). These children were born to Mary and Joseph after the birth of Jesus. The Pauline identification of James as "the Lord's brother" (Gal. 1:19) confirms this conclusion.

Since his name heads the list of Jesus' brothers and sisters (Matt. 13:55; Mark 6:3), he was the oldest of the children born to Mary and Joseph. Evidently, he and his brothers did not believe in the deity and the messiahship of Jesus during either the latter's developmental years or His years of ministry (John 7:5). When Jesus was regarded as insane and as a blasphemer, they may have manifested a natural human concern for his physical welfare (Mark 3:21-31). Their absence at the Crucifixion may have been caused by their shame or embarrassment over the shameful death experienced by Jesus. In any case, they did not become believers until after Christ's death and resurrection. They were among the first to receive the news of Christ's resurrection from Mary Magdalene (John 20:17). Christ later personally appeared to James (I Cor. 15:7). Whether the other brothers saw Him during the forty days of post-resurrection ministry is uncertain, but all the brothers were numbered among the believers, including the apostles, during the ten-day interval between Christ's ascension and the descent of Holy Spirit (Acts 1:14). Within five years of Christ's ascension, James was known as an apostle (Gal. 1:19). When Peter was miraculously delivered from prison after the martyrdom of James the son of Zebedee, he was especially concerned

---

2. Compare this with the ill feeling of the half-brothers of Joseph to him (Gen. 37).

Interior view of the Golden Gate in Old Jerusalem. James was one of the key leaders of the New Testament church in Jerusalem.

that James should be informed about his release and his departure from Jerusalem (Acts 12:17). This may indicate that James by this time (A.D. 44) was acknowledged as the overseer of the Jerusalem church, especially in the absence of the apostles. Shortly after (A.D. 46), Paul regarded him along with Peter and John as the pillars of the Jerusalem church (Gal. 2:9). In fact, James was one of the three who recognized and approved Paul's apostolic credentials and message. At the council of Jerusalem (Acts 15), he was the final spokesman, gave the oral verdict, and recommended that letters incorporating the council's decisions be sent to the Gentile churches. When Paul came to Jerusalem at the end of his third journey, both James and the church elders suggested that Paul ceremonially purify himself as a testimony to Christian Jews who were zealous of the law (Acts 21:18-26). It was this event that led to Paul's seizure, arrest, and imprisonments (Acts 21:27—28:31). From this point on, Scripture is silent about the ministry of James.

Tradition is mixed about the death of James. According to Eusebius, an early church historian, Paul's conspirators turned on James after the apostle, under Roman custody, went to the imperial city. When James refused to renounce Christ under the pressures of the priests and

337

elders, he was forced to the temple roof and thrown over. For a short while after impact he lived, but he was finally beaten to death. Josephus, the early Jewish historian, claimed that James was martyred during a Jewish insurrection in the interval between the death of Festus, the Roman procurator of Judea, and the arrival of the new governor, Albinus. Death supposedly came by stoning. Both traditions have two common facts: James died a martyr's death and that event occurred about A.D. 62-63.

The book was slow in gaining canonical recognition. Eastern Church Fathers (Origen, Cyril of Jerusalem, Athanasius, Jerome, and Augustine) accepted its authenticity well before the leaders of the Western churches. In fact, it did not gain general recognition as a genuine, canonical book until the Council of Carthage (A.D. 397). Several reasons can be suggested for this delay in acceptance. The apparent contradiction of Paul over the relationship of faith to works probably caused some doubt. Since James was not well known outside of Palestine, the fact that he wrote an early book just to Jewish Christians might have disenchanted some Gentile churches.

Destination of the Letter

James wrote "to the twelve tribes which are scattered abroad" (1:1).[3] Some believe that this refers to the non-Christian Jews of the dispersion; however, the nature of the imperatives could only be directed at believers. Others feel that the book was written to all Christians, both Gentile and Jewish. The phrase "twelve tribes" would be synonymous with "spiritual Israel." The most plausible view is that James wrote to Christian Jews who were scattered throughout the Roman empire. They were perhaps once residents of Palestine, but persecution or lack of job opportunities forced them out of that locale. James would have personally known many who were driven out of Jerusalem in the persecution prompted by Stephen's martyrdom (Acts 8:1-4; 11:19). He would have also known those Jewish pilgrims who were saved on the day of Pentecost (Acts 2:9-11) and those diaspora Jews who worshiped in nationality-centered synagogues in Jerusalem (Acts 6:9). At this time Jews still knew their tribal ancestry (Luke 2:36; Phil. 3:5). Since Peter later wrote to the diaspora Jewish Christians "throughout Pontus, Galatia, Cappadocia, Asia, and Bithynia" (I Peter 1:1), it may be that James wrote to Christian Jews in the East, possibly Babylon or Persia. This would further explain the late acceptance of the book by the Western churches.

---

3. Literally, "to the twelve tribes, the ones which are in the diaspora."

JAMES

Time and Place

All critics and historians believe that the book was written rather early in the first century (A.D. 45). If so, it was the first book of the New Testament to be composed. There are some internal hints for this early date. The church leaders are called teachers and elders, not bishops and deacons as in later writings (3:1; 5:14).[4] The synagogue is mentioned as the meeting place of Christians (2:2). There are no references to doctrinal truths revealed in later Epistles: the Church as the body of Christ, the oneness of believing Jews and Gentiles, and the apostasy. The Judaizers' controversy over the necessity of circumcision had not yet arisen. The gulf between the rich and the poor, especially among the Jews, ended with the Jewish-Roman war (A.D. 66; 5:1-6); therefore, the book had to be written before that event. Some sense within James a familiarity with the teachings of Jesus, especially the Sermon on the Mount. If so, the parallelism is in concept rather than in direct quotation; this should be expected from a book written before the actual Gospel records. Since tradition places the martyrdom of James in A.D. 62, the book could easily have been written in the fifth decade (A.D. 45-50).

The place from which it was written is unknown. Various sites have been suggested: Rome, Antioch, Alexandria, and Jerusalem. The last one is the best possibility since in the Bible James is always placed in Jerusalem after his conversion.

Little is known about the historical background of the writing of the Epistle. The contents of the book suggest that the readers were in the midst of trials (1:2-12; 5:10-11), in moral laxity (1:22-25; 4:1-11), and in doctrinal confusion (1:13-16). James, aware of the situation, wrote thus to correct their moral and doctrinal problems.

Purposes

The general purpose of James was to exhort his readers to support with their lives what they said with their lips. Specifically, he wrote to explain the nature of trials and temptations (1:2-18), to appeal for religious practice (1:19-27), to rebuke them for their partiality (2:1-13), to show the necessity of works as the evidence of faith (2:14-26), to warn against the improper use of the tongue (3:1-12), to describe the nature of spiritual wisdom (3:13-18), to contrast worldliness with spirituality (4:1-12), to point out dependence upon the will of God for future plans (4:13-17), to warn the rich against improper use of wealth (5:1-6), to reinforce their need of patience (5:7-11), to instruct them about various types of prayer (5:12-18), and to give guidelines about the recovery of the sinning Christian (5:19-20).

---

4. "Masters" is literally "teachers" in the Greek text (3:1).

Distinctive Features

There is a striking similarity between the content of James' Epistle and Jesus' Sermon on the Mount. James either heard the Sermon personally or discussed it with those who did. Note these comparisons. Mere profession is not enough to get one into the kingdom of heaven (2:14-26; cf. Matt. 7:21-23). Hearing and doing go together (1:22; cf. Matt. 7:24-27). The character of a person is made evident by his actions (3:11-12; cf. Matt. 7:16-20). The warnings against judging (4:11-12; cf. Matt. 7:1), wrong use of wealth (5:1-6; cf. Matt. 6:19-24), and swearing (5:12; cf. Matt. 5:34-37) can also be seen.

James, like Jesus, liked to use Old Testament characters as illustrations: Abraham (2:21), Isaac (2:21), Rahab (2:25), Job (5:11), and Elijah (5:17).

He also had an affinity for illustrations from the world of nature and from the ordinary activities of mankind: wind-tossed wave of the sea (1:6), withering grass and fading flowers (1:10-11), burning heat of the sun (1:11), conception and birth (1:15), shadows caused by the sun's position (1:17), firstfruits (1:18), looking into a mirror (1:23), begging (2:15-16), breath of the body (2:26), bits in horses' mouths (3:3), helms of ships (3:4), fire (3:5), taming of creatures (3:7), fountain of water (3:11), figs and olives (3:12), sowing and harvesting (3:18), vapors (4:14), motheaten garments (5:2), rust (5:3), labor and wages (5:4), early and latter rains (5:7), anointing with oil (5:14), and drought (5:17).

In a New Testament book it is unique that the Savior is mentioned only twice directly and twice indirectly: "Lord Jesus Christ" (1:1; 2:1) and "the coming of the Lord" (5:7, 8). If the title "Lord" refers to the Son rather than to the Father, then He is seen elsewhere also (4:10, 15; 5:10, 11, 14, 15). There is no reference, though, to Christ's incarnation, death, or resurrection. The book, however, is saturated with the teaching of Christ instead of His imprinted name.

James was very concerned about the speech of the believer. He devoted almost an entire chapter to the use of the tongue (3:1-12). Throughout the book he used verbs pertaining to the right and the wrong uses of the tongue: "ask" (1:5, 6; 4:2, 3 [twice]); "say" (1:13; 2:3; 2:14, 16, 18; 4:13, 15); "speak" (1:19; 2:12; 4:11 [twice]); "tongue" (1:26; 3:5, 6 [twice], 8); "word" (3:2); "mouth" (3:10); "laughter" (4:9); "boasting" (4:16); "howl" (5:1); "crieth" (5:4 [twice]); "grudge" (5:9); "swear" (5:12); "sing" (5:13); and "pray" (5:13, 14, 16, 17, 18). The verb "said" is used of God or the Bible (2:11 [twice]; 4:5-6), and the verb "spoken" is used of the prophets (5:10).

JAMES

Outline

Survey

1:1-12

The book begins and ends with the subject of trials (1:2-3; cf. 5:10-11).[5] Such trials are designed by God to produce joy (1:2), patience (1:3), maturity (1:4), wisdom (1:5), stability (1:6-8), humility (1:10), blessing (1:12) and love (1:12) in the believer's life. Wisdom to understand the purpose of the test can be secured through believing prayer. God designs such tests for a certain period of duration. The believer must endure it completely and must continue to love the Lord throughout the trial in order to receive the crown of life. This could refer to the abundant life of present experience (John 10:10) and/or to a special reward to be given at the judgment seat of Christ.

1:13-18

Within a test planned by God there may come a temptation to do evil.[6] The believer must distinguish between the test and the temptation. He should never blame his sin on God because sin is contrary to the nature of God. God could never respond to a solicitation to do evil, nor would He ever tempt a believer to sin. Man himself bears the total blame for his own sin because it originates within the lusts of his sin nature. Note the order: lust—sin—death. A believer should realize that God is never the source of evil but that He is always the origin of good and perfect gifts. Since God is immutable ("no variableness neither shadow of turning"), evil will never proceed from His good, holy being.

---

5. The Greek word *peirasmos* can refer to tests that come from God or to temptations to evil that come from the sinful nature.
6. It was the will of God for Jesus to be tempted, but the temptation came from Satan (Matt. 4:1).

The sin of our lustful wills brings forth death, but His will gave us a new birth (cf. John 3:5). Since like begets[7] like, a good, holy God produces good, holy human lives, not sinful ones. As "firstfruits of his creatures," believers should be like Him.

1:19-27

James exhorted his readers to "be swift to hear, slow to speak, slow to wrath" (1:19). This contrast was to be developed in producing the righteous life (1:20-21). True righteousness involves not just the hearing of the Word, but the actual doing of it. If a man looks into a mirror, views his dirty face, and walks away without washing it, then why did he even look into the mirror? A nondoer of what he hears is in the same situation (1:22-25). Genuine religion does not involve hypocritical lip-profession (1:26), but it includes compassionate acts and personal purity (1:27).

2:1-13

There can be no partiality in the maintenance of genuine faith (2:1). To show preference for a rich visitor to the church service over a poor one is evil (2:2-4). Since God did not choose men to salvation on the basis of their economic condition, neither should Christians favor the rich over the poor. In Christ the poor man is just as wealthy as the rich man (2:5). The poor and the rich must be loved equally in order to fulfill the royal law of loving one's neighbor as oneself (2:8). James then pointed out that violation of this directive made the sinning Christian a transgressor (2:9-11). Christians are to speak and to do the truth consistently knowing that they will be judged for their exercise of mercy and partiality (2:12-13).

2:14-26

James argued that a living faith will produce living works of faith. He was critical of the man who claimed to have faith but who had no works to substantiate his claim. Can that kind of faith save anyone?[8] His implied answer was negative. A statement of compassion without actual help when one has the power of relief has no profit (2:15-16). Three times James emphasized that a mere profession of faith without works is dead (2:17, 20, 26). Such a faith is no different than the belief of demons in monotheism. Since their faith never issued in a

---

7. The translations "bringeth forth" (1:15) and "begat" (1:18) are both based on the same Greek verb apokuo.
8. Literally, the closing question of 2:14 is: "Is the faith able to save him?" Grammarians regard the article "the" as the article of previous reference. Thus, can that type of faith, spoken with the lip but not supported with the life, save the professor?

transformation of life, it was valueless. The faith of Abraham's lip in the covenant promises was made perfect in his action of offering Isaac as a sacrifice. James did not claim that Abraham was justified by faith and works; he argued that the patriarch was saved by a faith that wrought works (2:21-23). Rahab, likewise, demonstrated that she believed in the God of Israel as her own God when she hid the Jewish spies. James then equated the works of faith with the spirit of the human body. Human life is marked by the presence of breathing; genuine spiritual life is marked by the activity of works.

3:1-12

James warned against impromptu decisions to become teachers.[9] Since teachers influence their students not only in what they say but also in how they live, their accountability to God is much greater (3:1). He declared that those who can control the tongue can also control their behavior (3:2). To illustrate his thesis he pointed to the bit in the horse's mouth, to the helm of the ship, and to a spark that kindles a forest fire (3:3-5). He declared that the tongue was the one member of the body that Satan could use to defile the believer's body and to destroy other lives (3:6). Although men have trained animals, creeping things, and sea creatures, yet they are unable to tame the tongue because of its innate evil propensities (3.7-8). Within seconds men can use their tongues to bless God and to curse men. This paradox in man is contrary to the principles of nature (3:9-12).

3:13-18

A living faith and genuine wisdom are companions. If a person has both, he will "shew out of a good conversation [lit., behavior] his works with meekness of wisdom" (3:13). A life that manifests envy and strife reveals an earthly, sensual, demonic wisdom couched in confusion and evil works (3:14-16). Heavenly wisdom is characterized by purity, peace, gentleness, approachability, mercy, and good fruits, and is without partiality, and without hypocrisy.

4:1-12

A spiritual Christian manifests peace, not fighting (3:18; cf. 4:1). Dissension stems from the lusts of the sin nature, not from the Spirit of God. In a series of positive and negative statements (4:2-3), James revealed that his readers had committed spiritual adultery in that their friendship with the world made them the enemies of God (4:4). Envy was caused by their lustful human spirit, not by the Holy Spirit (4:5). In a series of imperatives, he then explained the essence of spiritual

---

9. Literally, the Greek *didaskaloi* means "teachers" rather than "masters."

wisdom and behavior: humility (4:6), submission to God and resistance of the devil (4:7), nearness to God (4:8a), cleansing of one's actions and attitudes (4:8b), contrition over sin (4:9), and self-abasement (4:10). He concluded by warning against evil speaking or judging one's brother. Such actions make a person a judge of the law, rather than a doer of it. Their responsibility was to do; it was God's work to judge (4:11-12).

4:13-17

He cautioned against presumptuous planning of one's life apart from the will of God. The question of where we go, how long we stay, and what we do should be answered under divine direction. Since life at its longest is very short, the believer should want to live every moment of it in the will of God. To ambitiously make one's plans without consulting God is evil boasting and sin.

5:1-6

Earlier, James stated that rich Christians should rejoice when they are made low through divine trials (1:10). The church apparently gave preferential treatment to the rich (2:1-7), and the wealthy members in their midst did not practice compassionate generosity (2:15-16). To those who lived for wealth, James now sounded a warning of judgment. Their riches would perish; their selfishness and fraud would affect their judgment; and their hedonistic practices would one day no longer be tolerated. There is a possibility that for the encouragement of his oppressed readers James echoed the words of Jesus in proclaiming divine judgment against the unsaved wealthy Jews who crucified Christ and who persecuted the Jewish Christians (5:4-6; cf. Matt. 6:19-24).

5:7-12

In the midst of persecutions and divinely ordained trials, the readers were exhorted to have patience (5:7, 8, 10, 11). The imminent coming of the Lord was to provide an incentive for mental and emotional stability (5:8) and for the elimination of personal grudges (5:9). Both the Old Testament prophets and the patriarch Job had suffered, bearing suffering patiently and rejoicing in it, and had been rewarded with divine blessing. The readers were exhorted to follow their examples. Their speech was to be above reproach as they endured their trials (5:12; cf. Job 1:22; 2:10).

5:13-18

In a series of questions and imperatives, James then explained various types of prayer that could be exercised in the midst of their trials. The mentally afflicted one was to utter a prayer of dependence; the happy

Christian was to sing psalms of praise; the physically sick was to summon the church's elders who were to pray over him and to anoint him. The initiative was with the sick person. The believing prayer of all of them would cause the Lord to heal the one who was sick probably because of persecution. If he had committed sins in the midst of his trial, then these would also be forgiven (5:14-15). Mutual confession and intercession were also commanded. The value of "the effectual fervent prayer of a righteous man" was aptly illustrated in Elijah (5:16-18).

5:19-20

The closing two verses deal with the restoration of an erring believer by a concerned fellow Christian. If no one had intervened in the sinning Christian's life, his sin could have led to the chastisement of premature physical death. Awareness and confession of his sins (I John 1:9) would hide his sin.

Increase Your Learning

By Doing

1. Circle the word "brethren" wherever found in the book.
2. Circle all words that deal with speech (e.g., "say," and "tongue").
3. Underline the word "works" wherever found.
4. Circle all proper names in the book.

By Discussing

1. What is the difference between testing and temptation? Give some specific illustrations of each.
2. What is sin committed in the mind of the believer? Relate the mind, the emotions, and the will to the critical point of sinful conception.
3. Do our churches today give preferential treatment to the wealthy? How can the gulf between rich and poor Christians be bridged?
4. How many works must a person produce to give evidence of genuine saving faith? Must they be done throughout one's lifetime? How does this harmonize with the concepts of carnality and immaturity?
5. Are Christian businessmen guilty of establishing economic goals without God's help? Is it possible to carry on a business based upon Scriptural principles?
6. Give specific ways by which a believer can manifest friendship with the world.

By Reading

Gaebelein, Frank. *The Practical Epistle of James.* New York: Doniger and Raughley, 1955.
King, Guy. *A Belief that Behaves.* London: Marshall, Morgan, & Scott, 1941.

Mayor, Joseph B. *The Epistle of St. James.* Grand Rapids: Zondervan Publishing House, 1954.

Ross, Alexander, *The Epistles of James and John.* Grand Rapids: Wm. B. Eerdmans Publishing Co., 1964.

Tasker, R. V. G. *The General Epistle of James.* Grand Rapids: Wm. B. Eerdmans Publishing Co., 1964.

24

FIRST PETER

Writer

The name of Simon Peter is well known. It is mentioned 210 times in the New Testament, whereas the name of Paul is recorded 162 times and the combined names of all the other apostles are found only 142 times.

A native of Bethsaida, a village on the northeastern tip of the Sea of Galilee (John 1:44), he made his living through fishing along with his father Jonas and his brother Andrew (Matt. 16:17; John 1:40). After his marriage, he and his wife apparently moved to a nearby town, Capernaum (Matt. 8:5; cf. 8:14). There is no record that they ever had children. His brother Andrew was a disciple of John the Baptist, and there is a strong possibility that Simon was also (John 1:35-40). Andrew became convinced of the messiahship of Jesus first, and then he introduced Simon personally to Jesus (John 1:41-42). On this occasion Simon was given the additional name of Peter (Greek) or Cephas (Aramaic), both meaning "a rock" (John 1:42). Shortly after this event Christ called Peter to become a full-time follower or disciple (Matt. 4:18-20).[1] From His multitude of disciples, Christ later chose twelve, including Peter and Andrew, to be with Him and to be sent forth by Him both to preach and to heal (Mark 3:13-15; Luke 6:12-13). This select group was given the new name of "apostles." In all of the lists of the apostles, Peter's name always stands first (Matt. 10:2-4; Mark 3:16-19; Luke 6:14-16; Acts 1:13). For the next three years or so, it was Peter's blessing to observe firsthand the preaching and healing ministry of Jesus.

---

1. So many events both in the Gospels and in the Epistles surround the person of Peter that it would be impractical to incorporate them all into this survey. Consult a concordance for a complete listing of Peter's activities.

In addition, he became a privileged member of the inner circle of three, along with James and John, who accompanied Christ to the Mount of Transfiguration (Matt. 17:1-5), into the bedroom of Jairus' daughter (Mark 5:37), and into the Garden of Gethsemane (Matt. 26:36-46). After Christ's arrest, he denied the Lord three times as predicted (Matt. 26:69-75), but later repented and was perhaps an eyewitness of Christ's crucifixion from a distance (I Peter 5:1). He was a witness to several of Christ's postresurrection appearances and to His ascension into heaven (Luke 24:34; Acts 1:9-10).

Not only was Peter the most prominent disciple during Christ's earthly ministry, but he became the leading apostle in the early years of the church. On the day of Pentecost, he was the chief spokesman for the small group of believers (Acts 2). It was he who opened the doors of the kingdom of heaven to the Jew, the Samaritan, and the Gentile (Matt. 16:19; cf. Acts 2:14-41; 8:14-25; 10:1-48). During these years, he restricted his activities to Palestine, mainly in Jerusalem but also in Lydda (Acts 9:32-35), Joppa (Acts 9:36-43), Caesarea (Acts 10:1-48), and Syrian Antioch (Gal. 2:11). He made a major contribution to the discussion of Gentile salvation at the council of Jerusalem (Acts 15: 1-21). After this event, however, his name disappears from the Book of Acts. Little is known about his activity in his later years, but he apparently traveled much with his wife (I Cor. 9:5), probably visiting

This structure along the shores of the Sea of Galilee dates from Roman times. It contained a flour mill powered by water entering from the aqueduct. The waters of Galilee were familiar to the apostle Peter.

such areas as the provinces of Asia Minor (1:1) and Babylon (5:13). Tradition states that he was crucified upside down in Rome[2] about A.D. 67-68, although some place his martyrdom as early as A.D. 64.

There has been no serious challenge to the Petrine authorship of the First Epistle. The early historian Eusebius listed it among the undisputed books. These Church Fathers also recognized its canonicity and ascribed it to Peter: Polycarp, Irenaeus, Tertullian, and Clement of Alexandria.

Their convictions were caused doubtless by the strong internal evidence of the Epistle. The author called himself "Peter" and claimed to be an apostle (1:1). He stated that he was an eyewitness of Christ's sufferings and postresurrection glory (5:1).[3] There are several autobiographical expressions which reflect Peter's intimate associations with Christ. The charge to the elders to feed the flock repeated Christ's postresurrection commission to Peter (5:2; cf. John 21:15-17). The command to be clothed with humility echoed the spiritual intent of the washing of the disciples' feet by Jesus (5:5; cf. John 13:3-17). There are also similarities between the language of the Epistle and that of Peter's recorded sermons in the Book of Acts: God is no respecter of persons (1:17; cf. Acts 10:34); the resurrection and ascension glory of Christ (1:21; cf. Acts 2:32-36); and Christ, the rejected stone, as the cornerstone (2:7-8; cf. Acts 4:10-11). Since Second Peter referred to itself as "this second epistle" (3:1), the First Epistle must have been First Peter (1:1; cf. II Peter 1:1). All evidence points to Simon Peter as the human author of this book.

Recipients of the Letter

Who were the readers? The opening verse reads: ". . . to the strangers scattered throughout Pontus, Galatia, Cappadocia, Asia, and Bithynia" (1:1). Does this refer to Jewish Christians mainly, or to Gentile Christians, or to both? It is difficult to determine exactly the answer to that question.

Many commentators believe that the recipients were chiefly Gentile converts with some Jewish believers numbered among them. It could be said of Gentiles that they once walked in ignorant lusts (1:14) and that they had a vain life-style received by tradition from their fathers (1:18). They had been saved out of pagan darkness (2:9). Their spiritual past was differentiated from God's covenant people Israel: "Which in time past were not a people, but are now the people of God" (2:10). Abominable idolatries were part of their past also (4:3). Peter's use of his

---

2. For a refutation of the view that Peter spent over twenty years in Rome, see the section "Establishment of the Church" under Romans.

3. The latter, though, could refer to the glory of Christ displayed on the Mount of Transfiguration (cf. II Peter 1:16-18).

Greek name rather than his Hebrew (Simon) or Aramaic one (Cephas) may suggest a Gentile readership (1:1). However, a close analysis of these passages could reveal the spiritual past of any unregenerate person, whether Jew or Gentile. Even the Jewish Peter included himself as one who did the will of the Gentiles, including lusts and idolatries (4:3; note "us" and "we").

In defense of a Jewish readership, it must be noted that Peter was known as an apostle to the Jews (Gal. 2:7). However, it must also be admitted that he had a ministry among the Gentiles as well (Acts 10:34-48; I Cor. 9:5; Gal. 2:12).[4] The phrase "strangers scattered" (literally, "elect pilgrims of the dispersion")[5] seems to refer to Jewish Christians, scattered as a result of the Babylonian captivity or the persecution of Palestinian churches. However, all believers are constituted as "pilgrims" on a hostile earth looking toward their heavenly home (2:11; cf. Heb. 11:13-16; 13:14). His appeal to the readers to have their behavior "honest among the Gentiles" (2:12) also lends credence to a Jewish readership. However, some have wondered about the meaning of "Gentiles." Does this term refer to non-Jews racially or to non-Christians spiritually? If the latter, it would be a synonym for all the unregenerate. The natural reading of the text, however, suggests the former. In conclusion, the evidence favors a Jewish Christian readership, with the possibility that some Gentile believers were numbered among them.

Time and Place

The Christians in the provinces of Pontus, Galatia, Cappadocia, Asia, and Bithynia were suffering for their faith (1:1, 5). The persecutions did not stem from the imperial government, but originated from the local populace in the form of verbal slander and social pressures (4:14-15). Quite possibly, they could have been ridiculed for their separated lives (4:4-5) and/or accused of being traitors (2:13-17). The church was also infected with some internal problems such as worldliness (2:11-16; 4:1-5) and greedy, autocratic elders (5:2-3).

There is no indication how Peter was informed about the spiritual condition of these believers. In fact, the evangelization of these provinces of northern Asia Minor remains somewhat of a mystery. A witness in Pontus and Cappadocia is not even mentioned in Acts. Paul was forbidden by the Spirit to preach in Bithynia (Acts 16:7). Galatia and Asia were evangelized by his missionary team (Acts 13-21). On the day of Pentecost, pilgrims from Cappadocia, Pontus, and Asia heard Peter's

---

4. Paul was known as the Apostle to the Gentiles, and yet he always preached to the Jew first.
5. The Greek word for "strangers" is *parepidemois,* translated elsewhere as "pilgrims" (2:11; Heb. 11:13).

sermon (Acts 2:9). This may have provided the contact between Peter and those provinces. Peter did travel outside of Palestine, perhaps as far as Greece (I Cor. 9:5). His itinerary could have easily included these Roman provinces. Somehow Peter heard about the plight of those believers, became burdened over them, and accepted the Spirit-given responsibility to encourage them.

The date of writing is difficult to determine. He probably wrote both Epistles before the outbreak of the imperial persecutions and the martyrdom of Paul. This would place the time of writing about A.D. 63-65.

There is some indication that Peter used an amanuensis in the composition of this book: "By Silvanus, a faithful brother unto you, as I suppose, I have written briefly ..." (5:12). Not only was Silvanus the messenger of the Epistle, but also the apostle's secretary. "Silvanus" is a lengthened form of "Silas," and doubtless this was the same individual as Paul's traveling companion (Acts 15:40; II Cor. 1:19; I Thess. 1:1; II Thess. 1:1). Silas was originally a member of the Jerusalem church so he would have been well known to Peter (Acts 15:22, 27, 32).

The geographic origin of the Epistle has raised several questions. Peter wrote: "The church that is at Babylon, elected together with you, saluteth you" (5:13). Three views of the meaning of "Babylon" have developed. First, there was a small town in Egypt with that name, but it was too insignificant to merit a visit by Peter. The second view is that "Babylon" is a symbolic name for the city of Rome. According to its many proponents, Babylon on the Euphrates was greatly deserted by New Testament times, so it would be highly unlikely that Peter would have journeyed to it. One of Peter's companions was Mark (5:13) who was also with Paul during the first Roman imprisonment (Col. 4:10) and who may have accompanied Timothy to Rome for the second confinement (II Tim. 4:11). It would be more logical to assume that Peter and Mark got together in Rome than in Babylon. Tradition does state that Peter spent his later years in Rome, but there is no indication from tradition or Scripture that Peter ever went to the ancient region of Babylon. The advocates also claim that a consultation with a map would disclose that the letter had to be sent from the west (Rome) because of the order in which the names of the provinces appear. Their final argument is that "Babylon" was a symbolic name for Rome (Rev. 17:3-5, 9, 18). Although the Rome view sounds convincingly plausible, the third view that the name refers to the literal Babylon on the Euphrates seems best. There is no reason to suspect that Peter inserted a symbolic name into a nonsymbolic context. The normal reading of the passage would cause the reader to think of the real Babylon. If Peter meant Rome, then why did he not write "Rome"? Actually, the symbolic use of Babylon for Rome was a mystery not revealed until years later

351

The Old Testament city of Babylon was nearly deserted in New Testament times. A settlement including Jews and Christian Jews, however, existed in the area of Babylon.

when John penned Revelation (Rev. 17:5). John could not have called it a mystery if it had been known for thirty years. As a result of the Babylonian captivity, a good number of Jews still resided in the East. The Magi came from that region (Matt. 2:2) and pilgrims from Mesopotamia heard Peter's sermon on the day of Pentecost (Acts 2:9). As an apostle to the circumcision, Peter could have had a genuine concern for that remote region. Until stronger evidence is forthcoming, the literal view must stand as the readable interpretation of the text.

Purposes

Peter, therefore, wrote to explain the relationship of trials to God's purposes in salvation (1:1-12); to provoke the readers to lives of holiness, love, growth, and testimony (1:13—2:12); to call for submission of believers to civil authorities (2:13-17), of servants to masters (2:18-25), and of wives to husbands (3:1-8); to discuss the proper attitude of believers in suffering (3:9—4:19); to give guidelines to the elders for the proper performance of their ministry (5:1-4); to call them to humility (5:5-7); to warn them against the tactics of Satan (5:8-11); and to send greetings (5:12-14).

Distinctive Features

The key word of the Epistle is "suffering." It occurs sixteen times (1:11; 2:19, 20, 21, 23; 3:14, 17, 18; 4:1 [twice], 13, 15, 16, 19; 5:1, 10). In those passages are six references to Christ's own sufferings (1:11; 2:23; 3:18; 4:1, 13; 5:1). Peter challenged the believer to follow

352

the example of Christ and to suffer patiently (2:20) for the sake of righteousness (3:14), for well doing (3:17), with rejoicing (4:13), as a Christian (4:16), and according to the will of God (4:19). The suffering motif permeates the Epistle and forms the background for Peter's exhortations.

Peter's literary style reveals a definite preference for the imperative. As an apostle, he used his authority to charge his readers with thirty-four commands (1:13 [twice], 15, 17, 22; 2:2, 13, 17 [four times], 18; 3:1, 7, 8, 14 [twice], 15; 4:1, 7 [twice], 12, 13, 15, 16 [twice], 19; 5:2, 5 [twice], 6, 8 [twice], 9).

The Epistle provides a New Testament commentary upon the Old Testament prophets' understanding of what they wrote:

> Of which salvation the prophets have inquired and searched diligently, who prophesied of the grace that should come unto you: Searching what, or what manner of time the Spirit of Christ which was in them did signify, when it testified beforehand the sufferings of Christ, and the glory that should follow (1:10-11).

This passage teaches that the prophets enjoyed the indwelling, revealing ministry of the Holy Spirit and that they did not understand completely everything revealed to them and recorded by them. In the same passage they wrote about the cross and the kingdom, but they did not realize that it would take two comings of the Messiah to accomplish these goals. They wondered: If Christ is to reign, why must He die? And, if He dies, how can He reign? The interval between the two comings was not disclosed until after the first coming of Christ.

The Epistle also provides excellent material for the doctrine of Christology. Within the book are references to the preordained purpose behind His incarnation (1:20), His sinless life (1:19; 2:22), His suffering and death (2:24), His resurrection (3:21-22), His ascension (3:22), His presence at the right hand of the Father (3:22), and His second coming (1:7, 13; 4:13; 5:1, 4).

One of the most difficult interpretative passages is found here (3:18-22). It has provoked many stimulating questions. Who are the spirits in prison? Are they men or angels? Why were they imprisoned? What did Christ preach to them? Did He give them a second chance to repent? What relationship did these spirits have to the days of Noah? What is the meaning of baptism? How can baptism save? Three major views have emerged. The first is that Christ preached through Noah to the patriarch's generation. The second is that Christ went to Hades between His death and resurrection and announced to the unsaved who had lived in Noah's day that their judgment was sure. The third view is that Christ after His resurrection went to Tartarus (cf. II Peter 2:4), declared to the angelic spirits that their attempts and subsequent ones to keep the Messiah from entering the world had failed, and announced the certainty of their eternal judgment.

Outline

SALUTATION (1:1)
   I. THE DESTINY OF THE CHRISTIAN (1:2—2:10)
     A. Plan of salvation (1:2-12)
       1. Its program (1:2-5)
       2. Its problem (1:6-9)
       3. Its prophecy (1:10-12)
     B. Products of salvation (1:13-25)
       1. Holiness (1:13-16)
       2. Reverence (1:17-21)
       3. Love (1:22-25)
     C. Purpose of salvation (2:1-10)
       1. Growth (2:1-3)
       2. Sacrifices (2:4-8)
       3. Testimony (2:9-10)
  II. THE DUTY OF THE CHRISTIAN (2:11—3:12)
     A. Subjection in the state (2:11-17)
     B. Subjection in the household (2:18-25)
     C. Subjection in the family (3:1-12)
  III. THE DISCIPLINE OF THE CHRISTIAN (3:13—5:11)
     A. Suffering as a citizen (3:13—4:6)
       1. Its blessing (3:13-17)
       2. Its example (3:18-22)
       3. Its purpose (4:1-6)
     B. Suffering as a Christian (4:7-19)
       1. Its responsibilities (4:7-11)
       2. Its consolation (4:12-19)
     C. Suffering as a shepherd (5:1-4)
     D. Suffering as a soldier (5:5-11)
CONCLUSION (5:12-14)

Survey

1:1-12

Peter began his Epistle by outlining the plan of God for the believer.[6] In eternity past God knew whom He would choose and on that basis elected His own. This choice was implemented by the Holy Spirit who set apart the elected sinner for a special work of grace. At the appointed time the sinner obeyed the call of God through faith, received the cleansing of Christ's blood, and was born again. Because of Christ's resurrection, he now has the hope of eternal life and a future inheritance, characterized in four ways (1:4). The believer is also kept or guarded by the power of God during his life so that he will possess his inheritance

---

6. Note the three Persons of the Trinity in 1:2.

in eternity future. Peter wanted to assure his readers that the heaviness of their trials was not inconsistent with their rejoicing over God's plan for their lives. It was His purpose that their faith would be purified through such trials, that their love for Christ would increase, that their rejoicing would abound, and that their total salvation would be received after suffering (1:7-9). Since Christ had to suffer before He could gain His glory, they had to do likewise (1:10-12). This order not only baffled the readers, but also the Old Testament prophets and the angels.

1:13-21

Using "wherefore" as his transition, Peter then appealed to his readers to gird up the loins of their minds, to be sober, to hope, to be obedient, to be holy, and to pass the time of their earthly pilgrimage in fear (1:13-17). These exhortations were to be carried out with the knowledge that their redemption was secured by the blood of Christ who knew in eternity that He would suffer on earth and who became incarnate nevertheless. Since He did that for them, they were to perform the eternal plan of God which included suffering for Him.

1:22—2:10

In the midst of their suffering, they were to achieve four purposes. First, in relationship to other Christians, they were to love without hypocrisy and in purity (1:22). Second, in reference to themselves, they were to grow, being nourished by the Word of God (2:2). The Bible was not only the means of their new birth (1:23-25), but also the sustenance of their spiritual life. For growth to take place, five sins had to be forsaken (2:1). Third, in relationship to God, they were to offer spiritual sacrifices (2:5). Peter then described the character of Christ, the believers' high priest: gracious, living stone, disallowed of men, chosen of God, precious, chief corner stone, elect, stone of stumbling, and a rock of offense. Believers were seen as living stones, a spiritual house, and an holy priesthood. Fourth, in relationship to the unsaved, they were to witness about their fourfold privileged position and about the work of Christ in calling them out of darkness into light, in making them into the people of God, and in giving them mercy (2:9-10).

2:11-17

In the middle section of his Epistle, Peter imposed the responsibility of submission upon all believers (2:11-17) and particularly upon slaves (2:18-25) and wives (3:1-7). All believers, as spiritual pilgrims, should abstain from fleshly lusts in order to manifest an honest life-style before the unsaved, to repudiate false charges against themselves, and to attract men to God (2:11-12). They should voluntarily submit themselves "to every ordinance of man for the Lord's sake" (2:13). They should obey the civil regulations decreed by kings and governors in order to convince the rulers that they were not traitors in spite of the false accusations made against them (2:14-15). They were to exercise their spiritual freedom as conscious servants of God by honoring all men, loving the brotherhood, fearing God, and honoring the king (Caesar).

2:18-25

Peter charged Christian slaves to be submissive to their masters regardless of the latter's treatment of them. He declared that suffering for wrongdoing was not Christian suffering; rather, to suffer patiently and wrongfully for welldoing would please Christ (2:18-20). As an illustration, he pointed to Christ. No one can enter into Christ's sufferings for sins, but one can experience the way in which He suffered. They were to imitate Christ in five ways in the midst of their submissive suffering: no sin, no guile in the mouth, no reciprocity in reviling, no threatening, and total commitment to God. Peter then listed four accomplishments of Christ's substitutionary atonement: bore our sins, caused those who were dead in sins to live unto righteousness, spiritually healed us, and caused straying sheep to return to their spiritual shepherd.

3:1-7

He then charged Christian wives to be submissive to their unsaved husbands and to win them to Christ more by their behavior than by their speech.[7] They should attract their husbands to Christ not by stylish clothing or good grooming, but by the development of inner spiritual graces: chastity, fear, a meek and quiet spirit, holiness, and submission. He then admonished Christian husbands to honor their saved wives and to recognize their equality in Christ in order to have effective prayer.

3:8—4:6

For prayers not to be hindered, Peter called for the presence of these spiritual realities: unity, compassion, brotherly love, pity, courtesy, giving of blessing for evil, no evil speaking, hatred of evil, doing good, and seeking peace (3:8-11). Ordinarily, no harm would come to them if they practiced these qualities, but they were to rejoice if they had to suffer for the sake of righteousness (3:13-14). He then admonished them not to be afraid of their oppressors, to be spiritually prepared through the acknowledgment of the lordship of Christ, to be mentally prepared to give a reasoned defense for their doctrinal beliefs and their

---

7. Literally, 3:1 reads: "... that, if any obey not the Word of God, they also may without a word spoken by the wife be won by the deportment of the wives."

willingness to suffer, and to have a good conscience. Again, Peter pointed to Christ as the perfect example of one who suffered in the will of God for welldoing (3:17; cf. 3:18-22). Just as Christ's suffering brought believing sinners to God, so Peter trusted that the suffering of his readers would bring some of their persecutors to God. He wanted them to possess the same mind or attitude that Christ possessed. Just as Christ's death potentially destroyed the power of the sin nature in their lives, so their sufferings should practically issue in a cleansed life (4:1-2). Their present experience should be so radically different from their past that their former sinful companions would wonder over their changed lives (4:3-4).

4:7-19

The imminence of eschatological events was used by Peter to exhort his readers to prayerful watching (4:7), love (4:8), hospitality (4:9), a faithful discharge of ministry (4:10), and the glorification of God in everything (4:11). Again, he asked them to rejoice over their sufferings for Christ. Just as Christ suffered to gain glory, they were to suffer to give glory to Him. Their sufferings were nothing in comparison with the eternal suffering that the unsaved would experience. He charged them to commit their lives to God and to trust His faithfulness in the midst of their sufferings.

5:1-4

Peter then charged the elders to feed or to shepherd their local churches. They were not to assume that responsibility out of peer pressure or out of a desire for money; rather, they were to do it with an open will and mind. They were to lead by example, not by dictatorial decree. Faithful pastors will receive the crown of glory at the coming of Christ and the subsequent judgment seat of Christ.

5:5-11

In closing, Peter charged the younger members to be submissive to the elder; but beyond that, he admonished all to be subject one to another. Humility, not pride, should mark their reciprocal relationships. The command to be clothed with humility no doubt reflected the lesson he learned from the washing of the disciples' feet by Jesus. All anxiety caused by their suffering was to be placed upon God because He would support them (5:7). He warned them about satanic attempts to destroy them and called for soberness, vigilance, and resistance. His benediction provided an excellent summary of the entire intent of the Epistle (5:10). The call of God to eternal glory takes a believer through suffering to achieve perfection, stability, and strength.

5:12-14

He ended the book by revealing the name of his amanuensis, Silvanus, by sending greetings to them from the church at Babylon and from Mark, and by instructing them about proper Christian mutual greetings.

Increase Your Learning

By Doing

1. Circle the words "suffering" and "subjection" with their cognates wherever found.
2. Circle the word "grace" wherever found.
3. Underline all of the imperatives charged in the book.
4. Make a list of all of the important doctrinal truths discussed in the Epistle.

By Discussing

1. Why do Christians not suffer more for their faith today? Does a lack of suffering mean that a believer's life will not be perfected in certain areas?
2. What can angels learn about God and His plan of salvation as they observe Christians?
3. What are the characteristics of genuine Christian fear (1:17)? Why do Christians lack this attitude today?
4. In what specific ways can saved wives manifest Christ to their unsaved husbands? What actions can keep their husbands from accepting Christ?
5. How can a pastor be a firm leader without being autocratic? How can a church cope with a dictatorial pastor?
6. Contrast pride with humility.
7. In what ways can Satan devour a Christian? How can believers protect themselves from his attacks?

By Reading

Bigg, Charles. *A Critical and Exegetical Commentary on the Epistles of St. Peter and St. Jude*. Edinburgh: T. & T. Clark, 1902.

Selwyn, Edward Gordon. *The First Epistle of St. Peter*. London: Macmillan Company, 1947.

Stibbs, Alan. *The First Epistle General of Peter*. Grand Rapids: Wm. B. Eerdmans Publishing Co., 1959.

Wuest, Kenneth S. *First Peter in the Greek New Testament*. Grand Rapids: Wm. B. Eerdmans Publishing Co., 1942.

25

SECOND PETER

Writer

On the basis of both external and internal evidence, the canonicity and the authorship of Second Peter have been attacked more than that of any other New Testament book. However, upon close investigation it can be demonstrated that these rejections rest more upon subjective speculation than upon positive proof.

It is true that second-century Church Fathers did not comment upon the Epistle in their writings, but their silence should not be used as an argument against the nonexistence of the book in their day or against its Petrine authorship. Silence must be looked upon as being neutral. Any suggested reason for their silence must be regarded as plausible speculation. Evangelicals generally explain their silence by the late date of its composition, its brevity, and its limited distribution; however, even this view cannot be proved to the satisfaction of all. Furthermore, no extant third-century writing denied its Petrine authorship. Eusebius quoted Origen as saying "Peter has left one acknowledged Epistle, and perhaps a second, for it is disputed."[1] The names of the disputers were not mentioned, so no one for sure knows who they were. In addition to Origen's probable acceptance, Methodius and Firmilian attested to its authenticity. Fourth-century writers (Jerome, Athanasius, Augustine, and Ambrose) accepted it and so did the famous church councils at Laodicea (A.D. 372) and Carthage (A.D. 397). Although objective proof in the form of direct patristic quotations is not as extensive as that for other New Testament books, the testimonies do favor the Petrine

---

1. *Ecclesiastical History,* VI, xxv, 8.

authorship of the Epistle. The argument of the opposition does not rest upon a variety of firm statements denying its authenticity, but rather upon silence.

In relationship to the internal contents, opponents of Petrine authorship usually point to contrasts of writing style and vocabulary between the two Epistles. This typical liberal argument can usually be explained by the differences in subject matter, in the circumstances that created the writing, and in the use of a different amanuensis. It may even be that Peter used Silvanus to write the First Epistle (5:12) and that the apostle wrote the second one by himself. Arguments based upon style and vocabulary are admittedly subjective. Actually, there is ample similarity between the two Epistles in content, grammar, and use of words to suggest a single author for both of them. Both salutations are identical as far as word choice and order: "Grace to you and peace be multiplied" (literal translation, I Peter 1:2; cf. 1:2). Several unique words are common to both books: "precious" (1:1, 4; cf. I Peter 1:7, 19; 2:6-7); "put off" or "putting away" (1:14; cf. I Peter 3:21); "eyewitness" or "behold" (1:16; cf. I Peter 2:12; 3:2); "supply" (1:5, 11; cf. I Peter 4:11); "conversation" (2:7; 3:11; cf. I Peter 1:15, 18; 2:12; 3:1, 2, 16); and "brotherly kindness" or "love of the brethren" (1:7; cf. I Peter 1:22).[2] The phrase "without spot, and blameless" or "without blemish and without spot" occurs in both (3:14; cf. I Peter 1:19; see also 2:13).

There is also a striking resemblance between the language of the Second Epistle and that of Peter's sermons recorded by Luke; "obtained" (1:1; cf. Acts 1:17); "godliness" or "holiness" (1:3, 6, 7; 3:11; cf. Acts 3:12); "unlawful" or "wicked" (2:8; cf. Acts 2:23); "reward of unrighteousness" or "iniquity" (2:13, 15; cf. Acts 1:18); and "the day of the Lord" (3:10; cf. Acts 2:20).

The writer identified himself as "Simon Peter" (1:1). He used *Sumeon* rather than the common *Simon* (cf. Matt. 16:17). If this book had been written by a forger or by a person using the pseudonym of Peter, he would have used the common Hebrew designation to avoid drawing attention to himself. Only the real Peter would have identified himself in this way to readers who knew him affectionately by that name. Many critics claim that pseudonymity[3] was a well-known literary practice in the ancient world; however, there is no indication that the church which believed in honesty and truth accepted its use. In fact, many

---

2. The latter two are English translations of single Greek words.
3. There is a difference between a pseudonym and a pen name. Samuel Clemens wrote under the fictitious pen name "Mark Twain." A pseudonym would be if a modern author wrote under the name of Ernest Hemingway, using the style and the name of that great writer to gain an audience for his book.

pseudepigrapha ("false writings") bearing the names of the apostles were rejected.

Within the book Peter made several references to his past personal relationships with Christ. He knew that his martyrdom was imminent as predicted by Christ during His postresurrection ministry (1:13-14; cf. John 21:18-19). He spoke of the significance of his eyewitness account of the transfiguration of Christ (1:15-18; cf. Matt. 17:1-13).

Peter identified this letter as his second one: "This second epistle, beloved, I now write unto you" (3:1). The fact that he did not locate the geographical home of his readers (1:1) would cause one to believe that he wrote to those he had addressed in his First Epistle (1:1). The strong authentication of the Petrine authorship of the First Epistle should therefore support his authorship of the second because of the continuity between the two books. They are two volumes of the same set. Jude apparently used Second Peter and recognized its author as an apostle (Jude vv. 17-18; cf. 3:1-3). Actually, the quotation by Jude serves as first-century evidence of the existence and the inspired, authoritative nature of the Epistle. The claim that the false teachers (2:1—3:5) represent second-century heretics cannot be supported objectively. The New Testament constantly warned against the present and future presence of apostates (Acts 20:29-31; Rom. 16:17-18; I Tim. 4:1; II Tim. 3:8; I John 2:18-19; 4:1). Peter was simply describing the false teachers of the middle of the first century.

In conclusion, it can be demonstrated that the alleged attacks upon the Petrine authorship are not as awesome as first voiced. Furthermore, a strong case for his authorship can be established by a careful study of both the patristic writings and the internal contents of the Epistle.

Time and Place

Peter knew that the provinces of Asia Minor would soon be invaded by false teachers (2:1; 3:3). These apostates were known to him and were already influencing Christians in other areas with their moral and doctrinal errors (2:12, 17, 18; 3:5, 16).[4] Their heresy involved a denial of Christ's deity, His atonement, and His second advent (2:1; 3:4), stemming from intellectual arrogance and immoral living. Peter had to write this Epistle, therefore, to warn the believers. It probably was composed shortly after the First Epistle and just months before his martyrdom, placing it somewhere in the A.D. 64-67 range. There is no indication where Peter was at the time of writing. Since tradition placed his martyrdom in Rome, he may have been in that city at that time.

---

4. The use of the present tense shows that the apostates were already on the scene in adjacent areas: "speak evil" (2:12); "These are" (2:17); "they speak" (2:18); "they are ignorant" (3:5); and "they wrest" (3:16).

Purposes

Peter knew that it was his responsibility to remind his readers of proper Christian doctrine and ethics (1:12-13). However, he also knew that he was about to die (1:14). In order for his readers to have a permanent, written record of his teaching after his decease, he purposed to write (1:15; 3:1). In this Epistle, therefore, he wanted to encourage his readers to grow into Christian maturity (1:1-11), to explain the imminence of his death (1:12-15), to show how the transfiguration of Christ guaranteed His second coming (1:16-18), to inform them that the truth of the second advent was not a human-originated concept (1:19-21), to describe the moral and doctrinal characteristics of the false teachers (2:1-22), to explain the delay in Christ's return (3:1-9), to describe the destruction of the universe in the Day of the Lord (3:10-14), to elaborate further the doctrinal ignorance of the false teachers (3:15-16), and to stimulate vigilance and growth on the part of his readers (3:17-18).

Distinctive Features

Peter emphasized knowledge as the best safeguard against the inroads of apostasy. Various cognate forms of the verb "to know" are found sixteen times in the Epistle (1:2, 3, 5, 6, 8, 12, 14, 16, 20; 2:9, 20, 21 [twice]; 3:3, 17, 18).

This Epistle contains one of the two key passages on the inspiration of Scripture (cf. II Tim. 3:16):

> Knowing this first, that no prophecy of the scripture is of any private interpretation. For the prophecy came not in old time by the will of man: but holy men of God spake as they were moved by the Holy Ghost (1:20-21).

No doubt Peter had in mind the Old Testament, but the principle underlying the composition of those thirty-nine books also pertains to the New. He linked together the ancient prophets with the present apostles (3:2) and specifically associated Paul's writings with theirs (3:15-16). Paul stated the fact that the Scripture was God-breathed at the very moment of human composition (II Tim. 3:16). Peter explained the method by which this could be accomplished. The Bible did not originate within the thought processes or the willful determination of any man or men. Rather, holy men of God (not unholy men or holy men of a false religion) spoke and wrote as they were borne along by the will and activity of the Holy Spirit.[5] Since the Scripture came into being in this way, no one by human determination or intelligence can understand it.

---

5. The phrase "as they were moved" is the translation of the Greek present passive participle *pheromenoi*. This word is used of sailing ships being driven or borne along by a wind.

The Holy Spirit must direct one in the interpretation of the text as well as in the inspiration of the text.

The book also contains a classic description of the destruction of the heavens and the earth by fire in the Day of the Lord (3:10-13). Jesus said that the heaven and the earth would pass away (Matt. 24:35); this passage gives the method. Astronomers claim that the sun and the stars are burning down and that eventually the entire universe will be cold and lifeless. However, Peter predicted that the world would end by a catastrophic, divine judgment. With the advent of the thermonuclear era, men's understanding of noise, melting, fervent heat, burning, and fire has increased. It is not unthinkable today to imagine a continuing series of thermonuclear explosions that could destroy the entire earth.

Peter also made a valuable comment upon Paul's Epistles (3:15-16). His mention of "all his epistles" does not mean that Peter was familiar with all thirteen of Paul's letters. Even though such was within the realm of human possibility, it is very highly improbable that he could have read all of them. It does reveal that the letters of the apostles were being copied and circulated among the churches even during the lifetime of the apostles. His mentioning "longsuffering" and "salvation" could mean that Peter was referring to First Timothy specifically (cf. I Tim. 1:15-16). In accordance with a previously stated principle (1:20-21), he acknowledged that Paul's spiritual wisdom was given to him by God and that this wisdom produced his writings. He also compared Paul's Epistles with the other Scriptures, namely the Old Testament. The use of "other" is all-important because this means that Peter regarded Paul's writings as Scripture, equal in authority and equal in difficulty of interpretation by unsaved men.[6] This demonstrates that one authenticated writer of inspired Scripture recognized the authority of another authenticated writer.

Outline

SALUTATION (1:1-2)
    I. SAFEGUARDS AGAINST THE APOSTASY (1:3-21)
        A. The maturity of believers (1:3-11)
        B. The testimony of an apostle (1:12-18)
        C. The authority of Scripture (1:19-21)
    II. DESCRIPTION OF THE APOSTATES (2:1-22)
        A. Their methods (2:1-3a)
        B. Their judgment (2:3b-13)
        C. Their character (2:14-22)

---

6. Compare these two sentences: "I read *Time, Newsweek,* and other magazines" with "I read *Time, Newsweek,* and other newspapers." The first is correct, but the second is wrong, because *Time* and *Newsweek* are magazines, not newspapers.

363

III. Refutation of the Apostasy (3:1-18)
    A. The attack (3:1-4)
    B. The defense (3:5-18)
        1. The past destruction of the world (3:5-7)
        2. The present delay of God (3:8-9)
        3. The future destruction by fire (3:10-14)
        4. The ignorance of the apostates (3:15-16)
        5. The stability of the readers (3:17-18)

Survey

1:1-11

The best defense is a strong offense. Peter illustrated that axiom by calling his readers to a life of maturity as the best safeguard against the inroads of apostasy. Maturity reflects a proper knowledge of Christ (1:2, 3, 5, 6, 8). All believers positionally have obtained like precious faith (1:1), have been given all things that pertain to life and godliness (1:3) and have been given exceeding great and precious promises (1:4). Practically, however, they need to develop these graces: faith, virtue, knowledge, temperance, patience, godliness, brotherly kindness, and love (1:5-7). A maturing Christian will not only produce positive spiritual fruit, but will also protect himself from falling from his steadfastness (1:10; cf. 3:17). Such maturity and vigilance will be rewarded and later manifested in the millennial kingdom (1:11).

1:12-18

Peter followed the pedagogical technique of repetition, even though his readers knew what he was about to reveal and were established doctrinally. He knew that he was to be martyred shortly, and he wanted his readers to have a record of his teaching after his decease (1:12-15). As one proof of the future reality of Christ's second advent, Peter pointed to his eyewitness experience of the transfiguration of Christ. Christ had said: "There be some standing here, which shall not taste of death, till they see the Son of man coming in his kingdom" (Matt. 16:28). In reflection upon the transfiguration that quickly followed (Matt. 17:1-13), Peter saw in it a premature and miniature picture or preview of Christ's coming to the earth to establish His kingdom in power and glory (1:16-18). He denied that the second advent concept was a humanly originated fairy tale (1:16).

1:19-21

There was another proof more sure than the empirical eyewitness account of an apostle. Sights and sounds at times are even deceptive to the most honest of men. Peter therefore pointed to inscripturated revelation. The Old Testament originated with the Spirit of God; therefore, its teachings are true. Its very pages are saturated with predictive prophecy about the second advent of the Messiah.

2:1-3

Peter then expressed the purpose of his writing: "But there were false prophets also among the people, even as there shall be false teachers among you..." (2:1). The imminent threat of proselyting apostates prompted Peter to warn his readers. To be forewarned is to be forearmed. He first of all described their methods: false teaching, pernicious ways, evil speaking of the truth, covetousness, feigned words, and merchandise-making of you. Their heresy involved a denial of Christ, probably the deity of His person, the nature of His atonement (2:1), and the reality of His second advent (3:4).

2:4-9

Peter then declared that their judgment was certain (2:1, 3). As proof, he cited the bondage of sinning angels in Tartarus,[7] the destruction of Noah's generation, and the overthrow of Sodom and Gomorrah. Note that Lot was declared to be just or righteous even though his life was vexed by the immorality of his neighbors. Just as God delivered him, Peter knew that He would deliver his godly readers and that He would judge and punish the moral reprobates or false teachers (2:9).

2:10-18

He then demonstrated that their moral character demanded the judgment of God. They were unjust (2:9), unclean, presumptuous, self-willed (2:10), beastly, ignorant, corrupt (2:12), riotous, spotted, blemished, deceived (2:13), adulterous, cursed (2:14), wells without water, and clouds (2:17). They habitually practiced sin (2:14; cf. I John 3:6, 8), forsook the right way, and went astray (2:15). Peter believed that they would be destroyed physically (2:12) and that they would experience eternal darkness (2:17).

2:19-22

These false teachers were not saved men who went astray and subsequently lost their salvation. Rather, they had escaped the pollutions of the world through a change in life-style that was according to the Christian norm. Their practice of life had been affected by Christianity, but their spiritual position remained unchanged. Like the dog and the sow, their inner essence had not been regenerated. Time and the return

---

7. The phrase "cast them down to hell" is the translation of one Greek participle *tartarosas*. This is the only place where this word occurs in the Bible. This has led to the conclusion that whereas unsaved men go to Hades to await the resurrection and judgment, angels go to Tartarus.

to the old ways revealed that they had not been saved in the first place.

3:1-9

Again Peter called his readers to the prophetic-apostolic word as the defense against the scoffing, lustful false teachers. The heart of their heresy was a denial of Christ's second advent. They cited two reasons for their position: the delay in Christ's return and the permanent, undisturbed nature of creation (3:4). Peter abruptly declared that the critics were ignorant of both God's Word and His world. The Bible openly declared that the world was convulsed by a cataclysmic flood in Noah's day (3:5-6; cf. Gen. 6-9).[8] Rock strata and fossil deposits confirm the view of a sudden, unexpected catastrophe that overtook all life forms. Peter then argued that the same God who judged the world in water declared that He would judge it again in fire. This will occur when the judgment of unsaved men takes place (3:7; cf. Rev. 20:11-15). To settle the problem of delay, Peter pointed to the relationship of time to a God of eternity. To God, one day is as a thousand years to man. God does not reckon time as man does. Actually, the delay in Christ's return is a blessing in disguise to the unsaved because it gives them more time in which to repent. Christ has not forgotten His promise nor is He impotent to fulfill His word; rather, His delay is an expression of grace and longsuffering.

3:10-14

However, just as time (120 years) expired for Noah's generation, God's period of longsuffering will end. The Day of the Lord will overtake the future generation by surprise just as the flood caught that ancient world unprepared. The Day of the Lord is any period of special divine blessing or judgment. Here it refers to the destruction of the present universe, polluted by the effects of both human and angelic sin. Since this event is certain, believers should look beyond to an eternity of righteousness and peace and should govern their present lives accordingly (3:13-14).

3:15-18

Just as God saved Paul, a false teacher, in demonstration of His longsuffering, Peter wanted his readers to know that God could also save the mockers of the Second Advent (3:15). At the same time, they needed to know that the false teachers were unlearned, unstable, and unable to perceive the real doctrine of Scripture. He concluded the book by reminding them why he warned them. To keep from falling from their

---

8. Some evangelicals relate these verses to a divine judgment upon the pre-Adamic earth (Gen. 1:1-2) and others to both Genesis 1 and Genesis 6.

stedfastness, they needed to be aware of doctrinal error and to grow in grace and in knowledge of Christ.

Increase Your Learning

By Doing

1. Circle the word "knowledge" with its cognates wherever found.
2. Make a list of all the characteristics of the apostates.
3. Underline every reference to Christ's second advent.

By Discussing

1. Relate knowledge of God and of His Word to faith. Are they dependent upon each other? Can a person be mature without one of them?
2. Describe the corruption of our present world. In what ways does a Christian life-style deliver one from such moral and physical pollution?
3. Discuss contemporary Christendom. Who are the false teachers today? How do they deny the Lord?
4. Is evolution disproved by chapter 3? Can Biblical catastrophism be harmonized with uniformitarian geology?

By Reading

Mayor, Joseph B. *The Epistle of St. Jude and the Second Epistle of St. Peter.* London: Macmillan Co., 1907.

Wuest, Kenneth S. *In These Last Days.* Grand Rapids: Wm. B. Eerdmans Publishing Co., 1954.

(See First Peter.)

26

FIRST JOHN

Writer

External evidence is very strong for the Johannine authorship of this book. All of these Church Fathers used the Epistle, regarded it as authoritative, and attributed it to the apostle John: Polycarp, Papias, Irenaeus, Origen, Cyprian, Clement of Alexandria, Tertullian, and Eusebius.

Although the book is anonymous, the similarities of vocabulary, thought phrases, and style of writing between it and the Gospel of John argue for the same author. For example, these distinctive words are common to both books: Father, Son, Spirit, beginning, Word, believe, life, keep, light, commandment, love, abide, and paraclete. In addition, these phrases are found in both volumes: to do truth (1:6; cf. John 3:21); to walk in darkness (2:11; cf. John 8:12); children of God (3:2; cf. John 11:52); to be born of God (3:9; cf. John 1:13); children of the devil (3:10; cf. John 8:44); to pass from death to life (3:14; cf. John 5:24); the Spirit of truth (4:6; cf. John 14:17; 15:26; 16:13); the only begotten Son (4:9; cf. John 3:16, 18); no man has ever seen God (4:12; cf. John 1:18); the Savior of the world (4:14; cf. John 4:42); and the water and the blood (5:6; cf. John 19:34).

The opening verse not only echoes the first verse of the Gospel (John 1:1), but reveals the fact that the author was an eyewitness to both the pre-Calvary and the postresurrection ministries of Christ: "That which was from the beginning, which we have heard, which we have seen with our eyes, which we have looked upon, and our hands have handled, of the Word of Life"(1:1).[1] John easily qualifies as this eyewitness (1:1-3; 5:6-10; cf. John 19:34-35).

---

1. The verbs "heard" and "seen" are both in the Greek perfect tense, whereas

Time and Place

Irenaeus claimed that John lived his senior years in Ephesus serving as the general overseer of the area churches. He became aware that anti-Christian teachers had penetrated the assemblies and/or developed within the ranks of the church membership (cf. Acts 20:29-30). After influencing many of the believers, some of these apostates had withdrawn physically from the churches (2:18-19). Their heresy centered about the person of Christ. They denied that Jesus was the Christ (2:22; 5:1) and that God the Son had become incarnate (4:2-3). In essence, it was a denial of the union of two natures, human and divine, into one person. The heresy possessed the nature of incipient Gnosticism that became mature in the second century. Some have equated it with either Docetic[2] or Cerinthian Gnosticism. The former taught that Christ appeared as a real man, but He was not. He did not have a real material body. Rather, His appearances were similar to the theophanies or

---

the verbs "looked upon" and "handled" are in the aorist tense. In refutation of the Gnostic heresy, John employed the change of tense to show that he heard and saw the incarnate Christ and that he looked upon and actually touched His resurrection body (cf. Luke 24:39).

2. The Greek verb *dokeo* means "to seem to be."

A figure of the goddess Diana of Ephesus.

Christophanies of the Old Testament. Cerinthus, on the other hand, taught that the spirit of the divine Christ descended upon the man Jesus at the latter's baptism, indwelt Him for the duration of His ministry, and left Him shortly before His crucifixion. He contended that Jesus was born naturally of both Mary and Joseph. Both views attacked the nature of the person of Christ, especially His incarnation, and indirectly the value of His atonement.

In addition to facing doctrinal attack, the individual believers were in poor spiritual condition. They had a tendency toward sin and worldliness (1:5—2:6; 2:15-17), a lack of love for the brethren and an indifference toward their physical needs (2:7-11; 3:13-24), and a lack of assurance of personal salvation (5:13). Irenaeus claimed that these errors of moral laxity stemmed from the Nicolaitans who originated from Nicolas (Acts 6:5; cf. Rev. 2:14-15).

Out of a genuine concern for the spiritual children for whom he was responsible, John wrote this Epistle. It was probably written as a circular letter from Ephesus about A.D. 85-95 to the believers of the Roman province of Asia, including the churches mentioned in the Book of Revelation (chs. 2-3).

Purposes

The book is difficult to outline because John did not move from one subject to another. Rather, he interwove several themes throughout the book. The concepts of love, obedience, assurance, and faith were discussed side by side. However, certain emphases, detectable at times, do provide some help for the listing of purposes. He wanted to present the physical reality of Christ's incarnate body (1:1-4), to outline the relationship of sin to the believer (1:5—2:6), to emphasize the necessity of love for the brethren (2:7-11; 4:7-21), to appeal for separation from the world (2:12-17), to warn against the false teachers (2:18-29), to stimulate moral purity (3:1-12), to present tests that would demonstrate the actuality of personal salvation (3:13-24), to show how to distinguish between truth and error (4:1-6), to set forth the results of faith in Christ (5:1-12), and to give assurance of salvation (5:13-21).

John did introduce four major purposes with such words as "These things write we unto you." In so doing, he dealt with the joy of spiritual fellowship (1:4), admonished them to sin less (2:1), warned against seducing heretics (2:26), and presented assurance of eternal life (5:13).

Distinctive Features

First John is an Epistle of assurance. The phrase "we know"[3] occurs thirteen times (2:3, 5, 29; 3:14, 16, 19, 24; 4:13, 16; 5:15, 18, 19, 20).

---

3. The translation of two Greek verbs *oidamen* and *ginoskomen*.

In fact, cognates of the verb "to know" appear at least forty times. Whereas the Gospel was written to create faith and life (John 20:31), the Epistle was penned to give certainty of faith and the possession of eternal life: "These things have I written unto you that believe on the name of the Son of God; that ye may know that ye have eternal life . . ." (5:13). If a person wonders whether he is really saved, he should carefully read this book and ask himself these questions:

1. Have I experienced spiritual fellowship with God and with others (1:3-4)?
2. Am I sensitive to sin (1:5-8)?
3. Have I experienced forgiveness, cleansing, and restoration after confession (1:9)?
4. Am I keeping His commandments (2:3, 5)?
5. Am I doing the will of God (2:17)?
6. Am I doing righteousness (2:29)?
7. Am I looking forward to the coming of Christ (3:1-3)?
8. Am I no longer marked by habitual sin (3:9)?
9. Do I love the brethren (3:14)?
10. Am I free from moral guilt (3:21)?
11. Have I experienced answered prayer (3:22)?
12. Do I have the inner witness of the Holy Spirit (3:24)?
13. Have I heard the word of God in the messages of men (4:5-6)?
14. Do I love God (4:19)?
15. Do I believe that Jesus is the Christ (5:1)?
16. Do I believe God's record (5:10-11)?

Affirmative answers should bring inward assurance that one is really a regenerated child of God.

The book contains a classic description of the concept of worldliness (2:15-17). The threefold problem of man (lust of the flesh, lust of the eye, pride of life) resulted in the moral destruction of Adam and Eve (Gen. 3:6) and was used by Satan in his temptation of Christ (Matt. 4:1-11). It may be that all human sin can be grouped under these three categories.

Outline

PREFACE (1:1-4)
I. THE MORAL BASES OF JOHN'S MESSAGE (1:5—2:2)
    A. Sin breaks fellowship with God (1:5-7)
    B. Sin exists in the believer's nature (1:8)
    C. Sin manifests itself in the believer's conduct (1:9—2:2)
II. THE TESTS OF ASSURANCE INTRODUCED (2:3-27)
    A. The moral test of obedience (2:3-6)
    B. The social test of love (2:7-11)
    C. Groups in the church (2:12-14)
    D. The believer and the world (2:15-17)
    E. The doctrinal test of faith (2:18-27)
III. THE TESTS OF ASSURANCE DEVELOPED (2:28—4:6)

A. The moral test (2:28—3:10)
B. The social test (3:11-18)
C. Assurance and the condemning heart (3:19-24)
D. The doctrinal test (4:1-6)
IV. THE TESTS OF ASSURANCE REVIEWED (4:7—5:5)
A. The social test (4:7-12)
B. The social and the doctrinal tests (4:13-21)
C. The three tests together (5:1-5)
V. THE WITNESSES OF ASSURANCE (5:6-17)
VI. SUMMARY OF ASSURANCE (5:18-21)

Survey

1:1-4

In the preface John immediately claimed that Jesus Christ was eternal ("from the beginning") and a person separate from the Father ("with the Father"), that He became incarnate ("was manifested"), and that there was empirical proof that He possessed a real material human body both before and after His death and resurrection ("heard," "seen," "looked upon," and "handled"; see footnote 1). True spiritual fellowship can only be experienced when one has a proper evaluation of Christ's person. Such fellowship involves at least two believers, the Father, and the Son in proper relationships with each other.

1:5—2:2

Light and darkness cannot coexist. There is not a single bit of moral darkness in God; He is moral purity personified (1:5). In a series of five conditional sentences (all introduced by "if"), John then outlined the dual relationships of a believer toward his sin and God. No one who is consciously walking in sin can have fellowship with God (1:6). Even when a believer is in fellowship with God, there is taking place a secret cleansing of unknown sins in his life (1:7). A believer is self-deceived if he thinks that he no longer possesses a sin nature (1:8). Restoration to fellowship occurs when a believer confesses his known sins and experiences God's forgiveness and cleansing (1:9). A believer who claims that he has not sinned rejects the truth of God's Word which states that he does sin (1:10). The goal of a believer is to sin not, but when he commits an act of sin, he can appeal to the advocacy and the propitiatory sacrifice of Christ as his basis of restoration (2:1-2).

2:3-17

Assurance of saving knowledge can be gained through a life-style of commandment-keeping (2:3-5).[4] To love one another as Christ loved

---

4. This does not mean that a person can keep all of the commandments all of the time. David was a commandment-keeper even though he committed terrible sins at times (cf. I Kings 3:14).

us is the new commandment. To be in fellowship with God, one must love his brother and not be an offense to him. In a series of six statements addressed to three groups within the churches (two each to the little children, fathers, and young men), John commended them for their victories over past sin and Satan and for their spiritual relationship to God (2:12-14). He then warned them against loving the world system and its things by succumbing to the desires of the flesh and eyes, and to proud ambition. Both a lack of love of the world and the presence of obedience to the divine will will bring assurance (2:15-17).

2:18-27

John then moved to an exposé of the heresy. He distinguished between *the* antichrist of the tribulation period and the antichrists of this present age. The latter could bear the name of the former in that both denied the essential deity of Jesus Christ and His incarnation. Lack of continuance in a correct doctrinal evaluation of the person of Christ is a sign that a person was never saved in the first place (2:19; cf. 2:24). The anointing, indwelling presence of the Holy Spirit is a guarantee of knowledgeable salvation and a safeguard against doctrinal deviation (2:20, 27).

2:28—3:10

Assurance of salvation can be gained through the development of moral purity. Lack of abiding in Christ or of total obedience will bring shame and embarrassment at His coming, but not rejection (2:28). Since like begets like, genuine righteousness can only be produced by those who have been born again of a righteous God (2:29). A genuine belief in and a love for the coming of Christ will produce moral purity (3:1-3). Since Christ died to take away sins, a genuine believer will sin less after his conversion than he did before. His life will not be marked by habitual sin.[5] The children of God and the children of the devil can be contrasted through their life-styles. The former is marked by habitual righteousness, whereas the latter is known by constant sinning.

3:11-18

A genuine child of God should expect to be hated by the world (3:11-13). Sincere love for the brethren is a mark of salvation (3:14). Lack of love for the brethren is a sign that one is still in the realm of spiritual death (3:14-15). If Jesus manifested His love by laying down His life for His own, then believers should do the same through benevolent acts of compassion. Real love must be demonstrated (3:18).

---

5. The verbs "sinneth not," "sinneth," and "committeth sin" are all in the Greek present tense (3:4, 6, 8, 9). These refer to a constant practice of sin rather than to isolated acts of sin.

3:19-24

Assurance should not be based upon the changeable feelings of the heart, but upon the testimony of God's Word. An assured heart, however, is necessary to gain answered prayer. Such assurance can be gained through faith in Christ, love for the brethren, obedience of Christ's commandments, and a desire to please Him. It is the witness of the Spirit, not the feelings of the heart, that secures assurance (3:24; cf. Rom. 8:14, 16).

4:1-6

The ability to discern doctrinal truth from error is an evidence of genuine salvation. John warned that believers should not be gullible, but that they should test what they hear. A proper definition of Christ's person is the key essential to doctrinal orthodoxy. A genuine believer will be able to sense the voice of God in the messages of men (4:5-6; cf. John 10:4-5, 27).

4:7-12

Since love is an eternal attribute of God, His children should love one another. Lack of love reveals a lack of salvation. Since God initiated His love toward us, believers should do likewise toward others. Love for an unseen God must be manifested through a love for visible men.

4:13-21

Again, John pointed to the witness of the Spirit (4:13), the confession of Christ's mission and person (4:14-15), and a life saturated by love for God and others (4:16) as guarantees of salvation. The secure position of the believer is seen in the phrase: "... as he is, so are we in this world" (4:17). The believer's certainty of eternal acceptance is just as real as Christ's presence in the third heaven. A believer can no more lose his salvation than Christ could be ejected from the Father's presence. The presence of love for God and the absence of moral guilt reveal a genuine spiritual relationship (4:18).

5:1-13

John then merged correct faith, love of God, love of the brethren, and obedience (5:1-3). He equated overcoming faith with the orthodox convictions that the man Jesus and the eternal Son of God were one and the same person (5:4-5). In refutation of the Gnostic tendencies, he pointed to the witness of the Spirit, the water, and the blood (5:6-8). The piercing of Jesus' side on the cross and the outflowing of water and blood (John 19:34-35) demonstrated that He had a real human body. At His baptism Jesus was declared to be the Son of God by the voice of the Father and by the descent of the Holy Spirit

(Matt. 3:16-17; John 1:33-34). He then argued that rejection of God's oral and written witness reveals a lack of eternal life. Acceptance of God's record leads to the acceptance of God's Son which bestows eternal life.

5:14-21

Assurance of salvation can also be gained through answered prayer in the will of God (5:14-15). John then distinguished between intercessory prayer for a brother sinning a type of sin that would not culminate in premature physical death and a lack of prayer for a brother who did persistently sin a type of sin that would bring severe divine chastisement (5:16). What is sin unto death? Commentators have been puzzled for generations over this concept. Perhaps it refers to conscious, persistent disobedience to the revealed will of God (cf. John 15:6; I Cor. 11:29; James 5:19-20). He concluded the book with a series of three "we know's" (5:18, 19, 20). A genuine child of God will be kept by Christ from habitual sin and from the eternal grasp of Satan (5:18).[6] The believer knows that he belongs to God and that the world lies in the lap of the wicked one, namely Satan (5:19). The believer has an understanding given by the Spirit that he knows the true God, even Jesus Christ (5:20).

Increase Your Learning

By Doing

1. Circle all forms of the verb "to know" wherever found.
2. Underline all references to "love."
3. Underline the terms "my little children" and "beloved" wherever found.
4. Using a colored pencil, mark all verses that deal with John's refutation of the Gnostic teaching about Christ.

By Discussing

1. What contemporary views parallel the Docetic and Cerinthian Gnostic heresies?
2. What is Christian fellowship? Do our church services and activities promote or hinder it? How do personal devotions relate to group fellowship?
3. What is worldliness? Is it an attitude, an action, or both? Relate the concept of Christian liberty in nonmoral issues to it. Why do Christians differ over their definitions of worldliness?
4. Contrast a person's love for God, for Christians, for his family,

---

6. The phrase "whosoever is born" is the translation of the Greek perfect passive participle *ho gegennemenos,* always used of the regenerate believer. The phrase "he that is begotten of God" is the translation of the aorist passive participle *ho gennetheis,* a reference to Christ, the only begotten Son of God. It is Christ who keeps the believer; the believer does not keep himself.

for his sweetheart, and for the world. What are the similarities and the differences?
5. How can believers test the spirits today? How can we distinguish between truth and error?
6. What should a person do if he cannot gain the assurance of salvation?

By Reading

Findlay, George G. *Fellowship in the Life Eternal*. Grand Rapids: Wm. B. Eerdmans Publishing Co., 1955.

Ross, Alexander. *Commentary on the Epistles of James and John*. Grand Rapids: Wm. B. Eerdmans Publishing Co., 1954.

Stott, J. R. W. *The Epistles of John*. Grand Rapids: Wm. B. Eerdmans Publishing Co., 1964.

Westcott, Brooke Foss. *The Epistles of St. John*. Grand Rapids, Wm. B. Eerdmans Publishing Co., 1955.

Wuest, Kenneth S. *In These Last Days*. Grand Rapids: Wm. B. Eerdmans Publishing Co., 1954.

27

SECOND JOHN

Writer

Because of its brevity and private character, the letter did not enjoy a wide circulation; therefore, quotations or recognition of it in the patristic writings are sparse. However, these used and attributed it to the apostle John: Irenaeus, Clement of Alexandria, Origen, and Cyprian.

Although the book is anonymous, the internal contents of the letter do support Johannine authorship. The author identified himself as "the elder" (1). This could refer to either the church office of bishop-pastor-elder or to his age, probably the latter because of his affinity for age descriptions (little children, young men, fathers). Such a designation should not be regarded as unique because even Peter called himself an elder (I Peter 5:1). There are similarities of style and vocabulary between this Epistle and the other two accepted writings of the apostle John (Gospel and the First Epistle). These words and phrases are common to all three: love in the truth; have known the truth; walking in truth; new commandment; love one another; deceiver; antichrist; and abideth. The moral and doctrinal problems discussed in the Second Epistle are the same as those mentioned in the first letter: the need of love for one another in obedience to Christ's commandments (4-6; cf. I John 2:7-11); and the heresy of the denial of Christ's theanthropic person (7-11; cf. I John 4:1-3).

Addressee

The opening verse reads: "The elder unto the elect lady and her children . . ." (1). The question is obvious: Who is the elect lady? Many are the suggested answers. The actual Greek words are *eklektei*

377

kuriai. Some identify these two words as a designation of the universal church (cf. Eph. 5:25, 32) or as a personification of an unknown local church. Others equate them with the church in Babylon (cf. I Peter 5:13), the phrase literally reading: "The jointly elected one in Babylon greets you." The Greek phrase *he sunekleke* is in the feminine gender; thus it could read "the jointly elected woman." If Babylon were a symbolic name for Rome, then John may have been writing to the local church at Rome. However, there is no indication that John was using allegorical language in this passage. Also, both the address and the salutation (1, 5, 13) imply a real woman with real children, an actual sister, and regular nephews and nieces. Some have suggested that one of the two words might be a proper name; therefore, she would either be the elect Kuria or the lady Electra. The most plausible explanation is that she was an unknown, saved woman, loved by all who knew her (1, 2). Her children with whom John had any contact were all obedient to the truth (4). Her home apparently housed the congregation of believers in her vicinity (10). She was well known for her hospitality, especially the entertainment of itinerant preachers (10, 11).

Time and Place

False teachers, who denied the incarnation of Jesus Christ, His theanthropic person, and possibly His physical return to the earth,[1] were in the vicinity of the elect lady, seeking opportunities to spread their heresy in the churches (7). John, aware of the situation, identified the teaching as deceptive and anti-Christian (7). This was doubtless the same heresy condemned in the First Epistle, a form of incipient Gnosticism. The apostle wanted the elect lady to be alert lest she unwittingly give opportunity to them to spread their error in her house (8-11). Because of the need for warning, he wrote this personal note to the woman and her children who probably lived in the area over which he had the general spiritual oversight. If John can be placed in Ephesus, where tradition located him, then she probably lived in the Roman province of Asia. The book was shortly written after the First Epistle, between A.D. 85 and 95.

Purposes

First of all, he wanted to commend the lady and her children for their love and loyalty to the truth (1-4). Then he desired to beseech

---

1. The phrase "is come in the flesh" (7) is the translation of a Greek present participle *erchomenon.* Since it is not an aorist or a perfect participle, it may be that these Gnostics were denying the reality of the Second Coming (cf. II Peter 3:3-4). Actually, when one denies either the First or the Second Advent, he usually denies the other as well.

378

her to continue her walk in love and in commandment-keeping (5, 6). Finally, he wanted to warn her about the false teachers (7-11), to inform her of his plans to visit her (12), and to send greetings from the children of her sister (13).

Distinctive Features

The unique contribution of this short Epistle to the canon is in its description of the attitudes and actions a Christian should manifest toward false teachers. The touchstone of heresy is an open denial of the truth that God became flesh in the person of Jesus Christ. A denial of the incarnation or virgin birth automatically leads to a denial of Christ's sinless life, His substitutionary atonement, His bodily resurrection, and His second advent to the earth. This denial does not come from an ignorance of the truth, but from a knowledge of it that is totally rejected. To such teachers no opportunities should be given to preach or to teach. No hospitality or greeting should even be given to them. Any encouragement of them will bring to the involved believer a loss of reward. In the area of fundamental doctrines, there cannot be any tolerance of error or academic freedom.

Outline

I. SALUTATION (1-3)
II. HIS REQUEST FOR RECIPROCAL LOVE (4-6)
    A. Cause of his rejoicing (4)
    B. Basis of the request (5)
    C. Essence of the request (6)
III. HIS WARNING AGAINST APOSTASY (7-11)
    A. Cause of the warning (7)
    B. Appeal of the warning (8)
    C. Explanation of the warning (9-11)
IV. HIS DESIRE TO VISIT (12)
V. CLOSING GREETINGS (13)

Survey

1-3

The relationship that existed between John and the elect lady was based upon love and truth. He loved the lady and her children in the truth; they who knew the truth also loved her in the truth; they all loved for the sake of truth which was in them and would be with them forever; and grace, mercy, and peace originated from God in truth and in love.

4-6

A contact with some of the lady's children caused him to rejoice because they were walking in truth and in love.[2] He appealed that their mutual love might continue, a love based on obedience.

7-11

He then informed her that deceiving, antichristian teachers were abroad. He cautioned her against being influenced by this false teaching. The church's doctrinal position on the person of Christ had already been revealed and defined. There was no need for an advancement upon the doctrine; rather, it needed to be defended. Neither doctrinal orthodoxy nor heresy were simple, academic issues; rather, they involved the possession or the absence of eternal life. She was not to allow her influential position to give the apostates an opportunity to preach to the believers that met in her house nor to extend any form of Christian kindness or hospitality to them. Such involvement would actually aid the cause of Satan.

12-13

He closed by saying that he would visit her soon and would give her additional information at that time. Greetings from her relatives ended the brief Epistle.

Increase Your Learning

By Doing

1. Circle the references to the elect lady.
2. Underline all uses of "love" and "truth."

By Discussing

1. Are centralized churches today doing the job? Could evangelization and edification better be served through the ancient concept of house-churches? How would a salaried pastor fit into this picture?
2. Should Christian colleges invite to their lectureships in the name of academic freedom theologians who repudiate the essential doctrines of evangelical Christianity? What is the difference between reading the books authored by apostates and inviting them to preach?
3. Should evangelicals cooperate with liberals who deny the essential theanthropic person of Christ even when an evangelical is the featured speaker?

By Reading

(See books under First John.)

---

2. Verse 4 does not imply that John found a few children who were not walking in truth or that he knew about all of her children. All of her children with whom he had any contact were obedient.

28

THIRD JOHN

Writer

The recognition of the canonical authenticity and the Johannine authorship of this Epistle is similar to that of the Second Epistle. Because of its brevity and private character, the letter did not have a wide geographical distribution; therefore, only a few quotations as to its acceptance are found in the patristic writings. These men recognized its genuineness: Irenaeus, Clement of Alexandria, Dionysius, Cyprian, and Cyril of Jerusalem. The entire church recognized its authenticity at the third Council of Carthage (A.D. 397).

There is a similarity of style and vocabulary between this book and the other three Johannine writings. These distinctive phrases are again seen: "love in the truth," "truth in you," "walk in the truth," and "hath not seen God." The repetition of the author's self-designated title, "the elder," inseparably links the Third Epistle to the Second. Arguments for the Johannine authorship of one, therefore, can serve for the other as well.

Identity of Gaius

The book was addressed "unto the well beloved Gaius, whom I love in the truth" (1). He was well known not only to John, but also to many Christians and to the church at Ephesus (1, 3, 5-6). But who was he? Gaius was a common name in the first century. Gaius of Macedonia assisted Paul in the apostle's ministry at Ephesus and was dragged into the ampitheater along with Aristarchus during the insurrection of the pagan silversmiths (Acts 19:29). Gaius of Derbe journeyed with Paul from Macedonia into the province of Asia in the latter months of Paul's third missionary journey (Acts 20:4). Gaius of Corinth was evangelized and baptized by Paul (I Cor. 1:14). Later he became Paul's host and his house became the meeting place of the Corinthian church (Rom. 16:23). The three aforementioned men could all be considered as possibilities for the addressee of this book; however, there is one major problem common to all three. They all were probably converts of Paul, whereas "the well beloved Gaius" seems to have been a convert of John (4).[1] Little is known about this fourth Gaius except that he was an influential, hospitable member of some church in the Roman province of Asia which was under the general spiritual oversight of John. Some have suggested that Gaius was its bishop-elder, but there is no firm support for this conjecture.

Time and Place

Trouble had developed in the church of which Gaius was a member. Diotrephes had usurped authority in the church, speaking ill against John, refusing to receive the apostle's representatives, and maltreating those who did (9-10). A previous letter sent to the church (either one of the two Epistles or a lost letter) had been totally disregarded by Diotrephes. News of Diotrephes' audacity reached John either through the return of his emissaries (10), the report of brethren who had been entertained in the home of Gaius (3),[2] or the report of Demetrius (12). John hoped to visit Gaius and the congregation to correct the situation personally, but he was unable to make the trip right away (10, 14). John thus wrote this epistle to encourage Gaius to cope with the situation himself (11). It may be that Demetrius was the bearer of the letter and that John wanted Demetrius to take charge of the work after Diotrephes had been disciplined (12). As with the other Epistles, this letter was penned somewhere in the period between A.D. 85 and 95 by John in Ephesus.

There is an early tradition worth mentioning here. Eusebius claimed that John returned from his banishment on the island of Patmos (Rev. 1:9) to Ephesus after the death of the Roman emperor Domitian in A.D. 96. He further said that John revisited the churches in the province of Asia at that time (cf. II John 12; III John 14). Because of this tradition, some have suggested that Second and Third John were written after the Book of Revelation. However, these two books could have been written before his exile in Patmos when he still had freedom of move-

---

1. The phrase "my children" would include Gaius as one of John's converts, nurtured under the latter's ministry. Compare this use with Paul's reference to Timothy or Titus as "my son."

2. The brethren and the emissaries may be the same group (3, 5; cf. 10).

ment on the mainland. No one can say with any certainty that John fulfilled his desires to visit the elect lady and Gaius.

Purposes

In this personal note John determined to inform Gaius of his love and prayers (1, 2), to express his joy over Gaius' stand for the truth (3, 4), to commend Gaius for his hospitality (5-8), to reveal his displeasure over the arrogance of Diotrephes (9, 10), to promote a rejection of Diotrephes' leadership and a following of Demetrius' example (11), to commend Demetrius (12), and to inform Gaius of his plans to visit him (13, 14).

Outline

SALUTATION (1)
    I. GAIUS, THE HOSPITABLE ONE (2-8)
        A. His prayer for Gaius (2)
        B. His rejoicing over Gaius (3, 4)
        C. His commendation of Gaius (5-8)
    II. DIOTREPHES, THE PREEMINENT ONE (9-11)
        A. His rejection of John (9, 10)
        B. John's rejection of him (11)
    III. DEMETRIUS, THE GOOD ONE (12)
CONCLUSION (13, 14)

Survey

1-8

As a distinctive signature of his literary style, John again merged the concepts of love, joy, and truth: love in the truth (1), truth in you (3), walk in the truth (3, 4), and fellow helpers to the truth (8). Gaius was not only known for his love (6) but he was greatly loved by all believers and by the apostle himself (1). Gaius may have been a physically weak person because John prayed: "I wish above all things that thou mayest prosper and be in health, even as thy soul prospereth" (2). He was stronger spiritually than he was physically. John then informed Gaius that he was the cause of the apostle's rejoicing because of his walk in the truth manifested by his hospitality. He commended Gaius not only for entertaining Christian laymen and itinerant missionaries but for giving financial support to them (5-8).

9-10

Diotrephes was just the opposite of Gaius. Full of pride, he rejected the apostolic authority of John by disregarding the exhortations of a previous letter, by speaking maliciously about John in public, by not receiving the brethren sent by John, by forbidding those church members who wanted to receive them, and by expelling those members from the church.

11-12

John then admonished Gaius to follow that which was good (as personified by Demetrius) and not to follow that which was evil (as personified by Diotrephes). The apostle then declared that Diotrephes was unsaved (11b). He stated that Demetrius had three testimonies to his spiritual goodness: all Christians, the truth itself, and the witness of John. Some have suggested that this was the same Demetrius, the pagan Ephesian silversmith, who persecuted Paul and his companions (Acts 19:23-41). There is no positive equation of the two, but if so, it demonstrates what the grace of God can do in a human life.

13-14

John wanted to write more, but since he planned to visit Gaius, he kept the letter short. He then concluded by sending greetings to Gaius and by asking Gaius to greet the apostle's friends there.

Increase Your Learning

By Doing

1. Circle the names of the three main persons mentioned in the Epistle.
2. Underline the word "truth" wherever found.

By Discussing

1. Compare physical health with spiritual vigor (2). If our souls were as healthy as our bodies, how spiritual would we be? Reverse the contrast.
2. What should bring the greater joy to a Christian parent—the salvation of his son or the developing Christian maturity of his son? Defend your answer. Where does modern evangelicalism place the emphasis?
3. How can a Diotrephes manage to gain so much power? What can be done in our churches to keep this type of man from gaining leadership?

By Reading

(See books under First John.)

29

JUDE

Writer

There are seven men in the New Testament who bear the name of Jude: one of the physical ancestors of Jesus (Luke 3:30); the traitor of Jesus (Mark 3:19); the son or brother of James, also called Thaddaeus, one of the twelve apostles (Luke 6:16; John 14:22; Acts 1:13); an insurrectionist from Galilee (Acts 5:37); a native of Damascus in whose house Paul stayed and prayed after his conversion (Acts 9:11); an emissary of the Jerusalem church who, along with Silas, bore the results of the church council to Antioch (Acts 15:22, 27, 32); and the brother of James and the half-brother of Jesus (Mark 6:3). It is quite evident that the last-mentioned person wrote the book. He identified himself as: "Jude, the servant of Jesus Christ, and brother of James" (1). If he had been the apostle, Judas Thaddaeus, he would have used that official title. If he had been one of the other possibilities, he would have further identified himself (e.g., Barsabbas, or, of Damascus). Since he indicated his relationship to James, he must have referred to the half-brother of Jesus who was the author of the Book of James.[1] He apparently did not consider himself to be a commissioned apostle (1, 17-18).

As one of the younger brothers of James, he did not believe in the messiahship of Jesus during the latter's earthly ministry (Mark 6:3; John 7:3-8). Since he was associated with Mary, his brothers, and the apostles in the upper room after the ascension of Christ, he must have been converted during the forty days of Christ's postresurrection minis-

---

1. See the section under James for a further discussion of Jude's physical relationship to Jesus.

try, perhaps through a personal appearance of the Savior (Acts 1:14). Later he had an itinerant preaching ministry during which he was accompanied by his wife (I Cor. 9:5). Nothing certain is known about his death.

Several of the early Church Fathers viewed the book with much suspicion, probably because of its brevity, the lack of renown of the author, and the inclusion of quotations from noncanonical sources (9, 14-15). In spite of this, the book had stronger external attestation than Second Peter, a strange fact since Peter was better known than Jude. Both Athenagoras and Clement of Alexandria accepted its canonical status and ascribed it to Jude. The Muratorian Canon included it. These later writers embraced its authenticity: Didymas, Athanasius, Augustine, and Jerome.

Relationship to Second Peter

There are obvious similarities between the major content of Jude (4-19) and the second chapter of Second Peter (2:1—3:3), but what is their connection? It is possible, but highly improbable, that they wrote on the same subject independent of each other. There just are too many similarities for that position to be held. A second view is that they both used a common source. This is conceivable, but there is no objective manuscript evidence of such a document. The most plausible view is that one writer, under the guidance of the Holy Spirit, incorporated some material from the other's book into his own Epistle. But who borrowed from whom? Did Peter write after Jude or did Jude use Second Peter? The second possibility is the more logical one. Jude indicated that his purpose in writing changed suddenly (3). The reading of Second Peter could have caused this change. Peter placed the advent of the false teachers into the future (II Peter 2:1), whereas Jude saw them as already present (4). Jude's reference to the apostolic warning about mockers (17-18) seems to refer to the counsel of Peter (II Peter 3:2-4) and Paul (Acts 20:28-30; II Tim. 3:1-9). The fact that Jude quoted from other sources (9, 14-15) makes it more likely that he borrowed from Peter than vice versa. Since all Biblical truth is divinely revealed truth, it is the Spirit's prerogative to direct two authors to write on the same subject for emphasis and/or to cause one to utilize another. In the final analysis, it is not one man copying another man's work; rather, it is God copying God or God writing twice.

Time and Place

The historical, theological occasion for this Epistle can be seen in this key verse: "Beloved, when I gave all diligence to write unto you of the common salvation, it was needful for me to write unto you, and exhort you that ye should earnestly contend for the faith which was once delivered unto the saints" (3). Jude had originally planned to write a treatise on salvation (e.g., justification by faith) to his readers, probably Jewish Christians, quite possibly the same readers as mentioned in James and the Petrine Epistles. Unknown to him, false teachers had quietly invaded the local churches, repudiating the doctrines of grace, holiness, and the lordship of Christ (4). When the Epistle of Second Peter came into his hands, Jude saw that the predicted heretics were already on the scene. Concerned over the heretical threat to the spiritual welfare of his readers, Jude wrote this Epistle to warn them about the apostasy so that they would defend the faith in the face of moral and doctrinal attacks.

The time and place of writing cannot be determined with certainty. Since it was written after Second Peter, any date between A.D. 66 and 80 would be acceptable.

Purposes

The purposes reflect the occasion. Jude wanted to urge his readers to contend for the faith (3), to warn them against the insidious tactics of the apostates (4), to describe the characteristics of the false teachers and their subsequent judgment (5-16), to remind them of past apostolic predictions about the rise of the apostasy (17-19), to stimulate them to spiritual growth and soul winning (20-23), and to assure them of God's protection (24-25).

Distinctive Features

Jude gained notoriety through his inclusion of concepts gleaned from apocryphal literature.[2] He quoted or alluded to the *Assumption of Moses* (9) and the *Book of Enoch* (14-15), both noncanonical volumes. This practice, however, was not unique. Paul orally quoted Aratus, a pagan poet, in Athens, and the condensed record of that sermon was incorpo rated by Luke into the Book of Acts (Acts 17:28). Paul later referred to a pagan Cretan poet (Titus 1:12) and doubtless used a noninspired source for the names of Moses' opponents, Jannes and Jambres (II Tim. 3:8). Mere quotation of an apocryphal piece of literature in an inspired book does not mean that the apocryphal book was inspired nor does it mean that the Biblical author approved of everything written in the apocryphal book. It simply means that the Biblical author, under the guidance of the Holy Spirit, selected the quotation because it was true (cf. Titus 1:13). Truth is truth no matter where it is found. However,

---

2. These pseudepigraphal writings should be distinguished from the Apocrypha that was incorporated into the Roman Catholic canon by action of the Council of Trent in A.D. 1545-1546. The two mentioned books are not in the Apocrypha.

when that true statement was penned into an inspired book, it then became the inspired, authoritative basis of faith and practice. The Bible does record the lies and errors of men accurately, but there is no indication that these two quotations contain historical or doctrinal error.

The book contains a classic description of the apostasy. Jude employed the wilderness generation of Israel, the angels, the inhabitants of Sodom and Gomorrah, Cain, Balaam, and Korah as historical examples and precedents for the apostates' sins. The sin of Israel was unbelief (5); the angels manifested rebellion toward the revealed will of God (6); the cities were judged for their sexual perversion; Cain was known for his bloodless sacrifice and self-righteousness; Balaam ministered for money; and Korah presumed to usurp authority that belonged only to God's appointed leader, Moses. Just as all six were punished for their sins in past ages, so Jude assured his readers that the apostates would be divinely judged in the future.

Jude's literary style shows an affinity for triads. He described himself in three ways: as Jude, the servant of Jesus Christ, and the brother of James (1). He saw his readers as sanctified, preserved, and called (1). His blessing included mercy, peace, and love (2). He claimed that the apostate dreamers defiled the flesh, despised dominion, and spoke evil of dignities (8). He cited three men as examples of past apostasy: Cain, Balaam, Korah (11). The three Persons of the Trinity have a part in the protection of the believer (20-21).

Outline

SALUTATION (1, 2)
I. THE WARNING OF APOSTASY (3, 4)
   A. Its content (3)
   B. Its need (4)
II. HISTORICAL EXAMPLES OF APOSTASY (5-7)
   A. Israel (5)
   B. Angels (6)
   C. Sodom and Gomorrah (7)
III. DESCRIPTION OF THE APOSTATES (8-16)
   A. Their actions (8-11)
   B. Their character (12-13)
   C. Their judgment (14-15)
   D. Their pride (16)
IV. THE DUTIES OF BELIEVERS (17-25)
   A. To the Scriptures (17-19)
   B. To themselves (20, 21)
   C. To others (22, 23)
   D. To God (24, 25)

Survey

1-2

In opening his book Jude assured his readers that their spiritual position was eternally secure[3] and that God's abundant provision for daily living was available (1). He ended the letter by assuring them of God's ability to preserve their daily practice and orthodoxy (24).

3-4

He then informed them of his change of purpose in writing. Instead of writing on the general topic of salvation, he deemed it necessary[4] to exhort them to contend for the faith. The phrases "the faith" and "once delivered" show that the doctrinal limits of orthodoxy had already been defined. Jude did not expect any further revelation on that subject; rather, he wanted his readers to defend that which was already given. He then notified them of the presence of false teachers who used sneaky tactics, who were ungodly, and who denied the concepts of divine grace and the deity of Christ.

5-7

Three historical examples of personal, moral, and doctrinal apostasy were listed to show the certainty of divine judgment upon those who practiced such sins. Note the phrases of judgment: "destroyed" (5); "hath reserved in everlasting chains under darkness unto the judgment of the great day" (6); and "vengeance of eternal fire" (7).

8-16

Jude described the character of the apostates: evil speakers, ignorant, beastly, corrupt (10), spotted, fearless, hypocritical, twice dead (12), unstable (13), ungodly (15), murmuring and proud (16). Their sermons manifested arrogance in an attempt to impress their listeners (8, 9, 10, 15, 16). Their judgment will be finalized at the second advent of Christ (14-15).

17-25

Jude outlined the proper defense of the believers in the face of such evil apostates. They were to remember the warning of past inscripturated revelation about the rise of the apostasy and the spiritual condition of the apostates (17-19). In relationship to themselves, they were to do four things: to fortify themselves in doctrinal orthodoxy; to pray in the Spirit; to keep themselves in the love of God; and to look for Christ's coming (20-21). They were to make a distinction between committed apostates and deceived apostates, seeking to win the victimized subjects of the false teaching (22-23). Finally, they were to commit themselves

---

3. Literally, the verse reads: "... to the, having been loved in God-Father and having been kept in Jesus Christ, called ones."
4. The phrase "it was needful for me" shows the human involvement in the writing of inscripturated revelation. The authors were active, not passive.

to God who alone could keep them from moral and doctrinal error. In themselves they could not do it. In all of their defense, they were to bring glory to God.

Increase Your Learning

By Doing

1. Circle the word "beloved" wherever found.
2. Underline the words "these" and "ungodly" wherever found.
3. Circle the names of the Old Testament examples of apostasy.

By Discussing

1. How can one contend for the faith without being contentious? How can evangelicals maintain a balance between a positive presentation of the gospel and a negative defense of the faith?
2. Can a genuine Christian ever apostatize? How can one distinguish between a backslidden believer and an apostate unbeliever?
3. How does one pray in the Holy Spirit?
4. How can evangelicals win to Christ the adherents of the various sects, such as Jehovah's Witnesses, Christian Science, Mormonism, etc.?

By Reading

Lawlor, George Lawrence. *The Epistle of Jude.* Nutley, N.J.: Presbyterian and Reformed Publishing Co., 1972.

(See also books under Second Peter.)

30

REVELATION

Writer

The author of this last canonical book called himself by the name of John five times (1:1, 4, 9; 21:2; 22:8).[1] He further identified himself as Christ's servant (1:1) and as a brother and companion in tribulation (1:9). He claimed that he was on the island of Patmos "for the word of God, and for the testimony of Jesus Christ" (1:9). Patmos was a small, rocky, barren island in the Aegean Sea about sixty miles southwest of Ephesus. Several early Church Fathers declared that John the apostle had been banished to the island by the Roman emperor Domitian who ruled A.D. 81-96.[2]

Admittedly, there are some differences of style and vocabulary between the Book of Revelation and the other Johannine writings, but it has also been demonstrated that there are some very striking resemblances between it and the Gospel.[3] To deny the Johannine authorship of Revelation simply on the basis of literary style is just too subjective. The similarities, in fact, outweigh the differences.

These Church Fathers recognized the canonical authenticity and the Johannine authorship of the book: Justin Martyr, Irenaeus, Tertullian, Hippolytus, Clement of Alexandria, and Origen. The book was also given a place within the Muratorian Canon.

Time and Place

During his exile on Patmos, John heard the voice of Christ speaking

---

1. The critical Greek text contains the name of John only four times, omitting the 21:2 reference.
2. Clement of Alexandria, Eusebius, and Irenaeus made this claim.
3. Consult E. F. Harrison, *Introduction to the New Testament*, p. 441.

to him: "What thou seest, write in a book, and send it unto the seven churches which are in Asia; unto Ephesus, and unto Smyrna, and unto Pergamos, and unto Thyatira, and unto Sardis, and unto Philadelphia, and unto Laodicea" (1:11; cf. 1:9). Tradition claims that John was the overseer of these churches when he lived in Asia during the latter years of his ministry. Now, through John, Christ wanted to communicate to these assemblies. Actually, John became a noninvolved observer of the future and a passive stenographer who recorded what he saw. The churches had moral and doctrinal errors that needed to be corrected (chs. 2-3), but beyond that, Christ desired to reveal the future aspects of God's program for the world (chs. 4-22). In clear obedience to the will of his Savior, John therefore wrote this book and sent it as a circular letter to the seven churches of the Roman province of Asia. The couriers of the letter may have been the *angeloi*[4] of the churches (1:20), either their pastors or emissaries sent to John by the churches or both. The revelation was received and the book was dispatched in the latter years of Domitian's reign, about A.D. 95.

Purposes

The basic purpose can be seen in the opening verses:

> The Revelation of Jesus Christ, which God gave unto him, to

4. The English transliteration of the Greek *angeloi* is "angels." The literal meaning is "messengers."

The isle of Patmos, the site of John's exile.

shew unto his servants things which must shortly come to pass; and he sent and signified it by his angel unto his servant John: Who bare record of the word of God, and of the testimony of Jesus Christ, and of all things that he saw. Blessed is he that readeth, and they that hear the words of this prophecy, and keep those things which are written therein: for the time is at hand (1:1-3).

In English editions the book has been erroneously titled "The Revelation of St. John the Divine." Technically, it is a revelation about Jesus Christ or a disclosure that came from Him.[5] As a book of prophecy (1:3; 22:6, 7, 10, 18, 19), it was designed to exalt the Lord Jesus Christ through disclosures of the future. It would reveal not only what Christ would do, but also that which would be done for Him. The goal of the book is to reveal the latter stages of God's eternal plan of redemption: the establishment of the messianic kingdom of righteousness and peace (11:15; 21:1-2). In all of this, Christ is central "for the testimony of Jesus is the spirit of prophecy" (19:10).

In his introduction John also purposed to pronounce a blessing and to impose a responsibility upon his readers. In fact, this is the only canonical book to contain within its pages a blessing for both the reading, hearing, and keeping of its contents (1:3; cf. 22:7). The concept of "revelation" should not be construed to be an unknowable mystery, for how could a reader *keep* the contents if he did not understand what to keep?

In his development of the basic theme, John purposed to exalt Christ as the living Lord of the churches (1:4-20), to correct the moral and the doctrinal problems that existed in the seven churches of Asia (2:1—3:22), to describe the nature of the Great Tribulation period with special emphasis upon the three series of divine judgments to be poured out then (4-1—19:10), to depict the second advent of Christ to the earth with its subsequent events (19:11—20:15), and to preview the establishment of the new heavens and the new earth (21:1—22:21).

Various Schools of Interpretation

The Book of Revelation has been hermeneutically approached in several ways, based upon various theological backgrounds and presuppositions. Even within each school there is a divergence of opinion as to the interpretation of many events, symbols, personages, and sequence of events.

The *preterist* school has produced a double approach to the book. The older proponents claimed that the symbolism referred only to the

---

5. The words "of Jesus Christ" are in the Greek genitive case. Grammatically, it could be either a subjective genitive (came from Him) or an objective genitive (about Him).

contemporary events of John's day. To them, the narrative depicted the defeat of both the religious (Jews) and the political (Roman empire) enemies of the church. Since the seventeenth century, the newer advocates have believed that the symbols expressed the clash between Judaism and Christianity (chs. 4-11), the conflict between the church and the pagan world (chs. 12-19), and the present triumph of Christendom in the world (chs. 20-22). Both views deny any real prophetic element in the book. Held by most liberals, this view establishes an arbitrary meaning for the many symbols and repudiates the basic prophetic intent of the book (cf. 1:19).

The *idealist* school is committed to an allegorical approach of spiritualizing the symbols. It identifies the sequence of events with the eternal struggle between good and evil and between Christianity and paganism. As such, it does not equate the symbols with any specific historical events or personages, either past, present, or future.

The *historicist* school reflected the viewpoint of the Reformers and the interpretation of the classic commentaries of past generations. To them, the symbolism outlined the course of church history from the day of Pentecost to the return of Jesus Christ to the earth.

The *futurist* school is held mainly by dispensational premillennialists and covenant premillennialists.[6] This view teaches that the first three chapters definitely refer to the apostolic period and that they may conceivably preview the course of church history from the first century to the beginning of the Great Tribulation period. It also claims that the great bulk of the book (chs. 4-22) is yet future to our present day since these chapters expound the Great Tribulation, the second advent of Christ, the Millennium, and the new universe.

Growing out of the hermeneutical approach to the Book of Revelation and other prophetic portions of Scripture are three major millennial views.[7] The *postmillennialist* view teaches that Christ will not come to the earth until after the kingdom has been established through worldwide evangelization of the pagan world. This view was very popular at the start of the twentieth century because many segments of Christendom believed that the world would become better through a spreading Chris-

---

6. Both groups hold to a literal one-thousand-year rule of Christ on earth after His second advent. The former makes a clear distinction between God's program for Israel and that for the church, whereas the second would generally identify the two entities. The former would hold to a pretribulational rapture of the church, whereas the latter would embrace a posttribulational position.

7. The word "millennial" is based upon a Latin word meaning "one thousand." The Greek word *chilios,* meaning "one thousand," is the basis of the English word "Chiliasm."

tian influence; however, two major World Wars, an economic depression, and various local wars have destroyed the optimism of that position. The *amillennialist* position teaches that Christ could come at any moment, that all of the dead would be raised to face a general judgment, and that eternity future would follow. This view denies a literal rule of Christ on the present earth for a period of one thousand years. The *premillennialist* adherents claim that after Jesus Christ returns, He will rule over the earth for one thousand years.

The premillennialist position, however, is divided over the relationship of the true church to the Great Tribulation period. The *posttribulationist* believes that the church will enter the Great Tribulation, will experience the persecution of the antichrist but not the wrath of God, will be raptured[8] to meet Christ in the air, and will return with Him to the earth to reign with Him during the Millennium.[9] The *midtribulationist* teaches that the church will go through the first half of the tribulation and that it will be raptured in the middle of that period. At the conclusion of the tribulation, the church will return with Christ to the earth to reign with Him. The *pretribulationist* claims that Christ could come at any moment, that the church will be raptured before the beginning of the seven-year tribulation period, that it will be in heaven during that period, and that it will return with Christ to the earth after the tribulation.[10] (The latter view is the approach of the author.)

Literary Format

The book naturally falls into three basic sections. This key verse reveals what those divisions are: "Write the things which thou hast seen, and the things which are, and the things which shall be hereafter" (1:19). The following chart graphically illustrates the scope of the book:

Have Been	Are	Shall Be Hereafter
Ch. 1	Chs. 2–3	Chs. 4–22
Past	Present	Future
Christ	Churches	Consummation

8. The word "rapture" is based upon the Latin equivalent of the Greek word translated "shall be caught up" (I Thess. 4:17).
9. Many covenant premillennialists are also traditional posttribulationists. Holding to the doctrine of imminency, they teach that when Christ comes, the preceding seven years will be known as the Great Tribulation and the leading persecutor of Christians as the antichrist.
10. The partial rapture theory teaches that only those Christians who are looking and living for Christ will be raptured before the tribulation and that carnal believers will enter the tribulation to be persecuted by the antichrist.

John had just seen a symbolic vision of the resurrected, sovereign Christ (1:4-18). Later he was commanded: "Come up hither, and I will show thee things which must be hereafter" (4:1). This would mean that the last nineteen chapters deal with the prophetic future and the climax of God's program for the ages. By process of elimination, the remaining two chapters (chs. 2-3) that contain the letters to the seven churches of Asia must be regarded as the present section. Twelve times throughout the book John was issued the command to write; once he was told not to write (10:4). Instead of writing the book at one sitting, John must have written at periodic intervals after viewing different visions given to him.

The bulk of the book is concerned with divine judgments that will be poured out in the Great Tribulation in preparation for the second advent of Christ to the earth (4:1—19:10). After two introductory chapters (chs. 4-5), John developed this section by dividing it into three series of seven judgments each: seven seals, seven trumpets, and seven vials (or bowls). This chart shows its literary construction:

SEALS	TRUMPETS	VIALS
1-6 ( ) 7	1-6 ( ) 7 ( )	1-6 ( ) 7 ( )

Between the sixth and the seventh judgment in each series, a parenthesis of additional information was inserted (7:1-17; 10:1—11:14; 16:13-16). Also, parentheses were inserted between the trumpet and the vial series (12:1—14:20) and between the vial series and the description of Christ's second coming (17:1—19:10).

The interrelationships of the seals, trumpets, and vials provide interpretative questions. Are they parallel? consecutive? The parallel arrangement views the three series as covering the same period of time with

Seals
_____

Trumpets
_____

Vials
_____

repetitive emphasis upon intensification of the judgments. The consecutive arrangement sees them as occurring one at a time throughout the

Seals	Trumpets	Vials

tribulation. In essence, there would be approximately twenty-one divine judgments poured out then. Recent dispensationalists embrace a tele-

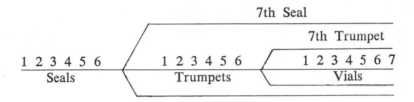

7th Seal

7th Trumpet

1 2 3 4 5 6 | 1 2 3 4 5 6 | 1 2 3 4 5 6 7

Seals | Trumpets | Vials

scopic arrangement of these three series. The seventh seal introduces the trumpet series and is explained by it. The seventh trumpet introduces the vial series and is explained by it. Thus the seven vials equal the seventh trumpet and the seven trumpets are the seventh seal. In support of this, it is said that the seventh seal was not described, but it simply introduced the seven angels with the seven trumpets (8:1-2). The last three trumpets are called the last three woes (8:13). The transfer of the kingdom to Christ occurs at the blowing of the seventh trumpet (11:15). The Battle of Armageddon is seen in the parenthesis between the sixth and seventh vials (16:13-16). The seven vials are called the seven last plagues (15:1) and the seventh vial begins: "It is done" (16:17). A correlation of these critical concepts and passages seems to support the telescopic arrangement rather than the parallel or consecutive ones.

Distinctive Features

Revelation contains more references to the Old Testament than any other book in the New Testament. Whereas Matthew has 92 and Hebrews has 102 references, estimates of allusions in Revelation to the Old Testament range from 278 to over 400.

This is a book of numbers. The numeral "seven" is very prominent. There are seven churches (1:11), seven lampstands (1:13), seven stars (1:16), seven letters (chs. 2-3), seven spirits (4:5), seven seals (5:1), seven trumpets (8:2), seven thunders (10:3), seven heads and seven

397

crowns (12:3; 13:1), seven angels (15:6), seven vials (15:7), seven mountains (17:9), and seven beatitudes (1:3; 14:13; 16:15; 19:9; 20:6; 22:7, 14). There are four beasts (4:6), four horsemen (6:1-8), and four bound angels (9:14). There are twelve tribes of Israel (7:4), twelve thousand of each tribe (7:4-8), twelve gates in the holy city (21:12), twelve foundations (21:14), and twelve fruits on the tree of life (22:2).

Revelation sustains vital relationships to other canonical books. A logical contrast would be that with the first book of the Bible, Genesis. The first rebellion could be contrasted with the final one; the entrance of sin versus its exit; the imposition of the curse with its removal; the beginning of death with its end; and the creation of the first heaven and earth with that of the new heaven and earth.

A prior understanding of Daniel is necessary to a proper exposition of Revelation because many symbols first mentioned by the prophet are repeated and clarified in John's book. Whereas Daniel was a sealed book (Dan. 12:8-9), Revelation is an open book, designed to be read and understood (1:3; 22:10).

In the Upper Room Discourse, Christ anticipated the development of the New Testament canon through the ministry of the Holy Spirit in the lives of the apostles. He claimed that the Spirit would "bring all things to your remembrance, whatsoever I have said unto you" (John 14:26); this refers to the Gospels. He also said that the Spirit would "teach you all things" (John 14:26); this refers to the Epistles. Finally, He predicted that the Spirit would "shew you things to come" (John 16:13); this would logically include the content of Revelation.

Outline

INTRODUCTION (1:1-8)
 I. THE THINGS WHICH YOU HAVE SEEN (1:9-20)
    A. Description of John (1:9-10)
    B. Command to John (1:11, 19)
    C. Vision of Christ (1:12-18, 20)
 II. THE THINGS WHICH ARE (2:1—3:22)
    A. Ephesus (2:1-7)
    B. Smyrna (2:8-11)
    C. Pergamos (2:12-17)
    D. Thyatira (2:18-29)
    E. Sardis (3:1-6)
    F. Philadelphia (3:7-13)
    G. Laodicea (3:14-22)
 III. THE THINGS WHICH SHALL BE HEREAFTER (4:1—22:5)
    A. The heavenly throne (4:1-11)
       1. Its occupant (4:1-3)
       2. The twenty-four elders (4:4-5)
       3. The four beasts (4:6-8)

4. The praise (4:9-11)
B. The sealed book (5:1-14)
   1. The book viewed by John (5:1-4)
   2. The book taken by Christ (5:5-7)
   3. Songs of rejoicing (5:8-14)
C. The seal judgments (6:1—8:1)
   1. First seal (6:1-2)
   2. Second seal (6:3-4)
   3. Third seal (6:5-6)
   4. Fourth seal (6:7-8)
   5. Fifth seal (6:9-11)
   6. Sixth seal (6:12-17)

     Parenthesis (7:1-17)
     a. The 144,000 (7:1-8)
     b. The great multitude (7:9-17)

   7. Seventh seal (8:1)
D. The trumpet judgments (8:2—11:19)
   1. First trumpet (8:2-7)
   2. Second trumpet (8:8-9)
   3. Third trumpet (8:10-11)
   4. Fourth trumpet (8:12-13)
   5. Fifth trumpet (9:1-12)
   6. Sixth trumpet (9:13-21)

     Parenthesis (10:1—11:14)
     a. The angel and the book (10:1—11:2)
     b. The two witnesses (11:3-14)

   7. Seventh trumpet (11:15-19)

     Parenthesis (12:1—14:20)
     a. The holy war (12:1-17)
     b. The marine beast (13:1-10)
     c. The land beast (13:11-18)
     d. Various announcements (14:1-20)

E. The vial judgments (15:1—16:21)
   1. The temple and the angels (15:1-8)
   2. First vial (16:1-2)
   3. Second vial (16:3)
   4. Third vial (16:4-7)
   5. Fourth vial (16:8-9)
   6. Fifth vial (16:10-11)
   7. Sixth vial (16:12)

     Parenthesis (16:13-16)
     a. The three unclean spirits (16:13-14)
     b. Armageddon (16:15-16)

   8. Seventh vial (16:17-21)

     Parenthesis (17:1—19:10)
     a. The harlot (17:1-7)

Survey

1:1-11

John opened the book by setting forth the sequence of revelatory transmission: God—Christ—angel—John—the book—the reader—and the listener (1:1-3). Greetings were then extended to the churches by John and a blessing by the triune God (1:4-5a).[11] The book was dedicated to Christ because of His past redemptive work, His future coming, and His eternal sovereignty (1:5b-8). John then explained why he penned the book. Because of his Christian witness and beliefs, he had been exiled to Patmos where Christ commissioned him to record the visions which he was about to see and to send the book to the seven churches (1:9-11). The phrase "in the Spirit" could refer either to an entrance into a trancelike state or to a worshipful attitude (cf. John 4:24).

1:12-20

When John turned to see the one who had spoken to him, he saw a symbolic vision of Christ in all His resurrection, moral, and divine glory standing in the midst of seven lampstands that represented the seven churches. His appearance manifested His deity and royalty (girdle), eternity and wisdom (white head and hair), omniscience (eyes of fire), righteousness (feet of brass), authority (sound of many waters), sovereignty (right hand), glory (countenance), and power (sword). John reacted by falling prostrate, but Christ reassured him with further identification of Himself (1:17-18). Christ again commanded John to write the book.

2:1—3:22

The second major section contains the seven letters to the seven

---

11. The phrase "seven spirits," because of its location between the Father and the Son, doubtless refers to the sevenfold perfection of the Holy Spirit (Isa. 11:2-3) rather than to seven angelic spirits (cf. 4:5).

churches of Asia. John did not write seven individual letters; rather he penned one book, containing seven brief letters, that was to be circulated among all of the churches. These letters have a threefold significance. First, they were real churches with genuine moral and doctrinal problems that Christ wanted to correct. Second, the problems of these churches have been present in every generation of the church age; therefore, every believer and church today can profit from these chapters (cf. 2:7). Third, most dispensational interpreters claim that these letters *may* contain a prophetic preview of the course of church history from the first century to the Great Tribulation.

The letters follow a common literary format for the most part. They contain an address, a description of Christ (usually taken from the first chapter), a commendation of works, a complaint, an exhortation, a warning, a promise to the overcomer, and an admonition to the spiritually sensitive.[12]

2:1-7

Although the church at Ephesus was marked by works, labor, patience, and a discerning intolerance of moral and doctrinal error, it had no love. It epitomized orthodoxy without love. Three commands were issued: remember, repent, and do. The threat centered in the removal of any future opportunity to serve Christ as a local church; the Ephesian church ceased to function in the sixth century. The overcomer is not a super-spiritual Christian; rather, it is a title for the individual believer (cf. I John 4:4; 5:1, 5; Rev. 21:7-8). Some dispensationalists believe that the principles of this church's life-style reflect first-century Christendom.

2:8-11

No complaint or threat was directed toward the church at Smyrna. It was marked by works, persecution, and financial poverty, and was under the threat of future oppression. To encourage the church, Christ was revealed as the controller of time and the victor over death. Two exhortations were: Do not fear the persecution, and be faithful unto death. Smyrna was a rich poor church, a suffering congregation. Some believe that it reflects Christendom that endured the Roman imperial persecutions in the second and third centuries.

2:12-17

The church at Pergamos was commended for its works, loyalty to Christ, and doctrinal steadfastness; however, it tolerated two errors, the doctrines of Balaam and that of the Nicolaitans. The warning to repent

---

12. No complaint is registered against Smyrna and Philadelphia. There is no commendation for Laodicea.

General view of the Asclepium at Pergamum.

involved the discipline of the false teachers. Some see in Pergamos the union of church and state that developed in the fourth through the sixth centuries.

2:18-29

The church at Thyatira was known for its works, love, service, faith, and patience, but it permitted moral error to be propagated in its midst. The faithful remnant within the church were cautioned to hold fast its doctrinal and moral integrity until Christ's return. The believer-overcomer was promised ruling authority in the millennial kingdom. Some feel that this church corresponds to the medieval Catholic church (600-1517).

3:1-6

Sardis was a dead church that gained a reputation from its past. Although there was no commendation, there was a recognition of a worthy remnant that was morally and doctrinally pure. Five exhortations were given: be watchful, strengthen, remember, hold fast, and repent. The believer-overcomer was promised a robe of divine righteousness, a guarantee of security, and a heavenly confession. Some identify this church with the Reformation period when individuals tried to strengthen the remaining good points of the Catholic church.

3:7-13

Philadelphia was the church of the open door of service opportunities. No complaint was leveled at it. Rather, it was commended for its strength even though it was little, its doctrinal preservation, and its loyalty to Christ. Because the members maintained a belief in the imminent return of Christ, they were promised deliverance from the time period of the Great Tribulation. This church may reflect the missionary-minded church of the past three centuries.

3:14-22

The church at Laodicea was a poor rich church. No commendation is found among the many complaints. It was lukewarm, totally complacent and self-sufficient. Counsel was given rather than a direct exhortation. The church lacked spiritual wealth, clothing, and sight. It was the church of the closed door with Christ on the outside trying to get inside. Many relate it to the contemporary ecumenical church. It is the church of outward profession without the internal presence of Christ.

The altar of Zeus at Pergamum, to which the apostle John referred when he spoke of "Satan's Throne." This reconstructed model stands in the State Museum at Berlin.

4:1-11

John then was caught up into heaven to view the prophetic future.[13] His translation was similar to that of Paul (II Cor. 12:1-7) or Philip (Acts 8:39). His attention was focused on the Father sitting on the sovereign throne of judgment. The jasper and sardine stones plus the emerald rainbow probably represent God's faithfulness toward His covenant relationship with Israel.[14] The elders represent either angels, the redeemed of all ages (cf. 21:12-14), or the church universal (cf. Acts 15:6; 20:17). The four living creatures[15] were probably angels of the cherubim or seraphim classes (cf. Isa. 6:2-3; Ezek. 1:5-28), guardians of God's holiness and His governmental relationships over the world. The emphasis in this chapter is upon God's sovereignty based upon His creative rights.

5:1-14

The seven-sealed scroll in the Father's hand then caught John's interest. To many, this represents the title deed to the earth. When no worthy person was found to open the scroll, John began to weep. His weeping was interrupted by one of the elders who claimed that Christ could open it because of His triumphant death and resurrection. Christ was then described in seven ways: as the lion of Judah (Gen. 49:8-10); as the root of David (Isa. 11:1, 10; 53:2); as a little lamb;[16] as having been slain (His crucifixion); as having stood (His resurrection); as having seven horns, symbols of strength and kingship (I Kings 22:11); and as having seven eyes (Spirit sent from Him; cf. John 16:7). When Christ took the scroll, three anthems of praise burst forth—by the four living creatures and the twenty-four elders (5:8-10), by the angels (5:11-12), and by all creation (5:13-14). Here their songs praise Christ for His redemptive work, rather than His creative activity.

13. The Greek prepositional phrase *meta tauta* is translated both as "after this" and "hereafter" (1:19; cf. 4:1 [twice]). The church age is over. The word "church" does not appear again until 22:16. The church as a body is not seen again until the marriage of the Lamb (19:7). The phrase "unto the churches" (2:7, 11, 17, 29; 3:6, 13, 22) is conspicuously absent in a later, similar admonition (13:9). If the elders represent the church or the redeemed of all ages, then the church is already in heaven before the tribulation judgments fall (cf. 13:6). These form arguments for a pretribulational rapture of the church.
14. The two stones garnished the first and sixth foundations of the holy city (21:19-20). They were also found on the breastplate of the Jewish high priest, representing the tribes of Reuben (firstborn) and Benjamin (last born). (See Exodus 28:17-21.)
15. "Living creatures" is a better translation of the Greek *zoa* than "beasts."
16. The Greek uses the diminutive form: "a small lamb." The concept is that Christ was crucified before achieving human longevity.

6:1-17

The first four seals reveal the coming of four horses. The first seal represented the coming of the antichrist; Christ's coming is much later (19:11). The white horse shows his deceptive, counterfeit policies; the bow without arrow shows his victory by negotiation and disarmament (Dan. 8:25); and his authority was given to him by Satan with God's permission (Dan. 8:24; Rev. 13:1). The red horse of the second seal pictured world war, civil anarchy, and great bloodshed. The black horse of the third seal symbolized famine, food rationing, and inflationary prices. It will take a day's wage to buy one meal for one person (cf. Matt. 20:2). The fourth seal brought forth the pale or yellowish-green horse with its rider Death and its companion Hell. The fourth part of the world's population will be destroyed through the means of war, famine, pestilence, and wild animals. The fifth seal revealed the presence of martyrs in heaven crying out for divine vengeance. The sixth seal contained six events: an earthquake, the blackening of the sun, the reddening of the moon, a meteorite shower, convulsions of the planets and stars, and the displacement of mountains and islands. These events cause great consternation among the wicked inhabitants of the earth. *No doubt!*

7:1-17

In the midst of these persecutions and judgments, God will seal 144,000 Israelites to be preserved from these physical calamities and to serve Him in this period. Although Dan will have a future inheritance in the kingdom (Ezek. 48:1, 32), it is not mentioned as having a ministry in the tribulation, probably because of past idolatry (Judg. 18:1-31). A great host of Gentiles will likewise be saved and martyred then. Ten provisions are promised to them (7:14-17).

8:1—9:21

After the short parenthesis (7:1-17), the seventh seal was opened and revealed a half hour of heavenly silence. John then saw seven angels with seven trumpets; thus the seventh seal introduced the trumpet series and was described by it. The first trumpet destroyed one third of the vegetation, either throughout the world or just in Palestine. The second trumpet revealed a burning meteor falling into the sea (Mediterranean or all salt oceans) and turning one third of the water into blood. In addition, one third both of the marine life and of the ships were destroyed. The third trumpet saw a burning meteor turn one third of fresh water into bitter poison. The fourth trumpet affected one third of the sun, moon, and stars so that the world would experience a sixteen-hour day. The last three trumpets are then called the three woes. The fifth trumpet or first woe manifested a display of locusts or demons. Men were afflicted by severe physical torment short of death. The sixth trumpet or second woe produced an invasion of two hundred million soldiers that accomplished the deaths of one third of the remaining population. In spite of these catastrophes, men persisted in their sin and repented not.

10:1-11

In the parenthesis between the sixth and seventh trumpets (10:1—11:14), John viewed an angel with a little book who thundered that time had run out on man. The final judgment was then identified with the seventh trumpet. The mystery of God refers to God's program of delay and longsuffering between the entrance of sin and the establishment of the millennial kingdom of righteousness. John was then instructed to take the little book and to eat it. The ministry of preaching judgment is paradoxically both bitter and sweet.

11:1-14

The parenthesis continued with the concepts that Israel would have a temple in the tribulation and that Jerusalem would once more be controlled by the Gentiles for forty-two months. In the first half of the tribulation, God will use two witnesses who will perform miracles and who will be divinely protected from physical harm. Some have identified these witnesses as Moses, Elijah, or Enoch; however, it seems more plausible to treat them as future, unnamed prophets. They will be martyred but their bodies will be resurrected after three and one-half days of public display by their oppressors. Accompanying their resurrection will be an earthquake that will kill seven thousand in Jerusalem.

11:15-19

The third woe is the seventh trumpet. When it sounds, the transfer of the world's kingdoms to Christ will take place. This causes joy for the believer and anger for the wicked. The seventh trumpet revealed an opened heavenly temple out of which will come seven angels with the seven vial judgments (15:5—16:1). Thus, the seventh trumpet introduces the vial series and is fully explained by it.

12:1-17

A lengthy parenthesis was inserted between the trumpet and the vial series (12:1—14:20). The first part manifested satanic hatred toward God's program for the Messiah and Israel (12:1-17). The woman in the vision represented Israel and possibly all of the messianic line back to Eve (Gen. 3:15). The sun, moon, and stars are symbols of Jacob, Rachel, and the twelve sons of Jacob (Gen. 37:9-10). The dragon, representing Satan, desired to destroy the child (Christ) as soon as He was born; this was attempted in the decree of Herod the Great to slay

406

the infants in and around Bethlehem (Matt. 2:16-18). After a brief mention of Christ's birth and ascension into heaven (12:5), the action moved to the middle of the Great Tribulation when Israel will flee into the wilderness to escape the persecution of the antichrist (12:6). The flight was caused by Satan's defeat in a heavenly war by Michael (12:7-12). Forced to the earth, Satan will take out his anger upon Israel through his human instrument, the antichrist; however, God will protect and sustain Israel for those three and one-half times or years (Dan. 7:25).

13:1-10

The first beast, representing the antichrist, will be a Gentile probably from the Mediterranean area (cf. Isa. 17:12; Dan. 7:2-3). The seven heads may represent the seven continents over which he rules, the seven Gentile powers that conquered Israel and held her in captivity (Egypt, Assyria, Babylon, Persia, Greece, Rome, and the antichrist's kingdom), or the seven hills of the city of Rome (17:9). The ten crowned horns refer to the ten-nation confederacy that gives allegiance to the antichrist (17:12-17; cf. Dan. 2:33, 41-44; 7:8). The multiple animal characteristics reveal that the antichrist will embody within himself all of the worst evil traits of past Gentile world rulers (Dan. 7:4-6). Actually, Satan will energize him (13:2). The healing of the death wound may refer to a counterfeit death and resurrection of the personal antichrist or to the revival of imperial government under his leadership. He will be worshiped and feared, will be an orator and a blasphemer, will persecute the saints, and will rule the world for forty-two months.

13:11-18

The second beast, representing the false prophet, will probably be a Jew. He will promote the worship of the antichrist through miracles, the erection of idol worship, and the control of commerce. He will force men to be marked with the number 666. Those who refuse to worship the antichrist's image will be killed.

14:1-20

The last section of the parenthesis contains various announcements about the remaining months of the Great Tribulation. John first saw Christ and the 144,000 on Mount Sion. If this anticipates an earthly scene, it refers to the millennial kingdom and the fulfillment of God's guarantee that the 144,000 would be preserved (7:3-4). However, it may refer to the heavenly Jerusalem (Heb. 12:22). The spiritual position of the 144,000 was described in five ways: virgins, followers, redeemed, without guile, and without fault. John then saw a flying angel who preached the everlasting gospel with a threefold emphasis: fear God, glorify Him, and worship Him (14:6-7). Then followed a prediction of the fall of Babylon (14:8) which will be graphically described later (chs. 17-18). An announcement that all image worshipers of the antichrist will suffer eternal wrath was then given (14:9-12). A blessing was pronounced upon all future martyrs (14:13). The chapter ends with a symbolic description of Armageddon in the form of a grape harvest (14:14-20). In that day, man's sins will be ripe for divine judgment.

15:1—16:1

John then saw "seven angels having the seven last plagues; for in them is filled up the wrath of God." Their appearance caused the martyrs to rejoice. The seven angels then came out of the heavenly temple, were given the seven vials[17] of judgment by one of the four living creatures, and went forth to "pour out the vials of the wrath of God upon the earth." These seven vials or bowls comprise the seventh trumpet.

16:2-21

The first vial produced an incurable, ulcerated sore upon the worshipers of the antichrist (16:2; cf. 16:11). The second vial caused the death of every marine creature in the oceans (16:3). The third vial turned all the fresh water springs and rivers into blood (16:4-7). The fourth vial increased the intensity of the sun's heat (16:8-9). The fifth vial brought darkness to both the capital and the kingdom of the antichrist (16:10-11). The sixth vial dried up the Euphrates River in order to permit the eastern armies to move into the Near East (16:12). The parenthetical insert revealed the gathering of the remaining wicked nations to Armageddon. Four forces will bring them there: the greed of the nations; the activity of demons; the united desire of Satan, the antichrist, and the false prophet; and the sovereign plan of God. The seventh vial brought the cry "It is done" (16:17). The threefold series of divine judgments is now over; the time is ready for Christ to claim the kingdoms of the world. The great earthquake belts or rifts will simultaneously split; Jerusalem will divide into three parts; topographical changes will occur; and great hail, weighing 100-125 pounds, will fall to the earth.

17:1-18

A lengthy parenthesis is inserted between the conclusion of the vial judgments and the second advent of Christ (17:1—19:10). Earlier, the fall of Babylon was briefly mentioned (14:8; 16:19); now it is described

---

17. The Greek word *phiale* is better translated "bowl" than "vial." The vessel was more like a saucer than a test tube.

in great detail. In this vision John saw a harlot sitting on many waters, a symbol of her worldwide influence (17:1; cf. 17:15). She also sat upon the beast (antichrist); this suggests a religious-political alignment in the first half of the tribulation. In John's day the woman represented Rome with its pagan political and religious power (17:18). Although the woman seems to be in control of the beast, the ten-nation confederacy over which he rules will turn on the harlot and destroy her. This may occur in the middle of the tribulation when the political antichrist establishes himself as God.

18:1-19

The previous chapter emphasized the religious-political power of the harlot; this chapter stresses her commercial influence. Four reasons were given for her judgment by God (18:8; cf. 18:3): she was demonic; she influenced the world to participate in her sin; she affected political leaders for evil; and she used her power for material gain. A call was then extended to tribulation believers to separate from her lest they receive the same physical judgments. Her destruction will be mourned by kings (18:9-10), merchants (18:11-16), and the sea merchants (18:17-19); note the triple mention of "Alas, Alas" (18:10, 16, 19).

18:20—19:6

Although earth mourns, heaven rejoices over her desolation because it fulfills its prayer of vengeance (6:9-11). The extensive nature of the judgment is seen by nine affected people or things (18:22-23). Two reasons were given for her fall: she deceived the nations with her sorceries, and she was morally and judicially liable for the martyrdoms of all the righteous (18:23-24). The call to rejoice (18:20) was answered with a fourfold response by many people (19:1-3), the elders and the four living creatures (19:4), a throne voice (19:5), and a great multitude (19:6).

19:7-10

Rejoicing continues because the marriage of the Lamb has come. The wife or bride of Christ (Eph. 5:22-32), the true church, is already in heaven and has been rewarded for her righteous deeds[18] at the judgment seat of Christ. The marriage apparently takes place in heaven after she has been rewarded, and the marriage supper will take place on earth shortly after Christ's advent. Out of gratitude for the revelations given to him, John fell at the feet of the ministering angel to worship

---

18. The Greek word is in the plural: "righteousnesses" or "righteous deeds." Because of the imputed righteousness of Christ, she is the Bride and she is in heaven. Because of earned righteousness, she has made herself ready.

him; however, he was corrected with these words: "Worship God: for the testimony of Jesus is the spirit of prophecy" (19:10).

19:11-16

The seven great events that will follow the Great Tribulation and will climax God's program for the ages is now presented in rapid sequence. The first is a symbolic description of Christ's return to the earth. Seven qualities are ascribed to Him—faithful and true to His promises, righteous judgment, fiery eyes of discernment, crowns of sovereignty, an unknown name, a blood-soaked vesture, and the name of the Word of God. By the power of His spoken word (Ps. 2:5; Isa. 11:4), He will smite the nations, will rule them with a rod of iron, will tread the wine-press of God's wrath, and will assert Himself as the sovereign King.

19:17-21

The supper of the great God is just the opposite of the marriage supper of the Lamb. The former is a synonym of Armageddon in which carnivorous birds will eat the flesh of the wicked. In that day the anti-christ, the kings of the earth, and their armies will be destroyed by Christ. The antichrist and the false prophet will be sent directly to the lake of fire and the remnant of their armies will be slain directly by Christ.

20:1-6

At this time Satan will be seized by an heavenly angel and will be bound with a chain in the abyss or the bottomless pit for one thousand years, the duration of Christ's millennial reign on the earth. Since he has no activity of deception on the earth at this time, no doubt his demons are also bound. John then saw those who would share Christ's reign. The tribulation martyrs, who had been beheaded, who refused to worship the antichrist, and who did not receive his mark, will be resurrected then. All of the righteous of all ages share in the first resurrection; the second resurrection, the raising of the wicked dead, will occur after the millennial kingdom. Certain blessings are ascribed to the participants of the first resurrection: blessed, holy, suffering no second death, priests, and co-rulers with Christ.

20:7-15

After the millennial reign of Christ, Satan will be released from the abyss. He will return to the earth to deceive the nations and to lead the rebels against Jerusalem. His millions of followers will come from the unregenerate population that was born during the past one thousand years. The army will be destroyed by fire and Satan will be sent directly to the lake of fire where the antichrist and false prophet are still in conscious torment.[19] When the wicked dead of all ages stand before Christ at the Great White Throne judgment, the present universe will be purged by fire to make way for the new heaven and the new earth. The book of life reveals the lack of regeneration and the books of works will determine the degree of punishment to be experienced in the lake of fire.

21:1-8

John then saw the newly created eternal state and the descent of the holy city. Several blessings of life in this state were enumerated: the presence of God, no tears, no death, no sorrow, no crying, and no pain. However, eight different life-styles will be excluded (21:8).

21:9—22:5

Some commentators argue that this description of the holy city (21:9—22:5) best suits the millennial conditions and that John, after describing eternity, goes back to expound the residence of the redeemed in the kingdom. However, the chronology of this closing section (19:11—

---

19. The Greek word *basanisthesontai* is third person plural: "they shall be tormented." It refers to all three, not just to Satan.

The Plain of Esdraelon, or Megiddo, was a strategic site in biblical times, where trading routes intersected and crucial battles were fought. This same valley is alluded to in the reference "Armageddon."

22:5) does not necessitate recapitulation. The city will bear various titles: the bride, the Lamb's wife, that great city, and the holy Jerusalem (21:9-10). She will have the glory of God (21:11). The city will have a wall with twelve gates bearing the names of the tribes of Israel (21:12-13) and twelve foundation stones bearing the names of the apostles (21:14). The city will be approximately fifteen hundred miles in length, width, and height, in the shape of a cube, tetragon, or pyramid (21:15-17). The streets will be of gold, the foundation stones of precious gems, and the gates of pearls (21:18-21). It will have no temple, no sun, and no moon. The glory of God will be the source of light (21:23-27). Inhabitants will drink at the river of life and will eat the twelve fruits of the tree of life (22:1-5).

22:6-21

In the epilogue, a blessing was again pronounced upon the keeper of the book's contents. John was warned not to worship the revealing angel nor to seal the book. A contrast was then made between the saved and the unsaved (22:11-15). Their eternal destinies become fixed at the time of their death or at Christ's second coming. An invitation was then given to the unsaved to experience salvation and a warning was likewise sounded not to tamper with inscripturated revelation. In response to Christ's promise to return, John concluded with an appropriate prayer: "Even so, come, Lord Jesus" (22:20).

Increase Your Learning

By Doing

1. Circle the names of the seven churches.
2. Circle the references to the seven seals, the seven trumpets, and the seven vials.
3. Circle the command to write wherever found.
4. Underline the phrase "and I saw" wherever found in the book.
5. Make a list of all the titles ascribed to Christ.

By Discussing

1. What causes Christians to leave their first love? What are the symptoms?
2. What does it mean to be a hot Christian? cold? lukewarm?
3. Compare the songs of the redeemed with those sung in churches today and with contemporary Christian folk and rock.
4. How can war be harmonized with God's character? Are there both holy and unholy wars?
5. How does Satan confer authority on men? through elections? through government overthrows?
6. From your study of Revelation, what new concepts about the person and work of Christ have you learned? How have these affected you spiritually?

By Reading

Barnhouse, Donald Grey. *Revelation*. Grand Rapids: Zondervan Publishing House, 1971.

Newell, William R. *The Book of Revelation*. Chicago: Moody Press, 1935.

Seiss, J. A. *The Apocalypse*. Grand Rapids: Zondervan Publishing House, 1957.

Strauss, Lehman. *The Book of the Revelation*. Neptune, N.J.: Loizeaux Bros., 1967.

Walvoord, John F. *The Revelation of Jesus Christ*. Chicago: Moody Press, 1966.

BIBLIOGRAPHY

General Reference Works

Blaiklock, E. M. *The Zondervan Pictorial Bible Atlas.* Grand Rapids: Zondervan Publishing House, 1969.

Davis, John D. *Davis Dictionary of the Bible.* Grand Rapids: Baker Book House, 1972.

Deal, William S. *Baker's Pictorial Introduction to the Bible.* Grand Rapids: Baker Book House, 1967.

Douglas, J. D., ed. *The New Bible Dictionary.* Grand Rapids: Wm. B. Eerdmans Publishing Co., 1971.

Grollenberg, L. H., comp. *Nelson's Atlas of the Bible.* New York: Thomas Nelson & Sons, 1956.

Harrison, Everett F., ed. *Baker's Dictionary of Theology.* Grand Rapids: Baker Book House, 1960.

Kraeling, Emil G. *Rand McNally Bible Atlas.* Chicago: Rand McNally, 1956.

Orr, James. *International Standard Bible Encyclopedia.* 5 vols. Grand Rapids: Wm. B. Eerdmans Publishing Co., 1939.

Pfeiffer, Charles F. *Baker's Bible Atlas.* Grand Rapids: Baker Book House, 1961.

Pfeiffer, Charles F., and Howard Vos. *Wycliffe Historical Geography of Bible Lands.* Chicago: Moody Press, 1967.

Scholer, David M. *A Basic Bibliographic Guide for New Testament Exegesis.* Grand Rapids: Wm. B. Eerdmans Publishing Co., 1973.

Tenney, Merrill C., ed. *The Zondervan Pictorial Bible Dictionary.* Grand Rapids: Zondervan Publishing House, 1963.

Unger, Merrill F. *Unger's Bible Dictionary.* Chicago: Moody Press, 1957.

Vine, W. E. *An Expository Dictionary of New Testament Words.* Old Tappan, N.J.: Fleming H. Revell Co., 1956.

Yohn, David Waite. *The Christian Reader's Guide to the New Testament.* Grand Rapids: Wm. B. Eerdmans Publishing Co., 1973.

Greek Lexicons

Abbott-Smith, G. *A Manual Greek Lexicon of the New Testament.* Edinburgh: T. & T. Clark, 1937.

Arndt, William F., and F. Wilbur Gingrich. *A Greek-English Lexicon of the New Testament.* Chicago: University of Chicago Press, 1957.

Gingrich, F. W. *Shorter Lexicon of the Greek New Testament.* Grand Rapids: Zondervan Publishing House, 1965.

Kittel, Gerhard, ed. *Theological Dictionary of the New Testament.* Translated by Geoffrey W. Bromiley. 9 vols. Grand Rapids: Wm. B. Eerdmans Publishing Co., 1964-74.

Liddell, Henry George, and Robert Scott. *A Greek-English Lexicon.* Oxford: Oxford University Press, 1940.

Moulton, James Hope, and George Milligan. *The Vocabulary of the Greek Testament.* Grand Rapids: Wm. B. Eerdmans Publishing Co., 1952.

Thayer, Joseph H. *Greek-English Lexicon of the New Testament.* Grand Rapids: Zondervan Publishing House, 1956.

Concordances

Bullinger, E. W. *A Critical Lexicon and Concordance to the English-Greek New Testament.* Grand Rapids: Zondervan Publishing House, 1957.
Clarke, Adam, ed. *Clarke's Bible Concordance.* Grand Rapids: Baker Book House, 1968.
Englishman's Greek Concordance of the New Testament. 9th ed. London: Samuel Bagster and Sons, Ltd., 1903.
Moulton, W. F., and A. S. Geden. *A Concordance to the Greek New Testament.* Edinburgh: T. & T. Clark, 1926.
Strong, James. *Exhaustive Concordance of the Bible.* New York: Abingdon Press, 1890.
The Zondervan Expanded Concordance. Grand Rapids: Zondervan Publishing House, 1971.
Young, Robert. *Analytical Concordance to the Bible.* Grand Rapids: Wm. B. Eerdmans Publishing Co., 1955.

Archaeology

Blaiklock, E. M. *The Archaeology of the New Testament.* Grand Rapids: Zondervan Publishing House, 1970.
Finegan, Jack. *Light from the Ancient Past.* Princeton: Princeton University Press, 1946.
Free, Joseph. *Archaeology and Bible History.* Wheaton, Ill. Scripture Press, 1956.
Pfeiffer, Charles F. *The Biblical World.* Grand Rapids: Baker Book House, 1972.
Thompson, J. A. *The Bible and Archaeology.* Grand Rapids: Wm. B. Eerdmans Publishing Co., 1962.
Unger, Merrill F. *Archaeology and the New Testament.* Grand Rapids: Zondervan Publishing House, 1964.
Wiseman, Donald J. *Illustrations from Biblical Archaeology.* Grand Rapids: Wm. B. Eerdmans Publishing Co., 1958.
Wright, G. Ernest. *Biblical Archaeology.* Philadelphia: Westminster Press, 1957.

Harmonies of the Gospels

Burton, Ernest Dewitt, and Edgar Johnson Goodspeed. *A Harmony of the Synoptic Gospels in Greek.* Chicago: University of Chicago Press, 1947.
Carter, John Franklin. *A Layman's Harmony of the Gospels.* Nashville, Tenn.: Broadman Press, 1961.
Cheney, Johnston M., and Stanley A. Ellisen. *The Life of Christ in Stereo.* Portland: Western Baptist Seminary Press, 1969.
Greenleaf, Simon. *The Testimony of the Evangelists.* Grand Rapids: Baker Book House, 1965.
Kerr, John H. *A Harmony of the Gospels.* Old Tappan, N.J.: Fleming H. Revell Co., 1903.
Robertson, A. T. *A Harmony of the Gospels for Students of the Life of Christ.* New York: Harper & Bros., 1950.
Wieand, Albert Cassel. *A New Harmony of the Gospels.* Grand Rapids: Wm. B. Eerdmans Publishing Co., 1953.

New Testament Introduction and Survey

Bruce, F. F. *The Books and the Parchments.* Old Tappan, N.J.: Fleming H. Revell Co., 1953.

Cawood, John. *Let's Know the Bible.* Old Tappan, N.J.: Fleming H. Revell Co., 1971.

Dunnett, Walter. *Outline of New Testament Survey.* Chicago: Moody Press, 1963.

Eason, J. Lawrence. *The New Bible Survey.* Grand Rapids: Zondervan Publishing House, 1963.

Gray, James M. *Synthetic Bible Studies.* Old Tappan, N.J.: Fleming H. Revell Co., 1923.

Gundry, Robert H. *A Survey of the New Testament.* Grand Rapids: Zondervan Publishing House, 1970.

Guthrie, Donald. *New Testament Introduction.* Downers Grove, Ill.: Inter-Varsity Press, 1961.

Hadjiantoniou, George A. *New Testament Introduction.* Chicago: Moody Press, 1957.

Harrison, Everett F. *Introduction to the New Testament.* Grand Rapids: Wm. B. Eerdmans Publishing Co., 1964.

Hiebert D. Edmond. *Introduction to the Non-Pauline Epistles.* Chicago: Moody Press, 1962.

————. *Introduction to the Pauline Epistles.* Chicago: Moody Press, 1954.

Luck, G. Coleman. *The Bible Book by Book.* Chicago: Moody Press, 1955.

Morgan, G. Campbell. *The Analyzed Bible.* Old Tappan, N.J.: Fleming H. Revell Co., 1971.

Phillips, John. *Exploring the Scriptures.* Chicago: Moody Press, 1968.

Scroggie, W. Graham. *A Guide to the Gospels.* London: Pickering and Inglis, 1948.

————. *Know Your Bible.* 2 vols. London: Pickering & Inglis, 1940.

————. *The Unfolding Drama of Redemption.* Grand Rapids: Zondervan Publishing House, 1970.

Shepard, J. W. *The Life and Letters of St. Paul.* Grand Rapids: Wm. B. Eerdmans Publishing Co., 1950.

Stott, John R. W. *Basic Introduction to the New Testament.* Grand Rapids: Wm. B. Eerdmans Publishing Co., 1964.

Tenney, Merrill C. *New Testament Survey.* Grand Rapids: Wm. B. Eerdmans Publishing Co., 1961.

————. *New Testament Times.* Grand Rapids: Wm. B. Eerdmans Publishing Co., 1965.

Thiessen, Henry C. *Introduction to the New Testament.* Grand Rapids: Wm. B. Eerdmans Publishing Co., 1943.

Vos, Howard F. *Beginnings in the New Testament.* Chicago: Moody Press, 1973.

Wright, Sara Margaret. *A Brief Survey of the Bible.* Neptune, N.J.: Loizeaux Bros., 1958.

Zahn, Theodor. *Introduction to the New Testament.* 3 vols. Grand Rapids: Kregel Publications, 1953.

New Testament Sets

Alford, Henry. *The Greek Testament.* 2 vols. Chicago: Moody Press, 1958.

Barnes, Albert. *Barnes' Notes on the New Testament.* Grand Rapids: Baker Book House, 1949-50.

Baxter, J. Sidlow. *Explore the Book.* 6 vols. Grand Rapids: Zondervan Publishing House, 1960.

Calvin, John. *Calvin's New Testament Commentaries.* Edited by T. F. Torrance and D. W. Torrance. 12 vols. Grand Rapids: Wm. B. Eerdmans Publishing Co., 1960.

Carter, Charles W., ed. *The Wesleyan Bible Commentary.* 6 vols. Grand Rapids: Wm. B. Eerdmans Publishing Co., 1965-69.

Erdman, Charles R. *An Exposition of the New Testament.* 17 vols. Philadelphia: The Westminster Press, 1948.

Everyman's Bible Commentaries. Chicago: Moody Press.

Gaebelein, Arno C. *The Annotated Bible.* Neptune, N.J.: Loizeaux Bros., 1970.

Grant, F. W. *The Numerical Bible.* Neptune, N.J.: Loizeaux Bros., 1944-53.

Lenski, R. C. H. *Interpretation of the New Testament.* 12 vols. Minneapolis: Augsburg Publishing House, 1933-46.

Maclaren, Alexander. *Expositions of Holy Scripture.* 11 vols. Grand Rapids: Wm. B. Eerdmans Publishing Co., 1944.

Nicoll, W. Robertson. *The Expositor's Greek Testament.* Grand Rapids: Wm. B. Eerdmans Publishing Co., 1961.

Robertson, Archibald Thomas. *Word Pictures in the New Testament.* 6 vols. Nashville: Broadman Press, 1930.

Shield Bible Study Series. 18 vols. Grand Rapids: Baker Book House, 1957—.

Spence, H. D. M., and Joseph S. Exell. *The Pulpit Commentary.* 8 vols. Grand Rapids: Wm. B. Eerdmans Publishing Co., 1959.

The Jamieson, Fausset and Brown Unabridged Bible Commentary. 6 vols. Grand Rapids: Wm. B. Eerdmans Publishing Co. ,1957.

The New International Commentary on the New Testament. Various single vols. Grand Rapids: Wm. B. Eerdmans Publishing Co., 1953—.

The Tyndale New Testament Commentaries. Various single vols. Grand Rapids: Wm. B. Eerdmans Publishing Co., 1957—.

Vincent, Marvin R. *Word Studies in the New Testament.* 4 vols. Grand Rapids: Wm. B. Eerdmans Publishing Co., 1957.

Wuest, Kenneth S. *Word Studies in the Greek New Testament.* 4 vols. Grand Rapids: Wm. B. Eerdmans Publishing Co., 1966.

One Volume Commentaries

Davidson, F. *The New Bible Commentary.* Grand Rapids: Wm. B. Eerdmans Publishing Co., 1953.

Ellicott, Charles John. *Ellicott's Bible Commentary.* Grand Rapids: Zondervan Publishing House, 1971.

Guthrie, D., et al. *The New Bible Commentary: Revised.* Grand Rapids: Wm. B. Eerdmans Publishing Co., 1970.

Halley, Henry H. *Halley's Bible Handbook.* Grand Rapids: Zondervan Publishing House., 1964.

Henry, Carl F. H., ed. *The Biblical Expositor.* Vol. 3. Philadelphia: A. J. Holman Co., 1960.

Howley, G. C. G., F. F. Bruce, and H. L. Ellison, eds. *A New Testament Commentary.* Grand Rapids: Zondervan Publishing House, 1969

Matthew Henry's Commentary on the Whole Bible. Grand Rapids: Zondervan Publishing House, 1961.

Morgan, G. Campbell. *An Exposition of the Whole Bible.* Old Tappan, N.J.: Fleming H. Revell Co., 1959.

Pfeiffer, Charles F., and Everett F. Harrison, eds. *The Wycliffe Bible Commentary.* Chicago: Moody Press, 1962.

Unger, Merrill F. *Unger's Bible Handbook.* Chicago: Moody Press, 1966.

Wesley, John, et al. *New Testament Commentary.* Grand Rapids: Baker Book House, 1972.

Williams, George. *The Student's Commentary on the Holy Scriptures.* Grand Rapids: Kregel Publications, 1971.

New Testament Charts

Boyer, James L. *Chart of the Period Between the Testaments.* Winona Lake, Ind.: Bible Charts.

———. *New Testament Chronological Chart.* Winona Lake, Ind.: Bible Charts.

417

New Testament Commentaries

Matthew

Brown, David. *The Four Gospels.* Carlisle, Pa.: The Banner of Truth, 1969.

Gaebelein, A. C. *The Gospel of Matthew.* Neptune, N.J.: Loizeaux Bros., n.d.

Gutzke, Manford George. *Plain Talk on Matthew.* Grand Rapids: Zondervan Publishing House, 1966.

Hobbs, Herschel H. *An Exposition of the Gospel of Matthew.* Grand Rapids: Baker Book House, 1965.

Ironside, H. A. *Expository Notes on the Gospel of Matthew.* Neptune, N.J.: Loizeaux Bros., 1948.

McNeile, Alan Hugh. *The Gospel According to St. Matthew.* London: Macmillan Co., 1955.

Morgan, G. Campbell. *The Gospel According to Matthew.* Old Tappan, N.J.: Fleming H. Revell Co., 1929.

Plummer, Alfred. *An Exegetical Commentary on the Gospel According to St. Matthew.* Grand Rapids: Wm. B. Eerdmans Publishing Co., 1956.

Rice, John R. *The King of the Jews: A Commentary on the Gospel According to Matthew.* Murfreesboro, Tenn.: Sword of the Lord Publishers, 1964.

Tasker, R. V. G. *The Gospel According to St. Matthew.* (Tyndale). Grand Rapids: Wm. B. Eerdmans Publishing Co., 1961.

Thomas, W. H. Griffith. *Outline Studies in Matthew.* Grand Rapids: Wm. B. Eerdmans Publishing Co., 1961.

Van Ryn, August. *Meditations in Matthew.* Neptune, N.J.: Loizeaux Bros., 1958.

Mark

Cole, R. A. *The Gospel According to St. Mark.* (Tyndale). Grand Rapids: Wm. B. Eerdmans Publishing Co., 1961.

English, E. Schuyler. *Studies in the Gospel According to Mark.* New York: Our Hope Press, 1943.

Hobbs, Herschel H. *An Exposition of the Gospel of Mark.* Grand Rapids: Baker Book House, 1970.

Ironside, H. A. *Addresses on the Gospel of Mark.* Neptune, N.J.: Loizeaux Bros., n.d.

Martin, Ralph P. *Mark: Evangelist and Theologian.* Grand Rapids: Zondervan Publishing House, 1973.

Morgan, G. Campbell. *The Gospel According to Mark.* Old Tappan, N.J.: Fleming H. Revell Co., 1911.

Swete, Henry Barclay. *The Gospel According to St. Mark.* Grand Rapids: Wm. B. Eerdmans Publishing Co., 1913.

Taylor, Vincent. *The Gospel According to St. Mark.* London: Macmillan Company, 1953.

Van Ryn, August. *Mediation in Mark.* Neptune, N.J.: Loizeaux Bros., 1957.

Wuest, Kenneth. *Mark in the Greek New Testament.* Grand Rapids: Wm. B. Eerdmans Publishing Co., 1957.

Luke

Geldenhuys, J. Norval. *Commentary on Luke.* (NIC series). Grand Rapids: Wm. B. Eerdmans Publishing Co., 1956.

Godet, F. *Commentary on the Gospel of St. Luke.* 2 vols. Edinburgh: T. & T. Clark, 1886.

Gutzke, Manford George. *Plain Talk on Luke.* Grand Rapids: Zondervan Publishing House, 1966.

Hobbs, Herschel H. *An Exposition of the Gospel of Luke.* Grand Rapids: Baker Book House, 1966.

Ironside, H. A. *Addresses on the Gospel of Luke*. Neptune, N.J.: Loizeaux Bros., n.d.

Morgan, G. Campbell. *The Gospel According to Luke*. Old Tappan, N.J.: Fleming H. Revell Co., 1928.

Plummer, Alfred. *A Critical and Exegetical Commentary on the Gospel According to St. Luke*. Edinburgh: T. & T. Clark, 1922.

Van Ryn, August. *Mediations in Luke*. Neptune, N.J.: Loizeaux Bros., n.d.

John

Gaebelein, Arno C. *The Gospel of John*. Neptune, N.J.: Loizeaux Bros., 1965.

Godet, F. *The Gospel of John*. Grand Rapids: Zondervan Publishing House, 1969.

Gutzke, Manford George. *Plain Talk on John*. Grand Rapids: Zondervan Publishing House, 1969.

Hendriksen, William. *John*. Grand Rapids: Baker Book House, 1953.

Hobbs, Herschel H. *An Exposition of the Gospel of John*. Grand Rapids: Baker Book House, 1968.

Hutcheson, George. *John*. Carlisle, Pa.: The Banner of Truth, n.d.

Ironside, H. A. *Addresses on the Gospel of John*. Neptune, N.J.: Loizeaux Bros., 1946.

Laurin, Roy L. *John: Life Eternal*. Chicago: Moody Press, 1972.

Morgan, G. Campbell. *The Gospel According to John*. Old Tappan, N.J.: Fleming H. Revell Co., 1911.

Morris, Leon. *Commentary on the Gospel of John*. (NIC series). Grand Rapids: Wm. B. Eerdmans Publishing Co., 1969.

Pink, Arthur W. *Exposition on the Gospel of John*. Grand Rapids: Zondervan Publishing House, 1945.

Tasker, R. V. G. *The Gospel According to St. John*. (Tyndale). Grand Rapids: Wm. B. Eerdmans Publishing Co., 1960.

Tenney, Merrill C. *John: The Gospel of Belief*. Grand Rapids: Wm. B. Eerdmans Publishing Co., 1948.

Van Ryn, August. *Meditations in John*. Neptune, N.J.: Loizeaux Bros., 1970.

Westcott, Brooke Foss. *The Gospel According to St. John*. Grand Rapids: Wm. B. Eerdmans Publishing Co., 1954.

Acts

Alexander, J. A. *Acts*. Carlisle, Pa.: The Banner of Truth, n.d.

Blaiklock, E. M. *The Acts of the Apostles*. (Tyndale). Grand Rapids: Wm. B. Eerdmans Publishing Co., 1963.

Bruce, F. F. *Commentary on Acts*. Grand Rapids: Wm. B. Eerdmans Publishing Co., 1954.

Carter, Charles W., and Ralph Earle. *The Acts of the Apostles*. Grand Rapids: Zondervan Publishing House, 1973.

Gaebelein, A. C. *The Acts of the Apostles*. Neptune, N.J.: Loizeaux Bros., n.d.

Gutzke, Manford George. *Plain Talk on Acts*. Grand Rapids: Zondervan Publishing House, 1972.

Ironside, H. A. *Lectures on the Book of Acts*. Neptune, N.J.: Loizeaux Bros., 1943.

Kent, Homer A., Jr. *Jerusalem to Rome*. Grand Rapids: Baker Book House, 1972.

Morgan, G. Campbell. *The Acts of the Apostles*. Old Tappan, N.J.: Fleming H. Revell Co., 1924.

Rackham, Richard Belward. *The Acts of the Apostles*. (The Westminster Commentaries). London: Methuen & Co., 1951.

Stagg, Frank. *The Book of Acts*. Nashville, Tenn.: Broadman Press, 1955.

Thomas, W. H. Griffith. *Outline Studies in Acts*. Grand Rapids: Wm. B. Eerdmans Publishing Co., 1956.

Van Ryn, August. *Acts of the Apostles*. Neptune, N.J.: Loizeaux Bros. 1961.

Romans

Barnhouse, Donald Grey. *Expositions of Bible Doctrines (Romans)*. 4 vols. Grand Rapids: Wm. B. Eerdmans Publishing Co., 1952-64.

Bruce, F. F. *The Epistle of Paul to the Romans*. (Tyndale). Grand Rapids: Wm. B. Eerdmans Publishing Co., 1963.

Godet, F. *Commentary on Romans*. 2 vols. Grand Rapids: Zondervan Publishing House, 1956.

Hodge, Charles. *Commentary on Romans*. Grand Rapids: Wm. B. Eerdmans Publishing Co., 1950.

Ironside, H. A. *Lectures on Romans*. Neptune, N.J.: Loizeaux Bros., n.d.

Lloyd-Jones, D. Martyn. *Romans*. Vols 1, 2, 3 (continuing series). Grand Rapids: Zondervan Publishing House, 1973.

McClain, Alva J. *Romans: The Gospel of God's Grace*. Herman A. Hoyt, ed. Chicago: Moody Press, 1973.

Mills, Sanford C. *A Hebrew Christian Looks at Romans*. Grand Rapids: Zondervan Publishing House, 1968.

Murray, John. *The Epistle to the Romans*. 2 vols. (NIC). Grand Rapids: Wm. B. Eerdmans Publishing Co., 1964.

Newell, William R. *Romans Verse by Verse*. Chicago: Moody Press, 1938.

Phillips, John. *Exploring Romans*. Chicago: Moody Press, 1971.

Plumer, William S. *Commentary on Romans*. Grand Rapids: Kregel Publications, 1971.

Schaal, John H. *The Royal Roman Road: Studies in the Book of Romans*. Grand Rapids: Baker Book House, 1972.

Stifler, James. *The Epistle to the Romans*. Old Tappan, N.J.: Fleming H. Revell Co., 1897.

Thomas, W. H. Griffith. *St. Paul's Epistle to the Romans*. Grand Rapids: Wm. B. Eerdmans Publishing Co., 1946.

Westwood, Tom. *Romans: A Courtroom Drama*. Neptune, N.J.: Loizeaux Bros., 1949.

Wilson, Geoffrey. *Romans*. Carlisle, Pa.: The Banner of Truth, n.d.

I Corinthians

Blair, J. Allen. *Living Wisely: A Devotional Study of the First Epistle to the Corinthians*. Neptune, N.J.: Loizeaux Bros., 1969.

Boyer, James L. *For a World Like Ours: Studies in I Corinthians*. Grand Rapids: Baker Book House, 1972.

De Haan, Martin R. *Studies in I Corinthians*. Grand Rapids: Zondervan Publishing House, 1956.

Godet, F. *Commentary on St. Paul's First Epistle to the Corinthians*. 2 vols. Grand Rapids: Zondervan Publishing House, 1957.

Grosheide, F. W. *Commentary on the First Epistle to the Corinthians*. (NIC series). Grand Rapids: Wm. B. Eerdmans Publishing Co., 1953.

Hodge, Charles. *Commentary on First Corinthians*. Grand Rapids: Wm. B. Eerdmans Publishing Co., 1950.

Ironside, H. A. *First Epistle to the Corinthians*. Neptune, N.J.: Loizeaux Bros., 1938.

Morgan, G. Campbell. *The Corinthian Letters of Paul*. Old Tappan, N.J.: Fleming H. Revell Co., 1946.

Morris, Leon. *The First Epistle of Paul to the Corinthians*. (Tyndale). Grand Rapids: Wm. B. Eerdmans Publishing Co., 1963.

Robertson, Archibald Thomas, and Alfred Plummer. *A Critical and Exegetical Commentary of the First Epistle of St. Paul to the Corinthians*. Edinburgh: T. & T. Clark, 1914.

Wilson, Geoffrey. *I Corinthians*. Carlisle, Pa.: The Banner of Truth, n.d.

BIBLIOGRAPHY

II Corinthians
Hodge, Charles. *An Exposition of the Second Epistle to the Corinthians.* Grand Rapids: Wm. B. Eerdmans Publishing Co., 1953.
Hughes, Philip Edgcumbe. *Paul's Second Epistle to the Corinthians.* (NIC). Grand Rapids: Wm. B. Eerdmans Publishing Co., 1962.
Ironside, H. A. *Second Epistle to the Corinthians.* Neptune, N.J.: Loizeaux Bros., 1939.
Moule, Handley C. G. *The Second Epistle to the Corinthians.* Grand Rapids: Zondervan Publishing House, 1962.
Plummer, Alfred. *A Critical and Exegetical Commentary on the Second Epistle of St. Paul to the Corinthians.* Edinburgh: T. & T. Clark, 1915.
Tasker, R. V. G. *The Second Epistle of Paul to the Corinthians.* (Tyndale). Grand Rapids: Wm. B. Eerdmans Publishing Co., 1958.

Galatians
Burton, Ernest D. *A Critical and Exegetical Commentary on St. Paul's Epistle to the Galatians.* Edinburgh: T. & T. Clark, 1920.
Cole, Alan. *The Epistle of Paul to the Galatians.* (Tyndale). Grand Rapids: Wm. E. Eerdmans Publishing Co., 1964.
De Haan, Martin R. *Galatians.* Grand Rapids: Zondervan Publishing House, 1960.
Hendriksen, William. *Galatians.* Grand Rapids: Baker Book House, 1969.
Ironside, H. A. *Messages on Galatians.* Neptune, N.J.: Loizeaux Bros., 1941.
Lightfoot, J. B. *Saint Paul's Epistle to the Galatians.* Grand Rapids: Zondervan Publishing House, 1957.
Ridderbos, Herman N. *The Epistle of Paul to the Churches of Galatia.* Grand Rapids: Wm. B. Eerdmans Publishing Co., 1961.
Skilton, John H. *Machen's Notes on Galatians.* Nutley, N.J.: Presbyterian and Reformed Publishing Co., 1972.
Stott, John. *The Message of Galatians.* Downers Grove, Ill.: InterVarsity Press, 1968.
Strauss, Lehman. *Devotional Studies in Galatians and Ephesians.* Neptune, N.J.: Loizeaux Bros., 1957.
Tenney, Merrill C. *Galatians: The Charter of Christian Liberty.* Grand Rapids: Wm. B. Eerdmans Publishing Co., 1951.

Ephesians
Bruce, F. F. *The Epistle to the Ephesians.* Old Tappan, N.J.: Fleming H. Revell Co., 1961.
Eadie, John. *Commentary on the Epistle to the Ephesians.* Grand Rapids: Zondervan Publishing House, 1883.
Foulkes, Francis. *The Epistle of Paul to the Ephesians.* (Tyndale). Grand Rapids: Wm. B. Eerdmans Publishing Co., 1963.
Hendriksen, William. *Ephesians.* Grand Rapids: Baker Book House, 1967.
Hodge, Charles. *A Commentary on the Epistle to the Ephesians.* Grand Rapids: Wm. B. Eerdmans Publishing Co., 1954.
Ironside, H. A. *In the Heavenlies.* Neptune, N.J.: Loizeaux Bros., 1937.
Lloyd-Jones, D. Martyn. *God's Way of Reconciliation.* Grand Rapids: Baker Book House, 1972.
Paxson, Ruth. *Wealth, Walk, and Warfare of the Christian.* Old Tappan, N.J.: Fleming H. Revell Co., 1939.
Robinson, Armitage. *St. Paul's Epistle to the Ephesians.* London: Macmillan Co., 1903.
Simpson, E. K., and Bruce, F. F. *Commentary on the Epistles to the Ephesians and the Colossians.* (NIC). Grand Rapids: Wm. B. Eerdmans Publishing Co., 1957.

Van Ryn, August. *Ephesians, The Glories of His Grace.* Neptune, N.J.: Loizeaux Bros., 1963.

Philippians

Blair, J. Allen. *Living Victoriously.* Neptune, N.J.: Loizeaux Bros., 1956.

Boice, James Montgomery. *Philippians.* Grand Rapids: Zondervan Publishing House, 1971.

Hendriksen, William. *Philippians.* Grand Rapids: Baker Book House, 1965.

Ironside, H. A. *Notes on Philippians.* Neptune, N.J.: Loizeaux Bros., n.d.

Lightfoot, J. B. *Saint Paul's Epistle to the Philippians.* Grand Rapids: Zondervan Publishing House, 1953.

Martin, Ralph P. *The Epistle of Paul to the Philippians.* (Tyndale). Grand Rapids: Wm. B. Eerdmans Publishing Co., 1959.

Motyer, J. A. *Philippian Studies.* Downers Grove, Ill.: InterVarsity Press, 1966.

Moule, H. C. G. *The Epistle of Paul the Apostle to the Philippians.* Cambridge: University Press, 1895.

Muller, Jac. J. *The Epistles of Paul to the Philippians and to Philemon.* (NIC). Grand Rapids: Wm. B. Eerdmans Publishing Co., 1955.

Strauss, Lehman. *Studies in Philippians.* Neptune, N.J.: Loizeaux Bros., 1959.

Tenney, Merrill C. *Philippians: The Gospel at Work.* Grand Rapids: Wm. B. Eerdmans Publishing Co., 1956.

Colossians (see also Ephesians)

Carson, Herbert M. *The Epistles of Paul to the Colossians and Philemon.* (Tyndale). Grand Rapids: Wm. B. Eerdmans Publishing Co., 1960.

Hendriksen, William. *Colossians and Philemon.* Grand Rapids: Baker Book House, 1965.

Ironside, H. A. *Lectures on the Epistle to the Colossians.* Neptune, N.J.: Loizeaux Bros., 1929.

Lightfoot, J. B. *St. Paul's Epistles to the Colossians and Philemon.* Grand Rapids: Zondervan Publishing House, 1879.

Martin, Ralph P. *Colossians: The Church's Lord and the Christian's Liberty.* Grand Rapids: Zondervan Publishing House, 1973.

Nicholson, William R. *Popular Studies in Colossians—Oneness With Christ.* Grand Rapids: Kregel Publications, 1951.

Simpson, E. M., and F. F. Bruce. *Commentary on the Epistles to Ephesians and Colossians.* (NIC). Grand Rapids: Wm. B. Eerdmans Publishing Co., 1957.

I and II Thessalonians

Frame, James Everett. *A Critical and Exegetical Commentary on the Epistles of St. Paul to the Thessalonians.* Edinburgh: T. & T. Clark, 1912.

Hendriksen, William. *Exposition of I and II Thessalonians.* Grand Rapids: Baker Book House, 1955.

Hiebert, D. Edmond. *The Thessalonian Epistles.* Chicago: Moody Press, 1954.

Ironside, H. A. *Addresses on 1st and 2nd Thessalonians.* Neptune, N.J.: Loizeaux Bros., n.d.

Milligan, George. *St. Paul's Epistles to the Thessalonians.* Grand Rapids: Wm. B. Eerdmans Publishing Co., 1952.

Morris, Leon. *The Epistles of Paul to the Thessalonians.* (Tyndale). Grand Rapids: Wm. B. Eerdmans Publishing Co., 1957.

—————. *The First and Second Epistles to the Thessalonians.* (NIC). Grand Rapids: Wm. B. Eerdmans Publishing Co., 1964.

Walvoord, John F. *The Thessalonian Epistles.* Grand Rapids: Zondervan Publishing House, 1958.

BIBLIOGRAPHY

I and II Timothy, Titus

Guthrie, Donald. *The Pastoral Epistles.* Grand Rapids: Wm. B. Eerdmans Publishing Co., 1957.

Hendriksen, William. *Exposition of the Pastoral Epistles.* Grand Rapids: Baker Book House, 1957.

Ironside, H. A. *Timothy, Titus and Philemon.* Neptune, N.J.: Loizeaux Bros., n.d.

Kent, Homer A., Jr. *The Pastoral Epistles. Studies in I and II Timothy and Titus.* Chicago: Moody Press, 1958.

King, Guy. *A Leader Led.* London: Marshall, Morgan & Scott, 1951.

————. *To My Son.* London: Marshall, Morgan & Scott, 1944.

Simpson, E. K. *The Pastoral Epistles.* Grand Rapids: Wm. B. Eerdmans Publishing Co., 1954.

Wuest, Kenneth S. *The Pastorals in the Greek New Testament.* Grand Rapids: Wm. B. Eerdmans Publishing Co., 1952.

Philemon (see also Philippians and Colossians)

Gaebelein, Frank. *Philemon: the Gospel of Emancipation.* Neptune, N.J.: Loizeaux Bros., 1960.

Moule, H. C. G. *Colossians and Philemon Studies.* London: Pickering & Inglis, n.d.

Hebrews

Bruce, F. F. *The Epistle to the Hebrews.* (NIC). Grand Rapids: Wm. B. Eerdmans Publishing Co., 1964.

De Haan, Martin R. *Hebrews.* Grand Rapids: Zondervan Publishing House, 1959.

English, E. Schuyler. *Studies in the Epistle to the Hebrews.* Neptune, N.J.: Loizeaux Bros., 1955.

Hewitt, Thomas. *The Epistle to the Hebrews.* (Tyndale). Grand Rapids: Wm. B. Eerdmans Publishing Co., 1960.

Ironside, H. A. *Studies in the Epistle to the Hebrews.* Neptune, N.J.: Loizeaux Bros., 1946.

Kent, Homer A., Jr. *Epistle to the Hebrews: An Expository Commentary.* Grand Rapids: Baker Book House, 1972.

MacDonald, William. *The Epistle to the Hebrews.* Neptune, N.J.: Loizeaux Bros., 1972.

Newell, William R. *Hebrews Verse by Verse.* Chicago: Moody Press, 1947.

Owen, John. *Hebrews: The Epistle of Warning.* Grand Rapids: Kregel Publications, 1968.

Thomas, W. H. Griffith. *Hebrews: A Devotional Commentary.* Grand Rapids: Wm. B. Eerdmans Publishing Co., 1962.

Westcott, Brooke Foss. *The Epistle to the Hebrews.* Grand Rapids: Wm. B. Eerdmans Publishing Co., n.d.

Wilson, Geoffrey. *Hebrews.* Carlisle, Pa.: The Banner of Truth, n.d.

James

Gaebelein, Frank. *The Practical Epistle of James.* New York: Doniger & Raughley, 1955.

Gutzke, Manford George. *Plain Talk on James.* Grand Rapids: Zondervan Publishing House, 1969.

Ironside, H. A. *Notes on James and Peter.* Neptune, N.J.: Loizeaux Bros., n.d.

King, Guy. *A Belief That Behaves.* London: Marshall, Morgan & Scott, 1941.

Manton, Thomas. *James.* Carlisle, Pa.: The Banner of Truth, 1962.

Mayor, Joseph B. *The Epistle of St. James.* Grand Rapids: Zondervan Publishing House, 1954.

423

Mitton, C. Leslie. *The Epistle of James.* Grand Rapids: Wm. B. Eerdmans Publishing Co., 1966.
Ross, Alexander. *The Epistles of James and John.* Grand Rapids: Wm. B. Eerdmans Publishing Co., 1964.
Strauss, Lehman. *James, Your Brother.* Neptune, N.J.: Loizeaux Bros., 1956.
Tasker, R. V. G. *The General Epistle of James.* (Tyndale). Grand Rapids: Wm. B. Eerdmans Publishing Co., 1956.

I and II Peter

Bigg, Charles. *A Critical and Exegetical Commentary on the Epistles of St. Peter and St. Jude.* Edinburgh: T. & T. Clark, 1902.
Blair, J. Allen. *Living Faithfully.* Neptune, N.J.: Loizeaux Bros., 1961.
———. *Living Peacefully.* Neptune, N.J.: Loizeaux Bros., 1959.
Greene, Michael. *The Second Epistle of Peter and The Epistle of Jude.* (Tyndale). Grand Rapids: Wm. B. Eerdmans Publishing Co., 1957.
Jowett, J. H. *The Epistles of St. Peter.* Grand Rapids: Kregel Publications, 1970.
Leighton, Robert. *Commentary on First Peter.* Grand Rapids: Kregel Publications, n.d.
Mayor, Joseph B. *The Epistle of St. Jude and the Second Epistle of St. Peter.* London: Macmillan Company, 1907.
Nieboer, Joe. *Practical Exposition of 2 Peter.* Neptune, N.J.: Loizeaux Bros., n.d.
Selwyn, Edward Gordon. *The First Epistle of St. Peter.* London: Macmillan Company, 1947.
Stibbs, Alan. *The First Epistle General of Peter.* (Tyndale). Grand Rapids: Wm. B. Eerdmans Publishing Co., 1959.
Wuest, Kenneth S. *First Peter in the Greek New Testament.* Grand Rapids: Wm. B. Eerdmans Publishing Co., 1942.
———. *In These Last Days.* Grand Rapids: Wm. B. Eerdmans Publishing Co., 1954.

I, II, and III John

Bruce, F. F. *The Epistles of John.* Old Tappan, N.J.: Fleming H. Revell Co., 1970.
Candlish, Robert. *I John.* Carlisle, Pa.: The Banner of Truth, n.d.
Findley, George G. *Fellowship in the Life Eternal.* Grand Rapids: Wm. B. Eerdmans Publishing Co., 1955.
Ironside, H. A. *Addresses on the Epistles of John and Jude.* Neptune, N.J.: Loizeaux Bros., n.d.
Ross, Alexander. *Commentary on the Epistles of James and John.* (NIC). Grand Rapids: Wm. B. Eerdmans Publishing Co., 1954.
Stott, J. R. W. *The Epistles of John.* (Tyndale). Grand Rapids: Wm. B. Eerdmans Publishing Co., 1964.
Strauss, Lehman. *The Epistles of John.* Neptune, N.J.: Loizeaux Bros, n.d.
Westcott, Brooke Foss. *The Epistles of St. John.* Grand Rapids: Wm. B. Eerdmans Publishing Co., 1955.
Wuest, Kenneth S. *In These Last Days.* Grand Rapids: Wm. B. Eerdmans Publishing Co., 1954.

Jude (see also 2 Peter)

Lawlor, George Lawrence. *The Epistle of Jude.* Nutley, N.J.: Presbyterian and Reformed Publishing Co., 1972.

Revelation

Barnhouse, Donald Grey. *Revelation.* Grand Rapids: Zondervan Publishing House, 1971.

BIBLIOGRAPHY

Cohen, Gary G., and Salem Kirban. *Revelation Visualized*. Chicago: Moody Press, 1972.

Criswell, W. A. *Expository Sermons on Revelation*. Grand Rapids: Zondervan Publishing House, 1969.

De Haan, Martin R. *Revelation*. Grand Rapids: Zondervan Publishing House, 1956.

Gaebelein, Arno C. *The Revelation*. Neptune, N.J.: Loizeaux Bros., 1960.

Hendriksen, William. *More Than Conquerors*. Grand Rapids: Baker Book House, 1968.

Ironside, H. A. *Lectures on the Revelation*. Neptune, N.J.: Loizeaux Bros., n.d.

Morris, Leon. *Commentary on Revelation* (Tyndale). Grand Rapids: Wm. B. Eerdmans Publishing Co., 1957.

Newell, William R. *The Book of Revelation*. Chicago: Moody Press, 1935.

Ottman, Ford C. *The Unfolding of the Ages in the Revelation of John*. Grand Rapids: Kregel Publications, 1967.

Scott, Walter. *Exposition of the Revelation of Jesus Christ*. Old Tappan, N.J.: Fleming H. Revell Co., n.d.

Seiss, J. A. *The Apocalypse*. Grand Rapids: Zondervan Publishing House, 1957.

Strauss, Lehman. *The Book of the Revelation*. Neptune, N.J.: Loizeaux Bros., 1967.

Swete, H. B. *The Apocalypse of St. John*. Grand Rapids: Wm. B. Eerdmans Publishing Co., 1908.

Talbot, Louis T. *An Exposition of the Book of Revelation*. Grand Rapids: Wm. B. Eerdmans Publishing Co., 1937.

Tenney, Merrill C. *Interpreting Revelation*. Grand Rapids: Wm. B. Eerdmans Publishing Co., 1957.

Walvoord, John F. *The Revelation of Jesus Christ*. Chicago: Moody Press, 1966.

General Index

Scripture Index

Scripture passages treated in sequence within the chapters on books of the Bible are not included in this index.